Managing across cultures

SUSAN C. SCHNEIDER AND JEAN-LOUIS BARSOUX

HEC University of Geneva
INSEAD

FINANCIAL TIMES
Prentice Hall

An imprint of **Pearson Education**

Harlow, England · London · New York · Reading, Massachusetts · San Francisco
Toronto · Don Mills, Ontario · Sydney · Tokyo · Singapore · Hong Kong · Seoul
Taipei · Cape Town · Madrid · Mexico City · Amsterdam · Munich · Paris · Milan

Pearson Education Limited
Edinburgh Gate
Harlow
Essex CM20 2JE
England

and Associated Companies throughout the world

Visit us on the World Wide Web at:
http://www.pearsoneduc.com

Typeset in 9¹/₂/12pt Sabon
by Dorwyn Ltd, Rowlands Castle, Hants

Printed and bound in Great Britain by
Biddles Ltd, *www.biddles.co.uk*

Library of Congress Cataloging-in-Publication Data

Schneider, Susan.
    Managing across cultures / Susan Schneider and Jean-Louis
    Barsoux.
        p. cm.
    Includes bibliographical references and index.
    ISBN 0-13-272220-8 (pbk.)
        1. Management—Social aspects. 2. International business
    enterprises—Management—Social aspects. 3. Intercultural
    communication. I. Barsoux, Jean-Louis. II. Title.
    HD38.S3623 1997
    658.3′041—dc20   96–32283
                                                              CIP

British Library Cataloguing in Publication Data

A catalogue record for this book is available from
the British Library

ISBN: 0-13-272220-8 (pbk)

10 9 8
05 04 03 02 01

Contents

Preface

This is a book about managing across cultures: the threats and opportunities, the problems and possibilities. Rather than experiencing cultural differences as threats to be overcome or as unfortunate remnants of history to be endured, we challenge the reader to experience and enjoy the richness of cultural differences. Rather than creating a cultural melting pot, we need to design organizations as cultural mosaics in which each element preserves its unique value.

Those concerned with *managing across cultures* are no longer just the jet-setting elite, the corporate trouble-shooters, and battle-scarred expatriates. International responsibilities and contacts are increasingly widespread through companies, and need not even imply international travel. The office of today (and even more so of tomorrow) consists of people of many different cultures working together. Appreciating and being able to manage cultural differences at home and abroad is becoming more and more a part of everyone's job.

This book is not only for the novice preparing for the first time to jump into the sea of international business. It is also for those experienced swimmers who have ridden the waves and have battled the force that was trying to pull them under. Often the realization of the power of culture comes only in retrospect. Many of those who survived, and those who did not, can take this opportunity to reflect on their experience, to crystalize the learning so that it can be passed on to others.

This learning can be used not only for helping to develop other international managers but also for helping teams and organizations to navigate better in global waters. Many experienced international managers are often quite frustrated with head office, and particularly Human Resource (HR) departments, in their lack of appreciation of what it takes to be effective in international business endeavors.

In this book we draw upon a broad and growing literature on culture and management. Bringing together past observations and research, we discover national differences in management practice, which in fact, have attracted attention at different times in the international business community. For example, "Japanese" emphasis on "corporate culture" gained popularity in the 1980s as did "just in time" and total quality management (TQM) in the 1990s. The "American" practices of scientific management at the beginning of the ninteenth century, and performance management at the end of the nineteenth century have also been widely diffused.

Given the current dramatic changes in the ways of doing business, the economic and political upheavals, and the greater interdependencies called for in doing business across borders, there is the never-ending search for a "new" model of management. Current contenders (in addition to the Japanese and American models described above) are the Chinese family business model for its use of networks, the "northern European" model for its concern for employee and social welfare, and the "Latin" model for its emphasis on flexibility and resourcefulness.

However, rather than to name the winner in this "best practice" contest, the book seeks to explore the cultural assumptions underlying these models. By exploring these assumptions we are forced to question to what extent these models *can* travel across borders. We have to consider whether these models should be introduced, if and how they have to be adapted, and to what extent they may even be refined and improved by local practice, thus bringing back to headquarters (HQ) something other than a contribution to profits.

We need to recognize that these underlying, and often hidden, cultural assumptions give rise to different beliefs and values about the practice of management. These assumptions are also manifest in the behavior of managers and employees, as well as in our everyday working environment, from the design of the buildings we enter, the interior office, to the very design of job descriptions, policies and procedures, structures and strategies. We need to realize that these values and beliefs, behaviors and practices have different meanings making them more or less acceptable in different cultures. Different behavior and artifacts may be needed to produce the desired effect.

Two potential traps in managing across cultures are to assume similarities and to assume differences. The first trap is often the case in British/American collaboration, where shared culture tends to be overestimated on the basis of shared language, and perhaps even more so between Americans and Canadians. Also, managers who have been successful in "dealing with the natives" on previous assignments in one part of the world may assume that the same behavior will be successful elsewhere. An example of the second trap would be a German manager negotiating in São Paulo, Brazil assuming that the culture will be very different, expecting a carnival atmosphere having been briefed on Brazilian culture before leaving home.

Our intent is *not* to rank countries on a set of cultural dimensions nor to provide readers with handy tips for doing business in Paris or Tokyo. Arriving at headquarters in France, we cannot assume that because we are in a French company we can expect, for example, greater emphasis on formality and hierarchy. After all, this company may be atypical of French companies, or unique due to the influence of differences in regional (north versus south, Paris versus provinces), industry (cosmetics versus banking), corporate (marketing versus R&D driven), and function (manufacturing versus finance) cultures. Culture can cut many ways. Rather than knowing *what* to do in country X, or whether national or functional cultures are more important in multicultural teams, what is necessary is to know how to assess the potential *impact* of culture, national or otherwise, on performance.

With the aim of improving effectiveness in international business, this book focuses on *national* culture. Our purpose is to provide a framework for analyzing culture, which can nonetheless be applied in other contexts, as will be discussed in Chapter 3. The proposed framework provides a map, a guide, suggesting where to look, what questions to ask (how and of whom), and how to interpret the pattern of responses and observations. Only then can we consider the implications for designing structure, strategy, and human resource management (HRM) and devise strategies to manage cultural differences as managers, as teams, and as companies facing the challenge of globalization.

While much has been written comparing management practice in the United States and Japan, we would like to focus more attention on Europe. This is not just for the sake of Americans and Asians with an interest in Europe, to recognize the diversity within, but also for Europeans themselves, who often recognize these differences, but do not understand the reasons behind them and fail to consider the consequences.

Furthermore, we draw upon our own experience of living with cultural differences on a daily basis, either through personal circumstances – born and raised in one country now living in another, having lived with parents and partners of different cultural backgrounds, or professional circumstances – working at INSEAD (European Institute for Business Administration) where multiculturalism is a way of life, interacting with students, managers, and professors from around the world, and where multiculturalism is considered to be a competitive advantage. This experience has forced us to challenge our own assumptions, to consider how our culture influences our behavior, and to anticipate the reactions of others.

As teachers and researchers in the field of cross-cultural management, we must constantly confront how culture influences our own work, and, in particular, the writing of this book. Our own cultural footprints can be detected in what follows. Sometimes we are aware of them, but not always. They are particularly evident in our prescriptions, such as the emphasis on the importance of self-awareness, the value of diversity, making culture explicit, confronting and negotiating differences, and looking for win–win solutions in responding to both global and local interests.

For many, this book will seem too instrumental in stressing the impact of culture on the effectiveness of organizations and managers. The very notion that culture can be "managed" is, in itself, culture-bound. For example, in discussing corporate culture, American managers tend to see culture as something organizations *have*; European managers are more likely to see it as something that organizations *are* and thus more dubious about being able to change it. The American assumption of being able to control one's destiny and the propensity to take action have created quite a market for how-to, self-improvement books and for books about managing across cultures, like this one. For all our attempts at impartiality, our own American, Anglo–French footprints can be traced.

In writing for an international managerial audience, we are acutely aware of the conflicting demands and expectations of our readers. American managers tend to be more pragmatic, and want to know implications for action, "what to do". French managers want to know more about the context, including the history and theory behind these ideas. What British managers may recognize as an obvious implication for management, Americans may want more clearly spelled out. Thus we must navigate between the theoretical and the practical, the abstract and the concrete, the implicit and the explicit.

Given our training and experience, as academics and clinicians, we are especially interested in exploring the meaning underlying behavior. We believe that the insights derived from observing behavior, from questioning values and beliefs, and from challenging assumptions will better equip managers to think through the consequences of their actions and allow them to frame their responses and actions better within different cultures.

The book is divided into three parts. Part I argues why we need to know about culture, and provides a framework which helps not only to organize what we already know (previous cross-cultural management literature), but can also serve as a guide for how to go about discovering and analyzing culture. This framework can be applied not only to national culture, but also to other cultural spheres – regional, industry, corporate, and functional/professional. Any business encounter, in effect, represents the interaction of several cultural spheres. This is particularly the case, for example, of strategic alliances where distant industry or corporate cultures, in addition to national cultures, meet head on. The challenge is even greater for the cross-functional teams charged with making that strategic alliance work!

Part II demonstrates how national culture influences management practice: organizational structure, strategy, and human resource management. Here we integrate the evidence from research in order to describe how these practices differ across countries and then to explain why – what the possible underlying cultural reasons are for these differences. We also discuss the implications of what these differences mean for managers and their companies, for example in considering the transfer of so-called "best practice" across national borders, and in appreciating the potential value-added of alternative models, or other ways of managing.

Part III focuses on how to manage cultural differences more effectively. Managers, teams, and organizations have to confront cultural difference, to learn from them, and to devise ways of utilizing them creatively in order to benefit from their potential value added.

Finally, it is important to realize that one's world-view is conditioned from a very early age. Try to remember the world map that hung on the wall in your school. How does that compare with the map shown opposite? Most likely it looks different. Most likely your country was in the middle, with the rest of the world distributed somehow around. The world seen through the eyes of an Australian or Korean, an Argentinian or Canadian, an African or Greenlander looks very different. Only by realizing that we cannot take our way of seeing the world for granted can we begin to recognize and appreciate how others see the world, and what that might mean for our working together.

The book aims to develop the reader's understanding of how culture influences management practice and how managers perceive their organizations and their careers. It also raises awareness of how culture guides the way managers look at problems, the solutions they find, the way they deal with others, and how others may react. Besides providing insight into other cultures, it will provide managers with something more precious – an increased awareness of their own culture. Exploring culture is an exciting endeavor, as it involves a never-ending process of discovery. Not only is it the discovery of others, but in that discovery of others, a rediscovery of self.

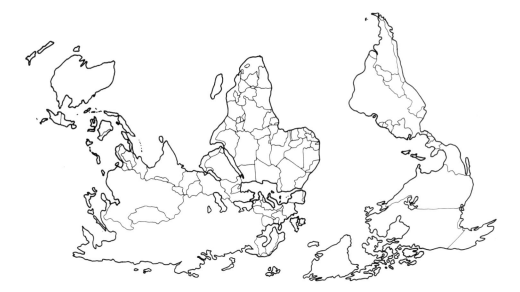

Another world-view

Acknowledgements

We would like to thank a number of colleagues (both academic and practitioners) whose advice and ideas have helped us improve the manuscript: Ariane Berthoin Antal (WZB Berlin, Germany), Sue Canney-Davison (London Business School, UK), Anne Donnelon (Babson College, USA); INSEAD Professors Paul Evans, Dominique Heau, Manfred Kets de Vries, and André Laurent, as well as a number of senior executives, notably Jose F.P. Santos (Universidade Catòlica Portuguesa and Segafredo), Julie Friedman (HR Givaudon-Roure), Paul Orleman (HR Rhône-Poulenc Rorer), Irene Rodgers (Inter-cultural Consultants, Paris).

We would also like to thank INSEAD for funding this project, and the numerous colleagues at INSEAD and CEDEP, in particular Jean-François Manzoni, for their support and encouragement.

Finally we would like to thank our families and friends who make managing across cultures an intrinsic part of our daily lives.

PART ONE

The meaning of culture

> Managers who readily accept that the cuisine, the literature, the music and the art of other countries run parallel to one another, must also learn to accept that the art of management differs in other countries.
>
> (André Laurent, Professor INSEAD)

Part I of the book comprises three chapters. Chapter 1 argues that culture is a powerful undercurrent in international business. Despite evidence of converging behavior among countries, we challenge the myth of the "global village" or "melting pot". We also challenge the notion that "business is business", that management, like science and engineering, is immune to the influence of culture, or culture-free.

The chapter then considers how culture plays a key role in the effectiveness of nations, companies, functions, and managers faced with the challenge of operating in a globalizing economy. Although somewhat difficult to detect, culture can be a powerful force that can undermine or propel business success. Its presence needs to be brought to the surface and its consequences anticipated. We need to develop awareness of how our own culture influences the way we behave and how others perceive and respond to that behavior. This means acknowledging stereotypes, but then getting beyond them. We have to surface cultural differences and make them open to discussion in order to avoid the risks of getting caught in the undertow.

Chapter 2 tackles the meaning of culture. It proposes a framework that can be used as a guide to discovering this meaning. This framework highlights key cultural dimensions that are most commonly used and referred to in the management literature. Knowing these dimensions enables us to look for the relevant cues that can help to direct our behavior, to anticipate the preferences or reactions of others, and to question the underlying reasons for the differences we encounter. This framework thus provides a map and a method of exploring culture differences – both within and between countries – guiding us through different approaches: observation, questioning, and interpretation.

Although the main focus of this book is national culture, Chapter 3 is concerned with recognizing other cultural spheres of influence including the region, industry, company, profession, and function. The framework proposed in Chapter 2 also serves to diagnose these cultural spheres. This chapter describes the potential interaction and the implications for managing across boundaries, that are other than national.

By emphasizing the importance of culture and providing a framework for analyzing different spheres of cultural influence (for example, national as well as corporate), we can anticipate better the impact and implications of managing across cultures.

CHAPTER ONE

The undertow of culture

All people are the same. It's only their habits that are so different.

Confucius

This is a book about the impact of culture on management. Our argument is not that culture is the most important influence on management, just that it is the most neglected. Part of this neglect may be due to the problem of recognizing the presence and the force of culture. Managers taking the plunge into the sea of international business need not only take account of the waves, but more importantly need to assess the depth and force of the undertow, which are more difficult to detect. Failure to do so can pose a serious threat to survival.

In this chapter we get a glimpse of the power of culture in the practice of management and the dangers associated with ignoring its impact. Here we begin to provide a way of bringing cultural differences to the surface. Before defining what we mean by culture (in Chapter 2), we first sound an alert for the need to recognize and assess the potential impact of culture. To do so, two enduring myths have to be challenged. The first is that since the world is getting smaller, cultural differences are disappearing. The second is that "management is management", and that, like science, its practice is universal.

Converging cultures?

Convergence myth #1: the world is getting smaller . . .

We are often told that the world is getting smaller. Thanks to advances in television, telecommunications, and transportation we are en route towards what Marshall McLuhan called the "global village".[1] So by the year 2000, we would all look alike and act alike wearing Levi jeans, Lacoste (alligator) shirts, Adidas running shoes, and Swatch watches while watching CNN on Samsung televisions, drinking Heineken, eating at MacDonalds, and singing in karaoke bars. Yet this is a vision that few find appealing, and many find appalling. And while it may be true that on the surface we appear to be converging in our dress (jeans and T-shirts) and even eating habits (fast foods), the pull of culture runs deep, and cannot be easily detected.

The same observation can be made about the proverbial melting pot. Large cities like Paris, London, Toronto, or Bombay attract people from many different origins. But wandering through New York City, reputed as the quintessential melting pot, we find clearly distinct neighborhoods. Little Italy sits alongside Chinatown, and the Ukranian restaurant on East 10th street has the menu in Ukranian. Uptown on East 86th street there is Germantown. In fact, rather than a cultural melt-down, we discover distinct cultural fragments, with differences so clearly defined that to the French philosopher, Jean Baudrillard it seemed that, "In America, each ethnic group, each race develops a competitive language and culture".[2]

A European melting pot was expected in 1992, when with the creation of an economic union all business people would look and act alike, as shown in Figure 1.1. But the magic moment came and went, adding little to the creation of a common European culture. Throughout Europe walls have collapsed, border guard posts have been vacated, and airport passport control booths for Europeans are supposed to have disappeared. But the promise of global products, uniform standards, and equal access to jobs or markets remains more theory than practice. Violent protests and demonstrations block the transportation of produce, meat, and fish across borders. The pressures to preserve political and economic sovereignty, as well as cultural identity and integrity, have remained, and have even grown stronger as evidenced by regional tensions in Spain, Ireland, Belgium,

Figure 1.1 Eurothérapie. (*Source: Le Monde,* 27 May 1994. Reproduced by permission of *Le Monde*; artist: Serguei.)

and most dramatically in former Yugoslavia. Indeed, it seems that the pressure for convergence or integration may in fact create an equal if not stronger pressure for divergence, or fragmentation.[3]

Convergence myth #2: management is management

Belief in the convergence of management practice and the creation of a global corporate village is strongly held among many managers and management scholars. Their core argument is that management is management, consisting of a set of principles and techniques (like management by objectives) that can be universally applied. Management is considered to be similar to engineering or science, and therefore transcends national boundaries. And yet even in science and engineering, this assumption may be misplaced.

For example, while it may be true that civil engineers designing road systems have an inherent logic with regard to speed and safety, this has not prevented them from implementing different systems, even in ostensibly similar environments. Take the simple problem of crossing roads. Depending on where you are in the world, there is preference for simple stop signs, traffic lights, roundabouts (with priority to those going on or those coming off), or an overpass. Each solution corresponds to a different mind-set: either collective or individualistic, contractual or negotiated, everyone's responsibility or no-one's.

Even the science of medicine is influenced by culture.[4] For example, in France the most common medical complaint is *crise de foie* (liver crisis) while in Germany it is *herzinsuffizienz* (heart insufficiency). Prescriptions to soothe the digestive system are higher in France, while in Germany digitalis is prescribed six times more frequently to stimulate the heart. These differences have been attributed to the French cultural obsession with food, and the German cultural quest for romanticism. In other words, different countries have very different approaches to medicine. If the practice of medicine is shaped by its cultural origins, why should the practice of management be any different?

Forces for and against convergence

Those who argue for the universality of management practice may concede that management differs in Malaysia or Poland. This, they argue, is due to an economic or technological lag. The assumption is that once those countries catch up, then it will be business as usual. In fact, the pace of technological and economic development in eastern Europe and southeast Asia has been quite impressive, and indeed bears evidence of convergence.

Convergence is also encouraged through management education, which is being exported wholesale to these regions. This training not only provides the tools and techniques of finance, accounting, and marketing, but also transmits a particular business philosophy and ideology, such as notions of the free market, the divine rights of shareholders, and the bottom line. Teaching the meaning of free enterprise in the former Soviet Union carries with it a set of business norms, as shown in Figure 1.2, that may or may not be particularly relevant or useful in the local context.

Figure 1.2 Doing lunch. (Reproduced by permission of the Cartoonists and Writers Syndicate; artist: Gable.)

This economic, technological, and managerial development, however, has not necessarily led to a warm embrace of Western style (or Asian style) management, but can in fact trigger a forceful reassertion of local values and beliefs. In eastern Europe, for example, despite initial eagerness to adopt new ways of management, the potential for a backlash against these management practices is strong, particularly when these are experienced as imposed. Given the history of foreign occupation and of forced ideology, there is a heightened sensitivity, if not ambivalence, towards the invasion of foreign companies and their business ideologies and practices. In addition, national pride and the desire to develop their own style of management, one that is more congruent with cultural values, are a natural outcome of knowledge transfer and an increasing sense of self-confidence and efficacy.

Even given similar levels of technological and economic development, convergence of management practices is not necessarily apparent. Comparing Japanese with American firms, French with British firms, or German with Swedish firms, we find clear evidence of different accounting practices, economic policies, and management approaches. Recently, German companies such as Daimler-Benz had a shock when trying to get listed on the New York Stock Exchange. Using American accounting practices revealed a very different profit picture. Apparently not even accounting is accounting.

Indeed, Rosabeth Moss Kanter (former) editor of *Harvard Business Review* acknowledged that management practice is not as global as once hoped. Following a massive survey conducted of 11,678 managers in 25 countries, she concluded that "the idea of a corporate global village where a common culture of management unifies the practice of business around the world is more dream than reality".[5]

Thus, despite technological and economic forces for integration, or convergence, there are equal or perhaps greater forces for fragmentation, one of them being culture. For this reason we need to consider how culture can be a powerful force, undermining or shoring up our effectiveness as nations, as businesses, and as managers. We need to be able to recognize the undertow, the presence and power of culture, in order to keep our heads above water and to better navigate through the rough seas of international business. We also need to discover how to harness the power of culture in order to gain competitive advantage.

Culture as a source of competitive advantage/disadvantage

Rather than seeing culture as a problem to be solved, there is evidence that culture can provide a source of competitive advantage. Michael Porter has argued that nations derive competitive advantage from a set of country-level factors such as the availability of resources, the size and sophistication of the market, the nature of government intervention, and the type of strategic linkages or networks. For example, he attributes the success of the shoe industry in a particular region in northern Italy to the network of relationships between suppliers, manufacturers, and distributors. The strategic link between business and university research centers is credited with the development of insulin in Denmark. And Holland is the world's export leader in the flower business due to unique resources, such as top research institutes.[6]

Many argue that it is these types of unique institutional arrangements that are responsible for the success of "Japanese management". This model is considered effective, not because of anything unique to Japanese culture, but because of the role of government, the nature of ownership and methods of financing, the structure of unions, and the linkages among Japanese businesses.[7]

Nevertheless, culture, although difficult to separate out, is deeply embedded in these institutional arrangements.[8] For example, given the importance placed on the collective or group, it is not surprising to find such linkages among businesses, or between business and government which in more individualist countries would be considered unjust collusion or undue interference. Similarly, in Japan the existence of *Keiretsu*, the networks of tight relationships between customers and suppliers, relies on a high degree of mutual trust, which is rare in countries which place more value on individual initiative and independence. Thus culture and institutional configurations work interactively to create potential competitive advantage or disadvantage.

France's many industrial innovations (the TGV high-speed train, the Minitel videotext system, the Ariane space rocket, and the extensive nuclear power program) can be attributed to the nature of the education system which places high value on engineering and administration and the close relationship between state and industry. These very features considered responsible for technological success, however, are being challenged given a more competitive and international business environment as potential impediments to commercial success.

Critics now say that this very system of education (which is heavily based on math and science, focusing on abstract knowledge instead of concrete experience) is too narrow. As a result, alumni of the *grandes écoles* tend to be "too inflexible and hierarchical", not taking initiative nor having the "communication, negotiation or imaginative skills" thought necessary for "the fast-changing scenarios of modern economic warfare".[9]

France's reputation for having one of the most efficient bureaucracies in the world, run by technocrats, is also being called into question. Criticism is rising towards the role of government and the governing elite now considered responsible for some of the problems which have arisen in the banking sector and in privatization efforts.[10]

German engineering is also highly regarded, made internationally famous by Audi's advertising slogan, *Vorsprung durch Technik* (In the lead through engineering). This concept has traditionally served German manufacturing industry well, contributing to its reputation for high quality and reliability, notably in the auto industry. According to Daniel Goeudevert, French boss of Volkswagen, "Germany's main advantage was its superior technical and professional training, and its higher esteem for manual work".[11] On the other hand, the emphasis on traditional engineering skills may be responsible for German firms not taking the lead in the high-tech sectors such as computers, telecommunications, electronic media, biotechnology, or fiber optics.[12]

Technik exerts a pervasive influence in German firms and on German managerial thinking. It is considered to be one explanation for German lack of interest in foreign investments, mergers, and takeovers.[13] German firms have traditionally been expected to make money by *making* things, not by buying and selling companies. That is the banks' business. In fact the close relationship between banks and business (where the banks hold shares and sit on the company's board) has been a unique feature of German industry, and was once regarded as a source of competitive advantage, but is now considered a liability, in part responsible for recent industrial scandals.

In Denmark, the concern for the impact of culture on competitive advantage was raised by the daily newspaper, *Morgenavisen*. It warned that the competitiveness of Danish companies entering the common market could be constrained by the cultural influence of *Janteloven*. *Janteloven* means that you are supposed to keep a low profile and not to act superior to anyone else. (In Sweden, it is called "Royal Swedish Envy", and in Dutch it is loosely translated as "Act normal, that's crazy enough"!) They argued that, as a result, Danish companies would not be aggressive enough in marketing and in competing with their European rivals.

When Jan Carlzon took control of SAS, *Janteloven* did not help his efforts to create an internationally competitive airline. First of all, his market-driven approach caused a certain discomfort among Scandinavians: fancy cabin interiors and uniforms designed by Pierre Cardin were considered too flashy, and the promotional activities were considered excessive – overdone and expensive.

Furthermore, the focus on business clients was resented – why treat them specially? The strategy of targeting the business customer did not sit well with Scandinavian sense of egalitarianism. In Norway, there is a sign above the SAS check-in counter for business class which reads: "Euroclass – FULL PRICE", in other words, *not* special treatment. This may have been designed to make the class distinction more culturally acceptable.

The point of these examples is to demonstrate that each country has its unique institutional and cultural characteristics, which can provide sources of competitive advantage. However, what may have provided a source of competitive advantage in the past can become an Achilles heel in the future. Managers therefore need to evaluate the extent to which national culture can interfere with their company's efforts to respond to strategic requirements, now and in the future.

When cultures clash

There is no shortage of evidence of cross-cultural friction between businesses. In every cross-border alliance there are seeds of potential cultural conflict and misunderstanding. One survey conducted by a consulting firm in Europe has found that "cultural differences are the biggest source of difficulty in integrating European acquisitions". Another found that 35 percent of senior executives ranked cultural differences as the number one problem in foreign acquisitions (compared with 20 percent who ranked unrealistic expectations, and 13 percent who attributed poor management).[14]

The problem is that this cultural malaise may go unrecognized. It may therefore be some time before cultural differences are surfaced and diagnosed. In one Franco–American joint venture the problem was only recognized after eight years of collaboration. Called in to investigate problems of cooperation, a French consultant interviewing American managers was shocked at the litany of complaints aimed at their French counterparts. Such complaints may seem trivial at first glance, but were apparently rather important, as eight years of collaboration had not resolved them. The belated realization that cultural problems were responsible for poor cooperation alerts us to the need to anticipate potential misunderstanding. Failure to pay attention to culture can, in fact, have disastrous consequences.

Consider the example of the shoe store in Leicester, England.[15] Eager to attract customers from the large local Muslim community, it advertised its footwear with the saying in Arabic, "There is no God but Allah". A subsequent arson attack on the store, with a car ramming through the front window, was claimed to be a protest. Although the desire to attract the local Muslim market was well-intended, the implementation was ill-conceived due to lack of understanding that it was insulting to associate the name of Allah with products (shoes) that were to be trampled in the dirt.

In another instance, an American oil company set up a drilling operation on a Pacific island and hired local labor. Within a week, all the foremen were found lined up on the floor, their throats cut. Only afterwards did they understand that hiring younger men as foremen to boss older workers was not acceptable in a society where age indicates status.[16] Using their own cultural criteria for recruitment, they failed to anticipate the deadly consequences.

While the reaction was far less dramatic, the next example demonstrates that subtle differences can still have far-reaching impact. This was the case of an American firm that purchased a textile machinery company near Birmingham, England, in the hope of using it as a bridgehead into Europe. Shortly after the takeover, the US manager set about tackling what he perceived to be a major production problem, the time lost on tea-breaks:

> In England, tea breaks can take a half-hour per man, as each worker brews his own leaves to his particular taste and sips out of a large, pint size vessel with the indulgence of a wine taster . . . Management suggested to the union that perhaps it could use its

good offices to speed up the "sipping time": to ten minutes a break . . . The union agreed to try but failed . . . Then one Monday morning, the workers rioted. It seems the company went ahead and installed a tea-vending machine – just put a paper cup under the spigot and out pours a standard brew. The pint-sized container was replaced by a five-ounce one imprinted – as they are in America – with morale-building messages imploring greater dedication to the job and loyalty to the company . . . The plant never did get back into production. Even after the tea-brewing machine was hauled out, workers boycotted the company and it finally closed down.[17]

The reason behind the preceding disasters, is not only that behavior, values, and beliefs are different across cultures, but also that their importance to those cultures should not be underestimated. What people in one culture value or perceive as sacred (seniority or tea) may be considered irrelevant in another culture. The trouble is that it is difficult to recognize just what matters (and how much) to another culture – especially when we find it so hard to recognize what is important in our own. The complaints expressed by the American managers about their French joint-venture partner tell as much, if not more, about what is important to the Americans.

Whether engaging in strategic alliances, setting up operations abroad, or attracting the local market, companies need to discover how culture can be harnessed to drive business forward. Companies also need to analyze the potential for cultural clashes that can undermine good intentions. Managers involved in these cross-border adventures need to recognize the symptoms of cultural malaise and to find out what is causing the irritation. To capture the potential benefits while limiting the potential misunderstanding, managers must be prepared to articulate how they see their own culture and to recognize how others may experience it. This, however, is not as easy as it seems.

Recognizing culture

As we see us/as they see us

If you were asked to describe your own culture, what would you say? Describing one's own culture is, in fact, not an easy task. It is a bit like asking a fish in water what it is like to swim in the water. Washed up on the beach, the fish quickly recognizes the difference, but may not be able (nor inclined) to describe it. Its immediate objective is to get back into the water.

We only begin to perceive our culture when we are out of it, confronted with another. "I understand my country so much better", said Samuel Johnson, the eighteenth century British writer, "when I stand in someone else's". Or in the words of French philosopher, Jean Baudrillard, "To open our eyes to the absurdity of our own customs is the charm and benefit of travel".[18] Another way of exploring our own behavior and values is to introduce an outsider, someone from an alien culture who, unfettered by preconceptions, could point out the absence of the Emperor's new clothes. Such was the story of *Gulliver's Travels* by Swift or Voltaire's *Candide*, outsiders or innocents who questioned what they observed.

Culture serves as a lens through which we perceive the other. Like the water surrounding the fish, culture distorts how we see the world and how the world sees us. Furthermore, we tend to use our own culture as a reference point to evaluate the other. For instance, as far as many continental Europeans are concerned the **British do not drive on the left side of the road; they drive on the *wrong* side of the road.**

It is easy when encountering differences to evaluate them according to what we take as normal. This can give rise to a perceived hierarchy of civilization, whereby some cultures are seen as only slightly less civilized than our own, while others are considered primitive, as shown in Figure 1.3. For example, Chinese negotiators, among themselves, often refer to their Western counterparts as "harmless barbarians".[19]

Recognizing cultural differences is the necessary first step to anticipating potential threats and opportunities for business encounters. But in order to go beyond awareness and to create useful interaction, these differences need to be open for discussion. One model known as the "Johari window" provides a way of discussing and "negotiating" the different perspectives, as shown in Figure 1.4.[20]

The Johari window tries to shed light on what I know and do not know about myself and what others know and do not know about me. Through self-disclosure and feedback, we can become more aware of the potential blind spots in how we see ourselves and how others see us that may interfere with effective interaction. This technique, popular in the 1960s era of sensitivity training in the United States, may be helpful in making cultural differences discussable.

For example, an American colleague tends to be rather direct and explicit when making a point. Her Belgian colleagues often try to advise her to be more subtle or

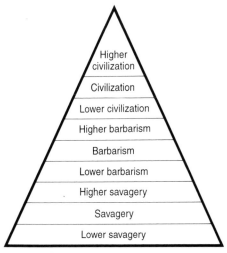

Lewis Morgan's "Pyramid of Human Development"

Figure 1.3 Levels of barbarism. (*Source*: L.R. Kohls (1979) *Survival Kit for Overseas Living*, Intercultural Press, Yarmouth, ME.)

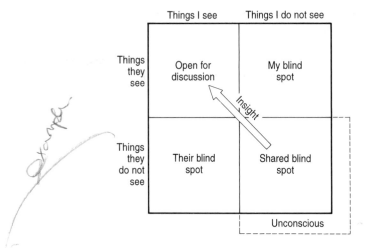

Figure 1.4   Johari window. (*Source*: adapted from S. Jourard (1964) *The Transparent Self*, Van Nostrand Reinhold, Princeton, NJ.)

diplomatic. This characteristic of being direct is one that both parties are aware of and which can therefore be discussed and joked about. In other respects, she may be seen as "typically American" in ways that she does not even suspect. To be told "That's so American!" can be quite disconcerting when she is not sure why, and tends to elicit a defensive response.

On the other hand, there are features of American culture which she knows but they either do not know or may have misapprehended. This provides opportunities to learn about the cultural richness of the other. Finally, despite the best intentions of both parties, a business relationship can turn sour because of something cultural of which neither side is aware. Thus they can discuss differences that are plain to see (obvious to both), and begin to explore or shed some light on what she cannot see (her blind spot), what they cannot see (their blind spot), and try to imagine what it is that both cannot see (shared blind spot).

Stereotypes: for better or for worse

In trying to describe one's own culture, we often call up stereotypes that others have of us. In fact, while we may find it difficult to describe ourselves, characterizing someone else's culture seems relatively easy. Stereotyping comes naturally. However, many of us have been brought up to think of stereotyping as bad – as ignorant and immoral – as evidence of prejudice and bigotry, and far from being politically correct. Stereotypes can indeed be wrong, based on misinformation, and hurtful, used to discredit the other. But they can also be used in a positive way to sort out what William James, a prominent turn-of-the-century psychologist, referred to as the "buzzing confusion".

Stereotypes represent mental "files" that are used to help process new information by comparing it with past experience and knowledge. When we meet someone from the

United States, we are apt to think, "This is an American" (much to the consternation of Canadians and South Americans). What is happening is that we are calling up the mental file of our experience or knowledge of Americans. We then evaluate the present encounter as compared with past experience. This process undeniably simplifies the current reality, but is necessary given the uncertainty and ambiguity inherent in cross-cultural encounters. However, although stereotypes may be necessary, they are far from sufficient.

The problem with stereotypes is not their existence but the way they are used.[21] For example, if on meeting an American I assume that "**All Americans are alike**", then I have simply imposed my mental file, or stereotype, on the current reality, cramming new data into old boxes. New input is distorted to fit the file – a bit like the Procrustean bed, wherein the visitor's arms and legs were cut off or stretched to fit. Or, this encounter can serve as an opportunity to enrich the cultural file on Americans.

Research indicates that managers are ineffective in cross-cultural situations when they either deny having stereotypes or get stuck in them. **Managers rated most effective by peers were those who admitted having stereotypes**, using them as a starting point, but continually revising them as they gained more experience.[22] These managers were constantly checking and rechecking, always updating the files against first-hand information. They were willing to question themselves and their stereotypes, to consciously unlearn, and to redefine their experiences. This requires careful observation, suspending judgement, and looking for explanations – reasons that make sense from the "native" perspective.

Getting beyond stereotypes

A famous American comic of the 1960s, Lenny Bruce, would start his routines by using every bad name for ethnic groups. Having shocked his audience, he would then say, "Now that I have your attention, let's get down to business". The purpose of the above discussion is to encourage managers to recognize and accept the existence of stereotypes in order to consciously go beyond them. In your next business encounter with Russians, the point is *not* to say, "Let me tell you about my stereotypes of Russians", but rather to call up the file and be ready to modify it. Furthermore, you do not have to *become* a Russian to do business with one. Consider the example in reverse. Figure 1.5 shows an American journalist interviewing the former head of the USSR, Gorbachev, on his views of opening up trade with the United States. Gorbachev, based on his stereotype of Americans, has come prepared. The point, then, is not to act out the stereotype of the other, but rather to be aware of how the differences may influence business interactions.

Cultural briefings are used with increasing frequency for managers; therefore, two parties coming into an international negotiation are likely to have a rudimentary understanding of each other's business customs. This is a useful starting point. But unless each party moves beyond that, one can imagine a rather bizarre scenario taking place: Japanese managers showing up, slapping the backs of their American counterparts, and saying, "Call me Kaz"; while the American managers look on bemused, bow their heads, and quietly introduce themselves as Smith-desu. However unlikely, the more we understand each other's culture, the more important it will be to arrive at a shared way of

The Brokaw interview.

Figure 1.5   Call me Mike. (Reprinted by permission, Tribune Media Services.)

working together, rather than imposing our ways, or adapting to theirs. As we will discuss in Chapter 7, this mutual adjustment is especially important given the "hybrid" of cultural experiences and backgrounds of an increasing number of international managers.

Normal curves

The problem with stereotyping is that it conjures up an image (from type setting) of stamping the same type on every blank face. It may be more useful to think rather of prototypes, which allow for variation around a set of core characteristics. Therefore, on any given cultural dimension there is a hypothetical "country" mean and variation around that mean, a normal curve. Thus when comparing these hypothetical means of countries, we expect to find significant differences and less variation within cultures than between them. In other words, members of the same culture are expected to have more in common than with members of the other.

For example, when comparing Swedes and Italians in terms of their levels of expressed emotionality, it may be possible to find some Italians who are more reserved and some Swedes who are quite expressive. But overall we can expect Swedish managers to be more reserved and more like other Swedes than their Italian counterparts, as shown in Figure 1.6.[23]

Depending on the homogeneity of a particular culture, this bell curve may be flatter or steeper, indicating more or less variation. Thus in comparing the United States with Japan, for example, the curve of a particular cultural dimension for the United States

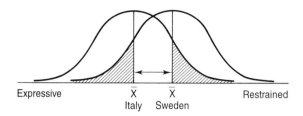

Expressive   X̄   X̄   Restrained
                            Italy   Sweden

Figure 1.6   Normal curves.

would be flatter, given a greater cultural heterogeneity (more variation), while in Japan it would be steeper, given the greater cultural homogeneity.

It is also important to recognize that specific individuals may more or less behave in line with their own cultures.[24] For example, a particular American may be considered atypical in his or her culture by being reserved, or over the top by talking to everyone in the street. On the other hand, he or she may be quite the norm by referring to people in an informal manner. Thus, it is important to know which traits may be more relevant to the issue at hand and to consider the extent to which one reflects the country norm on that particular issue.

Discovering cultural advantage

The Johari window, described earlier, can be used to stimulate awareness, first by asking managers to describe their culture as they see it (as we see us), then as others see it (as they see us).

Describe your culture as *you* see it:
_____
_____
_____

Describe your culture as *others* see it:
_____
_____
_____

Often managers find that it is far more difficult to complete the first part of the exercise than the second. They report difficulty in describing their own culture, and have to rely on what others have said about their culture as a point of reference. Those who find it less challenging tend to have had experience abroad. They acknowledge that it is in confrontation with other cultures that they have come to recognize themselves.

Although recognizing the difficulty in describing one's own culture, managers are surprised at how easy it is to describe the other's culture. And although acknowledging stereotypes, they are at the same time rejecting them. After all, business is business, or we are all engineers, bankers . . . . Yet when asked to give tips to others about to embark on a business endeavor in their country, the advice can be pretty specific. Through this exercise, managers begin to recognize that what they expect and what they take for granted in doing business may not be shared.

Furthermore, managers can be asked to indicate which aspects of their culture are seen as a plus, which might be leveraged to achieve competitive advantage in conducting business, and which may prove a hindrance. In this way managers can begin to think through the implications of national culture for competitiveness.

For example, managers from a British travel business identified "being traditional" as part of their (British) culture. They were then asked to work through how this could get in the way of their success (with potential partners for example) or could be used to enhance their success. This led to brainstorming on how being traditional could be used in a way to attract customers and to strengthen links with suppliers.

For example, being seen as traditional, this travel company could promote itself as having been in the business for a long time, as being interested in establishing long-term relationships with customers and suppliers, and as being reliable. They could position themselves against some fly-by-night operations that could leave you stranded on the other side of the world.

A similar challenge can confront an American consulting firm based in London. When, for example, developing strategies to internationalize, it needs to help its British clients to recognize their company's strengths and weaknesses (including cultural ones). At the same time, this consulting firm must question its own value-added (in terms of culture) to the British client firm. What value-added does their being an American firm bring to British industry? In what ways could being an American consultancy be viewed negatively by potential clients? In other words, what are the potential *cultural* competitive advantages and disadvantages for the client as well as for themselves?

Again, our aim here is to alert managers to the potential risks, or missed opportunities, of ignoring the impact of culture. In each interaction across cultures there are cues which signal potentially powerful undercurrents which can either undermine or propel our efforts. Very often our initial reactions and stereotypes of others can provide important signals to help surface cultural differences. By allowing these differences to be open to discussion we can achieve insights instead of accumulating blind spots. Not only do we begin to appreciate the other person's culture, but we begin to understand our own better. By being alert to these cues, we can then anticipate the potential impact of culture, and consider alternative approaches to management. But what is this thing called culture anyway? The next chapter tackles that question.

Notes

1. McLuhan, M. (1968) *War and Peace in the Global Village*, New York: Bantam Books.
2. Baudrillard, J. (1986) "En Amérique, chaque éthnie, chaque race developpe une langue, une culture competitive", *L'Amérique*, Paris: Grasset, p. 164.
3. Fayerweather, J. (1975) "A conceptual scheme of the interaction of the multinational firm and nationalism," *Journal of Business Administration*, 7, 67–89; Webber, R.H. (1969) "Convergence or divergence?", *Columbia Journal of World Business*, 4(3), pp. 75–83.
4. Payer, J. (1986) *Medicine and Culture*, New York: H. Holt.
5. Kanter, R.M. (1991) "Transcending business boundaries: 12,000 world managers view change", *Harvard Business Review*, May/June, pp. 151–64.
6. Porter, M.E. (1990) "The competitive advantage of nations", *Harvard Business Review*, March/April, pp. 73–93.
7. Westney, D.E. (1987) *Imitation and Innovation*, Cambridge, MA: Harvard University Press.
8. Child, J. (1981) "Culture, contingency and capitalism in cross national study of organizations" in L.L. Cummings and B.M. Staw (eds) *Research in Organizational Behavior*, Vol. 3, Greenwich, CT: JAI Press, pp. 303–356.
9. "France acknowledges its competitive failings", *International Herald Tribune*, April 18, 1990, p. 10.
10. "Enarchy", *The Economist*, April 15, 1995, p. 27.
11. James, B. (1992) "New skills are knocking on French firms' doors", *International Herald Tribune*, February 6.
12. Wever, K.S. and Allen, C.S. (1992) "Is Germany a model for managers?", *Harvard Business Review*, September/October, pp. 36–43.
13. Lawrence, P.A. (1980) *Managers and Management in West Germany*, London: Croom Helm.
14. Buchanan, S. (1989) "Cultural gaps can sink cross-border acquisitions", *International Herald Tribune*, January 12.
15. "Arson target: 'Allah' shoes in U.K. shop", *International Herald Tribune*, April 22, 1992.
16. "Mad dogs and expatriates", *The Economist*, March 3, 1984, p. 67.
17. Stessin, L. (1979) "Culture shock and the American businessman overseas" in E.C. Smith and L.F. Luce (eds) *Towards Internationalism: Readings in Cross Cultural Communication*, Rowley, MA: Newbury House, pp. 214–225, p. 223.
18. Baudrillard, J. (1986) "Tournons les yeux vers le ridicule de nos propres moeurs, c'est le bénéfice et l'agrément des voyages', *Op. cit.*, p. 209.
19. Kohls, L.R. (1979) *Survival Kit for Overseas Living*, Yarmouth, ME: Intercultural Press.
20. Jourard, S. (1964) *The Transparent Self*, Princeton, NJ: Van Nostrand.
21. Adler, N.J. (1991) *International Dimensions of Organizational Behavior*, 2nd edn, Boston, MA: PWS Kent.
22. Ratui, I. (1983) "Thinking internationally: A comparison of how international executives learn", *International Studies of Management and Organization*, XIII(1–2), Spring–Summer, pp. 139–50.
23. Laurent, A., Lecture.
24. Brannen, M.Y. *Negotiating Cultures: Dynamics of Work Culture Formation in a Japanese Takeover*, Oxford: Oxford University Press, forthcoming.

CHAPTER TWO

Exploring culture

> . . . Man is an animal suspended in webs of signifi-
> cance he himself has spun. I take culture to be those
> webs, and the analysis of it to be therefore not an
> experimental science in search of law but an interpre-
> tive one in search of meaning.
>
> Clifford Geertz[1]

Now aware of the powerful impact that culture can have on our business endeavors, and the need to detect its presence, we have to know what we are looking for. In this chapter we will provide a framework to guide readers in discovering the meaning of culture. The framework summarizes and organizes many of the cultural dimensions that have been found useful to managers, and indicates which of those may be most important and most relevant to the business at hand. This framework assists readers in knowing what clues to look for and what questions to ask.

Some of these cultural dimensions are easy to detect; others require diving below the surface. A few may be quite difficult to drag up from the seabed, hidden in the depths and shadows, beyond awareness. These can only be inferred by interpreting patterns of behavior and responses. The proposed framework provides a map through which we can better explore the cultural flora and terrain. Surfing, swimming, snorkeling, and deep sea diving require different skills and different equipment, as shown in Figure 2.1.

Exploring culture can be compared to exploring the ocean. On the surface, riding the waves, we can observe *artifacts*, *rituals*, and *behavior*. These provide clues as to what lies underneath. But to verify this, one has to look below. That means asking questions to discover the reasons: the *values* and *beliefs* which are given to explain that behavior. But further down rest the *underlying assumptions* which are difficult to access and need to be inferred, through interpretation. This requires sophisticated sounding equipment (inter- pretation) to discover potential lurking dangers as well as buried treasures. Here we discover the powerful undertow, the force of culture, both of the other and of our own.

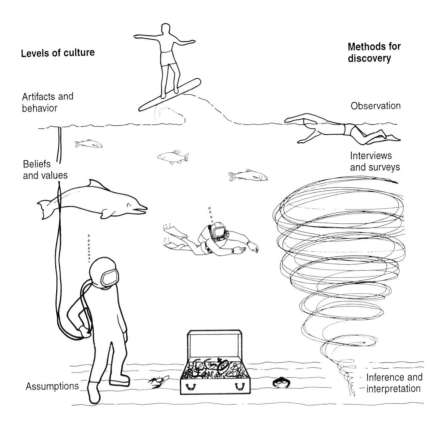

Levels of culture

Artifacts and
behavior

Beliefs
and values

Assumptions

**Methods for
discovery**

Observation

Interviews
and surveys

Inference and
interpretation

Figure 2.1   Navigating the seas of international business.

The search for meaning

Part of the problem in recognizing the impact of culture on management stems from the proliferation of definitions and from the nature of the tools and equipment used in exploration. Anthropologists, it seems, disagree about the precise meaning of culture. They have proposed over 164 different definitions. Some definitions embrace everything from law and religion to art,[2] while others focus on specific "value orientations" such as individualism/collectivism.[3] In a business environment driven by numbers (ROI, ROE, and P/E ratios), culture is often seen as too soft, or too vague, and hard to grasp. Culture eludes precise definition or measurement.

Culture has been defined as "shared patterns of behavior" as proposed by anthropologist Margaret Mead, when studying native rituals in Samoa.[4] However, observing behavior is not enough. What is important is the meaning of that behavior. This distinction is important as the same behavior can have different meanings and different behaviors can have the same meaning.

For example, maintaining eye contact in Western cultures signifies paying attention, being open and honest ("The eyes are the windows of the soul"). In Asia and in Latin America, maintaining eye contact may be taken as a sign of disrespect and aggression, particularly between people of different status levels. Therefore, Asians are quite uncomfortable when Europeans seem to insist on direct eye contact, and Europeans may feel they cannot trust someone who "won't look them straight in the eye". Yet within Europe the amount of eye contact considered acceptable also varies. An American in Paris may experience discomfort, feeling stared at, while in London may experience discomfort, feeling ignored. Culture determines the "intensity of looking" permitted.

Thus rather than defining culture as shared patterns of behavior, anthropologists such as Claude Lévi-Strauss and Clifford Geertz (cited above) define culture as "systems of shared meaning or understanding" ("web of signification") which drive or explain the behavior observed.[5] Observing cockfights in Bali as well as other rituals of daily life, Geertz derived possible interpretations, such as the importance of status, of personal ties and loyalty, and how emotionality, particularly aggression, is managed. Whether observing cockfights, or trading pits at the stock exchange, it is necessary to go beyond what we see, to search for the meaning beneath the activity.

But the meaning may not be readily apparent. Although explanations may be offered in statements of values or beliefs, the underlying assumptions are far from obvious. This is the difference between *espoused theory* and *theory in use*[6] – what people *say*, how they explain their behavior – and what people *mean* – what really drives their behavior. Thus underlying assumptions of cultures are difficult for outsiders to detect, as they are not easily expressed or even understood by insiders. Culture is like a code; what is observed must be deciphered.

Management scholar Ed Schein defines culture as

> a set of basic assumptions – shared solutions to universal problems of external adaptation (how to survive) and internal integration (how to stay together) – which have evolved over time and are handed down from one generation to the next.[7]

While these problems are considered universal (*emic*) in that every group needs to resolve them, the solutions are considered to be unique to that particular group (*etic*). These solutions are internalized, and like habits become taken for granted and difficult to articulate. They are, however, manifested in the way people behave, and in what they believe and value. They represent the "why" – why people behave the way they do, and why they hold the beliefs and values they espouse. These basic assumptions represent our taken-for-granted *Weltanschauung*, or world-view.

The appeal of Schein's definition is that it directly addresses the key challenges facing managers: finding solutions to problems of external adaptation – developing **strategies**; and of internal integration – designing **organizations** and determining **HR practices**. These solutions – strategies, structures, and HRM practices – are thus deeply embedded in culture as will be demonstrated in Chapters 4–6 (Part II).

Method of discovery

When exploring culture the search for meaning calls for an *interpretive* approach. This approach, common to clinical or ethnographic (field) research,[8] involves extensive observation and interviewing to provide detailed, or "thick", descriptions.[9] From the patterns and themes that emerge, theories are developed, so-called "grounded theory".[10] Further exploration involves digging up evidence to support or modify the theory. The interpretive approach involves building a case through inference (as in law or medicine) rather than providing scientific proof (as in engineering or science).

This approach may involve participant observation which requires "living the life", as did MIT professor, John Van Maanen, when he joined the police force to get a "native" perspective, the idea being to understand the meaning of culture through the eyes of the other.[11] This approach requires constantly checking for one's own biases, discovering one's own culture in studying others'.

It is also an iterative process which can include the people involved in the process of interpretation, as is often the case, say when providing feedback of the results of employee morale surveys (or climate audits). In this way, interpretation hits closer to home, and plans for action can then be formulated together. This is sometimes referred to as **action**, or **clinical research**.[12]

Discovering the meaning of culture calls for an approach which is problem-solving and action-oriented and which actively involves participants and observers to work together to discover that meaning. This sets the stage for working through these differences. Discovering the meaning of culture requires learning how to build theories as well as test them. This means playing detective, searching for clues, piecing together the evidence that begins to explain what we observe and why, developing theories, testing them, and then constantly revising them over time as we gain more experience.[13]

Providing a map

Schein's framework serves to integrate different definitions of culture as well as to provide tools for discovering culture. This framework organizes meanings of culture as behavior, as artifact, as values and beliefs, as systems of meaning, and as ways of knowing, going from the most accessible to that which can only be inferred. For example, art and architecture, symbols and rituals, represent artifacts, the concrete expressions or embodiment of culture. Like behavior, these can be observed. But their meaning is not obvious. Meaning has to be derived by questioning, and by again questioning the responses given. Thus culture can be detected at multiple levels which require different approaches: observation, interviews and questionnaires, and interpretation.

For example, we observe two Japanese businessmen facing each other and leaning forward, one more so than the other. Curious, we go and ask the one who is leaning more what he is doing. He responds, "bowing". Why is he doing that? He responds that the other person is his boss. "So what?" we ask. "So I have to show respect", he answers, slightly puzzled. Again we ask "Why?" Trying not to show his irritation, he responds that one should show respect to one's seniors. And again when asked, "Why?" he answers "because they have wisdom". Now confused, we ask "Why?" He looks at us, unsure if we are mad or just stupid, and snaps, "Because that is just the way it is and everyone knows it".

This leaves us perplexed because in our American youth-oriented culture, older managers are often considered "dead wood", not up to date on the latest financial techniques, and blocking career paths. In other words, we have hit the basic assumptions level, where things are taken for granted, neither challenged nor questioned. Here we need to correct for our own biases in order to properly interpret the deeply embedded meaning for the other.

Culture is founded upon these basic assumptions. They give rise to different beliefs and values, and manifest themselves in different behaviors and artifacts. For example, assumptions about space can be seen in architecture and design, and in the amount of physical and psychological distance between people as expressed in greeting rituals and ways of interacting. They manifest themselves in beliefs and values about the need for privacy and formality. Nevertheless, the underlying reasons for the artifacts and behavior are not necessarily obvious.

Thus while the underlying assumptions remain hidden, their manifestations in behavior and artifacts are more readily observable, and in values and beliefs more or less easily articulated. Experienced managers will quickly recognize some of the outward signs and signals described in the next section. What is crucial, however, is to understand the underlying rationale and its impact on daily business life. In the next section we will discuss what is most observable, saving for later the discussion of the underlying meanings, or basic assumptions.

Artifacts and behavior

Cultural assumptions can be observed in artifacts and behavior such as architecture and interior design, greeting rituals, dress and codes of address, and contracts. So to discover the meaning of culture, we need to start with observations, of artifacts and behavior.

Architecture and design

Entering an organization the most obvious artifact is the architecture and design of the building. In Japanese companies one often finds large, open, crowded offices where everyone, including the boss, sits together.

> Business offices in Japan in general are not partitioned. Junior employees work in teams sitting face to face at rows of desks. Section chiefs work at the head of the row. The department chief sits slightly apart, overseeing a number of sections.[14]

For unaccustomed Europeans, it may have the look and feel of a trading room in a bank: open, noisy, cramped, intense interaction, with everyone knowing what everyone else is doing. In the United States, open space office design is also popular, but this space is more likely to be partitioned off by half walls. The individual cubicles are personalized with cartoons, photos, aphorisms, or plants. A sense of privacy is established by not being able to see the others.

In Germany, on the other hand, one is more likely to find private offices with closed doors bearing official titles. Germans often have difficulty working in open-plan offices, since being able to hear others is experienced as a lack of privacy.

These differences led to problems in a research joint venture between IBM, Toshiba, and Siemens located at IBM in New York. The Japanese were unhappy, wanting to knock out some walls which they thought inhibited informal communication. The Germans complained about not having exterior windows which would allow them to see outside, and were uncomfortable with the interior windows which allowed people to look into their offices. They hung their coats over the interior windows in their office to gain privacy.[15]

At Mercedes Benz, German managers and engineers about to be transferred to Alabama underwent special preparation:

> To prepare for the move and begin the necessary acculturation, the team designing the new operation has been segregated from Mercedes' main headquarters here in a small warren of buildings intended to be much more intimate than is common in German businesses. Work spaces are open, doors left ajar. Privacy, a cherished commodity in densely populated Germany, is being eradicated.[16]

The need for privacy however is not necessarily signaled in the same way. In the United States, open doors commonly signal being accessible and available. Open door policies are intended to encourage interaction among people, and open communication. For the US manager, closed doors indicate the desire for privacy. Therefore, one is expected to knock and to be invited in. In France, closed doors however do not signal the same need for privacy. So a quick knock before entering is quite normal. This infuriates Americans, who experience this as "barging in".[17]

Not only are there striking differences in the use of space or artifacts, but what appear to be similarities may actually conceal differences. For instance, in Western firms, the offices with the most window space and the best views are typically reserved for those with the highest status. In Japan, on the other hand, finding yourself with a window seat does not auger well. *Mado-giwa zoku* means "those by the window" and indicates that you have been moved out of the mainstream, or side-lined. "*Beranda zoku* refers to employees who have had to give their desk by the window to newcomers and move out onto the corporate veranda."[18]

Other aspects of layout, such as the number of executive dining rooms, elevators, washrooms, or reserved parking spaces also indicate the importance attached to hierarchy and status within a particular firm or country. These may well be reinforced by artifacts such as cars, office furnishings, and plants, that send clear messages regarding ranking order.

The architecture and design hint at the underlying assumptions regarding internal integration – bringing people together or keeping them apart; and external adaptation – harmonizing with nature or dominating nature. They indicate the importance of hierarchy, of collective rather than individual effort, the preferred type of activity and interaction between people.

Greeting rituals

More clues can be found in formalized exchanges such as greeting rituals. The importance of these rituals should not be overlooked. Some countries, such as the United States, tend to pay less attention to protocol, but for others it is taken quite seriously. For example, failure to show respect by carefully exchanging and inspecting business cards in Japan can get business negotiations off to a very bad start.

In France, greetings are highly personal and individual. A general wave of the hand to say hello to everyone when arriving at the office, as in the United States, is considered insulting to French co-workers who expect to be greeted individually by name, *Bonjour Nathalie*, shaking hands and making eye contact. Should you say *Bonjour* again, when passing later in the hallway, you will be corrected: *Rebonjour*. Otherwise, you have signaled that you do not remember having greeted that person in the first place, and therefore that they are not important to you. Leaving rituals follow the same procedure.

Another part of the ritual that generates a fair amount of confusion is the degree of body contact expected in greeting. Are women supposed to shake hands? Are men expected to embrace one another? One MBA student from Hong Kong was quite distressed and uncomfortable when her French male colleagues insisted on kissing hello and goodbye. The French are, however, taken by surprise when, in the United States, mere acquaintances might greet them with a hug. One Brazilian executive attending a seven-week international management seminar lamented the coldness of the farewell rituals – handshaking and kissing – missing the *abruca* (two-armed hug) that would have demonstrated for him the close feelings of comradery.

Forms of address

The degree of formality in addressing business relations sends important signals, that may not be intended, anything from respect, to friendliness, to disdain. Formality is expressed in the use of last (family) names, the formal version of "you", and titles. For example, addressing business counterparts by their first name may be intended to create a friendly atmosphere for discussion by being informal. But Europeans may be put off by what appears to them as excessive familiarity, or as condescending. In many countries, the use of the first name (or Christian name) is reserved for family only, or children.

This confused one American MBA at a German subsidiary of an American consultancy firm. Although the American practice of using first names was the norm at the office, when German colleagues bumped into each other outside a meeting room or outside work they would greet each other by their last names. And although Japanese MBA students at INSEAD may use nicknames (such as Kaz) in the classroom, outside class they refer to each other by last name, *Takeshita-san*.

Similar to the use of first/last name is the informal and formal use of "you" which exists in many non-Anglo cultures, including French, German, Dutch, and Spanish, as well as Asian cultures. English speakers do not make this distinction. In cultures that do, the use of the formal or informal "you" may indicate not only seniority (children are referred to as *tu*, adults often as *vous* in France) and hierarchy, but also who is in and who is out, representing a powerful way of forming a clique.

For example, the widespread use of the formal *vous* in French business circles means that any violation of the practice is highly significant. Using the informal "you" can be taken as presumptuous, assuming unwarranted familiarity. Using the formal "you", on the other hand, can indicate that you wish to keep distance from those around you, considering yourself apart, or superior.

In Germany, managers use the title, last name, and formal "you" (*Sie*) in social situations as well as in the workplace. The head of Deutsche Bank insisted that the board members, who had worked together for years and had a good working relationship, used the "full address code" so as to not to get too friendly.[19] In the United States, someone with a doctorate may even drop the title in the workplace for fear of appearing aloof or elitist. In Portugal and Italy the formal "you" and title (*Dottore, Ingenere*) are required, whereas in France you would most likely be addressed as *Monsieur* or *Madame*, not *Docteur* nor *Professeur*.

Making contact

Another aspect of the initial encounter is the amount of physical space considered necessary to be comfortable. As described by Hall,[20] northern Europeans tend to require a larger personal space or "protective bubble" than their Latin European counterparts. Northern Europeans feel more comfortable with somewhat greater than arm's length distance. Southern Europeans want to move in closer (within arm's length) in order to feel the connection. A Latin European feels rejected when a northern European steps back to re-establish "the bubble".

A northern European feels uncomfortable when people are standing or for that matter driving too close for comfort. This can also be observed in queueing behavior. While standing in line, northern Europeans who leave a space for comfort, should not be surprised if it quickly gets filled by a Latin European. These cultural differences in queueing behavior were clearly evident at Eurodisney (now Disneyland Paris), posing problems for crowd control normally practiced in the United States and Japan. The northern Europeans and Anglo-Saxon guests became quite annoyed with the Latin Europeans filling in the gaps, as they interpreted it to be breaking in line.

The idea of intrusion is not just physical. It is also psychological. Thus, what many North Americans consider a perfectly friendly line of questioning, may be deemed impertinent or overly familiar by non-Americans. This difference is particularly likely to manifest itself at the "getting to know each other" stage of an international negotiation or prospective collaboration.

For example, French executives will not appreciate inquiries into their personal lives, their family circumstances, or how they spent the weekend. Their professional life and their personal life are regarded as quite separate domains. A senior HR executive at Disneyland Paris expressed surprise at a French executive who, in 18 months of working there, had not once brought his family to visit the park – this, in spite of the provision of free passes and the staging of events for family members. Nor was this due to lack of time. The executive in question had no intention of mixing family and work, even though the corporate culture actively encouraged it.

Observations of how people get to know each other, the degree of formality and personal contact preferred, reveal underlying assumptions about what is considered to be public versus private space. Americans tend to be more open, informal, and easy to approach than Europeans or Asians. However, Europeans often complain that relationships with Americans tend to be superficial. While it may be more difficult to get to know a European, the relationship once established is often more enduring.

Dress codes

Another cultural artifact, the prevailing dress code, also differs in degree of formality and can serve as a subtle signaling mechanism. Northern European managers tend to dress more informally than their Latin counterparts. At conferences, it is not unlikely for the Scandinavian managers to be wearing casual clothing, eschewing the office uniform of tie and jacket. Meanwhile, their French counterparts are reluctant to remove their ties and jackets.

For the Latin managers, style is important, while Anglo and Asian managers do not want to stand out or attract attention in their dress. French women managers are more likely to be dressed in ways that Anglo women managers might think inappropriate for the office. The French, in turn, think it strange that American businesswomen dress in "man-like" business suits (sometimes with running shoes). In addition, corporate dress seems to be color-coded. Women working in the United Kingdom have been advised not to wear red, or brightly colored suits and dresses. Bankers at one Dutch bank eschew brown suits.

Dress code may also signal task orientation. For example, rolled up shirt sleeves are considered a signal of "getting down to business' (United States) or "relaxing on the job" (France). One very hot day, at an in-house company seminar at a beautiful lakefront conference center, a German manager arrived in a dark tie and jacket. His colleagues arrived in more casual attire. When asked why he was so dressed up, he replied, "We're here to work".

Ideas currently in vogue regarding dress code include "dressing down days" and "dressing for the customer". Some US companies have designated certain days, such as Fridays, as days when people are encouraged to come to work in more casual clothes, like those they would wear at home.[21] This created problems in London.[22]

> Trying to relax in the 1990s is just too stressful. City high-flyers who campaigned successfully for "dress-down Fridays", when they could swap pinstripes for jeans at the office, have found the casual look leads to style wars . . . Three months after starting its dress-down days, Nomura, the Japanese finance house, finds that a quarter of its workers prefer formal suits. The same has happened at IBM and Ford at Dagenham (UK) . . .
>
> BIFU, the banking staff union, said, "there is a feeling that dress-down days erode the line between work and home life, and management always comes off best. In informal companies such as Microsoft, . . . people appear to live at their desks".

According to this report, not only did they feel vulnerable before their peers, but they were also reluctant to give up their symbols of authority. "The British were not ready: it was too much too quickly."

Other companies are also encouraging workers to dress in ways to match the customer. Doing business with Levi-Strauss may mean going to head office wearing jeans (Levis of course), rather than a Chanel suit. However, efforts to encourage a particular dress code, at work or otherwise, may be rejected, particularly in France and Italy, where the style of dress is seen as an expression of the individual.

Written versus verbal contracts

Whether business agreements are sealed by being put in writing or by giving one's word is also highly important. American managers are seen as excessive when they arrive to negotiate a business deal with the contract already in hand and a team of lawyers at their side. When head office expects contracts to be signed, sealed, and delivered this can create problems for managers operating in other parts of the world where one's word is considered far more binding than what is on paper ("my word is my bond" versus "get it in writing"). After all, personal honor is at stake, and reputation is far more valuable than some legal document.

If the business deal falls through, Americans will have recourse to the legal department to retrieve the situation. In other countries, if there are problems with the deal, these issues must be sorted out through the relationship. These different expectations may be reflected in the number of lawyers per capita in America, Europe, and Japan (per 100,000: United States 279, United Kingdom 114, Germany 77, France 29, Japan 11).

Observing the artifacts and behavior described above provides clues to assumptions regarding external adaptation – how space is used, how strangers are dealt with, how contracts are established – and internal integration – how formal, what is the proper way of getting to know someone, and how much personal distance is expected. But the meaning of these types of behavior has to be understood through the eyes of the other. This means pursuing our exploration by asking questions.

Beliefs and values

When questioned about their behavior, managers respond stating their beliefs and values. Beliefs are statements of fact, about the way things *are*. Values are preferred states about the way things *should be*, about ideals. Studies of managerial values across cultures and the discussion of how they affect the practice of management began in the 1960s.[23] These studies often focused on how these values affected motivation and leadership in different countries.

Using questionnaires and surveys, management scholars such as Hofstede, Laurent and Trompenaars have provided more and more evidence for different organizationally re-lated beliefs and values of employees and managers from around the world.[24] The implications of their findings for management practice will be developed more fully in Part II. Here we focus more specifically on beliefs and values regarding what makes for success, both for the organization and the manager, which represent cultural solutions to problems of external adaptation and internal integration.

Criteria for success

National cultures differ in their perception of for whom the firm exists: the shareholders, customers, or employees. In American or American-inspired business schools, students are taught that a company exists for the benefit (the divine rights) of the shareholders. In Japan, this statement would be greeted with disbelief, not to say shock. It is the customer who has divine rights. In certain European countries, such as Germany or Sweden, it may well be the employees who have the divine rights (right to information, right to consultation, right to veto, right to job security and social welfare benefits).

Different stakeholders mean different criteria for success. Therefore beliefs and values differ in terms of what is considered to be important: product integrity, technological leadership, market share, customer satisfaction, or shareholder value. Although all these factors are relevant to corporate success, cultural preferences come into play.

Product quality

The German corporate obsession is products; their design, construction, and quality. When Germans are asked what makes them proud of their company, they tend not to mention profits, turnover, or market share. Rather they will emphasize product quality. The *raison d'être* of the manufacturing companies which dominate German industry is to design and manufacture high-quality and reliable products. "German companies do not make money, only the Mint does that; they make goods and services and if people want to buy them, profit ensues."[25] This means that product integrity is often considered more important than customer satisfaction.

Technological leadership

In French industry, the belief in the supremacy of technology has been described as *la technologie au service de la vanité nationale* (technology as the servant of national vanity). Nevertheless, this has contributed to successes in a number of fields, including the aeronautic and space industries, nuclear energy, telecommunications, and railways. This orientation, which is supported by the education system, permeates through French industry. The premium placed on engineering and science degrees encourages emphasis on technology, innovation, and grand design, sometimes at the expense of commercial relevance (the Concorde being just one example).

Market share

Japanese companies, for their part, have revered market share as the road to success. The limited domestic market encourages emphasis on the customer and searching for markets abroad. This translates into a real willingness, on the part of Japanese firms, to invest time and money in understanding customers overseas. For example, one Japanese manager from Yamaha was sent to Spain for a year to learn to play guitar, as a way of absorbing the culture.

What is management?

Trying to define the meaning of management also shows up differences in beliefs and values. Take this popular and pragmatic definition: "Management is getting things done through other people". This seemingly innocuous statement uttered by the grandfather of American management, Peter Drucker, can be deconstructed to reveal a number of cultural beliefs and values.[26] For example, it emphasizes the importance of achievement (getting things *done*). It also puts stress on the material (*things*), and implicitly considers people as a factor of production (*through* other people). Overall, it characterizes the task orientation which typifies the American approach to management.

Others may read this as lacking in appreciation for "being" or for the more spiritual aspects (what is so important about getting things done?), and as manipulative (why *through* rather than *with* other people?). This definition may be rejected in cultures that emphasize the spiritual over the material, and concern for people over concern for the task.

German managers might also take issue with the definition but for different reasons. Germans do not distinguish management from doing technical work. For German managers there is a perceived oneness, or inseparability, of technical duties and managerial responsibilities. Therefore management is partly about getting things done, but it also means doing it yourself.

Consider another definition of management: "Real management is developing people through work". This quote reflects the more spiritual and people-oriented beliefs and values of the Pakistani CEO of a major international bank. This definition reveals more concern with *who* people are and how they evolve, rather than *what* they achieve. The Anglo–Dutch company Unilever provides an example of this philosophy, referred to by its management as "a management development company financed by soap and margarine".

For others, these beliefs and values would raise serious concern about lack of business sense. After all, business is about making money, not developing people. And the idea that people are developed through work as opposed to outside it would be seen as an intrusion of privacy ("I don't need work to develop me personally!") in cultures where there is a greater separation of personal and work life. The idea of developing people through work is also related to the current widespread notion of "empowerment", which some would regard as manipulation by another name: "Empowerment doesn't develop me personally – it just allows the organization to do away with a couple of layers of supervisors".

The right person for the job

The beliefs and values regarding the right person for the job can be inferred from artifacts such as the executive job advertisement. While this may seem like a standard international item, a brief glance through the jobs pages of *The Times* of London, *Le Monde* in Paris and Germany's *Frankfurter Allgemeine Zeitung* suggests otherwise.

First, what British job seekers deem an essential piece of information – what the job pays and what perks are on offer – is conspicuously absent from French and German advertisements. If French and German adverts are vague about material rewards, they are precise about qualifications. In Germany, a technical director for a machine tool company will be expected to have a Dipl. Ing. degree in mechanical engineering. French adverts go even further, specifying not just the type of degree but also indicating a particular set of awarding institutions. An advert might demand, for example, *Formation supérieure (X, Centrale, Mines)*, these being the most illustrious engineering *grandes écoles*. All this contrasts with the vague call for graduates (or graduate preferred) which prevails in Britain. In Britain, qualifications beyond degree level may make employers wary, but in France or Germany it is difficult to become overqualified. All this points to different beliefs and values regarding the qualifications for management.

Beliefs about who is the right manager, what is management, and what constitutes success are ultimately linked to values which indicate what is considered to be important, and thus deserving of attention. For example, if technological innovation is considered to be the key to success, then innovative behavior will be valued and encouraged. If market share is deemed necessary, then the focus will be to provide value to the customer. If the reason for being is "creating shareholder wealth", then profitability is valued above all else. These values in turn influence the degree to which organizations are seen as task- or people-oriented. It will also indicate the types of behavior, values, and beliefs expected of the people it seeks to hire. But what is perhaps more interesting is to try to get a glimpse of the underlying world-view, in order to better understand the rationale for what is valued and what is believed to be true. Digging deeper leads us to basic assumptions.

Basic assumptions

The basic assumptions used to guide us further in our exploration of culture are derived from the work of anthropologists, Kluckholn and Strodtbeck. These are the dimensions most commonly used by management scholars as shown in Figure 2.2.[27] Our intention here is *not* to review or critique this literature, but to organize and synthesize the overlapping but fragmented dimensions of culture considered relevant to management.

The relationship between the various dimensions can be more readily grasped if we return to the definition of culture as shared solutions to problems of external adaptation and internal integration. This distinction provides a useful framework for organizing the relevant cultural assumptions shown in Figure 2.3. Managing "relationships with the environment" or solutions to problems of *external adaptation* include assumptions regarding control and uncertainty, the nature of human activity, and the nature of truth and reality, or the way we know the environment. Managing "relationships among people" (solutions to problems of *internal integration*) includes assumptions regarding the importance of relationships over task achievement, relationships with superiors and subordinates (hierarchy), and relationships with peers (individualism and collectivism). Assumptions regarding time, space, and language are related to both relationships with nature as well as relationships with people.

In the following discussion, we will briefly describe and illustrate each assumption. The purpose here is to provide an idea of the core assumptions or basic foundations of culture

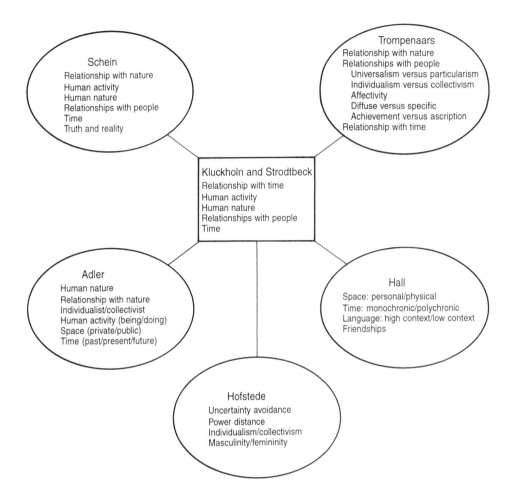

Figure 2.2 Key dimensions of culture. (*Source*: E. Schein (1985) *Organizational Culture and Leadership*, Jossey-Bass, San Francisco. Reproduced with permission.)

in order to be properly equipped to diagnose culture, and to discover coherence and meaning. Only then can we move on to understand the impact of culture on management practice. A deeper discussion of the implications for management in terms of organization, strategy, and HRM is reserved for Part II.

External adaptation

Relationship with nature

The very notion of "management" implies that managers have *control* over nature. American culture can be described as a "can-do" culture. Injunctions like "Go for it!" (or

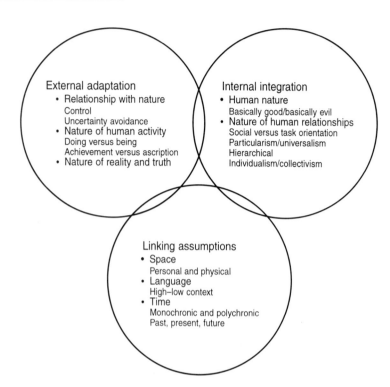

Figure 2.3 Underlying cultural assumptions.

as the Nike commercial says, "Just do it!") are manifestations of this profound belief that nothing is predetermined. This attitude is typically described by Europeans as "American enthusiasm", which they may consider refreshing if somewhat naive. While in some cultures nature may be seen as controllable, in others it is accepted as a given. Destiny, or fate, is predetermined. Rather than try to change things or *make* things happen, it is considered to be more natural to *let* things happen.

In countries where Islamic religion plays an important role, the attitude towards nature is best captured in the phrase, *Insh'allah* (if God wills), which implies that the events cannot be controlled. To try to do so is to be considered "insane or irreligious".[28] Similarly, in Portugal the expression, *se deus quiser*, is commonly used and has the same meaning, which again reflects the importance of religion in daily life, this time Catholicism, and the acceptance of fate, or one's destiny.

The importance of being in harmony with nature can be found in the following example. In China, in order to insure proper harmony, the *feng shui* expert will be summoned to advise on the construction and design of office buildings. Apparently, this was not the case when the Bank of China built its seventy-storey office building in Hong Kong.

Hong Kong residents also worried that triangles that give the building its distinctive design were an example of bad feng shui . . . the art of arranging buildings and other objects so they are in harmony with nature and bring good luck. Many feng shui experts say the sharp angles of the tower are like dangerous daggers pointed at businesses and homes in the area. Small mirrors have been placed in the windows of surrounding buildings to deflect the evil that is supposed to emanate from the bank. Neither the bank nor Mr. Pei [the world famous architect] consulted a feng sui expert.[29]

Dominating the Hong Kong skyline, this construction has been taken as an aggressive statement of control by Beijing over Hong Kong.

Closely linked with this desire for control over nature is the notion of "uncertainty avoidance" as discussed by Hofstede.[30] This refers to a society's discomfort with uncertainty, preference for predictability and control, and avoidance of risk. These assumptions about control over nature are reflected in planning rituals, the importance placed on schedules, and belief in taking initiative and responsibility.

In many eastern European countries, for example, the centralized control of the Communist regime served to reduce uncertainty. This experience, however, created a sense of learnt helplessness, a sense of being unable to make an impact, as well as a strong fear of making mistakes. This poses one of the biggest challenges to improving performance, at both individual and collective levels.[31]

Nature of human activity

The assumption of control over nature versus fatalism is connected to the desirability of taking action. For Americans, making things happen is assumed to be the way to survive. Taking time for reflection is seen as evidence of ineffective management. This is seen in the management injunction, "Don't just stand there, do something!"

But consider the alternative, "Don't just do something, stand there!" There is an old Chinese saying which goes, "Beyond the fine art of getting others to do things, is the even worthier art of allowing things to do themselves". French politician Henri Queuille went as far as to suggest: "Any problem, however complex can be solved by failing to take a decision".

American and northern European managers are more likely to initiate action, and to take decisions quickly. They value being active, and being decisive. "Better to make the wrong decision than no decision". Readiness to take action means willingness to take risks and to make mistakes, and then make the necessary adjustments. Compare this attitude with that of a French manager, confronted by a problem in his boss's absence. When asked whether he intended to take any action he replied, "It is better to do nothing than to disappoint".

French managers put more value on thinking than doing. They spend much more time analyzing and planning than their American counterparts. This frustrates American managers who prefer to take action and to figure things out along the way. The French regard the American approach as sloppy and unsystematic, as *bricolage* (tinkering). As they see it, it is better to get it right up front (figuring things out first) than waste time doing it the wrong way.

Japanese managers often dismiss this propensity for action and decision as impulsiveness. For them, taking quick decisions may signal a poor grasp of the importance of the decision at hand and insufficient reflection. Therefore, one's maturity as well as one's intelligence is placed in doubt.

When managers assume that they have control over nature, they are more likely to take action. In turn greater importance is placed upon *doing* versus *being*. When managers assume that they have little control over nature, they are more likely to take time to reflect and plan, to watch how events evolve, and to adapt to the emerging situation. Thus the quality of thinking (of education), and of personal character: who you are is more important than what you do. This difference is also referred to as *achievement* versus *ascription*.[32]

In America, the idea that "anyone can become President" sends a powerful message that what one accomplishes is more important than where one went to school or one's professional ties. In France, to become President, you will need to have attended the right *grande école* and to have the right connections. That pattern is replicated in French companies where access to senior executive level (*cadre supérieur*) is essentially determined by belonging to the elite – *grandes écoles* or *grands corps*. Who you are thus determines who you know, which is considered necessary for making it to the top.

In Japan your character, loyalty, trustworthiness, ability to get along with the group, may be more important than what you can achieve. While competitiveness within cohort groups may be intense, criteria for promotion may be more vague: being seen as hard-working and dedicated by spending extra hours at work, socializing with fellow employees, or playing golf with customers on weekends. Between levels, promotion is based on seniority, age, and gender (male). In cultures where seniority is important, such as Korea, it would be quite difficult for older managers to report to younger ones, or to earn less.

A senior HR executive at Rhône-Poulenc Rorer tells the following story.[33]

> At RPR Japan, a young Japanese was offered a job (by a German expatriate) at a director level within the Japanese affiliate. He turned down the offer. I asked him if he felt he had the skills to do the job. He replied, "Of course, but I am too young. I would have no credibility and would not be successful".

Whether managers are valued for what (and who) they know or what they are able to accomplish depends on assumptions regarding the relationship with nature. Nevertheless, it also influences assumptions regarding relationships among people, for example who has authority over whom. This will be further elaborated upon in the next section.

Nature of truth and reality

How truth is determined varies between cultures. In many Anglo-Saxon cultures, truth is synonymous with facts and figures. Harold Geneen, former CEO of ITT, referred to these as the "unshakeable facts", demanding to see the numbers of his European reports. The European managers remarked that they gave him the numbers all right but that they (not he) knew what the numbers meant. Interpretation and reasoning are seen as far more important than just numbers.

In France, a business decision will be based on serious analysis not only of the numbers but also the underlying logic. Based on Cartesian philosophy, this means that truth is established only when logically proven so. French managers use an inductive approach in problem-solving, deriving solutions from theory. This irritates American managers who feel that the French are too theoretical and abstract. The American approach is more deductive, theory is derived from data and experience. They are ready to go out into the field and experiment.

These differences can cause problems when making business presentations. For the French it is important to provide theory, history, and context. The Americans complain that these presentations are boring, and "too long-winded" – "just get to the point"! The French complain that American presentations are too much like "marketing" – too slick and superficial.[34]

American consultants are often trained to start presentations with the executive summary, or conclusions up front. This practice has unintentionally offended their clients, for example, in Poland where presenting conclusions first was viewed as arrogant or as precluding contribution to the solution by the other party. In Asian countries, once the conclusion is presented it is taken as given and then difficult to criticize.

Other cultures rely more on feeling, intuition, and spirituality. While presented with facts and figures, they are only convinced in their truth if it feels right. Brazilian managers, for example, say that they prefer to rely on intuition or emotions, as it is often difficult to get the facts and figures. And being faced with constantly changing situations has forced them to develop a finely tuned sense of intuition and to become highly resourceful. According to one report in *The Economist*, the astrological consulting business in Brazil, is worth $1 million a year.

> Not long ago, a São Paulo bank was weighing up a big decision: when to offer a big issue of debentures to the Euromarket. Did the managers look at the capital markets, examine exchange rates, and pore over economic statistics? No. After examining 15 different astrological maps, an astrological consultancy told the bank's vice president: "Jupiter is riding well, through the center of the skies". Translation: the time was right for a business venture abroad. Based on that celestial tip, the deal was a success.[35]

Europeans may be surprised when astrologists, wisemen, or fortune tellers assist in decision-making in Brazil or Asia. However, many French companies use graphology, handwriting analysis, to assist in making personnel decisions, for which there is little scientific evidence.

Thus the solutions to problems of external adaptation are revealed in assumptions regarding control over nature, human activity, and how truth is established. These solutions which determine the relationship with nature also have implications for how relationships among people are managed. For example, it may be that a perceived lack of control over nature increases the perceived need to have control over people. Under these circumstances, social controls would become more important than task controls, and change efforts would be geared to developing internal capabilities rather than re-engineering tasks. Thus lower perceived control over nature places greater emphasis on people (relationships) rather than task. Assumptions regarding human nature and how relationships are managed thus provide the solutions to problems of internal integration.

Internal integration

Human nature

What is the underlying assumption about human nature? Are people basically *good* or *evil*? Some religions take as their point of departure the idea that people are basically evil (original sin) and can only be redeemed through certain acts of religious faith. People are expected to sin, to confess, to ask forgiveness, and to repent. Others assume that people are basically good, that they live and work to fulfill or maximize their human potential. Hard work and task mastery or achievement are seen as ways of achieving these ends.[36]

In management this translates into the beliefs about workers: Theory X and Theory Y.[37] In Theory X, workers are assumed to be lazy, to need constant direction and supervision because they will try to get away with as much as possible. Managers, of course, are different. In Theory Y, workers are assumed to be self-directed, to be willing to take initiative and to do what has to be done without external control. Here, there is no perceived difference in the nature of workers and managers. Assumptions about human nature determine the willingness to delegate and the nature of control systems. The popular notion of empowerment depends very much on the assumption that people are self-directed and self-controlled.

These assumptions of whether people can be trusted or not are found in artifacts such as time punch clocks, the nature of reporting systems, and the degree of scrutiny of expense accounts. In many cases, the removal of time clocks has had a major impact on the nature of relationships between managers and employees, who feel for the first time that they are being treated as adults, and are trusted. The Danish CEO of Oticon, Lars Kolind, insists that his number one assumption is that he hires "adults". Adults, he says, know when to come to work, what to do, and how much to spend on travel. Therefore, there are no time clocks, job descriptions, nor accounting for travel expenses.

These assumptions regarding human nature relate to the nature of relationships. For example, if we assume that people are basically "good", we are more likely to give people greater autonomy, and to allow them to go off on their own way, to take initiative. This encourages a greater task orientation. If human nature is considered basically "evil", then there is a greater need for external controls and supervision. This encourages a more relationship-oriented culture, and a greater emphasis on hierarchy and other forms of social controls, such as group pressure. Thus assumptions regarding human nature influence assumptions regarding the nature of relationships, how important they are (for example, compared with task achievement) and how they are structured.

Relationships with people

Importance of task versus relationships

A key assumption differentiating cultures is the importance of *relationships* over *tasks*. The statement "Let's keep this strictly business" is likely to confuse, if not offend, managers in Asia, Latin American, and the Middle East. Here, managers prefer to do business with people they know. A relationship must be established before business can be conducted. Without that foundation, how could you trust this person to uphold the contract or perform their jobs? Companies often prefer to hire family members and relations because they believe that their character and trustworthiness have been vouched for by the employee. They can therefore rely on more informal social controls to keep employees in line. It is taken for granted that in order to get anything done you have to go through the relationships.

American and northern European managers prefer to focus on the task and to keep personal relationships aside. Americans pride themselves on having good business sense. They avoid doing business with friends and family, as these relationships are considered to interfere with sound judgement. People should be hired on merit (ability and past accomplishments) and not on "connections" (*Guanxi* in China and *le piston* in France). The idea that you need to develop relationships in order to accomplish tasks is viewed with suspicion, and dismissed as company politics.

In Latin cultures, family and friends come first, taking precedence over all else. Latin European managers responding to a survey differed considerably from their Anglo counterparts when asked whether they would lie to save a friend who had caused an accident from criminal prosecution. While almost nine out of ten Anglo managers refused to lie to save a friend, only two-thirds of Latin European respondents refused to do so.[38]

For the Anglo culture, objective "reality", the truth about what really happened, is more important than personal ties. In Latin cultures, reality must be considered in the context of the nature of the relationship and circumstances. This dimension is referred to as *universalism* versus *particularism*. In universalist cultures people believe that the rules and regulations should apply to everybody, and not just your enemies, as Brazilian managers would say.

Masculinity/femininity

Another difference relates to taking care of people versus taking care of business, referred to by Hofstede as *femininity versus masculinity*.[39] The concern for quality of relationships and of work life, nurturing, and social well-being in the Nordic countries, like Sweden and Denmark, have translated into initiatives such as Quality of Work Life and extensive social welfare programs. These countries are renowned for having among the highest standards of living, as well as the highest taxes, both of which caused concern in their decision to join the EU. It is perhaps not surprising that a world congress to deal with poverty recently took place in Denmark.

In masculine cultures, importance is placed on assertiveness, competitiveness, and materialism in the form of earnings and advancement, promotions and big bonuses. For the company profit counts above all, and the shareholder takes precedence over employee or customer interests. In Japan and the United States, both ranked high on masculinity according to Hofstede's findings, companies are now facing law suits from the families of managers who have died from overwork.

Hierarchy: the role of the boss

The nature of relationships also refers to how these relationships between people are structured, notably the extent to which *hierarchy* is revered. In France, for example, the boss is the boss. France has a singularity in terms of company law; it places in the hands of an individual what, in most countries is shared – deciding on, executing, and controlling policy. The French *Président-Directeur-Général* (PDG) is what Anglo–Saxons would regard as Chairman and Managing Director rolled into one. The status of a French PDG is sharply differentiated from that of the rest of top management. What is more, it is not a status which is lost on retirement: an ex-PDG expects to be addressed until his death as *Monsieur le Président*.

In northern Europe, on the other hand, the leader has considerably less importance. French managers would have a hard time believing that at Unilever, the Dutch–Anglo consumer products company, there are three CEOs; or that in Denmark and Sweden the boss is not supposed to act like the boss. Instead, hierarchy, power, and status are downplayed. The CEO of one large Danish bank was admired by his subordinates for driving a battered old car. The reaction of one Latin European MBA student to this was that he would not dream of putting money into a bank whose CEO drove such a car.

The Japanese position regarding hierarchy is more ambiguous. Conventional wisdom has it that Japanese manufacturing operations in the United States and Europe have been successful because the boss is seen as more directly involved with the workers, foregoing executive parking lots or dining rooms. Similarly, the use of uniforms in Japanese car assembly plants in the United States and United Kingdom is encouraged to blur the distinction between workers and managers. Workers are also encouraged to get involved in the decision-making processes and to come up with suggestions to improve how their job is done. While these practices reinforce the collective spirit, the boss is still very much the boss. Japanese employees spend many hours after work drinking and socializing with the boss to be able to decipher what it is that the boss really wants.

Peer relations or individualism/collectivism
The nature of relationships also includes how peers interact. Is the prevailing ethos one of cooperation or competition – group-oriented or "every man for himself"? In individualist societies people are supposed to take care of themselves and remain emotionally independent from the group. Self-interest is the dominant motivation. In collective societies, the concern is for the group rather than for the individual. Individuals define their identity by their relationships to others, through group membership, and strive for a sense of belonging.[40]

Consider, for example, the different forms of punishment meted out to youngsters in Japan and America. In Japan, ostracism is the most devastating punishment. This is evident in the fear of Japanese children of being locked out of the house; while for American children, punishment is being locked in ("go to your room"). Later in life, American children are expected to leave home at a certain age (between 18 and 21) and make it on their own. In contrast, Japanese children are expected, on reaching adulthood, to take care of their parents who have been taking care of them. This reflects the sense of mutual dependence, or interdependence (*amae*).[41]

This interdependence is also evident in Middle Eastern cultures. The idea that one's family could live 3,000 miles away is difficult for them to understand, never mind accept. This makes it difficult at times to recruit people for overseas assignments. One multinational in Egypt, very pleased to have found a high-potential local manager for foreign assignment and management development was frustrated because it was not possible for her, being single, to live alone, away from her parents.

Linking assumptions: space, language, time

Assumptions regarding space, language, and time as discussed by Ed Hall[42] relate to both issues of external adaptation and internal integration. For example, while language reflects and creates the relationship with nature (as in how skiers define snow, or how sailors describe the sea) it also provides the means for having relationships among people, in terms of what gets said and how it gets said. Assumptions regarding space can refer to how a group has managed its relationship with the environment through use of physical space, as seen in architecture and interior design, as well as how relationships are managed through personal space, how much physical and emotional distance exists between people. And our view of time and how we manage it is in part determined by the degree to which we assume control over nature, and in turn determines the importance placed on relationships versus tasks.

Space

Assumptions about space are expressed in many ways, both physical and personal, and at many different levels, from what can be observed to what must be inferred. Solutions to problems of the availability of space determines our use of space, again both physical and personal. For example, this is readily observed in architecture and interior design, at home and at work. In Japanese architecture and design the juxtaposition of interior/exterior space reflects less distinction and more harmony between people and their environment.

Differences can be found in how physical space (through architecture and interior design) as well as how public versus private space is managed in relationships. Compare Japan, where space is limited (island mentality) with the wide open spaces in the United States (frontier spirit).[43]

There is of course a high value placed on space in Japan, given the population and limited space available. This means that personal space is also carefully managed. It could be argued that the degree of formality, or personal distance, compensates for the lack of physical space. The Japanese do not appreciate touching or being touched and prefer bowing to handshakes.

In the United States there is less constraint with regard to physical space. The solutions which have evolved are therefore different from those in Japan. For example, there is less emphasis on living in harmony or respecting the other person's privacy. Abundance of space means that disputes can always be settled by moving on or "heading west". American mobility, both geographic and professional, is a manifestation of this "frontier spirit".

It can also be argued that American friendliness or readiness to make contact reflects the need to make greater efforts to reduce the impact of greater physical spaces and distances. Thus Americans more readily tend to share personal information and to inquire into the private lives of others.

Americans exchange personal information as currency, as evidence of goodwill, expect to be reciprocated, in order to build relationships, to establish trust. Europeans, however, tend to be more reserved than their American counterparts. Given the history of invasions and occupations, there is a greater suspicion of strangers, and a perceived need to keep their distance. First you need to demonstrate that you can be trusted.[44]

In this way assumptions regarding personal space determine the nature and degree of involvement with others, what is expected from friendships and family and from colleagues: relationship building versus getting down to business. It is expressed in artifacts and behavior such as the use of formal titles and address (formal versus informal "you"), what is discussed or not discussed, and how. It also reflects the degree to which information is embedded or direct, in other words, how much is left unsaid (high context or low context, as described in the next section).

Language

The use of language may represent the most visible yet the least understood influence on our world-view. It is through language that we formulate thoughts and that we experience the world and others. The oft-cited example of the Eskimos having multiple words for snow demonstrates that experience and language are intricately linked; our language is a reflection of our experience, but it also shapes what we experience.[45] Language determines what we see and fail to see, what we say and omit to say, and who is allowed to say what. It therefore influences both our relationship with the environment and our relationships with other people.

Hall makes the distinction between *high-context* and *low-context* cultures.[46] In low-context cultures, communications are expected to be clear and direct, or explicit. You are expected to come to the point, not to "beat around the bush". Nor are you expected to read between the lines. The person and the situation are not particularly relevant to the discourse. Everyone should be able to understand the message and have equal access to information.

In other cultures (high context), communication is highly dependent upon the person and the situation. Information is shared among people, and some people have more privileged access than others. Much is communicated in what is not said. Being able to read non-verbal signs and body language is crucial. Ambiguity and subtlety are expected and highly valued. You are not supposed to come right out and say it. This creates embarrassment and discomfort.

This difference between high- and low-context cultures can cause communication difficulties, even more so when the participants share the same mother tongue. For example, when communicating, Americans like to be direct and get to the point – to be made clear and explicit. British managers often complain that they find presentations by Americans exasperating because everything is spelled out when the meaning seems perfectly obvious. Americans for their part, have little patience for long-winded explanations and see language as functional rather than as an art form. The reverse is true in Britain, where speech is more suggestive. Mastery of the language is considered a sign of good breeding and intelligence.

Finally, assumptions regarding language determine what is said and how it is said. This can be observed in artifacts, such as appropriate subjects of discussion (family, religion, or politics) and the degree of expressiveness. In Asian cultures expressing emotion may be considered a sign of immaturity and dangerous impulsiveness. North American managers may find it easy to express anger but are surprised when their Russian counterparts become "sentimental". Scandinavian managers are often uncomfortable in observing discussion among Italian or French managers, expecting it to come to blows. For Americans, silence and reserve provoke intense discomfort, whereas in Japan, silence is an indication of deep mutual trust. Close friends drink silently together.

Time

Assumptions about time also influence our relationship with the environment and with people. While different attitudes to time are easy to detect, such as the *mañana* syndrome, their underlying meaning is difficult to appreciate. These assumptions have been described by Hall as *monochronic* versus *polychronic*.[47]

In Anglo–Saxon and northern European cultures, time tends to be seen as limited; time, like money, is regarded as a finite resource which is *spent*. Time is seen as "monochronic", structured in a sequential and linear fashion. Managers from these countries typically expect to have appointments scheduled in hour or half-hour slots. Indeed, if involved in a discussion, they will probably finish their conversation before acknowledging a new arrival. Monochronic managers are acutely concerned (some say obsessed) with starting meetings on time, and on spending time productively.

In Latin European and Middle Eastern cultures, time is experienced as unlimited and simultaneous, or "polychronic". Managers from these countries typically believe that time expands to accommodate activities, and that seveal activities can happen concurrently. As time is expandable, a Latin manager may be late to a business meeting because it would be unthinkable to pass a colleague or friend in the corridor without stopping to chat or make contact. The friend would be highly offended. Business meetings are likely to be more fragmented with many interruptions from phone calls and visitors, as well as several discussions going on at once. This reflects the importance of relationships, which more task-oriented managers find irritating.

Since time can be seen as either limited or expandable, this results in differences in the importance attached to being "on time". Thus it is not just the cultural views of punctuality which differ, but what is signaled by being "on time". As in the last example, time may be used as an indication of hierarchy. In Britain, for instance, the more important you are, the more permissible it is to keep others waiting. In other cultures, it signals reliability. In Germany, where punctuality is revered, the lateness of a boss is no more tolerable than that of a subordinate, in fact quite the opposite.

Cultural attitudes to time also differ in the relative importance accorded to **past**, **present**, and **future**. For example, Americans are fond of the expression "Don't cry over spilt milk". This means not to worry about what has happened in the past. Even the present is seen as relatively unimportant, compared to "what happens next". European and Asian managers often complain that Americans are too impatient and always in a hurry. In Europe or Asia, on the other hand, there is a greater emphasis on the past, and on the importance of tradition.

Time orientation also influences attitudes to change. Americans tend to view change as inherently good; there is a perpetual search for new and better ways of doing things, and the future is optimistically viewed as an improvement on the past. For Europeans, on the other hand, change may be seen as inherently dangerous, since it threatens long-standing traditions. In France, the past is often invoked as a reason for not doing something: "It's not possible, it's never been done that way before". This means that the present and the future are determined by what has happened in the past.

Interpreting patterns of culture

The basic assumptions outlined above are interrelated. For example, assumptions regarding control over nature are linked to assumptions regarding time and activity. In cultures where there is perceived control over the environment, time is likely to be seen as monochronic: time can be controlled by schedules and agendas. Perceived control over nature encourages doing and achievement. This in turn reinforces the importance of task performance versus relationships, and of purpose rather than position within a set of relationships, and of individual initiative rather than group belonging. The importance of performance will tend to align with universal truths, rules and regulations, and direct, or low-context language. It is important to follow procedures and to spell things out clearly to make sure they happen as planned.

On the other hand, cultures where there is little perceived control over nature do not believe that time can be actively managed, or put into boxes. Given little control over what happens, the kind of person you are is more important than what you do – being takes priority over doing and ascription over achievement. Task performance is seen as less meaningful than relationships. The group or collective thus becomes an important source of control; social control rather than task or performance controls. Given the importance of the group, there tends to be more interaction among people and greater cohesiveness within the group. Loyalty is valued and moving from group to group becomes unlikely (low mobility). Thus language tends to be high context, as there is a greater shared meaning that has evolved over time. As saving face becomes important to preserve harmony, there is more concern with feelings than absolute facts.

These patterns are not mutually exclusive or exhaustive. The dimensions can be taken to represent extremes along which different cultures can be placed. For example, André Laurent, Professor at INSEAD, uses the notion of Blue and Green cultures to designate the ends of a continuum of the set of interrelationships described above and as shown in Table 2.1.

This encourages a discussion of the strengths and weaknesses, competencies and pathologies, of these cultural prototypes without getting distracted by country-specific stereotypes. By focusing on the dimensions themselves, it also allows for the discussion and appreciation of cultural differences among the industries, companies, and functions

Table 2.1   Analyzing cultures

Blue		Green

External adaptation

Nature

Control over nature	├────┼────┼────┼────┼────┤	Fatalism
Tolerate uncertainty	├────┼────┼────┼────┼────┤	Avoid uncertainty

Activity

Doing	├────┼────┼────┼────┼────┤	Being
Achievement	├────┼────┼────┼────┼────┤	Ascription
Truth in numbers	├────┼────┼────┼────┼────┤	Feelings
Reality is material	├────┼────┼────┼────┼────┤	Spiritual

Internal integration

Human nature

Basically good	├────┼────┼────┼────┼────┤	Basically evil

Relationships

Task-oriented	├────┼────┼────┼────┼────┤	Relationship
Achievement	├────┼────┼────┼────┼────┤	Social welfare
Egalitarian	├────┼────┼────┼────┼────┤	Hierarchic
Individual	├────┼────┼────┼────┼────┤	Collective

Linking assumptions

Space

Public	├────┼────┼────┼────┼────┤	Private

Language

Explicit (low context)	├────┼────┼────┼────┼────┤	Implicit (high context)
Neutral	├────┼────┼────┼────┼────┤	Emotional

Time

Limited (linear, sequential)	├────┼────┼────┤	Unending (cyclical, simultaneous)
Future ├────┼────┼────┤ Present	├────┼────┼────┤	Past

Source: Adapted from A. Laurent. Reproduced by permission.

within as well as between countries. So, while a particular country may tend towards the blue end on one dimension, a given company within that country may lie more towards the green end. These differences will be the subject of discussion in the next chapter.

In this chapter we have provided a framework and a key set of dimensions for diagnosing culture. The framework organizes culture elements according to their visibility or accessibility and the method required to discern them; we can observe artifacts and behavior, question values and beliefs, and interpret underlying assumptions. For example, assumptions about time as monochronic (limited, sequential, and linear) are expressed in beliefs such as "time is money", the value placed on urgency. The corresponding behavior and artifacts can be observed in the presence of punch clocks, bells announcing coffee and lunch breaks, and people hurrying about, looking busy.

Basic assumptions represent the deepest level of culture, or our taken-for-granted world-view. It is at this level that we must search for the meaning of behavior, or beliefs and values. These assumptions are so embedded that it often takes a cultural outsider to detect them. Even then, they cannot be accessed through direct questioning, but have to be inferred. Once inferred, these assumptions need to be validated, tested with further questioning and close observation. Over time, patterns of behavior and artifacts, beliefs and values, begin to provide a coherent picture reflecting the inherent logic of the other culture. Webs of meaning are intricately woven between the various elements and layers, providing consistency and durability. Even if we do not always understand why, we begin to realize that what looks strange to us makes perfect sense to others.

Notes

1. Geertz, C. (1973) *The Interpretation of Culture*, New York: Basic Books, p. 5.
2. Tylor, E.B. (1924) *Primitive Culture*, Gloucester, MA: Smith.
3. Kluckholn, F. and Strodtbeck, F. (1961) *Variations in Value Orientations*, Evanston, IL: Row, Peterson; Triandis, H.C. (1972) *The Analysis of Subjective Culture*, New York: Wiley Interscience.
4. Mead, M. (1953) *Coming of Age in Samoa*, New York: Modern Library.
5. Lévi-Strauss, C. (1971) *L'Homme Nu*, Paris: Plon; Geertz, *Op. cit.*
6. Argyris, C. and Schon, D. (1974) *Theory in Practice*, San Francisco: Jossey-Bass.
7. Schein, E.H. (1985) *Organizational Culture and Leadership*, San Francisco: Jossey-Bass.
8. See Van Maanen, J. (1988) *Tales of the Field*, Chicago: University of Chicago Press.
9. Geertz, *Op. cit.*
10. Glaser, B.G. and Strauss, A.L. (1967) *The Discovery of Grounded Theory*, Chicago: Aldine.
11. Van Maanen, *Op. cit.*
12. Schein, E.H. (1987) *The Clinical Perspective in Fieldwork*, Beverly Hills: Sage.
13. Kets de Vries, M.F.R. and Miller, D. (1987) "Interpreting organizational texts", *Journal of Management Studies*, 24(3), pp. 233–47.
14. Sherman, C.D. (1986) "Seating surplus Japanese workers by the window: How Japanese firms put workers out to grass", *International Herald Tribune*, October 10, p. 21.
15. Browning, E.S. (1994) "Side by side", *Wall Street Journal*, May 3, p. 1.
16. Atkinson, R. (1994) "Mercedes immerses executives in 'Bama drawl", *International Herald Tribune*, pp. 1, 4.
17. Orleman, P.A. (1992) The global corporation: Managing across cultures, Masters thesis, University of Pennsylvania.
18. Sherman, *Op. cit.*
19. "The battle plans of Hilmar Kopper", *Euromoney*, January 1994, pp. 29–44.
20. Hall, E.T. and Hall, M.R. (1990) *Understanding Cultural Differences*, Yarmouth, ME: Intercultural Press, p. 11; Hall, E.T. (1960) "The silent language of overseas business", *Harvard Business Review*, May/June, 38(3), pp. 87–95.

21. Martin, R. (1995) "90's credo: Dress down for success", *International Herald Tribune*, March 18–19, p. 11.
22. Harlow, J. and Hamilton, K. (1995) "Hung-up staff turn backs on dressing down", *The Sunday Times*, December 10.
23. England, G.W. (1978) "Managers and their value systems: A five country comparative study", *Columbia Journal of World Business*, 13(2), pp. 35–44; Haire, M., Ghiselli, E.E. and Porter, L.W. (1966) *Managerial Thinking: An International Study*, New York: Wiley.
24. Hofstede, G. (1980) *Cultures Consequences*, Beverly Hills: Sage; Hofstede, G. (1980) "Organization, motivation and leadership: Do American theories apply abroad?", *Organization Dynamics*, 9, 42–63; Laurent, A. (1983) "The cultural diversity of western conception of management", *International Studies of Management and Organization*, 13(1–2), pp. 75–96; Trompenaars, F. (1993) *Riding the Waves of Culture*, London: Nicholas Brealey.
25. Lawrence, P.A. (1980) *Managers and Management in West Germany*, London: Croom Helm, p. 187.
26. Kohls, L.R. (1979) *Survival Kit for Overseas Living*, Yarmouth, ME: Intercultural Press.
27. Kluckholn and Strodtbeck, *Op. cit.*; Schein, *Op. cit.*; Adler, N.J. (1991) *International Dimensions of Organizational Behavior*, 2nd edn, Boston, MA: PWS Kent; Trompenaars, *Op. cit.*; Rhinesmith, S. (1970) Cultural Organizational Analysis: The Interrelationship of Value Orientations and Managerial Behavior, Cambridge, MA: McBer Publication Series, No. 5.
28. Copeland Griggs (1983) Going International Part II, Video.
29. Basler, B. (1990) "China's looming symbol", *International Herald Tribune*, March 23, pp. 1, 6.
30. Hofstede, *Op. cit.*
31. Cyr, D.J. and Schneider, S.C. (1996) "Implications for learning: Human resource management in East–West joint ventures", *Organization Studies*, 17(2), pp. 207–226.
32. Trompenaars, *Op. cit.*
33. Orleman, P.A., Personal communication.
34. Orleman (1992), *Op. cit.*
35. "Broomsticks and dollars", *The Economist*, February 11, 1995, p. 70.
36. See Furnham, A. (1989) *The Protestant Work Ethic*, Routledge: London.
37. McGregor, D. (1960) *The Nature of Human Enterprise*, New York: McGraw-Hill.
38. Trompenaars, *Op. cit.*, p. 34.
39. Hofstede, *Op. cit.*
40. Markus, H. and Kitayama, S. (1991) "Culture and self: Implications for cognition, emotion and motivation", *Psychological Review*, 98, pp. 224–53.
41. Doi, T. (1987) *Amae no shuhen*, Tokyo: Kobundo.
42. Hall (1960), *Op. cit.*
43. Wallin, T.O. (1972) "The international executive baggage: Cultural values of the American frontier", *MSU Business Topics*, (Spring), pp. 49–58.
44. Meyer, H.-D. (1993) "The cultural gap in long-term international work groups", *European Management Journal*, 11(1), pp. 93–101.
45. Whorf, B.L. (1967) *Language, Thought and Reality*, Cambridge, MA: MIT Press.
46. Hall and Hall, *Op. cit.*, p. 6.
47. *Ibid.*, p. 13.

CHAPTER THREE

Interacting spheres of culture

Culture is everywhere and always relevant in organizational life, but there is no obvious or natural level
of analysis from which to observe it.

John Van Maanen and André Laurent[1]

The influence of culture on business practice can be explored in several spheres. These
"cultural spheres of influence" interact in complex ways that limit the relevance of simple
recipes for doing business in any particular country. When arriving in France, for example, it is not enough to know at which end of the scale the French can be found on key
dimensions.

We have to recognize that providing consulting services to a pharmaceutical company
in Paris will be quite different from doing so to a tire company such as Michelin in
Clermont-Ferrand. We need to be able to recognize and assess which dimensions are
relevant, regardless of which cultural sphere of influence is operating – to know, for
example, how relationships are managed in that particular department or unit, of that
particular company, in that particular industry, in that part of the country, or region.

As such, culture can be discovered in many places: regional cultures within nations
(urban versus rural, north versus south), and among groups of nations (Nordic versus
Latin American), industry cultures (pharmaceutical versus automotive), and corporate
cultures and subcultures (such as professional or functional groups). Often it is impossible to know whether the boundary dividing one country from another is more meaningful than the boundary between companies, or even the boundary between functions
within the same firm. It may well be that a French engineer from Paris has more in
common with a Japanese engineer from another firm in Tokyo than with an accountant
from the company's office in Marseille. Yet attending a professional conference of, say,
engineers or accountants, national differences remain apparent.

Again, what is important is recognizing which dimensions of culture are relevant,
assessing their potential impact, and devising strategies for using them creatively. It may
not be possible or even useful to argue which of the many spheres of culture is more
dominant. The framework presented in the last chapter and the method of inquiry are the
same, regardless. Observing artifacts and behavior, asking questions to elicit values and

beliefs, and finally interpreting the underlying assumptions need to become reflex activities.

Let us take an example. When you enter a company, differences in architecture and interior design, dress and behavior, and styles of interaction are immediately apparent. For example, the style of architecture and design may emphasize tradition or modernity, and signal the importance of hierarchy or collegial relations. A telling clue would be the presence of an executive parking lot and dining rooms, of open office space or closed doors. Others include the dress code and form of address (the use of first or last names, titles, spoken deference), and the ease of interaction between senior and junior members, or between peers.

These observations provide clues to beliefs and values regarding the role of manager, the importance of rules and regulations, and the flow of communication and information. Underlying assumptions can then be brought to the surface regarding the nature of relationships among people, hierarchical and peer, and of the relationship with nature, for example, degree of perceived control. This diagnosis could apply to a company or business unit. The influence of industry culture or functional cultures would become clear from similarities observed among firms in the same sector, or among the same functions and professions in different firms.

The need to diagnose culture is clearly relevant in mergers and joint ventures, where managers from different countries, industries, and companies need to cooperate to achieve the benefits of these strategic alliances. Thus the aim of this chapter is to explore the multiple cultural spheres of influence and their complex interaction to better anticipate the impact of culture on management across whatever boundaries, as shown in Figure 3.1.

Each sphere of influence has its own set of artifacts and behaviors, beliefs and values, and underlying assumptions. Each has its own solutions to problems of external adaptation and internal integration. These different solutions may coincide or clash. The

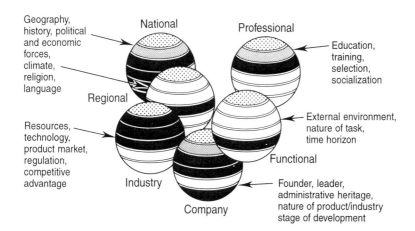

Figure 3.1   Interacting cultural spheres of influence. (J. Santos. Reprinted with permission.)

different cultural spheres may influence the business at hand to different degrees, and in more or less obvious ways, as some may be more deeply embedded than others.

In the next section we explore the different cultural spheres of influence: regional, industry, functional/professional, and corporate. The framework proposed in the previous chapter provides clues to assist us in deciphering which cultural dimensions are relevant. Reasons for differences are explored. We then describe how the various spheres may interact such that they can create problems or possibilities for gaining competitive advantage. Finally we draw out the implications for managers of different functional/professional cultures who must work together to deliver on the promised benefits of strategic alliances between companies in different industries, in different countries.

Cultural spheres of influence

Regional cultures

Regional cultures refer to differences **within** countries (such as the various *Länder* in Germany) and similarities **between** countries (such as in Scandinavia). It is important to recognize both, in order to avoid the assumption that doing business in Rome is the same as in Milan, or the assumption that doing business in Indonesia is so very different from Saudi Arabia. Recognizing regional cultures helps us to appreciate why certain industries flourish in different regions, and why trading partners may be more eagerly sought across some borders rather than others.

Within national borders

Regional cultures have evolved due to **geography, history, political and economic forces, language and religion**. Within countries, it is sometimes the east–west divide which is important, leading to cultural differences between, say, New York and California. In Germany, east–west differences exist for historical and political reasons, while in Turkey they are due to differences in levels of economic development. In other cases it is the north–south divide which indicates cultural borders, as in the case of doing business in Lisbon or Oporto (Portugal) where one finds Arabic or Celtic influences due to historical events, notably invasions.

Within countries, strong regional ties may compete with national identity as in the case of the Basques in the northeast of Spain fighting for independence, or the Québequois in Canada. In France, people maintain a strong sense of identity with a particular region, even if they have lived most of their lives elsewhere. Regional differences derive from *history* and *language*. In Brittany, for example, the local language, Breton, still evident on signposts, is similar to Welsh and derives from historical events which took place centuries ago. In the south, Provence, traces of Roman history are still visible, and the local language, Occitan, has recently been reinstated in some schools.

Regional differences within countries are also clearly evident in the case of Belgium and Switzerland, where different language groups coexist more or less amicably. The reasons for these differences within countries may also explain the similarities between countries. For example, cultural similarities of French-speaking Belgians and Swiss with the French themselves are attributed to historical events (the influence of Rome and Napoleon) which brought about shared religion, and language.

Cultural differences also exist between cities or between **urban-** and **rural**-based companies. Osaka and Tokyo (Japan) or São Paolo and Rio de Janeiro (Brazil) have differing reputations for being more task-oriented (hard-working) or more concerned about quality of life (relaxed). For example, one Indian executive described the culture of Bombay as very commercial, as it is a city where people come from all over India to make money. New Dehli, which houses the government, has a more administrative feel, and Calcutta is seen as the cultural center. A similar case could be made in Germany for Frankfurt, Bonn, and Berlin, respectively.

Companies located in large urban centers, whether Paris, New York, London, or Tokyo, tend to have different cultures from rural-based companies. Toyota consciously cultivates its image as a "country bumpkin"[2] and prefers to locate foreign operations in rural communities in the United Kingdom and the United States. Companies have also moved headquarters from large urban centers to improve productivity through enhancing quality of life, and not only for tax benefits.

With migration to the city in search of work, as is now the case in China, family ties are broken, weakening the importance of affiliation and reinforcing an achievement orientation. The move from rural to urban settings, or from agricultural-based to manufacturing-based or service-based industries, may also bring with it a gradual shift in a person's relationship with nature and time from a more harmonious one where time is seen as cyclical to one where there is greater perceived control and time is regarded as more linear.

Regional culture can have a strong influence on corporate culture as in the case of Michelin, the world's largest tire maker and technological leader (radial tires).[3] Michelin, the only major French company with headquarters outside Paris, plays on its home town (*la France profonde*) roots in its disdain for Paris as "superficial and faddish". It is located in the isolated, rural Auvergne region in central France known for being modest, austere, and pragmatic. Michelin makes a point of recruiting engineers from local universities and not from the *grandes écoles*.

Founded in the late 1800s by two brothers, André and Edouard, Michelin has been family run for three generations. Until recently, Michelin employees could expect to spend their entire working lives with the company, living in a company town (Clermont-Ferrand), complete with company housing, shops, and schools. This strong family culture encouraged dependency and an inward focus. Individualism was discouraged and criticism of the company strongly *déconseillé* (ill-advised).

Known for its secrecy, Michelin does not provide financial information despite being quoted on the Paris Bourse (stock exchange). The company is said to routinely fire people suspected of spilling secrets, and to exclude outsiders from its factories. Even a request by General de Gaulle to visit the factory was turned down. When Michelin goes abroad it chooses similarly isolated, rural sites, such as Greenville, South Carolina, or Newfoundland in Canada.

Particular regions within countries can create competitive advantages or disadvantages. One example is Silicon Valley, with its concentration of high-tech engineers and venture capital firms. Companies may choose to set up shop in particular regions because of such perceived advantages.

Japanese companies, for example, often choose to start operations in rural locations, particularly in the US Midwest: Honda in Maryville, Ohio; Nissan in Smyrna, Tennessee; and Mazda in Flat Rock, Michigan. Tennessee is considered particularly attractive to Japanese companies because of its similarities being non-union, having higher than US average productivity, a strong work ethic, racial homogeneity, and using courtesy to resolve conflicts. Being at the same latitude as Tokyo, the climate and the terrain are also similar. There is even similarity in symbols: the dogwood and the cherry blossom, the chrysanthemum and the magnolia.[4]

Beyond national borders

Similarities among countries create regional cultures beyond national borders. For example, around Stüttgart (Germany) the ethnic and linguistic heritage of the Alamann tribe crosses national borders to include parts of Alsace and Switzerland. Cultural affinities remain visible even after hundreds of years.[5]

Research on managerial values, work attitudes, and leadership styles in different countries has, in fact, confirmed these similarities, indicating this type of regional culture (see Figure 3.2).[6] This research indicates similarities between, say, French and Italian managers (Latin) which distinguish them from German and Austrian (Germanic) managers. These findings also imply that Swiss managers, whether French or German-speaking, are more similar in work attitudes to German than to French managers. And Belgian managers, French and Flemish-speaking, seem to have more in common with their French neighbor to the south than with their Dutch neighbor to the north. In fact a proposed merger between the Flemish Générale de Banque and a Dutch partner was called off, citing cultural differences as a prime reason.

It is revealing that Brazil, Israel, and Japan tend to fall outside of the main clusters, which is probably explained by their unique historical and cultural heritages. For example, Brazil's uniqueness derives from its history as a Portuguese colony and therefore being the only Portuguese-speaking country in South America, a predominantly Spanish-speaking continent. In Brazil one finds a greater mix of different backgrounds and races, but with more integration. Close by in Argentina, one finds predominantly Spanish spoken, a greater identification with Europe, and less mixing of races and religions.

Country clusters have *geographical, religious, linguistic,* or *historical ties* which cut across national boundaries. For example, geographical proximity would seem to account for the Nordic and Germanic clusters. Religion also seems to play an important role: the influence of Catholicism may be responsible for similarities within and between Latin Europe and Latin America; while the influence of Islam accounts for similarities in Malaysia, the Middle East, and North Africa; and Confucianism for similarities among Asian countries. The Anglo cluster, though geographically dispersed (United States,

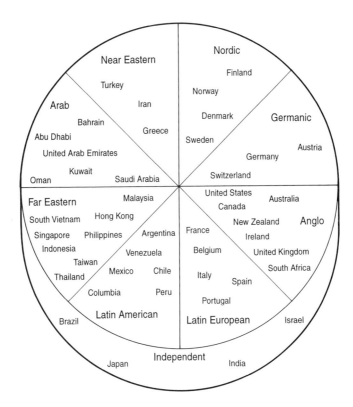

Figure 3.2 Country clusters. (*Source*: S. Ronen and O. Shenkar (1985) "Clustering countries on attitudinal dimensions: A review and synthesis", *Academy of Management Review*, 10(3), pp. 435–54.)

Canada, Australia, New Zealand, South Africa, Britain), is a product of a shared linguistic and colonial heritage.

Cultural similarity has an obvious bearing on patterns of trade and on the likely success of alliances or mergers between companies from those countries. For example, relations between Spain and Latin America are historically strong, with many family and educational ties. In practice, this shows up in the representation and market interests of Spanish publishers in South America. It also manifests itself in the Spanish pharmaceuticals industry, where the South American connection saves having to go through complicated, slow, and expensive drug registration procedures. Most South American countries will accept Spanish certification.[7]

For similar reasons American companies often view Britain as the ideal bridgehead into Europe. But, they can run into unexpected difficulties when assuming that there is a shared culture, or, for that matter, a shared language. In fact while cultural similarity among countries sometimes has the potential for creating competitive advantage as described above, it can also be a potential disadvantage.

When Electrolux, a Swedish company, acquired Zanussi in 1983, many Italians and, in particular, the union accused Zanussi of selling out to the "Vikings of the North". They would have preferred independence, or even an alliance with the French group Thomson, with whom they perceived greater cultural similarity. This prompted Swedish management to deny similarity among the Scandinavian countries by declaring, "We are not the Vikings, who were Norwegians anyway".[8]

Cultural similarities within clusters are often much more significant in international business than formal economic groupings, such as the European Union (EU). For example, Denmark has weaker economic links with its EU partner Germany, than it does with its Nordic neighbors, Norway (non-EU) and Sweden (which joined the EU only recently). In fact, some of the reluctance of Denmark to join the European Economic Community (EEC) as it then was, was said to reflect the ambivalence of embracing a European versus Scandinavian identity, as seen in the initial "NO" vote for Maastricht.

Industry cultures

One can also identify industry cultures. Advertising is culturally remote from banking, construction from consulting, and retailing from pharmaceuticals. While industry differences between banking and, for example, advertising may be quickly recognized, they may be less obvious in others. The recent trend towards "financial supermarkets" which sought to encourage alliances between banking and insurance ran into difficulties when bankers and insurers realized that they did not share similar world-views on managing a business.

For example, compared with banking, the insurance business is more customer-driven, and sales-oriented. There is an old industry saying, "Insurance is sold, not bought". In France, for example, they say Sicavs – banking products – are bought not sold. The insurance culture is more performance-driven as there are clearer links between individual effort and company performance and between individual reward and performance. Banking does not share the same aggressive, sales orientation. And the meaning and measurement of risk are quite different. Concerns regarding trust and reputation make banks wary of such alliances.[9]

Efforts to diversify may therefore run into trouble due to cultural differences between industries. One Dutch bank decided to exploit their branch network as a distribution system to go into the travel business. They quickly realized that selling travel packages was not the same as selling loans. Ciba-Geigy, a Swiss pharmaceutial company, encountered similar problems when it acquired AirWick, a product which deodorized bathrooms and kitchens. The idea of pushing consumer products was at odds with Ciba-Geigy's perceived mission of "saving the world". The scientists complained, "Those things aren't even products!".[10] Eventually the business was sold off.

General Electric's (GE) diversification into the financial industry, although reasonably successful in GE Capital Finance, created a nightmare with the acquisition of investment bank, Kidder Peabody.[11] This was attributed to the cultural belief instilled by CEO Jack Welch that every GE business should be #1 or #2 in their markets. The "profit at any price" GE culture was perhaps not appropriate to investment banking. GE's acquisition of television network, NBC, also created cultural static.

Industry culture can be demonstrated using the example of high-tech industries. Here we are more likely to find large open spaces which encourage information exchange and interaction. Dress codes tend to be more relaxed. Eccentric behavior may be more readily tolerated, and may even go unnoticed. Core values and beliefs have to do with the technological imperative, advancing science, and developing perfect, sophisticated products. A common belief is that the product will sell itself, and that therefore marketing is not necessary. The name of the game is technology push rather than customer pull. There exists a fundamental belief that customers are not able to appreciate the full value of the technology or product. After all, how many consumers realized beforehand how personal computers would change their lives both at work and at home?

High-tech industries rely on innovation. Thus underlying assumptions regarding external adaptation may emphasize control over nature, proactive behavior and risk-taking, and longer term time horizons. Assumptions pertaining to internal integration may include minimal hierarchy, individual effort as well as peer cooperation and interaction, and task (scientific discovery) versus social concerns (for example, in genetic engineering). In addition, relationships will be seen as important because interaction among people is believed to maximize **information exchange** which in turn fosters knowledge creation.

Reasons for differences

Differences in industry culture are due to different task environments such as nature of decision-making, the nature of the products or services, rates of technology change, degree of state intervention, and market characteristics.

Nature of decision-making

For example, the **nature of decision-making** in day-to-day business can be characterized by the degree of risk involved in each decision and the amount of time it takes to know the consequences of that decision. *Degree of risk* and *speed of feedback* (originally discussed by Deal and Kennedy[12] with regard to corporate culture) provide a useful framework to highlight cultural differences at the industry level, as shown in Figure 3.3.

Figure 3.3   Industry cultures. (*Source*: T. Deal and A. Kennedy (1982) *Corporate Cultures: The rites and rituals of corporate life*, Addison-Wesley, Reading, MA.)

For example, in biotechnology a large investment of resources, time and money, may be required without knowing for several years whether the investment will pay off. This creates a "bet your company" type culture, where risks have to be carefully assessed, since turning basic research into product development can take years, or may never come to fruition.

In other industries, such as bond trading, the stakes are big (high win/high loss) but the payoff is quick. This creates a "macho" type culture (and heavy drinking at *Harry's Bar* next to the New York Stock Exchange), not for the risk-averse. In investment banks, these differences are often sources of friction between the corporate bankers and the traders (relationship versus transaction-driven). In fact, the downfall of Lehman Brothers, a New York investment bank, was partly attributed to this culture clash.[13]

An example of an industry where the degree of risk of any particular decision is low but the speed of feedback is high would be retailing. This is sometimes referred to as a "sales culture" wherein "work hard play hard" is the name of the game and there is a heavy reliance on promotionals, and where socializing with customers and other colleagues is encouraged.

Where both degree of risk and speed of feedback are low we have what may be referred to as a "process culture". This may be the case with professional service firms, such as accounting or consulting firms, where prescribed method, processes, and procedures are to be followed religiously. This is not meant to imply that there is no risk or consequence in decisions taken, simply that how things are done may be more important than the outcome.

Product/market characteristics
Product and **market characteristics** determine whether patents or standards provide more value. The need to protect patents rather than standardize products will influence the degree of information sharing. Recent attempts to come up with shared standards in the computer software industry (UNIX) have encouraged information sharing between rival companies. This need for information sharing in order to arrive at shared standards can be contrasted to other industries, such as pharmaceuticals, where secrecy is a key concern, as patents are the drivers of competitive advantage.

At one pharmaceutical company this concern for security resulted in the "clean desk policy" – no papers were to be left on desks overnight. At one Swiss pharmaceutical company, the rule (unspoken of course) was to give information only if asked for it. It was considered rude to offer information. Messages in fact were not passed on. Information sharing was further restricted by the office design, individual offices with closed doors bearing rank and title, and a hushed atmosphere.[14]

Regulation
The **nature of regulation** influences industry culture, as it has an impact on market conditions, such as level of competition. This in turn influences the degree of customer orientation. Protected environments with little competition do not encourage companies to develop customer-oriented cultures. The telecommunications and banking industries have had a rude awakening to the newly competitive market conditions and demands of increasingly sophisticated customers.

Technology

Government regulation also influences the degree to which **technology** is developed and protected. This sends clear signals as to which industries are more highly valued and believed to be crucial to national security or economic sovereignty. In Brazil, for example, government regulation determines which technologies can be imported and exported.

In France, the government promotes (subsidizes) high-technology industries, such as the high-speed train (TGV) and the satellite launcher (Ariane). The success of the French videotext system, Minitel (6 million subscribers) where American (NYNEX), British (Prestel/Oracle), and German (Bildschirmtext) have all failed to establish themselves widely[15] is attributed to the unwavering state commitment through three changes of government, the ability to create one standard and enforce it, and the aggressive distribution policy (giving away terminals to subscribers). This led to a rapid build up of information services and generated greater interaction between information providers and consumers. Nevertheless, this success is now threatened by competition, the Internet.

Sources of competitive advantage

Sources of competitive advantage also influence industry culture. Concerns for efficiency over customer satisfaction, or cost effectiveness over quality, may predominate in heavy industry versus service industries. Need for resources, or different sorts of capital – financial, human, intellectual – drive cultural differences in **capital-, labor-,** and **knowledge-intensive** industries. In capital-intensive industries, investment decisions are taken for the long term, business is regarded as cyclical, with predictable upturns and downturns, that can be managed proactively.[16] Developing people is considered less important than is the case in knowledge-intensive industries, such as consulting, where the most valuable assets are people as "knowledge workers".

Interaction effects

National culture can interact with industry culture to provide competitive advantage. In the knitwear industry, Scottish companies, with their international reputation for good quality/price ratios, have found themselves competing with Italian companies' reputation for style.[17] Problems of gaining such advantage can be seen in what happens when a Japanese company famous for developing the Walkman, goes to Hollywood and buys a movie company. The Sony and Columbia Pictures case is an example of where it is easier to be wise after the event.[18]

The story starts in 1989, when Sony acquired Columbia Pictures for $3.4 billion, insisting on the marketing and technological synergies expected to result from the marriage between Hollywood's software and Japan's hardware. But in order to realize these expected synergies, Sony had to bridge a dual cultural divide, one relating to national culture and one relating to industry culture.

To start with, in purchasing Columbia Pictures Sony was getting not only a bit of Hollywood but also a large chunk of American culture. The entertainment industry was dominated by America.

... American movies and American culture had simply been accepted by vast sections of the world's population. Whether it was the diversity of the American experience, the exuberance, or the underlying emphasis on individual freedom and potential, U.S. films won a global approval that foreign competitors had not even been able to approach. In the eyes of many foreign viewers, movies and television were Hollywood, and Hollywood was America.[19]

Because of the close identification of the movie industry and American culture, Americans became alarmed at the "Japanese invasion into the soul of America". Fearing Japanese take-over and cultural imperialism, one California law maker went to the extent of proposing legislation to limit foreign ownership in the cultural and entertainment industries (that of course does not apply to American movies trying to break into the EU theater).

Perhaps even more problematic than the national culture divide was the difference in industry cultures. For one thing, the usual Japanese concern for financial controls was severely tested by accounting practices prevailing in the film-making industry. "Under the idiosyncratic accounting conventions, a film studio could report big profits but have no cash. This gave Columbia pictures $200 million in profits, and negative cash flow."[20] Sony's strength in technological innovation did not readily translate into the business culture of film-making, which is driven by market hits, mercurial personalities, and highly mobile talent. Indeed, Sony's recognition that it lacked the necessary industry knowledge led it to take a hands-off approach, relinquishing its usual controls, "determined not to interfere with the creative and intuitive art of movie-making". In November 1992, Sony was forced to announce a $2.7 billion write-down on the value of Sony Pictures and Entertainment.

Professional cultures

The idea of management as a profession and the need to create a "professional" culture are becoming more important to companies today. As decision-making is pushed down the ranks, and as employees are being empowered, there is greater autonomy and responsibility. This means that there is a greater reliance on judgement, knowing not only how to do things right, but also what is the right thing to do.

Professionals acquire judgement through intensive training, supervision, and socialization. Law firms, hospitals, and universities hire those who are thought to have the appropriate training and development, i.e. come from the "right" schools. This means having met certain standards of skills and abilities as well as having absorbed the appropriate professional norms and values (ethics).[21]

Companies hiring Harvard-trained MBAs find that recruits have a different perspective from those trained at MIT.[22] According to MIT professor John Van Maanen, those MBAs trained at Harvard are more likely to have a generalist approach and to work well in teams, and are hired by large companies into general management positions. MIT trained MBAs are more likely to be specialists, perform well in individual assignments, often taking staff roles in smaller companies. Or again, companies recruit INSEAD MBAs because of the international background and experience as well as their intensive cross-cultural exposure throughout the program.

The growing need for professionalism is pushed even further by the trend for organizations to become networks of specialists.[23] This is becoming an important issue in banking, for example, where it may no longer be possible for the generalist managers to adequately supervise specialists. This tension between specialists and generalists in professional service firms, or between scientists, research engineers, and managers can result in potential clashes with regard to who is formally (through promotion) or informally more highly valued.

Professional cultures differ in what is considered "proper behavior". For example, until recently professionals in the United States, such as doctors or lawyers, were not allowed to advertise their services. Professions also have dress codes, doctors in white coats and judges in black robes, codes of conduct – confidentiality in medicine and law, and oaths to uphold justice or to do no harm.

Doctors may learn to be cautious and not too aggressive in their bedside manner or in surgery. However, for lawyers aggressiveness, at least in court, may be encouraged. Law assumes adversarial relationships between conflicting parties while in medicine it is a joint effort to defeat a common enemy, the disease. For a lawyer, being convincing (establishing truth) may be more related to displaying and evoking emotions rather than remaining cool, calm, and collected. Even within the field of health care, different professions have different rules for expression of emotions. For example, social workers more readily admit to feeling stressed, as it is seen as a normal adjustment reaction, while doctors see it as a symptom of disease, and are therefore less likely to talk about it.[24]

Professionals also differ in their values and beliefs. For example, medical doctors and lawyers, scientists and engineers differ in their mission and method. In pharmaceutical companies, a task force assigned to approve the development of a new treatment or medication provides the opportunity to see these differences in action. The medical doctors may be more concerned with patient's comfort and well-being, while the scientists may be more concerned with having the opportunity to develop or test new drugs. The lawyers worry about compliance with government regulation and potential law suits. This reflects different stakeholders' demands and underlying assumptions regarding, say, the importance of relationships over task achievement.

In terms of method, scientists may be more excited by abstract theory, while engineers are impatient to work out the practical application. Medical doctors and lawyers have been trained to look for evidence in previous cases, while scientists have been taught to look for truth in large samples and statistical significance. For engineers, the proof is in making it work. Such differences reflect assumptions about how truth is established.

Interaction effects

The choice to study law or medicine, business or science is not only driven by personal abilities, interests, and values. Society signals which professions and occupations are valued over others. This is reflected in the status accorded, as well as the salaries.

Consider the following caricatures which demonstrate the interaction of national and professional cultures. Professors in Germany and Japan are seen as those with expertise or wisdom, and are often asked to comment on issues well beyond their domain. In

America, the professor is often considered to be someone who is out of touch with the real world. The entrepreneur in America is considered to be a latter-day frontiersman, and therefore a local hero. In Europe, entrepreneurs, or self-made men and women, are viewed with skepticism as *arrivistes* (pushy and unscrupulous). In France, someone who has made it without the proper education is always a little suspect (*louche*). In France, those who are unable to achieve the necessary grades to become an *ingénieur* might opt for dentistry, while in Britain the professions cream off the top talent, and an engineer is someone who fixes things.

In addition, some professional or occupational cultures are closely linked with particular countries: American MBAs, British accountants, German engineers, and French *cadres*. The notion of *cadre* is an assignation unique to France. To be considered *cadre* (or executive) at the outset of one's professional career, one has to graduate from a *grande école*. University graduates (non-*grande école*) may be named *cadre* only after a certain number of years of experience. Without the appropriate educational background, it is impossible to achieve this rank, rather like non-commissioned officers in the army.

The importance of qualified accountants in British companies – they outnumber their German counterparts by a factor of thirty and their Japanese colleagues by a factor of twenty – also has a historical component. The primacy of the accountant was tied up with the fact that they frequently had the most thorough training related to business at a time when British management attracted very few graduates. Accountancy was established as a sure route into general management and, even today, about 10 percent of British undergraduates seek to become accountants.[25]

The MBA is seen largely as an American product. This qualification is not offered in most European universities as business is considered to be a trade (commerce) rather than a profession. In fact, in France, the business schools fall under the jurisdiction of the Chamber of Commerce, not the Ministry of Education. Business education lies outside the domain of universities, as it is not considered (like economics, for example) to be discipline based. In many European countries, being "commercial" still has negative connotations.

Professional cultures can interact with national and regional cultures to provide competitive advantage. For example, one is more likely to find doctors and lawyers in the United States, engineers in Europe, particularly France and Germany, and accountants in the United Kingdom. The same is true by region – software engineers in Silicon Valley, financial analysts on Wall Street, film producers in Hollywood.

Professional cultures interact with industry culture, such that certain professionals may be valued above others. For example, in the pharmaceutical industry, where developing new drugs and preserving patents provides competitive advantages, the scientists may reign supreme. In the computer industry, the need to quickly develop new technology means the engineers are highly regarded. In some managed health care facilities, the doctors complain that they are now treated like lackeys, as the administrators or professional managers have taken over.

The health care industry, in particular, can benefit from positive interaction with professional culture. Cross-functional teams in pharmaceutical firms need to appreciate these differences in order to develop products that will satisfy several stakeholders:

patients and regulators. Health care management and service delivery, such as hospitals, can benefit from positive interaction between doctors and professional managers. In professional service businesses, such as accounting and consulting, the clash between generalists and specialists can create tensions which undermine the potential value-added of bringing the two cultures together.

Functional cultures

The importance of understanding differences in functional cultures becomes apparent when cross-functional teams are created to develop new products, design new policies, or explore new markets. Here it becomes clear that the different functions – finance, production, marketing, and R&D – have different cultures. For example, one member of an R&D committee vehemently objected when it was proposed that research money would be awarded subject to past track record rather than merit of the project. This reveals different values often found in finance versus R&D functions: the importance placed on reliability versus creativity, and of past results (reputation) versus future potential.

Take the simple comparison of production managers and finance specialists. Production managers are more physically active and tend to take a more down-to-earth, hands-on approach. Their work is more action-oriented. They operate in noisy, dirty places, and they, or at least those they are responsible for, are occasionally exposed to physical danger. Compare that with finance people, who interact in quiet offices, from behind a desk, primarily with other staff people, and manipulate numbers rather than machines.

Clashes in functional cultures can lead to friction, which is expressed in the stereotypes functional managers have of one another. At one end of the scale, the people in accounting and control may be written off as bean counters. At the other end, there are the sales people who are said not to mind which way they are going, as long as they are getting there fast (see Figure 3.4).

Reasons for differences

The reasons for these differences can be found in the **external environment**, such as stakeholder demands, and the **nature of the task**. Different stakeholders influence what is considered to be important and what is considered to be the best way to achieve success. For instance, the marketing function is more concerned with customer demands or needs, while R&D is more concerned with state of the art technology. Meanwhile, finance worries about return on investment and stock prices, the primary concerns of the financial community.

The nature of the task also differs.[26] For production, tasks are more routine and exceptions (*task variability*) are to be avoided in the interests of efficiency. These concerns can prove counter-productive in marketing and R&D. Differences in work flow integration are apparent in marketing (such as in developing an advertising campaign) and manufacturing on assembly lines. The nature of **task interdependence** – reciprocal versus sequential – requires different degrees of interpersonal interaction to achieve mutual adjustment. What is more, the lead (or lag) time for developing products is quite

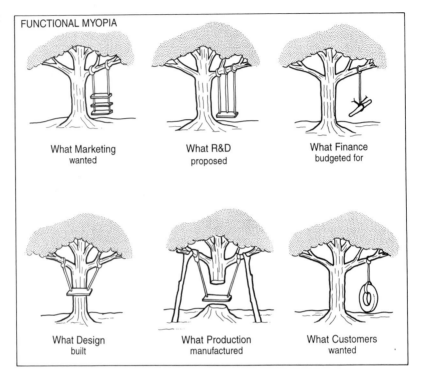

Figure 3.4 Functional caricatures. (*Source*: J.-L. Barsoux (1993) *Funny Business*, London: Cassell. Reprinted with permission.)

different than that for manufacturing them. Thus different functions have different cultures due to task requirements, time frames, and customers.

Different functions will hold positions of power in companies at different times in history because of changing strategic requirements.

> Up until the early 1950s, many top corporations were headed by former production line managers or engineers who gained prominence because of their abilities to cope with the problems of production. Their success, however, only spelled their demise. As production became routinized and mechanized, the problem of most firms became one of selling all those goods they so efficiently produced. Marketing executives were more frequently found in corporate boardrooms. Success outdid itself again. . . . During the 1960s, financial executives assumed the seats of power . . . [then] legal experts as regulation and anti-trust suits became more and more frequent in the 1970s. . . . [The] future, dominated by multinational corporations, may see former secretaries of state serving as corporate figureheads.[27]

Interaction effects

Which functions are most highly valued is in part determined by the nature of the industry. In high-tech and pharmaceutical companies, R&D may be the most valued. In consumer goods, marketing often has the biggest say. In fact, although many technology-driven companies such as pharmaceuticals and computers have now had to become more market-driven, the shift in power and status towards the marketing function is lagging.

Functional culture may also interact with corporate culture such that some functions, for example R&D and marketing, are valued over others. Even within the same industry, such as computers, different values are placed on marketing as demonstrated by Apple, Digital Equipment, and IBM. Recognizing the value of marketing led Steve Jobs, founder of Apple, to recruit John Sculley, based on Sculley's marketing experience as former CEO of Pepsi Co., with no experience in the computer industry. Ken Olsen of Digital was known to refer publicly to marketing as Harvard BS (nonsense), and refused to have a department named to that effect. IBM is so well known for its marketing capabilities that AT&T hired ex-IBMers to try to create a more market-driven culture.

The interaction between functional and national culture can be seen in the way functions are valued by different countries, as reflected in the salaries of department heads.[28] Take finance, for example. It heads the list in Britain, but ranks fifth in Germany, and sixth in The Netherlands. Instead, the Dutch award the biggest salary to sales. The French place a premium on marketing. Germany ranks R&D highest, while Britain consigns it to the bottom of the heap.

The British emphasis on finance is fairly easy to account for. It relates to the historical pre-eminence of chartered accountants, described earlier. Germany's emphasis on R&D is a manifestation of its concern with *Technik*, and is consistent with the high status of engineers in general. And the sales orientation of the Dutch can be seen as a legacy of Holland's trading culture. But explaining the French emphasis on marketing presents more of a challenge. Perhaps marketing (like finance) is seen as a more abstract and intellectual activity, while sales and production are considered more "hands-on", as they require direct contact with the customer or product.

Corporate culture

Perhaps the most frequently discussed cultural sphere is corporate culture. For this reason we will devote more time and attention to this sphere and use it as point of departure in discussing interaction among other spheres of influence. Many managers more quickly recognize the differences between companies than between countries. Indeed, it is not easy to separate these spheres of influence, to assess to what extent the corporate culture of IBM is "very American", or that of Volkswagen "very German". Corporate culture is also influenced by the nature of the industry, business, and product, as mentioned earlier. Thus it is difficult to say to what extent, say, the culture of Paris-based French cosmetics firm L'Oréal is due to national, regional, or industry influences. Indeed, it may be that corporate culture represents the intersection of these other spheres.

In many ways the interest in corporate culture, which began in the early 1980s, was triggered when American business started trying to explain the competitive advantage of the Japanese. Corporate culture was believed to be the secret weapon responsible for their success. The popularity of *Theory Z* and *The Art of Japanese Management* attest to this suspicion.[29] However, in their bestseller, *In Search of Excellence*, Peters and

Waterman[30] insisted that you did not have to be Japanese to have excellence, and provided examples of strong corporate cultures in US companies, such as IBM, Disney, and Delta.

This reinforced the belief that strong culture, widely shared and deeply held values and beliefs, resulted in exellent performance. Unfortunately, within a few years, several of the excellent companies cited had fallen off their pedestal. Worse still, corporate culture was often considered the culprit. Corporate culture is often cited as the reason for failed strategic change efforts, failed strategic alliances, and for failed attempts to international-ize, usually after the event.

In many ways, the interest in corporate culture was also a reaction to the overemphasis in many US firms on strategic planning, structure, and systems in the previous decade. With the failure of this approach to guarantee success, attention shifted to the "soft" side of business. There was a need for a sense of purpose to provide inspiration, a sense of mission to provide a direction, and a guiding philosophy to provide coordination and integration.

In Europe, business interest in corporate culture took off somewhat later. Deregulation and increased competition, which forced American business to reconsider their ways of doing things in the early 1980s, were also the prime reasons for interest in Europe. These industry changes helped drive interest in corporate culture in the late 1980s, and early 1990s. Companies such as British Airways, SAS, ICI, Daimler-Benz went through signifi-cant culture changes over this period. In addition, more and more mergers within domestic borders are bringing these issues to a head. Consider the following case of a bank merger.

Double Dutch

When the announcement was made that two Dutch banks, previously major rivals, would merge, the challenge posed by cultural differences became clear. Despite protests to the contrary ("We're all Dutch. We're all bankers. We went to the same schools"), the difference in corporate culture between the two banks was clear from the moment this visitor arrived. Consider her testimony.

> Entering the head office of one partner on a busy Amsterdam street I was struck by the imposing facade, the thick stone walls and barred windows. It had the feel of a vault. Climbing the circular stairway past a glass enclosed security station, I was subjected to intense scrutiny. (It turns out that the entrance by the front door is restricted to certain level of director, and certain clients.) Once past the guards, I arrived in a large open empty space where I was greeted by a man in a tuxedo with tails. I was then "allowed" into the elevator (which I was informed was reserved usually for important people) and shown to a wood panelled office with mahogany table. Here coffee or tea with cookies were served from a silver service by a man wearing white gloves. Lunch followed in a private dining room.

A subsequent visit to the future partner provides quite a contrast.

> I waited patiently at the security desk, where people seemed more interested in talking to each other than in attending to me. I was finally directed to a huge lobby that felt like

an airport lounge – decorated with interesting modern paintings and sculptures. The amount of open space was particularly striking, as was the variety of people in all sorts of dress (men and women, jeans with high heels). After a lengthy wait (45 minutes), I was led through a series of corridors and buildings (resembling Legoland), to the personnel office. The office was shared by several people, with partitions to divide up the space. When asked if I would like coffee, I was pointed in the direction of the nearest coffee machine: price 2 florins.

These initial impressions provide several indications about the beliefs and values, such as the importance of status and power, the ease of interaction and flow of communication, activity levels, the extent of formal or informal rules of behavior, the nature of controls, and the importance of the past and tradition.

On questioning insiders and informed observers, some of the underlying values and beliefs emerge more clearly. The first bank was seen as traditional, more aristocratic, run by "gentleman" bankers. There was evidence of a strong old boy network and a corresponding emphasis on developing personal relationships. Social controls were thus strong, and there was less emphasis on formal policies and procedures. Top management was seen as paternalistic, "father knows best", but was forgiving.

The second bank was seen as more aggressive, and more performance-driven, run by "street fighters". On average, key executives were ten years younger than their counterparts in the other bank. While this bank looked more informal in terms of dress and style of interaction, there were more formal policies and procedures and clearer reporting relations and controls. There was greater delegation but top management was perceived as a demanding task master, "tough".

Different sets of behavior and practices, beliefs and values, and underlying assumptions thus emerge. For one, the nature of banking was considered to be relationship-oriented while for the other it was transaction-based. Being relationship-driven had consequences in terms of occasionally showing greater concern for clients and employees than for business results. Training and development programs were provided, and employees rotated through several positions not only to develop a more generalist knowledge of the bank, but also to build up a network of relationships. This strengthened social controls and reinforced the importance of trust. Employees were thus encouraged to be part of the family, and were rewarded for belonging and loyalty (promotion was based on seniority).

The other bank considered banking to be transaction-oriented. Here there was more concern with business results than people (whether customers or employees). Bright individuals were hired, trained on the job; there was little outside training offered. Once assigned to a unit they were not likely to be rotated as specialized knowledge and expertise were valued. Control was based on reporting and budgeting systems. Rewards depended on performance.

These different sets of assumptions about the nature of investment banking created different values and beliefs. These in turn were reflected in different practices and behavior. The challenge in merging these two banks was for each bank to understand and appreciate the different underlying assumptions and their consequences in order to be able to craft a new culture appropriate to the current environment and to the needs of the different business units. Within the context of seminars held for the newly merged bank, members described the culture of their own areas, such as corporate finance and private banking, and discussed the different cultures needed by each unit, given the nature of their business. This allowed them to get beyond the "we–they" attitude of the former banks, and to appreciate both the need for differences between units as well as the need to create an overall culture that would provide a *raison d'être* for the bank as a whole. What has emerged is a more powerful and successful bank.

Reasons for differences

Corporate culture derives from the influence of founding figures and turnaround leaders, its unique company history, and stage of development. The nature of the market and product characteristics also contribute, as do the industry and national contexts.

Role of founder

The role of the **founder** is particularly important; founders influence the culture of the company through their values and beliefs.[31] Entrepreneurs such as Edwin Land of Polaroid, Ken Olsen at Digital Equipment, and Anita Roddick of the Body Shop demonstrate their values in their actions. The strong sense of social responsibility at the Body Shop, the concern for innovation and community relationships at Polaroid, and the emphasis on technology and entrepreneurial behavior at Digital are all examples.

Leaders

Strong leaders can also change a culture as in the case of Jan Carlzon whose experience in the travel business helped to turn SAS from a production- into a market-driven company. In Britain, Sir John Harvey-Jones redefined the meaning of ICI, Imperial Chemical Industries, to Innovative, Competitive, and International.

Administrative heritage

Administrative heritage also influences the culture. Different structures, standard operating procedures, or routines that evolve over time shape culture by prescribing specific behavior and reinforcing certain values and beliefs. Compare the cases of Ford and General Motors (GM).[32] Ford Motor Company started with a functional structure and grew through vertical integration, both backwards and forwards, in order to have better control over supply and distribution. At Ford, control was highly centralized, in particular in the person of Henry Ford. General Motors began with a divisional structure as it was created by merging several smaller companies, and grew through related diversification. At GM, divisional structures meant that control was passed further down the line.

Stages of development

The **stages of development** also influence corporate culture. For example, many start-up ventures in the computer industry have had a particular focus on technology, as their birth was dependent on developing new products or technologies. However, over time, market concerns became increasingly relevant, as beautifully engineered new technologies did not necessarily match customer needs.

Furthermore, as companies grow in size and scope, earlier more organic forms of organization need to become more structured and systematic. Thus companies move from being more entrepreneurial or professional, or more science or engineering driven, to being more managerial. At some stage, however, the managerial focus risks becoming bureaucratic, stifling the innovation and creativity that initially launched the company. At this point, the culture may return to a more entrepreneurial or technological orientation.[33]

Digital Equipment's former CEO, Ken Olsen, had promoted a company that was entrepreneurial, technology-driven, and consensus-oriented. This created problems later on when there was a greater need for market orientation and cost effectiveness, for greater coordination, and for faster decisions. Even when being forced out by the board, Olsen was still proclaiming, "Let a thousand flowers bloom", insisting that entrepreneurship should continue to flourish. Despite new management (some even recruited from IBM), efforts to make the company more market driven and efficient proved very problematic.

Nature of product

The **nature of the product** is important in creating the corporate culture and in shaping its evolution through subsequent interactions. Thus, a telecommunications company, such as Alcatel, would have a different culture from a cosmetics company, such as L'Oréal, although both are headquartered in Paris and rely heavily on new product development. The difference derives in part from the nature of their respective products and customers. Given differences in history of government regulation and therefore experience with market competitiveness, the culture of L'Oréal is more marketing-oriented. However, as competition heats up in the telecommunications market, the culture of Alcatel has been forced to become more customer-oriented.

But even two companies with a strong marketing orientation may differ due to the nature of their respective products. Take, for example, detergent and liquor. Crispin Davis was forced to resign as managing director from United Distillers Guinness because, "the hard-nosed marketing methods Davis learned from his previous career at Procter & Gamble, the world's biggest detergents manufacturer, did not fit a business which lives by premium pricing and exclusive brand image".[34]

Interaction effects

National culture interacts with corporate culture in ways which may converge, creating opportunities for competitive advantage. The culture and image of companies such as Louis Vuitton Möet Hennessy (LVMH – luxury goods, champagne and spirits) reflect very much their French origins, in the importance of refinement and elegance. BMW and Audi cultures derive in part from the importance of German engineering. MacDonalds profits from being seen as American. In spite of French complaints about MacDonalds destroying French cuisine (not only *what* you eat but *how*), French kids have not stopped insisting on family outings to "MacDo" (as it is affectionately known). Despite some local adaptation, both the product and the corporate culture remain very American.

The interaction of national and corporate culture as a source of competitive advantage or disadvantage is clearly seen in the case of Disney's adventures in Japan and France. The success of Tokyo Disneyland is attributed to a good fit between national (Japanese) and corporate (Disney) culture. What appears to be a monument to American values is, in fact, the embodiment of the Japanese drive towards perfection. As Van Maanen and Laurent put it, "Japan has built a Disneyland that surpasses its model in terms of courtesy, size, efficiency, cleanliness and performance".[35]

Efforts to make Tokyo Disneyland more Japanese were in fact rejected, as their partners (Oriental Land Company) wanted "an exact replica of the original" and "really wanted Japanese visitors to feel they were taking a foreign vacation". Opened in April 1983, attendance had reached 50 million by 1988, making it the number one attraction in Japan. In fact, Tokyo Disneyland now replaces traditional outings to shrines and temples for graduation and new year celebrations.[36]

The same Disney culture, however, created problems when France was chosen as a site for further international expansion. When EuroDisney opened in April 1992, it faced much resentment from the media and local population. Disneyland Paris was referred to by the French press as a "cultural Chernobyl", despite French kids' love affair with Mickey Mouse. Smiling faces, friendly service, the obsession with cleanliness and efficiency were behavior and values not particularly shared by French employees. Local employees resented and resisted the strong social controls for which Disney culture is famous.[37]

Initial attempts to make Disney more "European" did not help much. Attempts were made to downplay their Americanness using French and European castles, themes, and fairytales (Pinocchio). More sit-down restaurants were created, based on market research which indicated that Europeans preferred to sit for meals. However, it became apparent that the Europeans came for "an American experience" and preferred to spend their time at attractions rather than sitting at tables.

The EuroDisney adventure was not a success at first, as it was in Japan. With 11 million in attendance predicted for the first year, less than 3 million showed up, creating a loss of $920 million. And Disney has had to deal with a host of legal proceedings instigated by disgruntled employees. Despite financial restructuring and even a Saudi prince coming to the rescue, the park reported a loss of $1.5 billion at the end of 1994.[38]

The future however looks brighter for what is now called Disneyland Paris. Profits are predicted for 1996. Now they have reasserted the American image. Philippe Bourguignon, Chairman of EuroDisney SCA,

> . . . realized that the customers want the same kind of Disney experience as at the Disney parks in the United States, but at the same time he is eliminating some of Disney's by-the-book management rules to give the "cast members" more responsibility and autonomy . . .
>
> The product should be like the Disney product everywhere else, but the way we manage should be European.[39]

Thus the interaction of corporate and national culture can provide opportunities for competitive advantage or serious threats to survival. Furthermore, it must be kept in mind that corporate culture can be reinterpreted in different countries.[40] The same symbols can be locally redefined to have different meanings. Thus efforts to export logos, images, or company heroes may be interpreted in ways not intended, for better or worse. A Mercedes sedan, considered a luxury item in the United States, is likely to be hailed as a taxicab in Paris. In Japan, Mickey Mouse is used to sell money market accounts.

Corporate culture as homogenizer?

It is argued that the culture of certain multinational companies is the glue that holds geographically dispersed units together. Corporate culture, particularly where selection, socialization, and other such corporate practices are rigorous, is supposed to overcome the influence of national identity. However, while some insist that IBM employees are internationally recognizable, research suggests that this remains a surface resemblance. Although not designed with that aim in mind, Hofstede's classic study[41] is a striking testament to the persistence of national cultures in the presence of a strong corporate culture. His research showed that even within the distinctive corporate culture of IBM, national culture continues to play a major role in differentiating work values.

This was subsequently confirmed by Laurent's research[42] which showed greater national differences regarding beliefs about organization among managers working for the same company than between managers working in different companies. For example, a group of French and American managers working for a chemical division of a major US oil company with a very strong corporate culture and highly standardized policies and procedures showed greater divergence when questioned about the role of the manager than did a group of managers from different companies.

Hofstede[43] argues that while business practices (corporate behavior) across companies may look very similar, the underlying national values remain divergent. National cultural differences reside mostly in values and less in practices, while for organizations, the reverse is true. This is due to differences in socialization experiences. Basic assumptions and values are acquired early in life by virtue of upbringing and schooling. Organizational practices, on the other hand, are acquired through socialization at work, by which time most of the fundamental values are firmly in place.

Greater mobility (changing jobs and companies), and multiple associations (family, church, social clubs, etc.) weaken the impact of any one company culture. For this reason, the influence of corporate culture is stronger in places where the company is closely linked to the community. This can be seen in the case of Toyota city, an isolated, sprawling complex of factories (both Toyota's and its more than 300 parts suppliers) where 90 percent of industry and 80 percent of the work force is auto-related. At Toyota employees are encouraged to choose fellow workers as friends, and are actively discouraged from associating with the few non-Toyota locals.

> Toyota goes to extraordinary lengths to encourage loyalty. "Every employee is a brother", says one company slogan. Toyota runs extensive programs and sponsors clubs to keep workers together on weekends. It runs stores for employees and offers low-interest housing loans.[44]

This may indeed be an intentional strategy when Japanese companies select locations or set up greenfield sites in the United States and United Kingdom where they are the only show in town.

Company country clubs, vacation sites, and in-house training centers encourage employees to interact with one another. This is thought to strengthen ties with the company. In addition, job rotation within firms weakens the influence of professional or functional cultures and reasserts that of corporate culture. Identification is encouraged with the company, not with the profession. This in turn limits mobility as employees gain broader, company-specific knowledge rather than more narrow, function-specific knowledge.

Superficial changes in behavior, stated beliefs, and values may be apparent as pressures for convergence across industries increase due to changes in the competitive and global nature of the business environment. Bank tellers and branch managers, telephone operators and telecommunications executives may indeed become more "friendly" to customers, and insist that the company needs to be more service-oriented. However, underlying assumptions about the nature of relationships (in this case with clients) may remain unchanged, or difficult to modify.

As André Laurent puts it, national culture may shift, but very slowly. Like an iceberg, the tip can melt, but below the surface the reach of culture remains profound. He argues that while organization culture may be more amenable to change, real changes in national culture may take generations.[45]

Paradoxically, national culture may come through more forcefully in the face of a strong corporate culture. The pressures to conform perhaps create a backlash, a need to reassert autonomy and identity. Thus strategies to overcome differences in national or functional culture by creating a strong corporate culture may indeed backfire, as will be discussed in Part III.

Creating competitive advantage: interacting spheres

What emerges from the preceding discussion is that there are multiple cultural spheres of influence which interact in ways that can provide competitive advantages or disadvantages. Any cross-border venture harbors potential for cultural threats and opportunities among multiple spheres.

As new business opportunities open up, as alliances with other companies become possible, if not crucial to survival, and as potential partners, as well as markets, customers, suppliers, and producers may live on the other side of the border (national or industry), companies need to be able to detect the different cultural spheres of influence in order to anticipate and plan for their impact and interaction.

Unfortunately, many businesses are acquired or partnerships arranged without attention to these issues beforehand. It is only in the implementation phase that the problems become apparent, and only at the break-up point that they are properly articulated, and offered up as "excuses" to the financial press and business community.

Crossing borders of nations and regions, industries, companies and functions is the crux of strategic alliances. Whether joint ventures such as AT&T with Olivetti ran into difficulties due to national culture differences (American and Italian), or between the industry cultures (communication and computing), or corporate cultures (public service versus market-driven) is difficult to know. Nevertheless, cultural analyses are absolutely necessary to recognize the potential difficulties as well as the potential benefits, and to plan strategies for addressing them.

New business opportunities due to changing technologies lead to convergence of communications, information, and multimedia. This brings together very different industries: telecom, computers, consumer electronics, entertainment, and publishing. AT&T's efforts to break into the computer business took years and the recent breakup into three different companies may attest to the cultural difficulties in creating the previously hoped-for synergies.

New business opportunities are being created due to changing regulations in banking and insurance, across state, regional (in the United States) and national boundaries (in the European Union). In order to benefit from these possibilities, banks and insurance companies have to understand and work through their differences. This is the challenge facing Eureko, an alliance of banks and insurance companies from Portugal, Sweden, The Netherlands, the United Kingdom, and Denmark coming together to take advantage of changes in EU regulations to create a pan-European service company.

New business opportunities are also being created due to changing economic and political conditions; new markets are emerging in central and eastern Europe and China. These opportunities often result in joint ventures across different political and economic systems as well as cultures, both national and corporate. It is often difficult to know whether collective spirit in Russia is due to Communism, or more deeply embedded, and to what extent entrepreneurship can be nurtured in countries like Hungary. These are the challenges facing companies in their efforts to apply HRM practices, such as pay for performance or socialization techniques, in these countries.[46] Nevertheless GM found success in East Germany.

> Not in spite of, but because of their experience and lingering ideals, the East Germans embraced what G.M. is straining to teach workers worldwide – the Japanese approach with its emphasis on team work and constant improvement.
>
> The East Germans, G.M. discovered, are delighted to work in small teams like the "brigades" they knew in the Communist days. And they are happy to strengthen their bonds by socializing after hours, at the company's urging, with fellow team members.[47]

In these first three chapters, we have argued that culture is important to effectiveness for the organization and the manager. We have put forth a framework to help us recognize cultural differences from its most obvious signs and to uncover differences where they are most hidden. This framework can be used to diagnose other spheres of culture, such as corporate and industry, their complex interaction making simple recipes of limited value for managing across national cultures.

Despite these other spheres of influence, differences in national culture seem to persist. They are most deeply anchored in taken-for-granted assumptions which means we cannot ignore them. In the next section we will focus primarily on the impact of national culture on management practice in strategy, structure, and human resource systems.

Notes

1. Van Maanen, J. and Laurent, A. (1993) "The flow of culture: Some notes on globalization and the multinational corporation" in S. Ghoshal and D.E. Westney (eds) *Organization Theory and the Multinational Corporation*, New York: St. Martin's Press, pp. 275–312.
2. "Toyota's fast lane", *Business Week*, November 4, 1985, pp. 40–46, p. 42.
3. Barsoux, J.L. and Lawrence, P. (1990) *Management in France*, London: Cassell, p. 157.
4. Cuff, D.F. (1985) "Tennessee's pitch to Japan", *New York Times*, February 27, pp. D1, 6.
5. Bergmann, A., Professor of Human Resource Management, University of Lausanne, Personal communication.
6. Ronen, S. and Shenkar, O., (1985) "Clustering countries on attitudinal dimensions: A review and synthesis", *Academy of Management Review*, 10(3), pp. 435–54.
7. Calori, R. and Lawrence, P. (1991) *The Business of Europe: Managing Change*, London: Sage.
8. Ghoshal and Haspeslagh, Zanussi Electrolux.
9. Walter, I., Professor INSEAD, Personal communication.
10. Schein, E.H. (1985) *Organizational Culture and Leadership*, San Francisco: Jossey-Bass.
11. "The fall of the house of Kidder", *Euromoney*, January 1995, pp. 30–4.
12. Deal, T. and Kennedy, A. (1982) *Corporate Cultures: The Rites and Rituals of Corporate Life*, Reading, MA: Addison-Wesley.
13. Auletta, K. (1986) *Greed and Glory on Wall Street*, New York: Warner Books.
14. Schein (1985), *Op. cit.*
15. Jelassi, T. (1994) "The French videotext system Minitel: An example of a national information technology infrastructure", *Management Information Systems Quarterly*, March, pp. 1–20.
16. Rumelt, R., Professor of Strategy, INSEAD, Personal communication.
17. Porac, J.F., Thomas, H. and Baden-Fuller, C. (1989) "Competitive groups as cognitive communities: The case of the Scottish knitwear manufacturers", *Journal of Management Studies*, 26, pp. 397–416.
18. Kou, J. and Spar, D. (1994) "Being there: Sony Corporation and Columbia Pictures", HBS case 1994; Landler, M. (1994) "Sony's heartaches in Hollywood", *Business Week*, December 5, p. 11.
19. Kou and Spar, *Op. cit.*, p. 7.
20. *Ibid.*
21. Van Maanen, J. and Barley, S. (1984) "Occupational communities" in B. Staw and L.L. Cummings (eds) *Research in Organization Behavior*, Vol. 6, Greenwich, CT: JAI Press, pp. 287–365.
22. Van Maanen, J. (1983) "Golden passports: Managerial socialization and graduate education", *The Review of Higher Education*, 6(4), pp. 435–55.
23. Drucker, P.F. (1988) "The coming of the new organization", *Harvard Business Review*, January/February, pp. 45–53.
24. Meyerson, D.E. (1994) "Interpretations of stress in institutions: The cultural production of ambiguity and burnout", *Administrative Science Quarterly*, 39, pp. 628–53; Barley, S. and Knight, D.B. (1992) "Toward a cultural theory of stress complaints" in B.M. Staw and L.L. Cummings (eds) *Research in Organizational Behavior*, Vol. 14, Greenwich, CT: JAI Press, pp. 1–48.
25. Handy, C., Gordon, C., Gow, I. and Randlesome, C. (1988) *Making Managers*, London: Pitman, p. 170.
26. Lawrence, P.R. and Lorsch, J.W. (1967) *Organizations and Environment*, Homewood, IL: Irwin; Perrow, C. (1979) *Complex Organizations*, New York: Random House; Thompson, J.D. (1967) *Organizations in Action*, New York: McGraw-Hill.

27. Salancik, G.R. and Pfeffer, J.R. (1977) "Who gets power – and how they hold on to it: A strategic-contingency model of power", *Organizational Dynamics* (Winter).
28. Dixon, M. (1987) "Jobs", *Financial Times*, May 27, p. 8.
29. Ouchi, W.G. (1981) *Theory Z*, New York: Avon; Pascale, R.T. and Athos, A.G. (1981) *The Art of Japanese Management*, New York: Warner Books.
30. Peters, T. and Waterman, R. (1982) *In Search of Excellence*, New York: Harper & Row.
31. Schein, E.H. (1991) "The role of the founder in the creation of organizational culture", in P.J. Frost, L.F. Moore, M.R. Louis, C.C. Lundberg and J. Martin (eds) *Reframing Organizational Culture*, Ch. 1, Newbury Park, CA: Sage, pp. 14–25; Westney, F. and Mintzberg, H. (1989) "Visionary leadership and strategic management", *Strategic Management Journal*, 10, pp. 17–32.
32. Brief, A.P. and Downey, H.K. (1983) "Cognitive and organizational structures: A conceptual analysis of implicit theories of organizing", *Human Relations*, 36, pp. 1065–90.
33. Greiner, L. (1972) "Evolution and revolution as organizations grow", *Harvard Business Review*, July/August, pp. 37–46.
34. de Jonquières, G. and Summers, D. (1993) "Of soap and Scotch", *Financial Times*, October 21, p. 10.
35. Van Maanen and Laurent, *Op. cit.*, p. 297.
36. Brannen, M.Y. (1992) "'Bwana Mickey': Constructing cultural consumption at Tokyo Disneyland" in J.J. Tobin (ed.) *Remade in Japan: Everyday Life and Consumer Taste in a Changing Society*, New Haven, CT: Yale University Press, pp. 216–234.
37. Van Maanen, J. (1990) "The smile factory: Work at Disneyland" in P.J. Frost, L.F. Moore, M.R. Louis, C.C. Lundberg and J. Martin (eds) *Reforming Organizational Culture*, Ch. 4, Newbury Park, CA: Sage, pp. 58–76.
38. Brannen, M.-Y. and Wilson, J.M. (1995) "Transferring core competencies abroad in people-dependent industries: A lesson in semiotics from the Walt Disney Corporation", presented at the Academy of Management Meetings, Vancouver, BC.
39. James, B. (1994) "Euro Disney throws the book away", *International Herald Tribune*, October 20, pp. 9, 11.
40. Brannen and Wilson, *Op. cit.*; Wooldridge, A. (1995) "Insider trading", *The Economist*, June 24, p. 11.
41. Hofstede, G. (1980) *Culture's Consequences*, London: Sage.
42. Laurent, A. (1983) 'The cultural diversity of western conceptions of management", *International Studies of Management and Organization*, 13(1–2), pp. 75–96.
43. Hofstede, G. (1991) *Culture and Organization: Software of the Mind*, London: McGraw-Hill.
44. "Toyota's fast lane", *Business Week*, November 4, 1985, pp. 40–6, p. 42.
45. Laurent, A. (1989) "A cultural view of organizational change" in P. Evans, Y. Doz and A. Laurent (eds) *Human Resource Management in International Firms*, Ch. 5, London: Macmillan, pp. 83–94.
46. Cyr, D.J. and Schneider, S.C. (1996) "Implications for learning: Human resource management in East–West joint ventures", *Organization Studies*, 17(2), pp. 207–226.
47. Bennet, J. (1994) "G.M. success in an unlikely place", *The New York Times*, October 31, pp. D1, D5.

PART TWO

Culture and management practice

> Japanese and American management practices are 95 percent the same, and differ in all important respects.
>
> Takeo Fujisawa, cofounder Honda Motor Company

In Part I we argued that culture can have a profound impact on the effectiveness of managers and organizations navigating the seas of international business. We proposed a framework which can serve to explore different levels of culture through observation, questioning, and interpretation. We also provided a set of the key dimensions along which cultures can be analyzed. Furthermore, we discussed how managers and organizations are subject to multiple spheres of cultural influence, whether functional/professional, corporate, industry, regional, or national. These multiple spheres can be discovered and analyzed using the same framework and the same set of key dimensions.

In Part II we demonstrate more specifically **how** national culture influences management practice – structure, strategy, and human resource (HR) systems – in order to have a better understanding of the threats and opportunities that culture presents in international business. We draw upon the experiences of managers and their companies, and integrate the discoveries of a rather large field of comparative management research to demonstrate the differences in management practices across countries.

Beyond showing that differences exist, we explore the underlying cultural explanations for these differences. Management practices, in effect, represent the tip of the iceberg. In order to understand the meaning of these practices we need to uncover their cultural roots. Only then can we arrive at an appropriate approach to both formulating *and* implementing company structures, strategies, and HR policies abroad.

Chapter 4 presents evidence of national differences in organizational structure and processes. By pulling together the fragmented and somewhat disparate studies in the field of comparative management, we arrive at an emerging and more coherent picture or country profile of how companies located in that country may operate. The purpose of creating such **country profiles** is not to argue for or reinforce stereotypes. These country profiles do, however, serve as a reminder that managers in different countries (not to mention companies and industries) tend to have consistent preferences for ways of organizing.

For example, country profiles reflect different preferences for hierarchy and formalization. These differences are apparent not only in organizational structures, but also in organizational processes, such as how policies and procedures are formulated and implemented, how planning and control takes place, and how decisions are made. These preferences reveal underlying cultural dimensions regarding power and uncertainty.

Thus by focusing on the key cultural dimensions underlying country profiles we can broaden our perspective to consider the implications of these dimensions in other spheres of cultural influence: industry, company, and functional. In this manner we can create more specific profiles, which indicate preferences for organizational structure and process, taking into consideration the particular situation and people at hand. Furthermore we can then consider the implications for transferring organizational structures and processes and for learning across borders.

Chapter 5 argues that culture will also have an important impact on corporate strategy. "Rational analytic" approaches to strategic management often assume that managers are faced with an objective environment which lends itself to standardized methods of assessment and response. Thus the process of strategic management and its outcome is considered to be culture-free. We, however, argue that the assessment and response to the environment is *subjective*, open to differences in perception and interpretation. These differences are driven by underlying cultural dimensions, for example regarding uncertainty and control, or the relationship with nature.

Thus multiple interpretations and responses are possible. Indeed, that is what makes the "competitive ballgame". What companies look for, what they fail to notice, what they see but ignore, what they consider feasible or desirable, are all driven by cultural assumptions, both corporate and industrial, as well as national. Awareness of cultural differences can help to anticipate the strategic responses of international competitors, and help to discover complementarity in cross-border partnerships, international or otherwise.

Chapter 6 examines how culture influences the practice of human resource management (HRM). Country differences are described and underlying cultural dimensions are sought to explain the reasons for these differences. Examples are given of the impact of culture on HR practice in selection and socialization, management training and development, appraisal and compensation, and career development.

In order to become more international, many companies will have to re-examine their own HRM practices, which are often strongly embedded in the home country culture. Above all, the importance of HRM practices in creating and reinforcing the corporate culture needs to be recognized in order to assure that desired changes in structures and strategies can be implemented, both at home and abroad. This is, in effect, the very meaning of *strategic* HRM and the reason for its central role in creating strategic change.

The strategic role of HRM, however, creates dilemmas in managing human resources internationally, in deciding which HR practices should be designed centrally, and which ones need to be adapted locally. Companies have to simultaneously consider the needs of the company in terms of its global aspirations, while remaining in tune with local needs and realities. For example, the ability to recruit and develop people for international responsibility may be constrained by the availability or willingness of talented local managers or by an "ethnocentric head-office" view which fails to recognize or effectively utilize talented managers from outside its own national borders.

The most striking evidence of this is the failure of expatriates and of HR policies sent from head office. Companies will have to broaden their definition of, and search for high potentials, to enable people from overseas operations to move into positions of corporate responsibility. It is no longer just a question of how to develop international managers, but also how to internationalize the HRM function, not to mention the corporation.

Thus by looking at differences in management practice – structure, strategy, and HRM – we begin to understand how managers in different cultures have come to solve problems of external adaptation and internal integration.

CHAPTER FOUR

Culture and organization

> Intuitively, people have always assumed that bureaucratic structures and patterns of action differ in the different countries of the Western world and even more markedly between East and West. Practitioners know it and never fail to take it into account. But contemporary social scientists . . . have not been concerned with such comparisons.
>
> Michel Crozier[1]

Just how does culture influence organization structure and process? To what extent do organizational structures and processes have an inherent logic which overrides cultural considerations? Given the nature of today's business demands, do we find convergence in the ways of organizing? To what extent will popular techniques such as team management and empowerment be adopted across cultures? With what speed and with what possible (re)interpretation? What cultural dimensions need to be recognized which may facilitate or hinder organizational change efforts?

In order to demonstrate the impact of culture on organizational structure, systems, and processes, we present the evidence for national differences and consider the cultural reasons for these differences. Examining the degree to which organizations have centralized power, specialized jobs and roles, and formalized rules and procedures, we find distinct patterns of organizing which prevail despite pressures for convergence. This raises concerns regarding the transferability of organizational forms across borders and questions the logic of universal "best practices".

Different schools, different cultures

While many managers are ready to accept that national culture may influence the way people relate to each other, or the "soft stuff", they are less convinced that it can really affect the nuts and bolts of organization: structure, systems, and processes. The culture-free (or *emic*) argument is that structure is determined by *organizational* features such as size and technology. For example, the famous Aston studies,[2] conducted in the late 1960s in the United Kingdom and widely replicated, point to size as the most important factor influencing structure: larger firms tend to have greater division of labor (specialized) and more formal policies and procedures (formalized) but are not necessarily more centralized. Furthermore, the nature of technology, such as mass production, is considered to favor a more centralized and formal (mechanistic) rather than decentralized and informal (organic) approach.[3]

Other management scholars argue that the *societal* context creates differences in structure in different countries (*etic*).[4] In effect, the "structuralists" argue that structure creates culture, while the "culturalists" argue that culture creates structure. The debate continues, with each side arming up with more sophisticated weapons: measurements and methodologies.

Taking an historical perspective, theories about how best to organize – Max Weber's (German) bureaucracy, Henri Fayol's (French) administrative model, and Frederick Taylor's (American) scientific management – all reflect societal concerns of the times as well as the cultural backgrounds of the individuals.[5] Today, their legacies can be seen in the German emphasis on structure and competence, the French emphasis on social systems, roles and relationships (unity of command), and the American emphasis on the task system or machine model of organization, now popularized in the form of re-engineering.

Indeed, many of the techniques of modern management – performance management, participative management, team approach, and job enrichment all have their roots firmly embedded in a particular historical and societal context: *scientific management* in the United States at the turn of the century; *human relations*, brought about by Hawthorne studies (1930s) in the United States; *socio-technical* brought by the Tavistock studies of the coal mines in the United Kingdom (1930s); and *human resources* brought about in Sweden (1970s) with Saab Scania's and Volvo's redesign of auto assembly into autonomous teams.

These approaches reflect different cultural assumptions regarding, for example, human nature and the importance of task and relationships. While the scientific management approach focused on how best to accomplish the task, the human relations approach focused on how best to establish relationships with employees. The human resources approach assumed that workers were self-motivated, while earlier schools assumed that workers needed to be motivated by more or less benevolent management.

These models of management have diffused across countries at different rates and in different ways. For example, mass-production techniques promoted by scientific management were quickly adopted in Germany, while practices associated with the human relations school transferred more readily to Spain.[6] For this reason the historical and societal context needs to be considered to understand the adoption and diffusion of different forms of organization across countries. While some theorists focus on the *institutional arrangements*,[7] such as the nature of markets, the educational system, or the relationships between business and government, to explain these differences, we focus here, more specifically, on the cultural reasons.

This does not mean that institutional factors are irrelevant. In effect, it is quite difficult to separate out the influence of institutions from culture as they have both evolved together over time and are thus intricately linked. For example, the strong role of the state and the cultural emphasis on power and hierarchy often go hand in hand, as in the case of France. Or in the words of the French *roi soleil* Louis XIV, *L'état, c'est moi* ("The state is me"). Our argument (the culturalist perspective) is that different forms of organization emerge which reflect underlying cultural dimensions.

Culture and structure

Hofstede's findings

One of the most important studies which attempted to establish the impact of culture differences on management was conducted by Geert Hofstede, first in the late 1960s, and continuing through the next three decades.[8] The original study, now considered a classic, was based on an employee opinion survey involving 116,000 IBM employees in 40 different countries. From the results of this survey, which asked people for their preferences in terms of management style and work environment, Hofstede identified four "value" dimensions on which countries differed: power distance, uncertainty avoidance, individualism/collectivism, and masculinity/femininity.

Power distance indicates the extent to which a society accepts the unequal distribution of power in institutions and organizations. **Uncertainty avoidance** refers to a society's discomfort with uncertainty, preferring predictability and stability. **Individualism/collectivism** reflects the extent to which people prefer to take care of themselves and their immediate families, remaining emotionally independent from groups, organizations, and other collectivities. And the **masculinity/femininity** dimension reveals the bias towards either "masculine" values of assertiveness, competitiveness, and materialism, or towards "feminine" values of nurturing, and the quality of life and relationships. Country rankings on each dimension are provided in Table 4.1.

Given the differences in value orientations, Hofstede questioned whether American theories could be applied abroad and discussed the consequences of cultural differences in terms of motivation, leadership, and organization.[9] He argued, for example, that organizations in countries with high power distance would tend to have more levels of hierarchy (vertical differentiation), a higher proportion of supervisory personnel (narrow span of control), and more centralized decision-making. Status and power would serve as motivators, and leaders would be revered or obeyed as authorities.

In countries with high uncertainty avoidance, organizations would tend to have more formalization evident in greater amount of written rules and procedures. Also there would be greater specialization evident in the importance attached to technical competence in the role of staff and in defining jobs and functions. Managers would avoid taking risks and would be motivated by stability and security. The role of leadership would be more one of planning, organizing, coordinating, and controlling.

In countries with a high collectivist orientation, there would be a preference for group as opposed to individual decision-making. Consensus and cooperation would be more valued than individual initiative and effort. Motivation derives from a sense of belonging, and rewards are based on being part of the group (loyalty and tenure). The role of leadership in such cultures is to facilitate team effort and integration, to foster a supportive atmosphere, and to create the necessary context or group culture.

Table 4.1 Hofstede's rankings

Country	Power distance		Individualism		Masculinity		Uncertainty avoidance	
	Index	Rank	Index	Rank	Index	Rank	Index	Rank
Argentina	49	35–6	46	22–3	56	20–1	86	10–15
Australia	36	41	90	2	61	16	51	37
Austria	11	53	55	18	79	2	70	24–5
Belgium	65	20	75	8	54	22	94	5–6
Brazil	69	14	38	26–7	49	27	76	21–2
Canada	39	39	80	4–5	52	24	48	41–2
Chile	63	24–5	23	38	28	46	86	10–15
Colombia	67	17	13	49	64	11–12	80	20
Costa Rica	35	42–4	15	46	21	48–9	86	10–15
Denmark	18	51	74	9	16	50	23	51
Equador	78	8–9	8	52	63	13–14	67	28
Finland	33	46	63	17	26	47	59	31–2
France	68	15–16	71	10–11	43	35–6	86	10–15
Germany (F.R.)	35	42–4	67	15	66	9–10	65	29
Great Britain	35	42–4	89	3	66	9–10	35	47–8
Greece	60	27–8	35	30	57	18–19	112	1
Guatemala	95	2–3	6	53	37	43	101	3
Hong Kong	68	15–16	25	37	57	18–19	29	49–50
Indonesia	78	8–9	14	47–8	46	30–1	48	41–2
India	77	10–11	48	21	56	20–1	40	45
Iran	58	19–20	41	24	43	35–6	59	31–2
Ireland	28	49	70	12	68	7–8	35	47–8
Israel	13	52	54	19	47	29	81	19
Italy	50	34	76	7	70	4–5	75	23
Jamaica	45	37	39	25	68	7–8	13	52
Japan	54	33	46	22–3	95	1	92	7
Korea (S)	60	27–8	187	43	39	41	85	16–17
Malaysia	104	1	26	36	50	25–6	36	46
Mexico	81	5–6	30	32	69	6	82	18
Netherlands	38	40	80	4–5	14	51	53	35
Norway	31	47–8	69	13	8	52	50	38
New Zealand	22	50	79	6	58	17	49	39–40
Pakistan	55	32	14	47–8	50	25–6	70	24–5
Panama	95	2–3	11	51	44	34	86	10–15
Peru	64	21–3	16	45	42	37–8	87	9
Philippines	94	4	32	31	64	11–12	44	44
Portugal	63	24–5	27	33–5	31	45	104	2
South Africa	49	36–7	65	16	63	13–14	49	39–40
Salvador	66	18–19	19	42	40	40	94	5–6
Singapore	74	13	20	39–41	48	28	8	53
Spain	57	31	51	20	42	37–8	86	10–15
Sweden	31	47–8	71	10–11	5	52	29	49–50
Switzerland	34	45	68	14	70	4–5	58	33
Taiwan	58	29–30	17	44	45	32–3	69	26
Thailand	64	21–3	20	39–41	34	44	64	30
Turkey	66	18–19	37	28	45	31–3	85	16–17
Uruguay	61	26	36	29	38	42	100	4
United States	40	38	91	1	62	15	46	43
Venezuela	81	5–6	12	50	73	3	76	21–2
Yugoslavia	76	12	27	33–5	21	48–9	88	8
Regions:								
East Africa	64	21–3	27	33–5	41	39	52	36
West Africa	77	10–11	20	39–41	46	30–1	54	34
Arab countries	80	7	38	26–7	53	23	68	27

Rank numbers: 1 – Highest; 53 – Lowest.
Source: G. Hofstede (1991) *Cultures and Organizations: Software of the Mind*, McGraw-Hill, Maidenhead.

In countries ranked high on masculinity, the management style is likely to be more concerned with task accomplishment than nurturing social relationships. Motivation will be based on the acquisition of money and things rather than quality of life. In such cultures, the role of leadership is to ensure bottom-line profits in order to satisfy share-holders, and to set demanding targets. In more feminine cultures, the role of the leader would be to safeguard employee well-being, and to demonstrate concern for social responsibility.

Having ranked countries on each dimension, Hofstede then positioned them along two dimensions at a time, creating a series of cultural maps. He too found country clusters – Anglo, Nordic, Latin, and Asian – similar to those reported in the previous chapter.[10] While some concern has been voiced that the country differences found in Hofstede's research are not representative due to the single company sample, further research by him and others supports these dimensions and the preferences for different profiles of organization.

One such cultural map, as shown in Figure 4.1 (see also Table 4.2), is particularly relevant to structure in that it simultaneously considers power distance (acceptance of hierarchy) and uncertainty avoidance (the desire for formalized rules and procedures).

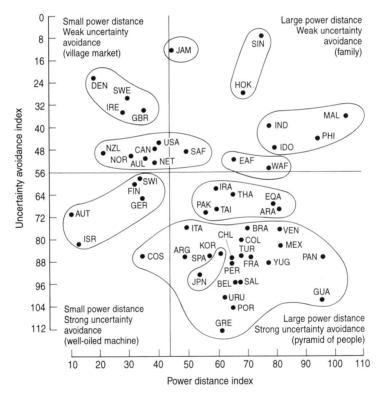

Figure 4.1   Hofstede's maps. (*Source*: G. Hofstede (1991) *Cultures and Organizations*, McGraw-Hill, Maidenhead.)

Table 4.2   Abbreviations for the countries and regions studied

Abbreviation	Country or region	Abbreviation	Country or region
ARA	Arab-speaking countries (Egypt, Iraq, Kuwait, Lebanon, Libya, Saudi Arabia, United Arab Emirates)	ITA	Italy
		JAM	Jamaica
		JPN	Japan
		KOR	South Korea
ARG	Argentina	MAL	Malaysia
AUL	Australia	MEX	Mexico
AUT	Austria	NET	Netherlands
BEL	Belgium	NOR	Norway
BRA	Brazil	NZL	New Zealand
CAN	Canada	PAK	Pakistan
CHL	Chile	PAN	Panama
COL	Colombia	PER	Peru
COS	Costa Rica	PHI	Philippines
DEN	Denmark	POR	Portugal
EAF	East Africa (Ethiopia, Kenya, Tanzania, Zambia)	SAF	South Africa
		SAL	Salvador
EQA	Equador	SIN	Singapore
FIN	Finland	SPA	Spain
FRA	France	SWE	Sweden
GBR	Great Britain	SWI	Switzerland
GER	Germany F.R.	TAI	Taiwan
GRE	Greece	THA	Thailand
GUA	Guatemala	TUR	Turkey
HOK	Hong Kong	URU	Uruguay
IDO	Indonesia	USA	United States
IND	India	VEN	Venezuela
IRA	Iran	WAF	West Africa (Ghana, Nigeria, Sierra Leone)
IRE	Ireland (Republic of)		
ISR	Israel	YUG	Yugoslavia

Source: G. Hofstede (1991) *Cultures and Organizations*, McGraw-Hill, Maidenhead.

Countries which ranked high both on power distance and uncertainty avoidance would be expected to be more "mechanistic"[11] or what is commonly known as bureaucratic. In this corner we find the Latin countries.

In the opposite quadrant, countries which rank low both on power distance and uncertainty avoidance are expected to be more "organic"[12] – less hierarchic, more decentralized, having less formalized rules and procedures. Here we find the Nordic countries clustered and to a lesser extent, the Anglo countries.

In societies where power distance is low but uncertainty avoidance is high, we expect to find organizations where hierarchy is downplayed, decisions are decentralized, but where rules and regulations are more formal, and task roles and responsibilities are more clearly defined. Thus there is no need for a boss, as the organization runs by routines. This is characteristic of the Germanic cluster.

In societies where power distance is high but uncertainty avoidance is low, organizations resemble families or tribes. Here, "the boss is the boss", and the organization may be described as paternalistic. Subordinates do not have clearly defined task roles and responsibilities (formalization), but instead social roles. Here we find the Asian countries where business enterprise is often characterized by centralized power and personalized relationships.

Emerging cultural profiles: converging evidence

These differences in structural preferences also emerged in a study conducted by Stevens[13] at INSEAD. When presented with an organizational problem, a conflict between two department heads within a company, MBA students from Britain, France, and Germany proposed markedly different solutions. The majority of French students referred the problem to the next level up, the president. The Germans argued that the major problem was a lack of structure; the expertise, roles, and responsibilities of the two conflicting department heads had never been clearly defined. Their suggested solution involved establishing procedures for better coordination. The British saw it as an interpersonal communication problem between the two department heads which could be solved by sending them for interpersonal skills training, preferably together.

On the basis of these findings, Stevens described the "implicit model" of the organization held by each culture. For the French, the organization represents a "pyramid of people" (formalized and centralized). For the Germans, the organization is like a "well-oiled machine" (formalized but not centralized), in which management intervention is limited to exceptional cases because the rules resolve problems. And for the British, it was more like a "village market" (neither formalized nor centralized) in which neither the hierarchy nor the rules, but rather the demands of the situation determine structure.

Going beyond questionnaires by observing the actual behavior of managers and company practices, further research reveals such cultural profiles as shown in Figure 4.2. Indeed, in studies comparing firms in France, Germany, and the United Kingdom,[14] French firms were found to be more centralized and formalized with less delegation when compared with either German or British firms. The role of the PDG (French CEO) was to provide coordination at the top and to make key decisions, which demands a high level of analytical and conceptual ability that need not be industry- or company-specific. The staff function plays an important role in providing analytic expertise. These capabilities are developed in the elite *grandes écoles* of engineering and administration.

The research findings confirmed the image of German firms as "well-oiled machines" as they were more likely to be decentralized, specialized, and formalized. In fact, German managers were more likely to cite structure as a key success factor, having a logic of its own, apart from people. German firms were more likely to be organized by function (sometimes to the extent that they are referred to as "chimney" organizations) with coordination achieved through routines and procedures.

Although German organizations tended to be flatter and to have a broader span of control when compared with the French, middle managers had less discretion than their British counterparts as they were limited to their specific technical competence. The

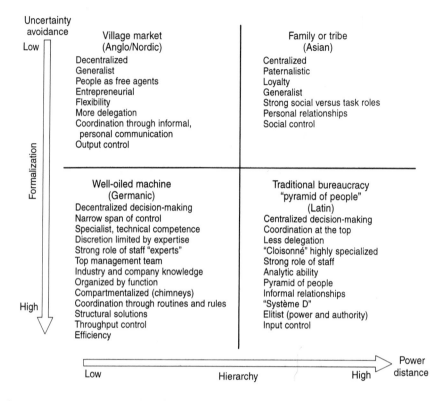

Figure 4.2   Emerging cultural profiles.

premium placed on competence was expressed in the concern to find competent people to perform specialized tasks, the strong role of staff to provide technical expertise, and expectations that top management not only has specific technical competence, but also in-depth company knowledge. Furthermore, top management typically consists of a managing board, *Vorstand*, which integrates the specialized knowledge of the various top managers (rather than in the head of a lone individual as in the case of France, Britain, or the United States).

In contrast to the well-oiled machine model with its greater concern for efficiency, the "village market" model reflects a greater concern for flexibility. Indeed, structure in British firms was found to be far more flexible, more decentralized and less formalized, when compared with the French and German firms. Organized by divisions, there is greater decentralization and delegation in the company and the role of central staff is far less important. Here, the burden of coordinating functions was placed on individual managers requiring a constant need for persuasion and negotiation to achieve cooperation.[15]

British managers, compared with Germans, were more ready to adapt the structure to the people working in it. Changes in personnel were often used as opportunities to reshuffle the jobs and responsibilities in order to accommodate available talent, and to create opportunities for personal development (free agents). Top management's role was to identify market opportunities and convince others to pursue them, underlining the importance of taking a more strategic view and of being able to communicate it persuasively.[16]

Studies in Asia have also found companies to fit the "family model", being more hierarchic and less formalized, with the exception of Japan. When compared with the Japanese, Hong Kong Chinese firms were less likely to have written manuals and Hong Kong Chinese bosses were also found to be more autocratic and paternalistic.[17] Another study of thirty-nine multinational commercial banks from fourteen different countries operating in Hong Kong found the Hong Kong banks to have the greatest number of hierarchical levels (eleven); the banks from Singapore, the Philippines, and India were also among those most centralized.[18]

A recent study of Chinese entrepreneurs found the Confucian tradition of patriarchal authority to be remarkably persistent. Being part of the family is seen as a way of achieving security. Social roles are clearly spelled out in line with Confucian precepts, which designate the responsibilities for the roles of father–son, brothers, and so on. Control is exerted through authority, which is not questioned. In 70 percent of the entrepreneurial firms studied, even large ones, the structure of Chinese organizations was found to resemble a hub with spokes around a powerful founder, or a management structure with only two layers.[19]

What begins to emerge from these various research studies is a converging and coherent picture of different management structures when comparing countries within Europe, as well as when comparing countries in Europe, the United States, and Asia. The primary cultural determinants appear to be those related to relationships between people in terms of power and status and relationship with nature, for example how uncertainty is managed and how control is exercised.

These underlying cultural assumptions are expressed in beliefs (and their subsequent importance, or value) regarding the need for hierarchy, for formal rules and procedures, specialized jobs and functions. These beliefs and values, in turn, are observable in behavior and artifacts, such as deference to the boss, the presence of executive parking and dining facilities ("perks"), and the existence of written policies and procedures, specific job descriptions, or manuals outlining standard operating procedures.

The research findings in the above-mentioned studies were based on observations as well as questionnaires and interviews of managers and companies in different countries. The same, of course, can be done comparing companies in different industries or within the same industry, and managers in different functions providing corresponding models of industry, corporate and/or functional cultures. From these findings, management scholars interpret underlying meaning.

The meaning of organizations: task versus social systems

André Laurent argues that the country differences in structure described above reflect different conceptions (or understandings) of what is an organization.[20] These different

Table 4.3 Management questionnaire

A = Strongly agree
B = Tend to agree
C = Neither agree, nor disagree
D = Tend to disagree
E = Strongly disagree

1. When the respective roles of the members of a department become complex, detailed job descriptions are a useful way of clarifying. A B C D E

2. In order to have efficient work relationships, it is often necessary to bypass the hierarchical line. A B C D E

8. An organizational structure in which certain subordinates have two direct bosses should be avoided at all costs. A B C D E

13. The more complex a department's activities, the more important it is for each individual's functions to be well-defined. A B C D E

14. The main reason for having a hierarchical structure is so that everyone knows who has authority over whom. A B C D E

19. Most organizations would be better off if conflict could be eliminated forever. A B C D E

24. It is important for a manager to have at hand precise answers to most of the questions that his/her subordinates may raise about their work. A B C D E

33. Most managers have a clear notion of what we call an organizational structure. A B C D E

38. Most managers would achieve better results if their roles were less precisely defined. A B C D E

40. Through their professional activity, managers play an important role in society. A B C D E

43. The manager of tomorrow will be, primarily, a negotiator. A B C D E

49. Most managers seem to be more motivated by obtaining power than by achieving objectives. A B C D E

52. Today there seems to be an authority crisis in organizations. A B C D E

Source: A. Laurent. Reproduced by permission.

conceptions were discovered in surveys which asked managers to agree or disagree with statements regarding beliefs about organization and management. A sample of the questions are shown in Table 4.3.

The results of this survey are very much in line with the discussion above in that they show similar cultural differences regarding power and uncertainty in views of organizations as systems of hierarchy, authority, politics, and role formalization. What would these different views of organization actually look like, were we to observe managers at work and even to question them? What arguments would managers from different countries put forth to support their responses?

Having a view of organizations as **hierarchical systems** would make it difficult, for example, to tolerate having to report to two bosses, as required in a matrix organization, and it would make it difficult to accept bypassing or going over or around the boss. The boss would also be expected to have precise answers to most of the questions that subordinates have about their work. Asian and Latin managers argue that in order for bosses to be respected, or to have power and authority, they must demonstrate expert knowledge. And if the most efficient way to get things done is to bypass the hierarchical line they would consider that there was something wrong with the hierarchy.

Scandinavian and Anglo managers, on the other hand, argue that it is perfectly normal to go directly to anyone in the organization in order to accomplish the task. It would seem intolerable, for example, to have to go through one's own boss, who would contact his or her counterpart in a neighboring department before making contact with someone in that other department.

Furthermore, they argue that it is impossible to have precise answers, since the world is far too complex and ambiguous, and even if you could provide precise answers, this would not develop the capability of your subordinates to solve problems. Thus a Swedish boss with a French subordinate can anticipate some problems: the French subordinate is likely to think that the boss, not knowing the answers, is incompetent, while the Swedish boss may think that the French subordinate does not know what to do and is therefore incompetent.

Those who view the organization as a **political system** consider managers to play an important political role in society, and to negotiate within the organization. Thus obtaining power is seen as more important than achieving specific objectives. Here again, Latin European managers are more likely to adhere to this view than their Nordic and Anglo counterparts.

In France, for example, executives have often played important roles in the French administration before assuming top positions in companies. Furthermore, Latin managers are acutely aware that it is necessary to have power in order to get things done in the organization. Nordic and Anglo managers, however, tend to downplay the importance of power and therefore reject the need for political maneuvering.

When organizations are viewed as systems of **role formalization**, managers prefer detailed job descriptions, and well-defined roles and functions. These serve to clarify complex situations and tasks. Otherwise it is difficult to know who is responsible for what and to hold people accountable. In addition they argue that lack of clear job descriptions or role definitions creates overlap and inefficiency. Nordic and Anglo managers, on the other hand, argue that the world is too complex to be able to clearly define roles and functions. Furthermore they say that detailed descriptions interfere with maintaining flexibility and achieving coordination.

From his research, Laurent concluded that underlying these arguments managers had different conceptions of organization: one which focused on the task, called **instrumental**, and one which focused on relationships, called **social**. For Latin European managers, organizations are considered as **social systems**, or systems of relationships, where personal networks and social positioning are important. The organization achieves its goals through relationships and how they are managed (as prescribed by Fayol). Roles and relationships are defined formally (by the hierarchy) and informally, based on authority, power, and status which are seen as attributes of the person, not the task or function. Personal loyalty and deference to the boss are expected.

However, getting things done means working around the system – using informal, personal networks to circumvent the hierarchy as well as the rules and regulations – what the French call *Système D*. According to sociologist Michel Crozier, it is this informal system that gives the French "bureaucratic model" its flexibility.[21] Organizations are thus considered to be necessarily political in nature. When asked to diagnose organizational problems, French social scientists and consultants typically start by analyzing the power relationships and power games (*les enjeux*).[22]

In contrast, for Anglo–Saxon, and northern European managers, the organization is a system of tasks where it is important to know what has to be done, rather than who has power and authority to do so (as in the socio/political view). This instrumental or functionalist view of organizations (very much in keeping with Taylor's scientific management) focuses on what is to be achieved and whether objectives are met (achievement orientation). Structure is defined by activities – what has to be done – and the hierarchy exists only to assign responsibility. It follows that authority is defined by function and is limited, specific to the job not the person.

Here, coordination and control are impersonal, decentralized, and reside in the structure and systems. Rules and regulations are applied universally. If the rules and regulations are dysfunctional, then they are changed rather than circumvented or broken. Management consultants are called in to figure out the best way to devise strategy, design structure, classify jobs and set salary scales, and develop concrete programs such as "total quality" or "performance management".

These different conceptions of organization were confirmed recently when Trompenaars[23] asked 15,000 managers to choose between the following statements:

> A company is a system designed to perform functions and tasks in an efficient way. People are hired to fulfill these functions with the help of machines and other equipment. They are paid for the tasks they perform.

> A company is a group of people working together. The people have social relations with other people and with the organization. The functioning is dependent upon these relations.

He too found large differences between Anglo and Nordic managers compared with Latin and Asian managers, as shown in Figure 4.3. These different beliefs reveal the underlying cultural meaning of organizations as task versus social systems.

As we see us . . . (revisited)

These findings can be further corroborated by asking managers to describe the approach to management in their countries, or "how we see us", as discussed in Chapter 1. For example, many of the research results discussed above place Scandinavian managers at

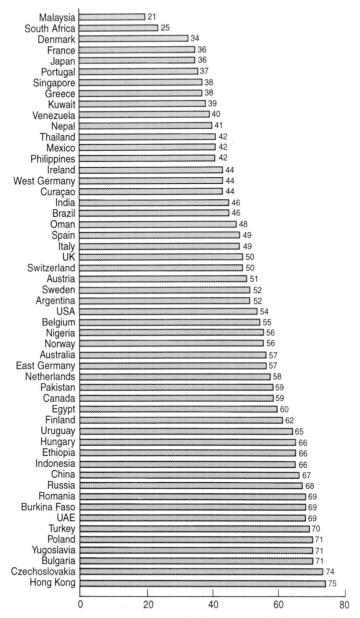

Figure 4.3   Organizations as task versus social systems. (*Source*: F. Trompenaars (1993) *Riding the Waves of Culture: Understanding cultural diversity in business*, Nicholas Brealey, London.)

one end of a continuum, with Latin and Asian managers at the other. Jan Selmer,[24] a Swedish management professor, proposed the following profile of "Viking Management". Compare this with the self-descriptions of Brazilian[25] and Indonesian managers in Table 4.4.

According to self-reports, clear differences and similarities emerge in terms of the nature of relationships (hierarchy) and the relationship with nature (uncertainty and control). For example, in keeping with the findings discussed above, Viking Management is characterized as decentralized (less hierarchy) when compared with the Brazilian and Indonesian views, which emphasize status and power or respect for elders.

On the other hand, in each case there is a strong emphasis on the importance of relationships: family (mother–daughter) and friends, avoiding conflict, being tolerant,

Table 4.4   As we see us . . . .

Viking management
Decentralized decision-making
Organization structure is often ambiguous
Perceived by others to be indecisive
Goal formulation, long-range objectives, and performance evaluation criteria are vague and implicit
Informal channels of communication
Coordinate by values not rules (normative versus coercive)
Case by case approach versus standard procedures
Consensus-oriented
Avoid conflict
Informal relationships between foreign subsidiaries and headquarters (mother–daughter
  relationships)

Brazilian management
Hierarchy and authority; status and power are important
Centralized decision-making
Personal relationships are more important than the task
Rules and regulations are for enemies
Flexible and adaptable (too much?) *Jeitiñho*
Anything is possible
Short-term oriented – immediatism
Avoid conflict – seen as win/lose
Rely on magic – low control over environment
Decisions based on intuition and feeling

Indonesian management
Respect for hierarchy and elders
Family-oriented
Group- versus individual-oriented
Friendly and helpful, hospitable
Tolerant
Decisions based on compromise – "keep everyone happy"
Importance of religion – (Islam)
Five principles
Bhinneka Tunggal Ika (unity through diversity)

seeking consensus, and "keeping everyone happy". For the Swedes, this corresponds to their keen concern for social well-being and quality of relationships, reflected in their number one ranking on Hofstede's femininity dimension.

In all three self-descriptions there is less emphasis placed on formalization. For the Swedes, organization goals and structures are experienced as vague and ambiguous. Uncertainty is managed with a "case by case" (and *not* a universal) approach, through informal communication channels, and "through values not rules". For the Indonesians, it is the "Five principles" established by President Suharto that provide the rules, rather than organizational ones. In comparison with the Swedes, however, the Indonesians perceive little control over their environment, *Insh'allah* (if God wills . . .)". Thus the Swedish approach to getting things done may be frustrated by the Indonesian sense of letting things happen.

Brazilian managers, faced with great uncertainty in the day-to-day business environment over which they feel they have little control, say that they have developed a finely tuned sense of intuition, having learned to trust their "gut" feel, as previously mentioned. For the Brazilians, the notion of *Jeitiñho* is similar to that of the French *Système D*, going around the system in order to get things done. This assures flexibility and adaptability such that anything is possible (although perhaps too much so as Brazilian managers themselves acknowledge).

Now imagine a Brazil–Sweden–Indonesia joint venture. This raises the possibility that three firms would have to resolve their differences on several fronts while using their similarities to create a shared sense of purpose. In particular, there would probably be a clash between the cultural assumptions underlying Swedish management – little concern with power and status and high perceived control over the environment – with those of Brazilian and Indonesian management – more emphasis on power and authority and less perceived control.

This would probably cause the biggest headaches for the Swedes when it came to efforts to delegate decision-making and to encourage individual responsibility and accountability. For the Indonesian and Brazilian managers, the frustration would come from confusion as to "who is the boss?" and "why isn't he/she making decisions?", and "how can I be held responsible when I have no control over what happens?". In decision-making, the Brazilians would find the Indonesians and Swedes interminably slow, seeking consensus or democratic compromise, while they in turn would see the Brazilians as impetuous, and too individualistic. On the other hand, the similarity in importance placed on relationships, on informal communication, and on avoiding conflict can help to work through these difficulties together, on a personal basis.

Although there are variations within countries, due to industry and corporate culture, as well as individual styles of key managers, the above research findings and self-descriptions point to different cultural profiles of organization. The underlying assumptions can be interpreted to reveal the nature of relationships, as seen in the importance of hierarchy, and control over nature, as seen in the need for formal or social rules and procedures. The underlying cultural meaning of the organization can then be interpreted as systems of tasks versus systems of relationships. These cultural profiles provide a starting point to explore different structural preferences and to begin to anticipate potential problems when transferring practices from one country to another or in forming joint ventures and strategic alliances.

On a less serious note, these differences have been caricatured in the organizational charts shown in Figure 4.4. Using these caricatures can provoke discussion of structural differences across countries in a humorous mode while allowing us to discover the grain of truth within and to imagine how our own organization chart might seem to others.

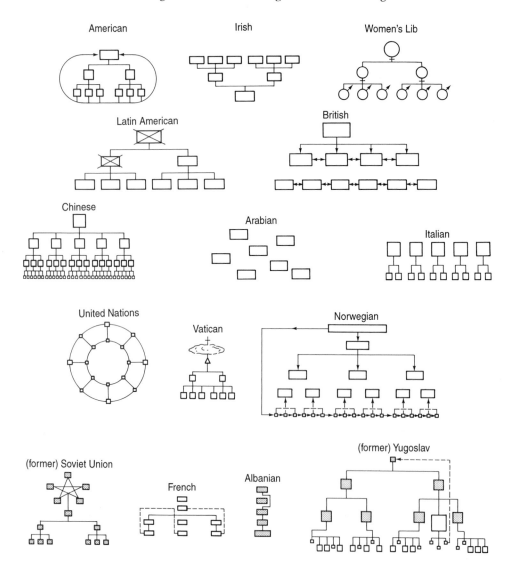

Figure 4.4   The organization chart. (*Source: International Management.* Copyright © Reed Business Publishing.)

Constructing cultural profiles enables us to appreciate the impact of culture on management as multidimensional. It would therefore be a mistake to base a prediction regarding structure or process on a single cultural dimension.

In addition, managers need to recognize that the relationships between cultural dimensions and structure (or processes) are not simple cause–effect links, but instead, are multidetermined. Similar approaches may exist for different cultural reasons, and different approaches may exist for the same reason. Thus formalized rules and procedures or participative management approaches may have a different *raison d'être* on different sides of the national border.

Having considered cultural differences in organization and structure, we can now turn our attention to organizational processes. In addition to cultural preferences regarding hierarchy and formalization, other cultural dimensions are considered to explain the reasons for some of the country differences that may seem contradictory. And to show why similar business practices may have different underlying cultural roots, or meaning.

Culture and processes

The characterization of organizations as pyramids, well-oiled machines, village markets, and family tribes, and the structural correlates are further reflected in the organizational processes. In effect, structures are similar to fossils, as they bear the traces of organizational processes over time. Thus the influence of culture can also be seen in organizational processes such as the nature of policies and procedures, planning and control, information processing and communication, and decision-making.

Policies and procedures

The formalization and standardization of policies and procedures may reflect low tolerance for uncertainty, as they can be clearly spelled out, leaving little room for doubt. Other cultural dimensions may also have a hand in explaining differences found between cultures. For instance, although the United States ranks low on uncertainty avoidance, European managers working for US multinationals often complain about the formal reporting systems, and volume of written policies and procedures that come down from headquarters.

This is perhaps more understandable given the contractual view of employment in the United States, an instrumental view of the firm, and low-context communication. All of these dimensions encourage a high level of explicitness which is evident in the ubiquitous standard operating procedures. Policies and job descriptions are thus written down and standardized so that anyone can perform them. Information is embedded in the system not in the person, as the organization is thought to exist independently from its members. This might seem contrary to the primacy of the individual, but in fact it is this standardization which allows individuals to move easily in and out of jobs/organizations and guarantees their career mobility in the village market. Also, given US commitment to universalism, rules and procedures are necessary to assure that all people are treated equally.[26]

A comparison of British and German firms[27] showed that all the British firms had detailed job descriptions while only one of the German firms did. This seems contrary to expectations, given the respective attitudes to uncertainty avoidance in the two countries (Germany high, Britain low). However, as German managers are specialists and tend to stay longer in one job, job descriptions are well-internalized, and there is less of a need to formalize them.

On the other hand, British managers are generalists, and tend to rotate jobs more often. One study found that in matched companies twenty-five out of thirty British managers had changed jobs within four years, compared with ten out of thirty German managers.[28] Therefore job descriptions are formalized to provide general guidelines to new incumbents.

Furthermore, British managers had a higher tolerance for mismatch between written expectations and actual responsibilities and thus did not feel constrained to follow the job descriptions. German resistance to written descriptions stemmed from the desire to preserve flexibility. Unlike the British managers, the German managers would have felt uncomfortable with any divergence between written procedures and practice (uncertainty).

Procedures or job descriptions are less likely to be made explicit where communication is more embedded in relationships and in situations (high context). Japanese managers tend to have broader general knowledge of the company, which is often tacit, having been gained through observation and on-the-job experience, like a craft.[29] In addition, tasks are assigned to groups not individuals, and individual accountability remains vague. This creates a stronger link between people, the group, and the organization, making knowledge company-specific, thereby reducing career mobility outside the organization, keeping it all in the family.

Systems and controls

Control systems also reflect different cultural assumptions regarding relationships with people (in terms of power and human nature) and relationship with nature (uncertainty and control). For example, French managers indicate that the most important function for a manager is to control, while British managers say it is to coordinate.[30] This reflects different attitudes towards power. For the French, control derives from the hierarchy; for the British, coordination is achieved through persuasion and negotiation, since the boss is not seen as all-powerful.

Furthermore, the nature of control depends on assumptions regarding human nature. When employees are seen as capable and self-directed (Theory Y),[31] there is more reliance on communication, rather than direct supervision. When managers assume that workers are basically lazy and need to be directed by others (Theory X), they are more likely to set up tight control processes.

Different types of control – input, throughout, and output – are also evident across cultures. The French are particularly careful about recruiting future senior managers from the top schools. This reflects input control – choosing the best and the brightest – and then assuming that they will manage and produce results. German companies are less concerned with hiring elites than with developing managers through rigorous apprenticeships and in-depth job-specific experience. The focus on detailed plans and operational controls also reflects the importance of throughput controls. In the United States and Britain, the emphasis is on budgets, financial controls, and reporting procedures, which reflects more output control.

This can be seen in different ideas regarding the purpose of budgets. One comparative study[32] of managers in US and French subsidiaries of the same firm found that for the American managers, budgets were treated as useful tools which provided concrete objectives against which performance could be measured. French managers, on the other hand, were more concerned with the overall logic and perfection of the budgeting system. These differences reflect American managers' confidence in their ability to control events by being pragmatic (instrumental) and results (achievement)-oriented, while French managers rely more on their analytic (Cartesian) capability, or the quality of thinking.

Planning practices also reflect underlying cultural assumptions. A study by Horovitz[33] comparing planning practices in the United Kingdom, Germany and France found that planning practices in the United Kingdom were more strategic in focus, more long term (six year horizon), with more participation in the process. In Germany, planning was more operational (including stringent, detailed one year plans), more short term (three year horizon), with little participation from the ranks. In France, planning was also more short term (less than half of the firms had long-range planning), more administrative (three year financial forecasts), and also less participative. The shorter term and the more operational/administrative orientation reflects the need to limit uncertainty to more manageable time frames and with more concrete outcomes. Thus the need to reduce uncertainty and to impose controls will result in planning that is more operational than strategic, more short term, and less participative.

Information and communication

Organizations must process information in order to make decisions, to communicate policies and procedures, and to coordinate across units. Yet what kind of information is sought or heeded, how information circulates, and what information is shared with whom, are likely to reflect cultural preferences for hierarchy, formalization, and participation.

For example, French companies are often characterized by French managers as *cloisonné* (compartmentalized), very clearly structured vertically as well as horizontally. This makes very clear the personal roles and responsibility, privileges and obligations, and hence the degree of discretion in performing one's job.[34] Thus the flow of information between groups is limited.

Furthermore, given the view of organization as a social system based on relationships, information may not be readily shared as it is viewed as personal, not public. Information is passed through personal connections. According to one French manager, "Information which is widely distributed is obviously useless".[35] In addition, the political nature of French organizations encourages information to be seen as a source of power, and therefore not easily given away.

For these reasons, it is not surprising that informal communication assumes considerable importance in French companies. A survey in the *Nouvel Economiste*[36] found that information was more likely obtained from rumours than from one's immediate boss.

Informal channels compensate for the centralized, formalized, and limited participative nature of information flows.

In contrast, managers in Sweden, which is more egalitarian and more tolerant of uncertainty, pay very little attention to formal structure or hierarchy. Communication patterns are much more open and informal. This is supported in the research findings of André Laurent that Swedish managers were far less inhibited than their French counterparts about bypassing the hierarchical line.[37] Given the Swedish view of organizations as instrumental rather than socio-political, there is a greater willingness to share information with anyone who has an interest in it. Information can be put to use; its value is instrumental, not social.

The Swedish insistence on transparency, or the open sharing of information, created initial difficulties for Electrolux when they acquired Italian company, Zanussi.[38] The Italian managers and labor unions, although first surprised by this transparency, came to respect and trust the "Viking" acquirers because of it. Nevertheless, Zanussi managers had trouble unlearning the previous habit of keeping information to themselves as a way of preserving power.[39]

In Japanese companies, intensive and extensive discussion is encouraged at all levels both within (among employees) and outside (with suppliers and customers) the organization. The adaptability of Japanese companies is often attributed to this cross-boundary, open flow of information. By maximizing the informal exchange of information, Japanese firms are able to generate and leverage knowledge, to create a "learning company".[40]

Consider the special case of Kao, the Japanese competitor of Proctor & Gamble and Unilever.[41] CEO Dr. Maruta strongly believes that,

> If everyone discusses on an equal footing, there is nothing that cannot be resolved . . . [As such,] the organization was designed to "run as a flowing system" which would stimulate interaction and the spread of ideas in every direction and at every level . . . [Thus] organizational boundaries and titles were abolished.

Kao's head office is indeed designed in such a way as to encourage the cross-fertilization of ideas.

> On the 10th floor, known as the top management floor, sat the Chairman, the President, four executive vice presidents, and a pool of secretaries. A large part of the floor was open space, with one large conference table and two smaller ones, and chairs, blackboards and overhead projectors strewn around; this was known as the Decision Space, where all discussions with and among the top management took place. Anyone passing, including the President, could sit down and join in any discussion on any topic . . . This layout was duplicated on the other floors . . . Workplaces looked like large rooms; there were no partitions, but again tables and chairs for spontaneous or planned discussions at which everyone contributed as equals. Access was free to all, and any manager could thus find himself sitting round the table next to the President, who was often seen waiting in line in Kao's Tokyo cafateria.

Furthermore, any employee can retrieve data on sales or product development, the latest findings from R&D, details of yesterday's production and inventory at every plant, and can even check up on the President's expense account.

Thus office design, building layout, and information technology can encourage managers to share information or to keep it to themselves, and can facilitate whether communication channels are open and multiple, or limited to a one-to-one basis, serial, and secretive. The Japanese scientists from Toshiba, assigned to a joint venture with IBM and Siemens, found it unproductive to be in separate little rooms. So they spent most of their time standing in the halls discussing ideas.[42] The German scientists preferred privacy.

This use of physical space and the consequent patterns of interaction are cultural artifacts which reveal different beliefs regarding the optimal degree of hierarchy, formalization, and level of participation. These beliefs influence the flow of information and communication within companies in different countries. Digging deeper, we find differences in the assumptions regarding the use of information under conditions of uncertainty, whether people are seen as trustworthy and capable, and whether information is used to preserve power or to be shared. In addition we find the underlying cultural meaning of information as serving instrumental versus political purposes.

Decision-making

The nature of decision-making is also culturally rooted. Who makes the decision, who is involved in the process, and where decisions are made (in formal committees or more informally in the hallways and corridors, or on the golf course) reflect different cultural assumptions. In turn, the very nature of the decision-making processes as well as different time horizons influences the speed with which decisions are taken.

It is perhaps not surprising that in countries such as Sweden and Germany, where power and hierarchy are played down, there is the greatest evidence of participation in decision-making. In Sweden, perhaps furthest along on the road of industrial democracy, union leaders often sit on the management board and are involved in making major strategic decisions, including decisions to relocate factories abroad. Everyone has the right to contribute to a decision. Decision-making means seeking consensus.

In The Netherlands and Germany, the works council, or labor representation, also plays an important role in deciding business affairs. The strong commitment to consensus, social equality, and human welfare reveals assumptions regarding collectivism and the importance of the quality of working life.[43]

In contrast, companies in cultures which emphasize power and hierarchy are more likely to centralize decision-making. In France, for example, the government plays an important role in determining company strategy and policy, often choosing top management. This has earned France the reputation of being "the father of industrial policy".[44] The PDG (CEO) may well have more experience in government than in business. Furthermore, he (in rare cases she) is expected to make decisions and is respected for it. Power is jealously guarded by each actor, such that management and unions often end up in violent confrontation, neither willing to concede to the other party. While industry is currently being privatized, and employees have become more involved through participation and through quality circles, French management is criticized for remaining centralized and elitist.[45]

The difference in decision-making between Nordic and Latin European firms was sharply illustrated when Sweden's Electrolux acquired Italy's Zanussi. The Swedish top management was often frustrated in its efforts to get Italian managers to arrive at a consensus among themselves in solving problems. The Italian managers, in turn, expected the senior management to settle problems such as transfer pricing between Italian product lines and the UK sales offices. According to one senior Italian manager, ". . . the key in this complex international organization is to have active mechanisms in place to create – and force – the necessary integration". However, the Swedish CEO preferred to let them solve their own problems; "Force is a word that is rarely heard in the Electrolux culture".[46]

Japanese firms, with their collectivist orientation, take yet another approach to decision-making. In the Japanese *Ringi* system, petitions (decision proposals) are circulated requiring individuals to "sign on". Signing, however, does not necessarily mean approval, but means that if the decision is taken, the person agrees to support it. While the opinions of superiors are sought, these opinions tend to be more implicit than explicit. Therefore, Japanese managers devote extra time in trying to "read their boss" to find out what is actually desired. In this way, Japanese firms reconcile the importance placed on both collectivism and the hierarchy.

Northern European and American managers often complain about the "slowness" with which Japanese companies *make* decisions. Japanese managers, on the other hand, often complain about the time it takes American and European companies to *implement* decisions. Although in Japan more time is taken to reach decisions, once the decision is taken it can be implemented more quickly as everyone has been involved and understands why the decision has been taken, what has been decided, and what needs to be done. Americans may pride themselves on being "decisive", making decisions quickly on their own. However, they then have to spend more time back at the office selling these decisions, explaining why, what, and how, and gathering support. Inevitably, implementation takes longer.

These different approaches to decision-making therefore have repercussions on the time taken to reach decisions, even in countries that appear to share cultural assumptions. For example, one study comparing strategic decision-making in Sweden and Britain demonstrated that it took twice as long in Sweden, not just to identify strategic issues (37 months versus 17 months), but also to decide what to do about those issues (23 months versus 13 months).[47]

These differences in the amount of time for reaching decisions was explained by the degree of involvement of others in the process and desire for consensus. In Sweden, more participants are involved in contributing information and more time is taken to collect information and compare alternatives. Also, strategic decisions were more often taken by the management board (a collective) in Sweden rather than, as in Britain, by the Managing Director (CEO), an individual. The Swedish consensus-driven approach (which includes government and union officials) results in the tendency to appoint commissions or special working groups which are often time-consuming.

The speed of decision-making reflects not just the process, but also the prevailing attitude towards time. Many Western managers complain that their sense of urgency is not shared in other parts of the world where the attitude seems to be "what's the big hurry?". Yet in Asia and the Middle East, a decision made quickly may indicate that it has little importance. Otherwise, more time for consideration, reflection, and discussion would be warranted. Thus taking quick decisions is not universally admired as a sign of determination and strong leadership but can be regarded as a sign of immaturity and irresponsibility, or even stupidity.

Furthermore, in cultures where the past plays an important role, traditions cannot be dismissed so quickly. Therefore, decisions need to be taken and implemented more slowly. While this may be more obvious in Asian cultures, important differences exist between countries with otherwise similar cultural profiles. American managers, who are less tradition-bound, may perceive European managers as rather slow in making decisions.

British society, for example, has been described as conservative and tradition-bound, with a marked reluctance to change.[48] The slower speed of decision-making in British firms is also attributed to its being more decentralized (assigned to standing committees) and more informal (guided by unwritten rules and procedures which are maintained through personal connections).[49]

A study comparing strategic decision-making in British and Brazilian firms found that Brazilian executives tend to take decisions more quickly.[50] This was attributed to their centralized power which enables them to take decisions individually. Also according to Brazilian managers, the greater perceived uncertainty and lack of control over the environment contributes to a strong sense of urgency (or as referred to in Table 4.3 "immediatism") and need for change.

Thus differences in approaches to decision-making can be attributed to multiple, interacting cultural dimensions. In addition to cultural preferences for hierarchy, and formalization, assumptions regarding time and change are important considerations in *how* and *how quickly* decisions will be made. In addition, the level of participation in decision-making may be similar but for different reasons. In some countries, such as the United States, participation may be seen as a way of integrating different individual perspectives and preserving everyone's right to decide. In other cultures, such as Japan, it is a way to preserve group harmony and relationships, while in The Netherlands and Sweden it serves to promote social welfare. This results in different underlying cultural reasons for empowerment.

In Sweden where interested parties have the "right to negotiate" (*forhandlingsratt*), and in Germany where they have the "right to decide" (*Mitbestimmung*),[51] "empowerment" signifies power sharing in order to arrive at a consensus regarding collective well-being. In countries, such as the United States, where you are supposed to be self-sufficient and take care of yourself (high degree of individualism), labor and management relationships are more characterized by distributive bargaining. Each actor insists on safeguarding their own interests at the expense of the others and having the resources, support, and authority to pursue individual well-being independently.[52]

Transferability of best practice? Alternative approaches

By pulling together the various experiences of managers and more systematic research studies, we have demonstrated how culture affects organization structure and process.

We have proposed different profiles or models of organizing which evolve from different underlying cultural assumptions. This raises questions about what is considered to be "universal wisdom" and the transferability of "best practice". For the most part, arguments for transferability are in line with convergence notions which claim universality; "Management is management and best practice can be transferred anywhere". This was the rationale behind the 1980s rush to copy Japanese management practice and current rash of American-style restructuring and re-engineering.

Those that question transferability point to differences in the cultural or national (institutional) context. The culturalists question the effectiveness with which Japanese quality circles, say, can be transferred to individualist countries, such as the United States and France. The institutionalists stress the nature of ownership, and the role of government, and of labour unions in promoting such practices. Whether the success of Japanese management practices is due to cultural or institutional factors remains a matter of ongoing debate.[53]

The transfer of best practice nevertheless assumes, to some extent, universality. For example, matrix structures were heralded in the 1970s as a means of combining the benefits of product, geographic, and functional structures. In theory, decentralized decision-making, overlapping roles and responsibilities, and multiple information channels were all supposed to enable the organization to capture and analyze external complexity, to overcome internal parochialism, and to enhance response time and flexibility.[54]

While matrix management may have promised more than it could deliver, Laurent found deep resistance to matrix structures among both French and German managers, but for different reasons.[55] For the French, matrix structures violated the principle of "unity of command" and clear hierarchical reporting relationships. The idea of having two bosses was undesirable, as it created divided loyalties and caused unwelcome conflict. On the other hand, German managers resisted matrix structures, as they frustrated the need for clear-cut structure, information channels, roles and responsibilities. Again, the principles underlying matrix management ran counter to the German need to reduce uncertainty.

Thus cultural differences often undermine the best intentions and the assumed rationality of best practices. Different logics of organization exist in different countries, which can be equally effective, if not more so, given different societal contexts. In fact, there seems to be little doubt that some contexts are more favorable to the success of certain management practices, and it need not always be the country where that practice originated. Japanese quality-control methods originally came from the American gurus, Demming and Juran. Quality circles were the Japanese value-added.

Effectively transferring management structures and processes relies on the ability to recognize their inherent assumptions and to compare them with the cultural assumptions of the potential host country recipient. Countries also differ in their readiness to adopt or adapt foreign models, or to manifest a NIH (not invented here) syndrome. Throughout their history, the Japanese have borrowed models from China and then Europe. Other countries, such as Germany, may be more resistant to importing alien management practices. In eastern European countries, such as Poland, and in the developing Asian countries, such as Thailand, the eagerness to adopt foreign models is tempered desire to develop their own models which are more culturally appropriate.

For example, managers in eastern Europe may reject "team" approaches looking for strong leadership and a sense of clear direction in an effort to break with the more collective approach of the past.[56] Despite the prevailing wisdom that organizations need to be less hierarchical and more flexible, some managers argue that faced with competitive threats and conditions of economic decline or instability, greater centralization and stronger controls are needed.

Indeed, companies in Hong Kong, Japan, and Singapore, where the hierarchy remains firmly in place, have performed well in industries, such as banking, which are facing turbulent environments. Here, other value orientations, not readily apparent in Western business, may be at work. For example, when trying to replicate Hofstede's original study in China, another dimension was discovered – "Confucian dynamism", thrift, persistence and a long-term perspective. This added dimension was considered to account for the competitiveness of the "Five Asian Dragons": China, Hong Kong, Taiwan, Japan, and South Korea.[57]

Consider this testimony regarding the entrepreneurial, family model characteristic of the overseas Chinese business community which has been quite successful whether transplanted to Malaysia or Canada.

> . . . The Confucian tradition of hard work, thrift and respect for one's social network may provide continuity with the right twist for today's fast-changing markets. And the central strategic question for all current multinationals – be they Chinese, Japanese or Western – is how to gather and integrate power through many small units. The evolution of a worldwide web of relatively small Chinese businesses, bound by undeniable strong cultural links, offers a working model for the future.[58]

Whatever the model of the future, be it team management or network organizations, we need to consider how culture may facilitate or hinder their diffusion. Will the more collective culture of Russia facilitate the team approach, while the greater relationship orientation of Chinese culture facilitates creating networks? Could it be that the greater emphasis on the task and the individual, which prevails in the performance management approach, will actually hinder American firms in their attempts to become more team- and network-oriented?

Given recent trends in the United States and Europe towards participative management and empowerment, the role of the leadership is changing. Rather than the more authoritarian notion of being the "boss", the role model is that of the "coach". Rather than directing and controlling, the new role calls for facilitating and developing. Notions of empowerment and the leader as coach, however, may not readily transfer.

Take, for example, two items from the Management Questionnaire designed by Laurent regarding the role of the boss (hierarchy) and of power as shown in Figure 4.5. Comparing the responses of managers attending training seminars from 1990 to 1994 with the results reported in 1980, we find some signs of convergence. According to self-reports, managers are becoming less authoritarian and more concerned with achieving objectives than obtaining power. Nevertheless, while country differences may have eroded, the different country rankings remain in place.

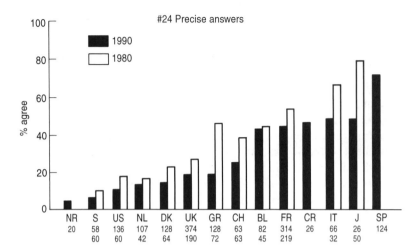

It is important for a manager to have at hand precise answers to most of the questions his/her subordinates may raise about their work.

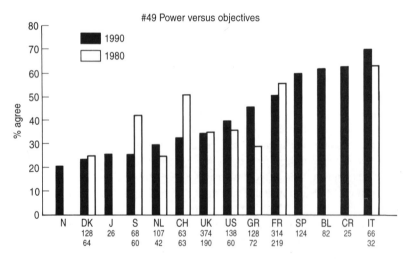

Most managers seem to be more motivated by obtaining power than by achieving objectives.

Figure 4.5   Convergence? (Reproduced by permission of A. Laurent.)

Even in countries which supposedly do not put much stock in hierarchy, such as The Netherlands and the United Kingdom, this new leadership behavior may be difficult to achieve. Therefore, what will that mean for countries in Asia where the hierarchy is still revered? What would the Asian version of empowerment look like? Perhaps there are different means of achieving this end. In the case of Japanese firms, the hierarchy is clearly, albeit implicitly, present. Nevertheless, there are apparently high levels of participation.

And as hierarchies collapse and as cooperation between units becomes more of a necessity, there is a greater need for negotiation and persuasion. Managers will increasingly have to elicit the cooperation of people over whom they have no formal authority. In fact this may demand a more political view of organizations to which Latin firms may be more attuned.

These are the challenges facing many companies as they remodel their corporate structures. They must not lose sight of the impact of national culture in their search for a model of organization that can respond best to the demands of the rapidly changing business context, and the pressures for internationalization. They must also recognize that the "best models" are not necessarily "home grown", but that other ways of organizing may be equally, if not more, effective.

Notes

1. Crozier, M. (1964) *The Bureaucratic Phenomenon*, Chicago: University of Chicago Press, p. 210.
2. Pugh, D.S., Hickson, D.J., Hinings, C.R., and Turner, C. (1969) "The context of organization structure", *Administrative Science Quarterly*, 14, 91–114; Miller, G.A. (1987) "Meta-analysis and the culture-free hypothesis", *Organization Studies*, 8(4), 309–25; Hickson, D.J. and McMillan, I. (eds) (1981) *Organization and Nation: The Aston Programme IV*, Farnborough: Gower.
3. Burns, T. and Stalker, G.M. (1961) *The Management of Innovation*, London: Tavistock.
4. Child, J. (1981) "Culture, contingency and capitalism in the cross-national study of organizations" in L.L. Cummings and B.M. Staw (eds) *Research in Organizational Behavior*, Vol. 3, 303–356, Greenwich, CT: JAI Press; Scott, W.R. (1987) "The adolescence of institutional theory", *Administrative Science Quarterly*, 32, 493–511; Lincoln, J.R., Hanada, M. and McBride, K. (1986) "Organizational structures in Japanese and US manufacturing", *Administrative Science Quarterly*, 31, 338–64.
5. Weber, M. (1947) *The Theory of Social and Economic Organization*, New York: Free Press; Fayol, H. (1949) *General Industrial Management*, London: Pitman; Taylor, F. (1947, first published 1912) *Scientific Management*, New York: Harper & Row.
6. Kogut, B. (1991) "Country capabilities and the permeability of borders", *Strategic Management Journal*, 12, 33–47; Kogut, B. and Parkinson, D. (1993) "The diffusion of American organizing principles to Europe" in B. Kogut (ed.) *Country Competitiveness: Technology and the Organizing of Work*, Ch. 10, New York: Oxford University Press, 179–202; Guillen, M. (1994) "The age of eclecticism: Current organizational trends and the evolution of managerial models", *Sloan Management Review*, Fall, 75–86.
7. Westney, D.E. (1987) *Imitation and Innovation*, Cambridge, MA: Harvard University Press.
8. Hofstede, G. (1980) *Cultures Consequences*, Beverly Hills, CA: Sage; Hofstede, G. (1991) *Cultures and Organizations: Software of the Mind*, London: McGraw-Hill.

9. Hofstede, G. (1980) "Motivation, leadership, and organization: Do American theories apply abroad?", *Organizational Dynamics*, Summer, 42–63.

10. Ronen, S. and Shenekar, O. (1985) "Clustering countries on attitudinal dimensions: A review and synthesis", *Academy of Management Review*, 10(3), 435–54.

11. Burns and Stalker, *Op. cit.*

12. *Ibid.*

12. Stevens, O.J., cited in Hofstede, G. (1991) *Cultures and Organizations*, London: McGraw-Hill, 140–2.

14. Brossard, A. and Maurice, M. (1976) "Is there a universal model of organization structure?", *International Studies of Management and Organization*, 6, 11–45; Horovitz, J. (1980) *Top Management Control in Europe*, London: Macmillan; Stewart, R., Barsoux, J.-L., Kieser, A., Ganter, D. and Walgenbach, P. (1994) *Managing in Britain and Germany*, London: Macmillan.

15. Stewart *et al.*, *Op. cit.*

16. *Ibid.*

17. Redding, S.G. and Pugh, D.S. (1986) "The formal and the informal: Japanese and Chinese organization structures" in S. Clegg, D. Dunphy, and S.G. Redding (eds) *The Enterprise and Management in East Asia*, Hong Kong: Center of Asian Studies, University of Hong Kong, 153–168; Vertinsky, I., Tse, D.K., Wehrung, D.A. and Lee, K. (1990) "Organization design and management norms: A comparative study of managers' perceptions in the People's Republic of China, Hong Kong and Canada", *Journal of Management*, 16(4), 853–67.

18. Wong, G.Y.Y. and Birnbaum-More, P.H. (1994) "Culture, context and structure: A test on Hong Kong banks", *Organization Studies*, 15(1), 99–123.

19. Kao, J. (1993) "The worldwide web of Chinese business", *Harvard Business Review*, March–April, 24–35.

20. Laurent, A. (1983) "The cultural diversity of western conception of management", *International Studies of Management and Organization*, 13(1–2), 75–96.

21. Crozier, M. (1964) *The Bureaucratic Phenomenon*, Chicago: University of Chicago Press.

22. Crozier, M. and Friedberg, E. (1977) *L'Acteur et le système: Les contraintes de l'action collective*, Paris: Seuil.

23. Trompenaars, F. (1993) *Riding the Waves of Culture*, London: Nicholas Brealey.

24. Selmer, J. (1988) Presentation, International Conference on Personnel and Human Resource Management Conference, Singapore.

25. Amado, G. and Brasil, H.V. (1991) "Organizational behaviors and cultural context: The Brazilian 'Jeitiñho' ", *International Studies of Management and Organization*, 21(3), 38–61.

26. Hampden-Turner, C. and Trompenaars, F. (1994) *Seven Cultures of Capitalism*, London: Piatkus.

27. Stewart *et al.*, *Op. cit.*

28. *Ibid.*

29. Nonaka, I. (1991) "The knowledge-creating company", *Harvard Business Review*, November–December, 96–104.

30. Laurent, A. (1986) "The cross-cultural puzzle of global human resource management", *Human Resource Management*, 25(1), 91—102.

31. McGregor, D. (1960) *The Nature of Human Enterprise*, New York: McGraw-Hill.

32. Perret, M.S. (1988) "The impact of cultural differences in budgeting", unpublished Ph.D. dissertation, University of Western Ontario.

33. Horovitz, *Op. cit.*

34. D'Iribarne, P. (1989) *La logique de l'honneur*, Paris: Seuil.

35. Orleman, P.A. (1992) The global corporation: Managing across cultures, Masters thesis, University of Pennsylvania.

36. "La communication dans l'entreprise", *Nouvel Economiste*, May 12, 1980, 42–7.

37. Laurent, *Op. cit.*
38. Haspeslagh, P. and Ghoshal, S. (1992) *Electrolux Zanussi*, INSEAD case.
39. Lorenz, C. (1989) "The Italian connection – a stark contrast in corporate manners", *Financial Times*, June 23, 20.
40. Nonaka, *Op. cit.*; Schütte, H. (1993) "Competing and cooperating with Japanese firms", Euro–Asia Center, INSEAD.
41. Ghoshal, S. and Butler, C. (1991) KAO Corporation, INSEAD case.
42. Browning, E.S. (1994) "Computer chip project brings rivals together, but the cultures clash", *Wall Street Journal*, May 3, A7.
43. Fry, J.A. (ed.) (1979) *Limits of the Welfare State: Critical Views on Post-war Sweden*, Farnborough: Saxon House.
44. Aubert, N., Ramantsoa, B. and Reitter, R. (1984) "Nationalizations, managerial power, and societal change", Working paper Harvard Business School.
45. Schmidt, V.A. (1993) "An end to French economic exceptionalism: The transformation of business under Mitterand", *California Management Review*, Fall, 75–98.
46. Lorenz, *Op. cit.*
47. Axelsson, R., Cray, D., Mallory, G.R. and Wilson, D.C. (1991) "Decision style in British and Swedish organizations: A comparative examination of strategic decision making", *British Journal of Management*, 2, 67–79.
48. Tayeb, M.H. (1988) *Organizations and National Culture: A Comparative Analysis*, London: Sage.
49. Mallory, G.R., Butler, R.J., Cray, D., Hickson, D.J. and Wilson, D.C. (1983) "Implanted decision making: American owned firms in Britain", *Journal of Management Studies*, 20, 191–211; Fry, *Op. cit.*
50. Oliveira, B. and Hickson, D.J. (1991) "Cultural bases of strategic decision making: A Brazilian and English comparison", presented at EGOS conference, Vienna.
51. Lawrence, P. and Spybey, T. (1986) *Management and Society in Sweden*, London: Routledge and Kegan Paul.
52. Irene Rodgers, Cross-cultural consultant, personal communication.
53. See Whitley, R.D. (ed.) (1992) *Business Systems in East Asia: Firms, Markets and Societies*, London: Sage.
54. Davis, S. and Lawrence, P.R. (1977) *Matrix*, Reading, MA: Addison-Wesley.
55. Laurent, A. (1981) "Matrix organization and Latin cultures", *International Studies of Management and Organization*, 10(4), 101–14.
56. Cyr, D.J. and Schneider, S.C. (1996) "Implications for learning: human resources management in east–west joint ventures", *Organization Studies*, 17(2), 207–226.
57. Hofstede, G. and Bond, M.H. (1988) "The Confucius connection: From cultural roots to economic growth", *Organizational Dynamics*, 16, 4–21; see also Hofstede, G. (1991) *Cultures and Organizations: Software of the Mind*, London: McGraw-Hill.
58. Kao, *Op. cit.*, p. 36.

CHAPTER FIVE

Culture and strategy

> It is as if there were a common set of issues in organizations that some of us choose to call culture and others choose to call strategy.
>
> Karl Weick[1]

The close link between culture and strategy, as noted above, was recognized by Karl Weick, a renowned organizational scholar, when he provided a set of statements to readers and asked them to decide whether the first word in each should be "strategy" or "culture". He demonstrated that by substituting the word culture in each statement (which were in fact traditional definitions of strategy), the meaning of the text remained unchanged.

Indeed, as stated earlier the definition of **culture** (provided in this book) as solutions to problems of external adaptation and internal integration could be taken as a fitting definition of **strategy**. In devising and implementing strategies, organizations need to assess their external environments as well as their internal capabilities. Strategic decisions are, in effect, intended to achieve external adaptation. Implementing these decisions requires configuring internal resources, including people, to achieve the necessary internal integration.

This chapter addresses the questions: How does national culture affect strategy? To what extent do different approaches to strategy, different ways of thinking about strategy, reflect different underlying cultural assumptions? Faced with similar business environments, how do managers from different cultures perceive and respond to that environment? In what ways does culture affect not only what decisions are taken (content), but also the way that these decisions are made (process)? And, in what ways does culture impact the interaction between strategic content and process? Having addressed these questions we then consider the implications for competitive analysis, for anticipating the strategic moves of different national competitors, and for the roles of headquarters and subsidiaries in both formulating and implementing strategy.

The cultural roots of strategy

Interest in strategy dates far back in history, often discussed in the context of war and the military. From the Greek *strategos* (commander of the army), to military maneuvers described in *The Art of War*,[2] and the personal maneuvers of Machiavelli's *Prince*,[3] strategies have been devised to achieve national or personal gain. For organizations too, strategy is considered to be the means for achieving corporate objectives.

In business, the notion of strategy became popularized in the 1960s when companies faced increased competition and limited resources. Strategic planning armies were mobilized to centralize and formalize the process. For companies like GE and Shell, strategic planning was sacrosanct, becoming something of a religious ritual. According to one former Shell executive, "Managers concerned with such [planning] systems fight a continuous battle to prevent them degenerating into a 'corporate rain dance' ".[4]

Corporate soldiers were trained to analyze organizational *strengths* and *weaknesses* and environmental *opportunities* and *threats* (SWOT) in order to create the appropriate strategic alignment, or "fit".[5] Strategic management weapons/tools, such as the Boston Consulting Group (BCG) matrices, were called upon to analyze the market (in terms of growth and position) and to assist in making strategic decisions as to where to attack (invest or divest). The language of SWOT analyses, cash cows, dogs, and stars became part of the shared corporate jargon.

Later on, models based on Industrial Organization economics, such as that of Michael Porter,[6] became the rage, and managers were off analyzing barriers to entry and exit, substitutability, desperately seeking other sources of competitive advantage. More recently, the search has been for "core competencies" and "strategic intent" with abundant examples taken from the Japanese management practices of Canon, NEC, and Matsushita.[7]

These strategic planning departments, rituals, tools, models, and jargon, in effect, represent cultural artifacts. The waves of fads and fashions which have carried strategic (as well as other) management practices promote certain sets of beliefs and values, such as "analytic rationality". However, it is important to understand the assumptions underlying these practices, beliefs, and values in order to question whether they have, in fact, the same meaning in different cultures. We need to consider alternative models of strategy formulation and implementation that may be equally viable. This has implications for developing strategies at the local and global levels, for communicating head office as well as local strategies, and for anticipating the strategic moves of local and global competitors and partners.

The rational/economic view

Many of the strategic management frameworks mentioned above, including the prescribed tools and techniques, affirm the belief and value of a "rational analytic" approach. This approach takes for granted certain assumptions. It assumes, for example, that the environment and the organization are objective realities that are similarly perceived and analyzed by intelligent managers.

Yet those managers making strategic decisions often find themselves confronted with environmental uncertainty, ill-structured problems, and socio-political processes.[8] In fact, rather than taking them as objective realities, it can be argued that both environments and organizations are *subjective* realities that are perceived and enacted in different ways.[9] This means that managers see different things, create different realities, and then act accordingly. Thus multiple interpretations of and responses to supposedly similar situations are likely. As such, national culture can play an important role in determining different types of strategic behavior.[10]

The rational analytic approach also assumes that managers making strategic decisions follow a similar route, gathering all relevant information, generating all possible alternatives, evaluating the costs and benefits of each alternative, choosing the optimal solution, and then acting upon it. While widely acknowledged that managers and organizations are limited in their capacity to digest all this information, thus subject to "bounded rationality",[11] the precise ways in which rationality in decision-making is limited, or more specifically culture-bound, have remained unexplored. In other words, how does culture influence the way managers gather and interpret information, choose between decision alternatives, and establish criteria for action?[12]

Clearly, much of the discussion to date regarding strategic management has been based on beliefs that environments and organizations are objective realities and that strategic decision-making is a rational and analytic process. Digging deeper, we discover underlying assumptions that environments are intelligible and predictable, and that by taking action, or doing, strategic objectives can be achieved. This functionalist, instrumental view of the world, however, may be challenged in other cultures.

Another view of strategy

Consider the speech given by the CEO of a major international bank, managed in accordance with Islamic principles.

> Strategy is a dynamic process, not a static perception, which is energized through feelings. It is not a bundle of facts, figures, and ideas assembled in order by the logical mind. Planning is the reflection of the flow of collective psyche synthesized with Purpose.

Underlying this notion of strategy we find dramatically different cultural assumptions. It highlights the role of feelings, or emotions, not just analytic rationality. It questions the nature of truth as determined by facts and figures, and logic, rather than by spiritual purpose. Furthermore, it views strategy as a collective process, and as dynamic – what is needed is to go with the flow.

Different cultural assumptions are also clearly evident in the approach of Matsushita. In 1932, the CEO announced a **250 year** corporate plan, divided into 10 segments of 25 years. He then codified the company creed, known as the "Seven Spirits of Matsushita", to explicitly articulate the following beliefs: harmony between man and nature, the need for co-prosperity and coexistence, the unlimited potential of people to grow and change, that the goal to improve life is never attainable, and that profit as an objective is a *means* not an *end*.[13] Here, underlying assumptions regarding the relationship with nature (harmony), human nature (unlimited potential), and the nature of human relationships (collective prosperity and existence) are easily surfaced.

According to Pascale,[14] coauthor of *The Art of Japanese Management*, Japanese companies adopt a broader notion of strategy. They challenge the Western view of strategic management, considering these rational analytic approaches to be "myopic" and "an oversimplification of reality".

> The Japanese are somewhat distrustful of a single "strategy", for in their view any idea that focuses attention does so at the expense of peripheral vision. They strongly believe that *peripheral vision* is essential to discerning changes in the customer, the technology or competition, and is the key to corporate survival over the long haul. They regard any propensity to be driven by a single-minded strategy as a weakness. (pp. 47–48)
>
> The Japanese have a particular discomfort with strategic concepts. While they do not reject ideas such as the experience curve or portfolio theory outright they regard them as a stimulus to perception.
>
> Western consultants, academics, and executives express a preference for oversimplifications of reality and cognitively linear explanations of events . . . We tend to impute coherence and purposive rationality to events when the opposite may be closer to the truth. (p. 57)

Here too, assumptions regarding the nature of truth and reality are different: that reality cannot be boxed into two-by-two matrices; and that truth cannot be determined by simplistic theories of cause and effect.

But other Western management scholars have also challenged the rational analytic approach. Consider these comments by Henry Mintzberg, who has been a rather outspoken opponent to the "strategic planning" approach. "Strategy formation is a process of learning only partially under the control of conscious thought . . . Strategies emerge informally, sometimes gradually, sometimes spontaneously, usually in a collective process."[15] Rather than planned, strategy is considered as *emergent*, or as *evolutionary*.[16] This view assumes that managers have less control over their environments which are difficult to know, and that taking action does not necessarily make things happen. Strategy unfolds in response to current events, within the historical as well as organizational context (structures and procedures). Thus the "intended" strategy and the "emergent" one may not necessarily coincide. Strategies designed at the top and those that emerge through more autonomous activities further down the organization may be more or less loosely coupled. Strategies as such are thought to emerge and to evolve over time, as "a pattern in a stream of decisions".

More recently in the field of strategic management, there has been a growing interest in developing organizational resources and capabilities.[17] These resource-based and core competencies views suggest that building "corporate" character (or developing resource bases) provides the capability and flexibility to respond to environmental events. These approaches reflect different underlying assumptions by placing the emphasis on what the company *is* versus what the company *does* (*being* versus *doing* at the corporate level). The focus is on having the "right stuff", or strategic traits, rather than necessarily making the "right moves", or strategic actions.

The success of Japanese companies such as Canon and NEC is attributed to developing such competencies which enables them to capitalize on unexpected opportunities and to create, or re-create markets. In fact, many Japanese companies have managed to resurrect markets previously written off as mature by Western firms. For example, while Honda entered the mature US motorcycle market intending to sell big bikes to the "tough guy" market, they ended up selling mini-bikes to the "nicest people" (their advertising slogan). "History has it that Honda 'redefined' the U.S. motorcycle industry. In the view of American Honda's start-up team, this was an innovation they backed into – and reluctantly."[18]

Indeed, many American and European companies, such as Xerox and Philips, became concerned when they realized that not only were their markets being invaded, but also that the technologies that they had developed were appearing as Japanese products. The apparent Japanese competitive edge forced companies to reconsider their own way of thinking about strategy. It provided dramatic evidence that strategy could be viewed through different lenses, shaped by different cultural assumptions.

The extensive body of research comparing Japanese and Western companies points to distinctive national patterns in strategic management.[19] Yet the underlying cultural reasons for these differences have not been sufficiently examined. While the emphasis in this chapter is on national culture, industry and corporate cultures also play an important role in determining strategy, which will be discussed further on.

Cultural models of strategy

Cultural assumptions regarding external adaptation are particularly relevant to strategy, as its very purpose is to align the organization with its environment. Assumptions regarding internal integration are relevant to questions such as who is involved and who takes the decision. For example, managers from different countries have different assumptions regarding uncertainty and control, as established in the previous chapter. Consider the potential consequences of these assumptions in the following hypothetical scenarios.

Managers from Nordic and Anglo countries are less likely to see environments as uncertain. They believe that environments can be analyzed and known. They therefore are attracted to analytic tools and techniques such as strategic forecasting or scenario planning. They call for industry reports and market research, and call upon industry experts to provide objective information to assist in making strategic decisions. Armed with this information and decision tools, they have faith in their ability to analyze and to predict their environments which provides a sense of control over the course of events. Thus strategic actions are taken to make things happen.

Managers from countries within Latin Europe or Asia are likely to perceive greater uncertainty when faced with similar environments, and perceive less control over what will happen. Thus they are more inclined to go with the flow, to adapt. Information is gathered through informal channels and personal relationships, and is thus more subjective. They prefer to interpret this information through intense, face-to-face discussion and debate, believing that multiple perspectives, broader involvement, and more extensive information sharing are necessary to comprehend the external uncertainty and ambiguity.[20] More time is required to analyze and to decide how to respond.

Thus assumptions having to do with the relationship with nature (control), human beings (as capable), the nature of truth and reality (facts and figures, logic), and the nature of relationships (the role of the hierarchy and the collective) influence the sources and type of information sought, and the methods of interpreting that information.[21] These assumptions also influence who is involved in the process, experts or colleagues, and the nature of strategic response. Different assumptions lead to different models of strategic management which can be categorized as "controlling" versus "adapting".[22]

In Table 5.1, we present these two models in more detail, albeit oversimplified, as they are intended to represent endpoints on a continuum along which different countries, or

Table 5.1   Cultural models of strategy

CONTROLLING		ADAPTING
Scanning is:		
Active search	├──┼──┼──┼──┤	Monitor
Focused and systematic	├──┼──┼──┼──┤	Broad and sporadic
Centralized (scanning department)	├──┼──┼──┼──┤	Decentralized
Planning is:		
Formalized (systems)	├──┼──┼──┼──┤	Informal (discussion)
Centralized (strategic planning department)	├──┼──┼──┤	Decentralized
Types and sources of information:		
Quantitative	├──┼──┼──┼──┼──┤	Qualitative
Objective	├──┼──┼──┼──┼──┤	Subjective
Impersonal	├──┼──┼──┼──┼──┤	Personal
Interpreting information relies on:		
Formal models and methods (e.g. strategic forecasting)	├──┼──┤	Informal methods ("home grown" models)
Scenario planning	├──┼──┼──┼──┤	Discussion and debate
People involved are:		
Mostly at the top	├──┼──┼──┼──┤	Across the ranks
Experts	├──┼──┼──┼──┼──┤	Employees
Decisions are made:		
Primarily at the top	├──┼──┼──┼──┤	On the front lines
Tend to be political	├──┼──┼──┼──┤	Consensual
Strategic goals and action plans are:		
Clearly defined and articulated	├──┼──┼──┤	Broad and implicit
Explicitly measured and rewarded	├──┼──┼──┤	Vaguely monitored
Time horizons are:		
Short term	├──┼──┼──┼──┼──┤	Long term
Action plans are:		
Sequential	├──┼──┼──┼──┼──┤	Simultaneous

indeed industries and companies, can be positioned accordingly. They are presented as "caricatures" to help surface and decipher the underlying cultural assumptions. These models are intended to help generate hypotheses, and to assist managers to know what questions to ask.

Controlling model

The "controlling" model can be characterized as centralized and formalized. Top management may call in expert consultants to assist in devising strategies. Formal strategic planning units may be established to devise plans to be submitted to top management or the board for deliberation. Formal scanning units may also exist that are responsible for tracking environmental events. Scanning is focused and in-depth in order to obtain the necessary information.

Information is often obtained from industry reports, or consultants, and tends to be quantitative and objective. Forecasting, econometric models, and structured scenarios are used to analyze the information. Based on this information and analysis, top management makes the decisions and then hands them down to be implemented. Implementation entails thorough planning, setting clear and specific targets (milestones), explicit communication of what is to be done and how, persistent follow through, and then linking performance goals with rewards.

What cultural assumptions are embedded in this model? First there is the assumption that the environment can be known (is intelligible and predictable). Specific information can be obtained (by active and focused scanning) and analyzed (interpreted) to reduce environmental uncertainty. Truth is determined by facts and figures manipulated by mathematical models. Strategic vision can be expressed as concrete targets ("$15 billion by the next year 2000"), explicit and tangible (low context). Even the vision of British Airways as "the world's favorite airline" is subject to be measured.

Decisions are taken by those presumed to have the most power or knowledge, namely top management. As the top managers are considered to be rational economic actors, or agents, they are assumed to make the best decisions in line with individual interests. Therefore they need to be held accountable, and controlled by systems (reporting) or supervisory boards. Given different individual interests, the decision-making process is seen as more political.

The monochronic view of time as linear and segmented means that strategic decisions are seen as discrete events, and action steps can be planned within a given timetable. Thus implementation is highly task- and achievement-oriented: concrete actions can be planned and the results measured. According to this perspective, the purpose of strategic management is to achieve control of what happens both outside as well as inside the organization, hence "controlling".

Adapting model

In contrast, the "adapting" model is more decentralized and informal. Responsibility for strategy is diffused throughout the organization. Scanning is broader based and less sytematic. Information is gathered from personal sources, friends and colleagues, and through observation (field visits) and thus tends to be more qualitative and subjective. Information is interpreted through "home grown" or intuitive models. Intense discussion is encouraged involving many people from all levels within the organization. Strategic decisions are expected to be reached through consensus (socially constructed).

Rather than a discrete strategic decision *per se*, a strategic direction tends to emerge. Implementation is then locally determined, keeping within this general strategic frame. Adjustments can then be made to unforeseen events and strategy can be refined on an ongoing basis. Responsibility and accountability are assigned to the collective.

The underlying assumptions in this model are that the environment cannot be readily known or controlled. Therefore the organization must be flexible and prepared to react to unforeseeable environmental events. A broad scan – peripheral vision again – is needed to detect subtle changes in the environment. Personal relationships and interactions are considered key to developing shared understanding, thus information sources are more personal and subjective. Truth and reality, or knowledge, are more likely to be arrived at through a "sixth sense", feelings or intuition. Strategic vision is often vague and philosophical. Strategy implementation is considered to hinge on the development of internal capabilities – knowledge, competencies, and learning – in order to be able to continuously improve, hence "adapting".

Returning to Japan . . .

In order to contrast the adapting and controlling models, let us return to Japan. Pascale explains the initial failure and subsequent success of Honda, as well as other Japanese companies, as follows.

> Their success did not result from a bold insight by a few big brains at the top. On the contrary, success was achieved by senior managers humble enough not to take their initial strategic positions too seriously. What saved Japan's near-failures was the cumulative impact of "little brains" in the form of salesmen and dealers and production workers, all contributing incrementally to the quality and market position these companies enjoy today. Middle and upper management saw their primary task as guiding and orchestrating this input from below rather than steering the organization from above along a predetermined strategic course.
>
> The Japanese don't use the term "strategy" to describe a crisp business definition or competitive master plan. They think more in terms of "strategic accommodation" or "adaptive persistence", underscoring their belief that corporate direction evolves from an incremental adjustment to unfolding events. Rarely, in their view, does one leader (or a strategic planning group) produce a bold strategy that guides a firm unerringly. Far more frequently, the input is from below. It is this ability of an organization to move information and ideas from the bottom to the top and back again in continuous *dialogdialogue that the Japanese value above all things.*[23]

Thus the strategy that emerges tends to be adaptive rather than being constrained by industry definitions, and fixed strategic plans. The success of Japanese firms is attributed to the absence of rigid planning systems, their willingness to adapt and shift to changing environments, and their use of intuition and feel as guides. Their success is also attributed to their taking a long-term perspective, being willing to invest time and effort without immediate results.

More recently, management scholars, both East and West, support Pascale's assertions. For example, Burgelman[24] describes Japanese strategy as "evolutionary", wherein top management sets an open-ended vision and "vaguely delineated fields of strategic action". He argues that innovation evolves from the tension created by ". . . setting ambiguous directions together with very challenging parameters which serve as criteria for supporting emerging projects".[25] In this way, peripheral activities are encouraged which provide opportunities for learning new capabilities.

Japanese management scholar Nonaka also supports this Japanese version of strategy. He argues that the role of middle management is to simultaneously translate the abstract philosophies of top management and the concrete practical experience of the front lines. Strategies evolve and knowledge is created through this "middle-up-down" management.[26] Furthermore, he argues that

> The centerpiece of the Japanese approach is the recognition that creating new knowledge is not simply a matter of "processing" objective information. Rather it depends on tapping the tacit and often highly subjective insights, intuitions, and hunches of individual employees and making those insights available to testing and use by the company as a whole.[27]

These examples from Japan provide evidence for a model of strategy that is adapting rather than controlling. The different cultural behaviors, beliefs and values, and underlying assumptions that support the two models can be surfaced and deciphered, as shown in Table 5.2.

In the West, current interest in developing core competencies and in creating learning organizations represents a shift towards the adapting model. The rapidly, and sometimes radically, changing business environments represent serious challenges to assumptions of environmental certainty and organizational control.

These challenges are strongly felt in traditionally stable industries such as banking, notably in Europe, where the creation of the European Union has dramatically changed the rules of doing business. For this reason, it is worth examining the strategic approaches of two large European banks, one in Spain and one in Denmark, faced with the arrival of 1992, the date set for the opening of a single European market when these new rules were to be put in place. As this research was conducted in the summer of 1989, the story will be told in the perspective of what was about to happen rather than what actually occurred.[28]

The tale of two banks (circa 1989)

The date was set. As of January 1, 1992, capital, goods, and labor would be allowed to circulate freely among the (then twelve) member states. For the banking industry this meant the possibility of setting up branches in other countries, of playing on a "level

Table 5.2 Cultural determinants of strategy

External adaptation	Strategy

Relationship with nature
  Uncertainty
  Control
	Controlling/adapting

Human activity
  Doing versus being
  Achievement versus ascription
	Right moves versus right stuff
	Actions versus competences

Truth and reality	Facts and figures Intuition and philosophy

Internal integration	
Human nature	Who is capable of making decision

Nature of relationships
  Power and status
  Individual/collective
  Task/social
	Who has the right, legitimacy
	Who is responsible/accountable

Language High context/low context	Goals are explicit Strategy clearly articulated

Time
  Monochronic/polychronic
 	
  Long term/short term
	Decisions discrete
	Step-by-step action plans
	Speed of decisions
	Time frames for implementing

field" (harmonization of standards and practices), and of being able to sell their own products and services abroad (mutual recognition and home country supervision). The establishment of a central European bank and a common currency was also envisioned. By the year 1989 there was "much ado" in the press, in national government debates, and among business consultants preparing for what became known simply as "1992".

In this context, senior executives were interviewed in two banks, one in Denmark and one in Spain, to explore how information was gathered and interpreted, and how strategic decisions would be taken with regard to "1992". Both banks were among the top three in their respective countries and were similar in the nature of their activities' retail (primarily) and commercial banking. Both banks had also gone through crises in the mid-1980s and subsequent organizational changes, including a new CEO. Neither bank had significant international experience, except for currency trading and taking care of private and corporate (national) clients abroad.

Both countries were "overbanked", meaning that the market was saturated but fragmented (although more concentrated in the hands of fewer players in Denmark, where the top four banks had 47 percent as compared with 21 percent market share in Spain). Competition was, nevertheless, greater in Denmark; Spanish bankers sat more comfortably with higher margins. The level of government regulation and involvement was somewhat greater in Spain.

While the banks were comparable in many respects, the economic and political contexts in which they were situated differed.[29] Denmark had just emerged from a recession with less than 1 percent growth predicted while the growth rate of the Spanish economy was over 5 percent. Politically, Denmark had been more ambivalent about joining the EEC (as was later to be evident in their initial NO vote to the Maastricht Treaty). This ambivalence was linked to their superior standard of living (despite accompanying higher taxes) and their strong Scandinavian identity. In Spain, there had been great excitement about joining the EEC, as it was symbolically linked with democracy, Spain having been denied entry under the Franco regime, and laying to rest an old fifteenth century saying that "Europe ends at the Pyrenees"!

The Danish approach to "1992"

Executives within the Danish bank, described "1992" as "business as usual". It was essentially seen as a political event external to the bank. The planning department was seen as primarily responsible for "1992". The interpretation and response to "1992" would be managed within the formal decision-making process: the planning department would provide input to the board and CEO, who would then take the final decision. Little information regarding "1992" was disseminated to the rest of the bank.

The primary sources of information were considered to be external, particularly from contacts within the government or in Brussels. Internal sources were given less attention. One executive had written a book about the Single Market in his "own time" and was permitted to give talks (outside the bank) on the subject of "1992" as long as it "didn't interfere with his job". Formal information about "1992" was not very actively sought. It was estimated that only 10 percent came from written documentation, and industry reports were not relied upon. Analyses of costs and budgets provided the framework for interpreting information. However, the CEO considered that having a vision was more useful than economic scenarios, as it was more open and adaptive to changing events.

According to senior managers, discussions regarding "1992" were expected to be political, open to "wild debate", but "like the Communist party, they would be loyal to the outcome". Although some expressed concern that the far-reaching consequences were ill-understood by top management, one senior executive stated, "We're pretty cocksure we can manage it".

The Spanish approach to "1992"

In the Spanish bank, "1992" generated much excitement and enthusiasm. It was viewed as stimulating, as an impetus for change. A task force, called "Project Europe 1992", was created to develop a strategy for the bank. This task force consisted of 15 middle managers drawn from throughout the bank, assigned on a full-time basis. Members of the task force then interviewed the top 100 managers regarding their views on what the strategy should be. Information was also gathered by talking to people at meetings and at other banks, visiting best practice companies, and attending seminars. Information was interpreted by meeting and talking and using home grown models emphasizing market share and customer profitability.

The CEO gave "1992" top priority by placing it as the first item on the agenda for each meeting. The debate around "1992" was seen as consensus-seeking. To discourage political behavior, the CEO encouraged open sharing of information with an explicit rule of "no secrets". Any member of the task force thought to be protecting "home turf" interests was asked to leave. The primary challenge was "the task of getting 15,000 people ready to accept the challenge of 1992".

Different approaches, different assumptions

While not fitting neatly into the two models of a strategy previously discussed, the Danish bank's strategy can be considered more in line with the controlling approach, while the Spanish bank took a more adapting approach. This raises several questions: Why these differences? To what extent can they be attributed to national culture? To what extent does the national context, beyond culture, play a role? What other spheres of influence may be involved?

The Danish bank's approach reveals cultural assumptions of environmental certainty ("business as usual") and of organizational control ("We're pretty cocksure we can manage it."). There were no committees specially created to address the issue, nor extra resources devoted to intelligence gathering. Responsibility was clearly assigned to the strategic planning unit, with limited involvement of others. Top management was expected to make the decisions, and individual interests were expected to result in political debate. Thus the Danish bank approach corresponds to the controlling model, in that it was formalized, centralized, and political.

The Spanish bank's approach to "1992" reveals assumptions of environmental uncertainty and little organizational control. Here we find broader based environmental scanning, a special task force was created to access input from employees at all levels, greater reliance on home grown models, and more intense discussion and interaction to socially construct the meaning of "1992". This approach corresponds to the adapting model, described as decentralized, informal, and consensual.

Thus different assumptions regarding environmental uncertainty and organizational control, and the role of the individual versus the collective may contribute to explaining the different approaches in the cases described above. The different assumptions are also in line with the cultural differences reported in the previous chapter.[30] Indeed, Spain and Denmark represent opposite ends of the spectrum on many cultural dimensions. The Danish are more tolerant of uncertainty and have greater perceived control over their environment compared with the Spanish. The Danes are also more individualistic. Furthermore, for Danish managers organizations are task systems, while for Spanish managers they are social systems.

The Spanish bank's approach appears closer to that of the Japanese described earlier in the chapter. In fact, Japan and Spain are quite similar on dimensions of uncertainty avoidance, hierarchy, and collectivism. They also share the view of organizations as social systems. The role of the boss is to orchestrate decisions, based on the input and interest of the collective.

The Danish bank's approach, on the other hand, appears to have more in common with the approach associated with US companies. They indeed share similar cultural assumptions about control over nature, and tolerance of uncertainty, individualism, and the view of organizations as task systems. The role of the boss is to make decisions based on expert, individual input and interests.

Although we have focused primarily on the role of national culture, the different assumptions underlying the controlling versus adapting models may derive from interaction with other spheres of cultural influence. The behavior, beliefs and values, and assumptions embedded in national as well as other cultural spheres are determined, in part, by the national context, as discussed in Chapter 3.

Interaction effects

The national context, or *institutional environment*, includes the role of government and unions (the degree and nature of regulation), the market conditions (protected versus free), economic and political systems, educational systems, and history.[31] These factors play an important role in determining strategy. Compare, for example, the 1980s strategies of cost-cutting and rationalizing in US firms with Japanese firms' strategies of R&D investment, market growth, and expansion.

The contrast was often attributed to cultural differences regarding short- versus long-term time horizons. However, differences in government policies (such as protectionism), ownership structures, strength of currency, and sources of financing (from banks versus equity market) were also considered to be some of the institutional reasons for differences in short-term versus long-term orientation.[32]

These institutional arrangements were also considered to be the cause of differences in the strategies of US and European firms. In Germany, for example, banks have an important influence on corporate strategy, and in France, it is the government which plays a key role. Longer term views, greater concern for social welfare, and larger investment in developing internal capabilities are more feasible when investors are committed to the company (as the shareholders are in fact the banks or the government) and are not demanding quarterly reports and short-term return on investment. Compare that with institutional investors in the United States and United Kingdom who, on average, hold on to stocks for less than two years.[33]

These institutional arrangements interact with national culture to encourage different strategies. In addition to the national context, the increasing cross-border economic and political integration, as in the cases of the European Union and North American Free Trade Area (NAFTA), creates institutional pressures that go beyond national borders, contributing to a supraregional culture. Thus the institutional environment determines the rules of doing business, both at the national or international level, and thereby shapes the different cultural spheres.

Let us examine how the national context interacts with national culture and other spheres of cultural influence which may help to explain the different strategic approaches in the cases of the Spanish and Danish banks. In Denmark, the economic recession, the previous ambivalence expressed towards joining the EEC, and the impending "shakeout" of the domestic market created an environment that was hostile and threatening. Indeed, research has shown that under conditions of threat, information flows are restricted, decision-making is centralized, and behavior reverts to well-known routines.[34]

In Spain, the economic and political context was different, marked by strong economic growth and a political climate that was pro-business and pro-integration. These conditions encouraged the Spanish bank to be more market-driven, to actively seek opportunities within the domestic market, and to develop internal capability. This is similar to the opportunity-driven, market-oriented, international strategies of Japanese companies in the 1980s.

Being faced with a hostile environment may have led the Danish bank to focus on costs and profitability, the bottom line. This corresponds to a strategic profile of *defender*, wherein efficiency and control are considered necessary to protect product/market niches and core businesses.[35] In the Spanish bank, the search for new product and market opportunities and the emphasis on flexibility and adaptability characterize organizations that are *prospectors*.[36] It can therefore be argued that these differences in the national context created conditions that encouraged the Danish bank to be defenders and the Spanish bank to be prospectors.

Organizations that are defenders tend to be more centralized and formalized, which would also explain the controlling approach. Prospector organizations tend to have structures that are more decentralized and informal, which reinforce an adaptive approach. Research has also demonstrated that organizations described as defenders are more likely to interpret strategic issues as threats, whereas entrepreneurial organizations, or prospectors, are more likely to interpret the same issues as opportunities.[37] This, in turn, reinforces the strategic actions noted above; seeking control and efficiency or seeking new products and markets. Thus the strategic process, content and profile interact in mutually reinforcing ways, as in Figure 5.1.

National context also helps to explain the different approaches to strategy through its effect on other spheres of cultural influence, such as corporate and industry cultures. *Corporate culture*, for example, is shaped in part by government regulation and resulting market conditions. Deregulation in the United States in the 1980s and in Europe in the 1990s, has forced companies on both sides of the Atlantic to become more competitive. This may mean becoming more cost-conscious and efficient on one hand, or more customer-driven and market-oriented on the other, or both.

The organization structures are adapted to meet these efforts by becoming either more centralized and formalized (in the name of efficiency), or more decentralized and informal (to be market-oriented), or by creating structures combining loose–tight properties in order to do both. The extent to which organization strategy drives structure or vice versa

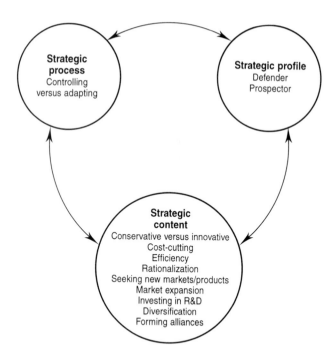

Figure 5.1   Interaction between strategic process, content and profile.

is open to debate.[38] Nevertheless, this interaction influences which strategies are pursued (content) and how they are chosen (process).

Industry culture is also driven by national context, or the institutional environment. For example, the degree to which technologies or markets are protected determines the level of competitiveness required as previously discussed. This can be seen in industries such as telecommunication, transportation, and banking. As a result of deregulation, many of these industries have had to become more customer-oriented and more efficient.

Industry culture is also being driven by broader, supraregional institutional pressures, such as EU regulations in the case of "1992". These pressures encourage the emergence of certain practices of strategic management either by coercion (through regulation or professionalization) or by copying best practices promoted by business consultants, professors, and the media to gain legitimacy.[39] For example, similar scanning practices found in Korean firms were attributed to their hiring the same US consulting firm.[40]

Industry recipes are passed on providing the key ingredients and the right procedures.[41] Evidence of this can be found in banking. In Norway, banks imitated each others' strategies, leading to greater decentralization and subsequent lessening of control, resulting in financial disaster.[42] In the 1980s, many US banks faced with intensifying competition, engaged in greater risk-taking, resulting in dramatic write-offs later on. Nor did following the fashion of financial supermarkets produce the anticipated synergies.

Further evidence may be found in the increasing number of domestic, or home-court, mergers in banking, in the United States, Europe, and Japan. These mergers continue, despite ongoing debates about whether the supposed benefits (such as economies of scale) outweigh the costs of integration, whether greater international competitiveness is derived by promoting greater competition at home, and whether developing assets and competencies within national borders neglects developing cross-border competencies.[43] Nevertheless, the uncertainties and anxieties that surround strategic issues, particularly in the current environment of economic recession and massive industry restructuring, provide fertile ground for the creation of business or industry myths that are often difficult to evaluate.

Thus corporate and industry cultures are influenced by both the national and supraregional contexts in ways that can influence which strategies are taken, as well as how those strategies are determined.[44] The prospectors of the 1980s became the defenders of the 1990s, with different emphases on expansion versus cost controls, risk-taking versus risk-minimizing, and innovative versus conservative actions. The controlling and adapting models of strategy may in fact represent alternative approaches that must be managed simultaneously in order to face the competitive challenge of being both market-oriented and cost-efficient.

Strategic implications of culture

In this chapter we have argued that assumptions regarding *external adaptation*, such as control and uncertainty, and those related to *internal integration*, such as hierarchy and individualism/collectivism, lead to different models of how organizations make sense of and respond to their environment. This can be observed in the way they gather, interpret and act on information about strategic issues: what is attended to and what is not, what kinds of information are considered useful, what models and methods are used to analyze this information, who is involved in the process, and what strategic decisions are taken.

These two models, called controlling and adapting, were illustrated by the example of how two banks in different countries, Denmark and Spain, went about making sense of a strategic issue – "1992". We further argued that this strategic process interacts with strategic profiles, such as defenders and prospectors, and strategic content, for example, cost-cutting or market expansion, in mutually reinforcing ways.

In addition, we discussed the way other cultural spheres may interact with strategy. We showed how the national context or institutional environment favors different approaches to strategy. We argued that the institutional environment, both at the national and supraregional levels, shapes corporate and industry culture, which in turn influences which strategies are chosen and how. We now need to consider the implications of these arguments in the roles of headquarters and subsidiaries in developing global strategies and in anticipating the moves of international competitors and partners.

The relationship between headquarters and subsidiaries

Different cultural assumptions drive different models of strategic process. In multinational corporations (MNCs), those at headquarters need to understand and appreciate how at the local level strategy is formulated and implemented in order to best integrate it with corporate-level strategic management. For example, if the predominant model at headquarters is controlling, the strategic planning staff are likely to be frustrated in their discussions with managers in subsidiaries that opt for the adapting model.

For one, requests for objective information, e.g. market research or industry data, may be ignored. Headquarters may also have difficulty in getting managers in these subsidiaries to use the same models or methods of analysis, such as strategic forecasting and scenario planning. Matrices depicting market growth and position, along with its cash cows and dogs, may be dismissed as having little credibility. The insistence on facts and figures may be met with insistence on gut feel and philosophical debate. Furthermore, it will be difficult to know whom to address, as responsibility for strategic planning may be more diffused. For these reasons strategies pursued by headquarters and those pursued by subsidiaries may be very loosely coupled.

On the other hand, headquarters, in cultures that prefer the adapting approach, may be equally frustrated by managers in subsidiaries where the controlling approach is preferred. Requests from these subsidiaries for greater precision regarding corporate goals and intended strategies, for concrete action steps, for implementation timetables, for clear-cut assignment of responsibility and accountability, and for ways of measuring follow-up may seem unnecessary, and even irritating.

The problems caused by this mismatch are illustrated by the case of a Japanese bank headquarters with an American subsidiary where managers on both sides were frustrated since nothing was happening. It turned out that the Americans were waiting for clear direction from the Japanese headquarters, while the Japanese were waiting for initiatives from the American subsidiary.[45] Therefore, it is important to know what information is considered relevant, what models and methods of interpretation are considered useful, and who expects to be involved or to take the decision.

Different assumptions will also drive different strategic content. Thus it is essential to recognize that strategies which are considered by HQ to be crucial to survival may not be similarly appreciated by the subsidiaries. For example, strategies to improve efficiency and control costs by reducing R&D budgets and head counts, may be seen as short-sighted, and considered "penny-wise and pound-foolish", if these actions are seen to undermine the development of competencies needed for long-term adaptability.

Nor will HQ strategies designed to develop organizational competencies, to enhance flexibility, and stimulate entrepreneurship necessarily be readily embraced at the local level. For example, heavily investing in management training and development, or allowing scientists to "tinker about in laboratories removed from the real world", in other words, to conduct basic research with no clearly defined product applications or market need, may be seen as a wasteful, inefficient use of resources. Engaging in peripheral activities which have little apparent value for the existing business might frustrate those looking for a clear-cut strategic direction, and for more resources to be devoted to core businesses.

Cultural assumptions will also influence the strategic profile, such as defender or prospector. Headquarters and subsidiaries may not share assumptions regarding the ability to impose control. Headquarters located in cultures that promote prospectors looking to develop new product market opportunities may feel blocked by subsidiaries located in cultures that encourage defenders, trying to protect market niches and core technologies. A defender head office may refuse to invest in, and thereby miss opportunities discovered by its prospector subsidiary.

The pursuit of greater efficiency through rationalization and restructuring may overlook the importance of market and customer knowledge. For example, when Xerox reorganized its US operations by product lines, it expected its European subsidiary, Rank Xerox, to follow suit. This caused problems in Europe, with the managing director reluctant to lose the specific market (customer) knowledge of the geographically organized units. In the end, Rank Xerox proposed a matrix structure which allowed it to retain its market focus.

The above discussion of the mismatch between headquarters and subsidiaries highlights the potential frustrations and misunderstandings that can occur in formulating and implementing strategies, especially when the strategic decisions are assumed to come primarily from the top; HQ decides what to do, and the subsidiaries are supposed to implement these decisions. This depiction is, or course, somewhat exaggerated. However, what it highlights is the need to question the roles of HQ and subsidiaries in formulating as well as implementing strategies. Research has shown that the more subsidiaries are involved in formulating the strategies, the more readily they are implemented.[46]

Furthermore, the mismatch, rather than provoking frustration and irritation can be used to set up creative tensions, so that alternative models can coexist and codetermine which strategies are pursued and how. Different pieces of the strategic puzzle may be best suited to one approach over the other. Having access to both approaches may help to solve the competitive dilemma of having to improve efficiency in the short term, while at the same time having to develop core competencies for the long run.

The existence of different approaches to strategy is also in tune with the view of multinationals as differentiated organizational networks.[47] This view encourages us to consider that strategies can be developed at the local level for local and global implementation. This means that global strategies do not necessarily have to come from the top, HQ. This notion seems to surprise some HQ managers, and some local managers who protest "not invented here!".

Anticipating competitive and cooperative relationships

As the same environmental event may be interpreted and responded to in different ways in different countries, understanding these differences can provide a competitive advantage in facing international competitors. Recognizing key cultural dimensions can help anticipate the way in which a competitor may interpret and respond to strategic issues such as new regulations or new market opportunities.

For example, interpretations of threat versus opportunity may have more to do with the degree of perceived environmental uncertainty and organizational control than with objective reality. Strategic issues are likely to be interpreted as a threat given perceptions of low control.[48] Furthermore, interpreting a strategic issue as a threat has consequences for strategic response, leading to more risk-taking behavior, more investment of time and money, and a greater internal orientation.[49]

Research has shown that Latin European managers were more likely to interpret issues as threats or even crises, when compared with northern Europeans. They were also more willing to invest resources in training and information technology, in other words, in developing internal capabilities.[50] In another study, Japanese managers were found to be more likely to identify a strategic issue as a threat than were American managers.[51] Thus interpretations of and reactions to threat are more likely among Japanese and Latin European managers as they are more likely to perceive greater uncertainty and less control over their environments than their US or northern European counterparts.

Again, this is supported in the case of the Danish bank, discussed earlier, where despite a hostile and threatening environment, "1992" was seen as "business as usual". Assumptions of control meant that "1992" was not interpreted as a threat, even if conditions may have warranted it. Furthermore, given this assumption, investing extra resources in gathering intelligence or developing additional capabilities was considered unnecessary. As a result, they were quite surprised when they merged with (some say "taken over" by) their arch-rivals (who lived literally next door in the same building), only three months later.

In the case of a joint venture, these different interpretations of strategic issues may cause problems. Latin European managers may be seen as overreacting by their colleagues from the north, while the Latin Europeans themselves may be frustrated because the northerners cannot be convinced that a situation is really a crisis. In addition, the shared interpretation of strategic issues across cultures is vital to the mobilization of resources and efforts in these alliances.

Thus by deciphering the underlying assumptions of uncertainty and control that influence the interpretation of strategic issues as threats or opportunities, the strategic actions, or non-actions, of competitors or partners might be better anticipated.

Other cultural dimensions have also been found to explain the strategic actions, such as the mode of entry into foreign markets. For example, Japanese companies, in their desire to reduce uncertainty, tend to prefer greenfield operations and joint ventures rather than acquisitions, especially when there is greater cultural distance.[52]

When entering the US market, companies from countries that are quite culturally different from the United States and more power-oriented tend to prefer foreign direct investment over licensing agreements.[53] In this way they are able to maintain control through hierarchies rather than bargaining.

Given cultural distance, they also tend to rely more on rules rather than value-based controls. When cultures are similar, companies can rely on shared values to create high degrees of trust, as in the case of Japan, where norms of obligation and reciprocity tend to reduce opportunistic behavior.[54] However, the high level of trust among insiders may not necessarily be extended to outsiders. In fact, the reverse may be true. Thus while licensing arrangements and networks (*keiretsu*) may be preferred within cultural borders, there is a preference for direct ownership, such as greenfield sites, outside cultural borders.

The impact of national culture on strategy needs to be further explored. It is only recently that the relationship of strategy and national culture has been demonstrated empirically. More research is needed to test the hypotheses presented above. The sudden interest in corporate culture was largely the result of failed strategic change initiatives and the realization that organization cultures could constrain the choice or implementation of strategy. The same could be said for national culture.

In fact, the growing interest in managing across cultures may be driven by difficulties encountered when trying to implement global strategies, or to initiate strategic change across borders. The recognition of national cultural differences enables us to question our own assumptions and ways of thinking about strategy, to recognize potential "competitive blinders",[55] as well as to anticipate the strategic moves of competitors and the strategic concerns of partners in other cultures.

Notes

1. Weick, K.E. (1985) "The significance of corporate culture" in P. Frost, L.F. Moore, M.R. Louis, C.C. Lundberg and J. Martin (eds) *Organizational Culture*, Beverly Hills: Sage, 381–90, 382.
2. Sun-Tzu (1988) *The Art of War*, Boston: Shambhala (translated by T. Clearly).
3. Machiavelli, N. (1958) *The Prince*, London: J.M. Dent and Sons (translated by W.K. Marriot).
4. Galer, G. (1994) "The elements of scenario planning", Presented at the Organizational Learning Kolleg, Ladenburg, Germany, April 5.
5. Hofer, C.W. and Schendel, D. (1978) *Strategy Formulation: Analytic Concepts*, St. Paul: West Publishing.
6. Porter, M. (1980) *Competitive Strategy*, New York: Free Press.
7. Hamel, G. and Prahalad, C.K. (1989) "Strategic intent", *Harvard Business Review*, 67(3), 63–76; Prahalad, C.K. and Hamel, G. (1990) "The core competence of the corporation", *Harvard Business Review*, 68(3), 79–91.
8. Lyles, M.A. and Mitroff, I. (1985) "The impact of sociopolitical influences on strategic problem formulation" in R. Lamb and P. Shrivastava (eds) *Advances in Strategic Management*, Vol. 3, Greenwich, CT: JAI Press, 69–82; Mintzberg, H., Raisinghani, D. and Theoret, A. (1976) "The structure of unstructured decision processes", *Administrative Science Quarterly*, 21, 246–75; Bower, J.L. and Doz, Y. (1979) *Strategy Formulation: A Social and Political Process*, Boston: Little, Brown & Co; Allison, G. (1971) *The Essence of Decision: Explaining the Cuban Missile Crisis*, Boston, MA: Little, Brown & Co.
9. Smircich, L. and Stubbart, C. (1985) "Strategic management in an enacted world", *Academy of Management Review*, 10(4), 724–36; Weick, K.E. (1979) *The Social Psychology of Organizing*, Reading, MA: Addison-Wesley.
10. See Schneider, S.C. and DeMeyer, A. (1991) "Interpreting and responding to strategic issues: The impact of national culture", *Strategic Management Journal*, 12, 307–20.
11. March, J.G. and Simon, H. (1958) *Organizations*, New York: John Wiley.
12. Schneider, S.C. (1989) "Strategy formulation: The impact of national culture", *Organization Studies*, 10(2), 149–68; Schneider, S.C. (1994) "Interpreting strategic issues: Making sense of 1992" in C. Stubbart, J.R. Meindl and J.F. Porac (eds) *Advances in Managerial Cognition and Organizational Information Processing*, Vol. 5, Greenwich, CT: JAI Press, pp. 243–74.
13. Lightfoot, R.W. (1992) "Philips and Matsushita: A Portrait of two evolving companies", Harvard Business School.
14. Pascale, R.T. (1984) "Perspectives on strategy: The real story behind Honda's success", *California Management Review*, 26(3), 47–72.
15. Mintzberg, H. (1995) *The Rise and Fall of Strategic Planning*, Englewood Cliffs, NJ: Prentice Hall.
16. Mintzberg, H. (1978) "Patterns in strategy formation", *Management Science*, 24(9), 934–48; Mintzberg, H. and Waters, J. (1985) "Of strategies deliberate and emergent",

Strategic Management Journal, 6, 257–72; Burgelman, R.A. (1983) "A process model of internal corporate venturing in the diversified major firm", *Administrative Science Quarterly*, 28, 223–44; Nelson, R. and Winter, S. (1982) *An Evolutionary Theory of Economic Change*, Cambridge, MA: Harvard University Press.

17. Prahalad, C.K. and Hamel, G. (1990), *Op. cit.*; Wernerfelt, B. (1984) "A resource based view of the firm", *Strategic Management Journal*, 5, 171–80; Bower, J.L. (1970) *Managing the Resource Allocation Process*, Boston, MA: Harvard Business School Press.
18. Pascale, *Op. cit.*, p. 56.
19. Pascale, R.T. and Athos, A.G. (1981) *The Art of Japanese Management*, New York: Warner Books; Pascale, *Op. cit.*; Kagono, T., Nonaka, I., Sakakibara, K. and Okumura, A. (1985) *Strategic vs. Evolutionary Management: A U.S.–Japan Comparison of Strategy and Organization*, Amsterdam: North Holland Elsevier Science Publishers, B.V.; Nonaka, I. and Johansson, J.K. (1985) "Japanese management: What about 'hard' skills?", *Academy of Management Review*, 10(2), 181–91.
20. (Law of requisite variety) Ashby, W.R. (1956) *Introduction to Cybernetics*, London: Chapman & Hall; Daft, R.L. and Lengel, R.H. (1986) "Organizational information requirements, media richness and structural design", *Management Science*, 32(5), 554–71.
21. See also Daft, R.L. and Weick, K.E. (1984) "Toward a model of organizations as interpretation systems", *Academy of Management Review*, 9(2), 284–95.
22. See Schneider, S.C. (1989), *Op. cit.*
23. Pascale, *Op. cit.*, pp. 63–64.
24. Burgelman, R.A. (1988) "A comparative evolutionary perspective on strategy-making: Advantages and limitations of the Japanese approach" in K. Urabe, J. Child and T. Kagono (eds) *Innovation and Management: International Comparisons*, Berlin: Walter de Gruyter, 63–80.
25. *Ibid.*, p. 73.
26. Nonaka, I. (1988) "Toward middle-up-down management: Accelerating information creation", *Sloan Management Review*, 29(3), 9–18.
27. Nonaka, I. (1991) "The knowledge-creating company", *Harvard Business Review*, November–December, 96–104.
28. Schneider, S.C. (1994), *Op. cit.*
29. Evaris, R.M. (1990) "Spain in the grip of Eurofever", *International Management*, February, 38–42; Caminal, R., Gual, J. and Vives, X. (1989) "Competition in Spanish banking" in J. Dermine (ed.) *European Banking in the 1990's*, Oxford: Basil Blackwell, pp. 261–305; Laurie, S. (1989) "Shoot-out in Danish city", *The Banker*, May, 38–43; Fairlamb, D. (1989) "The Nordic countries play-it-safe strategy for 1992", *Institutional Investor*, August, 99–106.
30. Hofstede, G. (1980) *Cultures Consequences*, Beverly Hills: Sage; Laurent, A. (1983) "The cultural diversity of western conceptions of management", *International Studies of Management and Organizations*, 13(1–2), 75–96.
31. Child, J. (1981) "Culture, contingency and capitalism in the cross-national study of organizations" in L.L. Cummings and B.M. Staw (eds) *Research in Organizational Behavior*, Vol. 3, Greenwich, CT: JAI Press, pp. 303–56; Scott, W.R. (1987) "The adolescence of institutional theory", *Administrative Science Quarterly*, 32, 493–511.
32. Westney, D.E. (1987) *Imitation and Innovation*, Cambridge, MA: Harvard University Press.
33. "A conversation with Michael Porter", *European Management Journal*, 9(4), 1991, 355–59.
34. Staw, B.M., Sandelands, L. and Dutton, J.E. (1981) "Threat rigidity cycles in organizational behavior", *Administrative Science Quarterly*, 26, 501–24; Billings, T., Milburn, S.W. and Shaalman, M.L. (1980) "Crisis perception: A theoretical and empirical analysis", *Administrative Science Quarterly*, 25, 300–15.

35. Miles, R.H. and Snow, C.C. (1978) *Organizational Strategy, Structure and Process*, New York: McGraw-Hill.
36. *Ibid.*
37. Meyer, A.D. (1982) "Adapting to environmental jolts", *Administrative Science Quarterly*, 27, 515–37.
38. Chandler, A.D. (1962) *Strategy and Structure*, Cambridge, MA: MIT Press.
39. Meyer, J.W. and Rowan, B. (1977) "Institutionalized organizations: Formal structure as myth and ceremony", *American Journal of Scoiology*, 83(2), 340–63.
40. Ghoshal, S. (1985) "Environmental scanning: An individual and organizational level analysis", Unpublished doctoral dissertation, Cambridge, MA, MIT Sloan School of Management.
41. Spender, J.C. (1989) *Industry Recipes*, Oxford: Basil Blackwell.
42. Reve, T. (1990) "Mimetic strategic behavior in banking", Presented at the 10th annual Strategic Management Society meeting, Stockholm.
43. Ballarin, E. (1988) "The process of concentration in Spanish banks: Theory and practice", Working paper, IESE; Porter, M. (1990) "The competitive advantage of nations", *Harvard Business Review*, March/April, 73–93; Dunning, J.H. (1993) "Internationalizing Porter's diamond", *Management International Review*, 33(2), 7–15.
44. Huff, A.S. (1982) "Industry influences on strategy reformulation", *Strategic Management Journal*, 3, 119–31.
45. Ouchi, W.G. and Jaeger, A.M. (1978) "Theory Z organization: Stability in the midst of mobility", *Academy of Management Review*, 3(20), 305–14.
46. Kim, W.C. and Mauborgne, R.A. (1993) "Making global strategies work", *Sloan Management Review*, Spring, 11–27.
47. Ghoshal, S. and Nohria, N. (1989) "Internal differentiation within multinational corporations", *Strategic Management Journal*, 10(4), 323–37.
48. Dutton, J.E. and Jackson, S.E. (1987) "The categorization of strategic issues by decision makers and its links to organizational action", *Academy of Management Review*, 12, 76–90.
49. Tversky, A. and Kahnemann, D. (1974) "Judgement under uncertainty: Heuristics and biases", *Science*, 185, 1124–31; Dutton, J.E., Walton, E. and Abrahamson, E. (1989) "Important dimensions of strategic issues: Separating the wheat from the chaff", *Journal of Management Studies*, 26, 379–96; Dutton, J.E., Stumpf, S.A. and Wagner, D. (1990) "Diagnosing strategic issues and the investment of resources" in R. Lamb and P. Shrivastava (eds) *Advances in Strategic Management*, Vol. 6, Greenwich, CT: JAI Press, 143–67; Milliken, F.J. and Dukerich, J.M. (1987) "Insights into issue interpretation: The effect of issue characteristics on judgements of importance and information search", Academy of Management Meeting, New Orleans.
50. Schneider, S.C. and DeMeyer, A., *Op. cit.*
51. Sallivan, J. and Nonaka, I. (1988) "Culture and strategic issue categorization theory", *Management International Review*, 28(3), 6–10.
52. Kogut, B. and Singh, H. (1988) "The effect of national culture on the choice of entry model", *Journal of International Business Studies*, 19, 411–32.
53. Shane, S.A. (1994) "The effect of national culture on the choice between licensing and direct foreign investment", *Strategic Management Journal*, 15(8), 627–42.
54. Black, J.S. and Mendenhall, M. (1993) "Resolving conflicts with the Japanese: Mission impossible", *Sloan Management Review*, Spring, 49–59.
55. Zajac, E.J. and Bazerman, M.H. (1991) "Blind spots in industry and competitor analysis", *Academy of Management Review*, 16, 37–56.

CHAPTER SIX

Culture and human resource management

The role of the Human Resource Manager, the "priest" in whose hands the company's "Ten Commandments" lie, is to ensure the survival of its soul. Far from merely providing a functional service determining salary rises and fringe benefits, the human resource management function forms the very heart of a company, and its manager exists to confirm the company's particular values and try to apply them in practice.

Michel Perez, Apple Computer, Europe[1]

Any international company hoping to implement a global strategy must choose the human resource policies and practices that will best support that strategy. This is, in essence, the meaning of **strategic international human resource management**. Or, as the HR Director of Honeywell Europe put it, "HRM is the local implementation of strategy". However,

If we accept the view that HRM approaches are cultural artifacts reflecting the basic assumptions and values of the national culture in which organizations are embedded, international HRM becomes one of the most challenging corporate tasks in multinational organizations.[2]

Unfortunately, the same policies will not produce the same effects in different cultural contexts. A major challenge facing companies with international or global aspirations is how to internationalize HRM, the policies, and the function. In keeping with the spirit of "war is too important to leave to the military", the task of internationalizing HRM may be, in the words of one Honda executive, too important to leave to the HR department.

This chapter discusses the influence of national culture on the development and transfer of HRM practices: selection, socialization, training, performance appraisal, compensation, and career development. Here we surface the basic assumptions underpinning the very notion of HRM, as well as the various HR practices (or artifacts such as socialization rituals), and beliefs (such as who is the right person for the job). This allows us to consider how HRM may be viewed differently through other cultural lenses and may thus have unintended consequences when transferred abroad.

Questioning these HRM practices can serve as a basis for dialogue between headquarters and subsidiaries, or between partners in strategic alliances, in their efforts to achieve a balance between global integration and local adaptation of HRM. The challenge is to determine where policies need to converge, where variety may prove more beneficial, and what local practices might be well-suited for global diffusion. Finally we consider the extent to which the HR function is equipped and prepared to handle these difficult international challenges.

The cultural meaning of HRM

The extent to which HRM can be considered *strategic* or *global* depends to a great extent on national context and culture. For example, in Europe, government, unions, and works councils have a greater impact on the strategic use of HRM practices than in the United States.[3] Different cultural assumptions regarding, for example, organizations as systems of tasks versus relationships, the role of the individual and the collective, and the importance of being versus doing (achievement versus ascription) make HRM practices culture-bound. Indeed many question whether the very notion of HRM is appropriate to other national contexts: "HRM can be seen as a contemporary manifestation of the American Dream".[4]

The idea of humans as resources assumes that people can be utilized like capital or raw materials, another factor of production which can easily be bought or sold, and whose value must be maximized and exploited. This view of human resource management (which some consider to be "very American"[5]) may cause genuine offense in cultures which take a less instrumental (task-oriented) view of organizations.

The approach to human resource management in the United States and Europe has evolved from different disciplines, psychology and sociology, which have different assumptions regarding the nature of the relationship between people and organizations.[6] In the United States, HRM has its roots in psychology, its prime concern being the improvement of worker motivation. This leads to focusing on the individual, analyzing employee needs, reward systems, and job enrichment. This approach is evident in the current interest in "performance management".

In Europe, HRM has evolved more from a sociological perspective, which pays more attention to the social system, the economic and political context, and the nature of the relationship between key actors, such as government, unions, and management. Here the primary concern is who has the power to decide, leading to efforts to promote industrial democracy (the workers decide) and industrial policy (the government decides). This results in legislation for worker representation on the board of directors, as in Germany and The Netherlands, quality of work-life councils in Sweden, and the *Code du Travail* in France. These issues are now being hotly debated at the European level in the EU, with differing concerns and opinions regarding the role of government and the welfare of workers.

As a result, the nature of the employment contract, which defines the relationship between the employer and employee both legally and psychologically, differs. Whether or not explicit, the psychological contract between the individual and the company establishes mutual expectations. The legal contract determines what is regulated and to what degree.

In the United States, this relationship is considered "contractual", based on notions of fair exchange, such that both parties, for example, guard their rights, preserving autonomy and independence (self-determination). Many HR practices, such as performance appraisals, equal opportunity recruitment and promotion, and training programs addressing ethics or diversity issues are in fact designed to avoid law suits.

In Europe, many aspects of the employment contract such as how to recruit, what salaries to pay, and how to terminate are decided outside the company walls. In The Netherlands, where legislation makes it extremely difficult to fire employees, court procedures and severance payments make the approval of lay-offs lengthy, costly, and traumatic. Employee rights are not only safeguarded by legislation, but are also vigorously protected by strong unions, as in Germany. Here, employment is seen more as a "social contract" based on a moral commitment: long-term employment promised by the company in exchange for loyalty or social welfare provided by the state. The European approach to HRM as such reveals a more social rather than instrumental view.

More recently many European companies have been faced with downsizing and restructuring activities, which has meant renegotiating these social contracts. Nevertheless, the underlying cultural assumptions remain firmly embedded, creating a demanding challenge as companies within Europe, America (North and South), and Asia are forced to deal with changing economic and political realities. The challenge remains: how to meet competitive demands without alienating their workforce or making matters worse, as in the case of France where massive strikes in late 1995 crippled transportation.

Given these cultural differences in the perceived relationship between employee and employer, it is easy to appreciate that certain subsidiaries or partners will be more or less receptive to particular HR initiatives or policies. The responsibility of the HR function is to navigate through the cultural differences in designing practices which will support specific strategies and develop the corporate culture.

Choosing from the HR menu

Companies can choose from a menu of HRM practices that concern selection and socialization, management training and development, appraisal and compensation, and career development. However, it is important to decipher the cultural assumptions underlying these choices in order to consider how these practices may need to be modified, or how their implementation needs to be managed.

Table 6.1 provides a set of questions which enables us to surface these cultural differences. The divergence of responses provides a basis for discussing the appropriate HRM strategy.

Selection

Finding the right people is often one of the most important challenges, particularly when unfamiliar with the nature of the local labor market or the available human resources. This makes difficult the task of finding those candidates who have the competence to get the job done and who seem likely to fit in with the existing corporate culture. This may mean that a company has to look in very different places to find the same kind of people in terms of abilities as well as behavior, beliefs, and values. What represents a standard profile in one country may be quite exceptional in another. For example,

> When K-mart bought the staid, state-owned Maj department store in Prague in 1992, some employees found the notion of service with a smile so repellent that they quit. "They felt that they had to be too nice to customers." . . . Czechs are notorious for what some call moodiness and others call cynicism. "This won't work with Czechs. We don't smile at people on the street."[7]

IKEA, the Swedish home furnishings company, uses extensive screening and hiring procedures to select people whose values are similar to those of the organization. An executive listed the characteristics of the successful new applicants to IKEA:

> They are people who accept our values and are willing to act on our ideas. They tend to be straightforward rather than flashy, and not too status-conscious. They must be hardworking and comfortable dealing with everyone from the customer to the owner to the cashier. But perhaps the most important quality for an Ikean is *ödmjukhet* – a Swedish word that implies humility, modesty and respect for one's fellow man. It may be hard to translate, but we know it when we see it. It's reflected in things like personal simplicity and self-criticism.[8]

This caused some difficulty for IKEA when it expanded into southern parts of Europe.

When recruiting internationally, companies need to understand how to access "equivalent" labor pools. Differences in education systems make it difficult to figure out who has the right profile. For example, the age of college graduates may differ due to the length of study. College graduates in Germany, due to the combination of long university courses (six years for economics students), apprenticeship, and national service, might not reach the job market until 28 years of age, compared to 22 years old for their British and Japanese counterparts.

This can create problems when someone younger with more experience is assigned to manage older employees with more education, as in the case of a 28-year-old American manager sent to work in Germany.

Local "talent" may also have very different types of skills and abilities owing to different national values placed on education: the amount and the subject. For example, in Spain, many top managers will have university degrees in law and/or economics, while in Germany many top managers have advanced engineering degrees or doctorates in science.[9] In Italy, the title of *Dottore* does not necessarily reflect the same level of education as in Germany, and a degree in philosophy earns more respect than it would in France.

In contrast, British recruiters pay very little attention to the actual subjects studied, with about half of all opportunities being open to graduates of any discipline. In the

Table 6.1   HRM menu: cultural determinants

HRM ISSUES	CULTURAL DETERMINANTS
Selection	
Who to hire? How to hire?	
• Desired behaviours – focus on skills/personality?	
• Specialists versus generalists?	
• Necessary qualifications?	
Level, discipline, or preferred institutions?	
• How important is "what you know" versus "who you know"?	Doing versus being Uncertainty avoidance Power/hierarchy Individual versus collective Task versus relationship
Socialization	
• What kind of "initiation rites" are acceptable? Team building?	Task versus relationship Individual versus collective
• What are the messages being sent? Competition versus cooperation? Individual versus team effort?	Private versus professional life High versus low context
• To what extent will people engage in/reject social events?	
• To what extent should efforts be made to ensure "corporate culture" is shared?	
• To what extent should the corporate culture be made explicit (pins, posters, slogans, etc.)?	
Training	
For what purpose?	
• Develop generalist versus specialist perspective?	Uncertainty avoidance
• Acquire company versus skill specific (technical) knowledge?	Individual versus collective Hierarchy
• Extent of job rotation?	Task versus relationship
• Role of mentorship?	
• Competences versus networking?	
How are training needs determined?	
• By company? By individual?	
• Who is sent for training? "High-flyers" versus "rank and file"?	
What training methods are most effective?	
• Case approach?	
• Reading and lecture?	
• Experiential exercise?	
• Professor versus student driven?	
• Groupwork?	
Performance appraisal	
• To what extent is individual versus team effort evaluated?	Individual versus collective
• To what extent is goal setting (MBO) useful?	Hierarchy
• To what extent do people expect feedback? And from whom?	Being versus doing Time monochronic versus polychronic
• To what extent will criticism be accepted?	High versus low context

Table 6.1 (cont.)

HRM ISSUES	CULTURAL DETERMINANTS
Compensation and rewards	
● Who gets what?	Equity versus equality
● To what extent should pay be linked to performance?	Doing versus being
● What degree of pay differential is acceptable?	Hierarchy
● To what extent are bonuses effective?	Control over nature
● To what extent should team versus individuals be rewarded?	Individual versus collective Uncertainty avoidance
● How much of salary should be fixed versus variable?	Masculinity versus femininity
● To what extent are financial versus non-financial rewards preferred?	
Career development	
● Who gets promoted?	Being versus doing
● What determines career success?	Individual versus collective
● What type of career paths are desirable?	Task versus relationship
Internal versus external hiring?	Uncertainty avoidance
Within functions/across functions?	
Within company/industry?	
Across companies/industries?	
Between government and business?	
● To what extent are people mobile? Willing to move?	
● At what stage are "high potentials" identified? At entry? After 5 years?	

United States, job candidates might hide their doctoral degree for fear of being rejected as overqualified for the position.

Not understanding the different educational systems can create obstacles to recruitment in that candidates with similar educational credentials may be neither able nor willing to do the same jobs. For example, in The Netherlands and Germany, having a vocational or technical education does not mean the same thing as it does in the United States. This created ill-will with a Dutch subsidiary of an American multinational when it tried to implement a program to "upgrade the workforce" using a college degree as the referent criterion. In Germany, the status accorded to *Technik* means that the applied sciences criterion taught in polytechnics is valued as highly as the "pure" sciences taught in the university.

In France, graduates of engineering schools, such as the Ecole Polytechnique or the Ecole Centrale, or schools of public administration (*Ecole National d'Administration*, ENA) are considered to be the elite. These graduates, however, may not be particularly interested in working for a foreign company, having loftier aspirations.

> [The] alumni of France's *grandes écoles* – of which the military-style Polytechnique views itself as the grandest – take leadership as a natural right. Whatever their subsequent performance, their diplomas guarantee them a lifelong career in government or at the head of large corporations.[10]

More than in any other western democracy, power in France is concentrated in the hands of a tiny elite. Every year, ENA (*Ecole Nationale d'Administration*) takes in fewer than

100 graduates . . . They spend 27 months there and, on graduation take up life-long employment in one of the grands corps (such as the Inspection de Finances, . . .). From these institutions – the inner sanctum of the French state, the *enarques* fan out to run the civil service, state-owned industries, banks, the arts, and of course, politics.[11]

As French companies are primarily interested in products of the foremost business or engineering *grandes écoles*, university graduates are often considered "second best" by many French corporate recruiters. For this reason, IBM-France has established a department called *Relations Grandes Ecoles*. So when French companies deliberately recruit university graduates instead, they are clearly distinguishing themselves from the norms of French industry and making a statement about the corporate culture. Michelin deliberately **does not** recruit from the *grandes écoles*. L'Oréal makes a point of hiring *personnes atypiques* (unusual people), reasoning that as a marketing company they need to encourage different perspectives.

Foreign multinationals may also have difficulty accessing the most exclusive labor pools, as competition from local companies may be quite intense. For instance, Japanese companies aggressively outbid each other to try to secure graduates from the most prestigious institutions. The rush to grab top students from Tokyo University has led to complaints about the "strong-arm tactics" used by prospective employers to prevent graduates from seeing competitors during the annual recruiting season.[12]

These local practices may in effect provide a source of potential competitive advantage by creating important pools of labor which are relatively neglected. For example, although women are well-represented among university graduates in Japan, they are not always well accepted in the Japanese corporate environment. This presents an opportunity for foreign firms. Some experts, in fact, advise that "Foreign firms should employ more Japanese female managers; they are more motivated than their male colleagues".[13] For example, Japanese women bankers have proved particularly successful in selling financial products to customers in Japan, as it was more often the housewives who handled the family finances.

Citibank in Taiwan, having been frustrated in their attempts to hire talented locals, began to recruit more local women to become private bankers. The bank was surprised at how successful these women were, having failed to recognize the importance of their being well-connected through family ties to high-income clients. Because of the assumed negative attitudes towards women, US multinationals have been reluctant to send women abroad as expatriates to countries like Japan. However, women expatriates are seen more as *gaijin* (foreigners) than as women, and they do not necessarily encounter the same barriers as their local counterparts.[14]

Cultural differences do not just influence *where* companies need to recruit, but also *how* they go about it. For example, hiring in China may require going through government agencies, or personal connections. This may make some managers, especially Americans, uncomfortable, as it is seen as nepotism. In the United States such practices would be avoided (or not openly admitted). What is considered to be important is the match between the person and the job description (task versus relationship orientation).

However, in more collectivist countries, nepotism is a natural outcome of the logic of interdependence. When an employer takes on a person, a moral commitment is established. There is an implicit understanding that the employer will look after the employee and quite possibly his/her family too. Family ties in turn provide social controls that are often more powerful than the organization hierarchy.

In summary, MNCs must discover and pick their way through these national differences in recruitment norms. They must find out what disciplines or schools are favored by would-be managers in those countries. They must consider whether the skills, experience, and values fostered by these institutions are compatible with the corporate values and job requirements. For example, hiring elite *grandes écoles* graduates may be at odds with a company's egalitarian culture, but may be the most effective choice for operating in France, especially if the company needs to rely on the strong personal network which cuts across French industry and government.

MNCs must also assess whether the national companies have a "blind spot" which means they are missing a potential source of talent (such as women in Japan, university graduates in France, or language majors in the United States). In other words, the MNC has to find a balance between imitating local firms and making its own path. It must learn about the local norms, values, and assumptions, in order to decide which ones must be respected and which, if ignored, may actually provide a competitive edge *vis-à-vis* local rivals.

Socialization

Once selected, employees have to learn the "company ropes". Socialization is the process by which new members absorb the corporate culture and become acquainted with the values and behavior expected of them. These are transmitted in a variety of ways: they may be learned through arduous training programs designed to foster an *ésprit de corps*; or they may be absorbed informally by observing other members, and learning the company language and folklore.

Socialization practices, however, may not be eagerly embraced abroad. Embedded in these practices are cultural assumptions regarding, for example, the nature of peer and hierarchical relationships. Furthermore, **how** they are transmitted, to what degree they are made explicit, is closely tied to use of language, high context/low context. These differences can become a source of friction.

As with initiation rites in the army or academic institutions (fraternity hazing or its French equivalent *bizutage*), socialization techniques aim to strengthen the identification of the individual with the group or organization. In Japan, newly recruited bankers are often given menial tasks, ringing doorbells to provide community service, or may undergo Zen training to teach them humility.[15] These initiation rites or tests of endurance are designed to make group membership more valuable. Once you have passed the test you are in. Thus they reinforce the importance of the group over the individual.

Socialization practices also transmit the importance accorded to the hierarchy. At Disney, every "cast member", including the sweepers, plays an important role in the show; even senior managers are expected to spend time in the park flipping hamburgers (including CEO Michael Eisner). One senior executive assigned to sweeping, irritated by the lack of respect shown to him, turned to his counterpart (the real sweeper) demanding, "Do you know who I am?". His counterpart replied, "Yes, you are a sweeper".[16] This reminds members, both senior and junior, that the hierarchy does not provide special privileges.

Not all initiation rituals are intended to foster mutual respect, comradery, and cohesiveness. Instead they may reinforce a corporate culture which is highly individualist ("every man for himself"), aggressive, and intensely competitive. For example, trainees at Salomon Brothers, the New York investment bank, were told they were "lower than whale [manure]" and had telephones thrown at them for asking too many questions. Company heroes were macho and aggressive, sporting nicknames such as "BSD" (referring to alleged sexual prowess) and the "Pirhana".

The spirit of competitiveness was embodied in the story of two very senior executives betting millions of dollars playing "liar's poker".[17] Recruits had to prove their nerve and competitiveness before being taken seriously. At Salomon Brothers, the underlying assumptions being reinforced were individual achievement, control over nature (or financial markets, regulators, and customers), masculinity, and the pre-eminence of task over relationships.

Even within the same industry (investment banking) and country (United States), socialization rituals can reveal a different set of cultural assumptions. At Goldman Sachs, another American investment bank, recruits were severely reprimanded for taking personal credit for achievements rather than acknowledging the contribution of others, reinforcing the importance of team work and cooperation. Junior members often spend weekends at retreats with senior mentors, called "rabbis".[18] This collective spirit might make it easier for Goldman Sachs to expand into certain parts of Asia, though perhaps not Hong Kong.

"Home" visits and seminars also present opportunities for socialization. "IKEA Way" seminars, a must for all employees, explain the company's roots and values, and how the name IKEA was derived (from the initials of the founder and of the farm and parish where he grew up). Included are trips to Sweden to visit the shed where the founder started the business and to witness at first hand the difficult farm land in order to get across the important values of frugality, hard work, and simplicity.[19]

Social events are also used to strengthen the ties between workers and the company. In Japan, young managers quickly learn that working long hours, drinking with the boss at karaoke bars, and playing golf on weekends with customers are not entirely voluntary activities. Japanese companies in France have been frustrated when trying to introduce the "*Bonenkai* party" (around Christmas) to create a sense of corporate community. The French employees preferred to have the money spent on the party put in their paychecks and they would rather party at home with friends and family, not colleagues.[20] While Japanese managers tend to derive their identity from the company (group), this is not true for the French, who are far more individualist.

Similarly, company rituals such as weekend company picnics, Friday night "beer busts" or the 7 a.m. "power breakfasts" which seem perfectly natural in America might be resented in countries such as France or Germany, where the line is more clearly drawn between work and private life. And the prospect of taking on the boss in a game of tennis at a company weekend retreat can be daunting, as it may not really be considered equal competition. The idea of mingling with colleagues from work (and from different company ranks) wearing shorts and swimsuits can be a source of further discomfort. Assumptions regarding the hierarchy remain firmly in place.

Other artifacts, such as booklets, posters, cards, and pins, are also supposed to remind employees of the visions, values, goals, and corporate identity. For example, many Disney executives are reminded of the company whenever they check the time, thanks to Mickey Mouse wrist watches or wall clocks. The SAS little red book or the blue book at Hafnia (a Danish insurance company) has important symbolic value apart from the actual content. Many managers, mainly in the United States but increasingly in Europe too, carry mission cards in their breast pockets (close to their hearts or wallets). Being a card-carrying member further strengthens identification and a sense of belonging.

European managers tend to view the use of these artifacts cynically as "terribly American" in their naivety, enthusiasm, and lack of subtlety. As one British HR manager of a US MNC, visibly embarrassed, stated, "Imagine having to put such things in writing!". Although agreeing with the principles, this British HR manager felt that it was "pretty pathetic to have them posted on the wall in every office". From a European perspective, their very explicitness may be considered condescending.

The need to spell things out, clearly and directly, reflects the low-context culture in the United States. In many European countries, where populations tend to be more homogeneous, there is more of a shared understanding and therefore less need to state the obvious. In the United States, the greater heterogeneity is managed through explicit pressures to fit in, to be American. Within European countries, given the homogeneity, the pressures to conform have already been internalized. Thus the use of socialization techniques to transmit the corporate culture is often regarded as manipulative and as an intrusion into the private or personal realm of the individual.

MNCs have to consider carefully the type of socialization practices used to diffuse or modify the corporate culture. Certain values are clearly core to the quality of internal communication or the company's global reputation. These should be upheld, at least in spirit, even if it means breaking local rules; indeed, breaking local rules may usefully distinguish the company and help it position itself against rival local firms. For example, efforts undertaken in Japanese greenfield operations in the United Kingdom to reduce the class distinction between workers and managers by wearing similar corporate uniforms and eliminating the trappings of managerial status, such as executive dining rooms, have been appreciated by the local workforce.

On the other hand, the company should be prepared to give way to local norms where corporate norms either cannot be justified or where they cause excessive disruption. There is no sense in pursuing a strong culture for the sake of it. If individuals are forced to comply with norms which seem arbitrary or out-of-touch with local ones, they may feel that these infringe on their integrity or freedom, leading to alienation rather than cohesion.

Training

Besides teaching the "rules of the game", companies have to train and develop technical and managerial competencies. Again, organizations develop their own specific programs in view of the perceived needs of their business and their managers. But cultural views differ on how training is provided, by whom, and for what purpose.

For what purpose?

Training is provided to develop the "know-how" thought necessary for success on the job and within the company. The type of know-how thought necessary, for example generalist or specialist knowledge, differs across companies as well as countries. The value placed on generalist or specialist know-how, as well as on the building relationships versus task competencies, will be reflected in the nature of job rotations and the extent to which training is conducted through in-house or external seminars.

To develop generalists, university recruits may be rotated between jobs for several months even years before finding a "home". This approach serves to acquaint trainees not only with a broad range of business activities but also helps to build an informal network by providing opportunities to establish personal connections. Seminars are then provided on more specific technical or managerial subjects. Developing specialists may involve recruiting those with previous business experience, and immediately assigning them to particular homes, so that they learn by doing, on the job.

For example, in the United Kingdom, job mobility across several functions and businesses is encouraged, as is attending external seminars.[21] Acquiring a broad range of skills and experience is considered to encourage versatility. (Unfortunately, the French connotation of "versatile" is fickle, inconsistent, and unpredictable.)

German managers tend to identify more closely with their technical background and to describe themselves as specialists – *Kaufmann* or *Techniker*. Career moves are carefully integrated with relevant technical training, and management training is almost exclusively conducted internally. This promotes more in-depth, company-specific knowledge.

The Japanese approach is designed to produce company generalists. Management, as the Japanese see it, is like a craft which can only be learned by watching, listening to and practising under more experienced colleagues. Knowledge acquisition is considered to be more tacit than explicit[22] (in keeping with high- and low-context language). Thus training is achieved on-the-job through a combination of mentorship and job rotation.

In many Japanese companies the role of mentor has actually been made into a formal requirement of every manager. It is a role which Japanese managers seem particularly inclined to take on, given the high esteem in which teachers are held in Japan, a legacy of Confucian respect for learning and wisdom. Recent efforts by US companies to assign mentors have met with mixed success, as achieving tasks often takes priority over developing relationships.

Who decides?

Cultural differences will also influence *who* decides on training needs – the firm or the individual. For example, at Apple Computer there is a strong commitment to the quality and availability of training. However, it is up to the individual to decide which courses to take. One French employee of Apple Europe was clearly overwhelmed by the choice:

It's help yourself time. It's self-help taken to the ultimate. But unless someone tells me that I'm going to be a good marketeer or sales guy or finance man by going on this or that course, I don't know which ones to go on.[23]

Apple helps those who help themselves. That philosophy is perfectly in tune with American belief in self-improvement; nothing is predetermined at birth and it is never too late to change. In addition, the American workforce is now being exhorted to develop a portfolio of skills that will guarantee employability, as they cannot expect to stay within the same company. Thus individuals are expected to take responsibility for their training needs and encouraged to proactively seek training opportunities.

This attitude may not be so eagerly received in cultures where people are less accustomed to taking responsibility for their own development, as shown by the above quote. In France, the top–down system is more prevalent. Here it is the company (line or HR manager) which nominates people to go on courses. Being sent on seminars often serves more to confirm managerial potential than to develop it. Being identified as having high potential is considered by French managers to be the most important criterion for company success.[24]

How to learn and from whom?

Cultural differences also assert themselves when it comes to how and what managers should learn and from whom. Different cultural responses to management education are particularly revealing.[25] For example, German and Swiss managers tend to favor structured learning environments with clear pedagogical objectives, course outline and schedule, and the "right answer" or superior solution. This is very much in contrast with the view typically held by Anglo–Saxons, "Most British participants despise too much structure. They like open ended learning situations with vague objectives, broad assignments and no timetables at all. The suggestion that there could be only one correct answer is taboo with them."[26]

The idea of working in groups may come more naturally to Asian managers than to the more individualistic Anglo–Saxons. On the other hand, Asian participants experience more difficulty having to "sell" their ideas in a group, with the potential for open disagreement and conflict, and therefore possible loss of face. Nor do they quite see the point of learning from other students who are no more knowledgeable than themselves. Wisdom resides in the hierarchy.

Class discussion may seem perfectly natural to American students who have been encouraged to express their own ideas and opinions, and are ready to jump in to add their "two cents" worth. British students have been educated to challenge and debate the ideas put forth by each other, including the professor. British culture values the ability to prove one's case, eloquently, even at the expense of others. Anglo–Saxon culture is more tolerant of confrontation and uncertainty, and is less concerned with status differences, either among participants or between themselves and the teacher. This is quite shocking to French and Asian students who are not used to either voicing their opinions in class, disagreeing with each other, or actively debating with the professor.

The extensive use of case studies, business games, and management exercises (role plays) favors learning by doing rather than learning by lecture and reading. It indicates a preference for experiential (active) rather than cognitive (more passive or reflective) learning.[27] It also reflects an inductive rather than a deductive approach, as cases or exercises are used to arrive at general principles or theories (the American approach) rather than starting with a theory or framework which is then applied to a given situation (the European approach). As a result, European managers often do not see the point of these exercises, and complain that seminars conducted by American trainers are not sufficiently abstract nor theoretical. American managers, on the other hand, want training to be more concrete and practical.

With each culture favoring different training and development practices, it may be difficult to integrate these into a coherent or consistent policy. Standardizing training methods may be important if the company needs to communicate specialized knowledge quickly across different units, or if the uniqueness of the company training programs is regarded as a major source of attracting new recruits.

On the other hand, MNCs may have a lot to gain from cross-fertilizing different approaches, and providing opportunities for training and development that appeal to people with different abilities, learning styles, educational backgrounds, and, of course, cultures. Working with groups of managers from different countries often requires a mixed pedagogical approach, and using trainers of different nationalities.

Companies are increasingly using management training to create a "one-company" mentality, as well as to enhance specific technical or conceptual skills among managers from different parts of the world. Very often these managers learn as much from each other as from the course material or professor. Often this training serves as an excuse for socialization and establishing relationships rather than the acquisition of formal knowledge. This intention may be more or less explicit. The CEO of one Hong Kong-based company opened a management seminar in France by explicitly stating that the purpose of being there was for the participants to get to know one another and to establish working relationships; the course content was of secondary value.

Performance appraisal

Performance management involves setting goals, measuring outcomes, and providing feedback to improve future performance. In theory, it is supposed to shape behavior in the desired directions and to motivate people, like ten-pin bowling, by having clear targets, and the possibility to correct behavior based on the feedback of results. Some even argue that goal setting and feedback are *the* most important contributions made by psychologists to management: "One of the clearest findings from 50 years of applied behavioral science research is that goal-setting procedures are the most powerful tool for performance management".[28] Yet the notion of managing performance is heavily embedded in an instrumental view of organizations which might have little appeal to those cultures that see organizations in terms of social relationships where what counts is managing people, not tasks.

Other cultural assumptions underlying performance management systems can also be recognized: that goals can be set and reached (control over the environment), that objectives may be given 6–18 month time frames (time can be managed), and that the attainment of goals can be measured (reality is objective). Bosses and subordinates are expected to engage in a two-way dialogue to agree on what has to be done, by when, and how. This assumes that power differences are not an issue, and that employees have the right of input in determining their goals, and are willing to take responsibility.[29] These assumptions were well-suited to the Germans who readily embraced management by objective (MBO) as it helped to reduce uncertainty by clarifying targets, roles, and responsibilities and to reduce status differences between boss and subordinate.[30]

In contrast, the idea of concrete, mutually established annual objectives may prove uncomfortable for many French managers, many of whom refuse to put these objectives in writing.[31] MBO largely failed in France because French managers felt that they had no control over the objectives they were being asked to achieve. Rather than empowerment, it was seen as entrapment – experienced by employees as signing their own punishment. Furthermore, the idea of having a two-way conversation ("between equals") with the boss seemed untenable.[32]

Cultural assumptions are also evident in the term "performance appraisal" which implies that "performance", what is done or achieved, is important, and can be measured objectively, that is, "appraised". In other words, what counts is results, not personality. This is even upheld in US law courts to protect employees from being evaluated based on who they are rather than what they do, unless it can be empirically demonstrated that personality is directly linked to performance. What is appraised is behavior and not traits; thus doing is more important than being.

In Asian firms, people are more likely to be judged on their integrity, loyalty, and cooperative spirit, not just on their ability to achieve high sales volume. Thus the very notion of performance appraisal may be at odds with the values of many cultures where "character appraisal" is considered to be more important. Indeed, the appraisal process itself may be interpreted as a sign of distrust or even an insult.[33] According to one French manager, "The French get offended by positive or negative feedback. If you question my job, you are questioning my honor, my value, and my very being".[34] For Americans, feedback serves to give them information on how they are *doing*. For the French, feedback serves as an unwelcomed commentary on who they *are*.

Giving feedback can thus present a cultural minefield. While giving and receiving feedback is not a particularly comfortable experience for any manager, different norms for being critical and being direct make it even more difficult. In one acquisition of a US firm by a Swedish company, American managers complained that the Swedes were far too critical, and never gave any positive feedback. Europeans, in turn, complain about the American "hamburger" approach to feedback: surrounding the criticism (the meat) with the soft stuff or empty praise (the bun).[35]

In Asia, the process of giving feedback often clashes with the need to "save face" (that is, guarding an individual's public reputation) which protects the person's "social capital" and preserves harmony. Thus confronting an employee with "failure" is considered to be very tactless and even dangerous. Western multinationals operating in certain Asian countries have had to adapt other approaches such as using a third party as a go-between. For example, in the Indonesian subsidiary of a large US multinational, negative feedback in performance appraisals was avoided as it was considered to bring about "an unhealthy pollution of harmonious hierarchical relationships".[36]

In addition, appraisal systems typically emphasize individual responsibility for assigned work. Yet this focus on the individual may seem inappropriate in collectivist cultures. In Japan, for example, there are festivals where dozens of people carry a heavy portable shrine known as a *mikoshi* through the streets. Because it is impossible to tell who is actually doing the lifting, some end up doing more carrying than others. This has given rise to the expression "*mikoshi* management" in Japanese companies. People work as a group, with the achievers often carrying the laggards along. This is considered normal, not free-riding.

The implications for managing performance and appraisal are twofold. It is crucial to recognize that the very notion of performance management is loaded with cultural assumptions that are not necessarily shared by others. Managers in different cultures will react differently to looking at objective performance data (the facts) and to having an open, honest dialogue. Insensitivity to these issues may alienate or demotivate local employees. MNCs also have to beware of relying strictly on the same criteria used for evaluation back home. Being assertive, showing initiative, and achieving results may count more in some cultures than others. These cultural biases may be responsible for the "glass ceilings" experienced by foreigners in many international companies.

Given the fairly universal discomfort (more or less intense) which surrounds feedback sessions, companies should probably encourage some local interpretation. What is more, companies may actually find that far-flung operations actually have novel ways of delivering or depersonalizing negative (or even positive) feedback, so that it does not demotivate. Nor should it be assumed that judging on merit will necessarily be rejected. In fact, as P&G found out in India, many local managers working for foreign multinationals which strongly believe in meritocracy are pleased that good performance is finally being recognized.

Compensation and rewards

Cultural differences also play a role in determining who gets rewarded and how. The belief that "money talks" in every language turns out to be far too simplistic to provide a basis for determining salary policy. The very notion of working for a bonus, of being motivated by money, might cause offense and be taken as demeaning ("After all, we're not trained seals."). Different cultures attach value to different types of reward, and vary in the extent to which they believe reward should be individual or collective.

The current trend of linking pay to performance is particularly culturally suspect. As one American expatriate in Paris discovered, "Quantifiable objectives freak out [French] executives. They don't want clearly defined objectives. Relating increased performance to increased bonus doesn't work. They're really turned off to discussions about finance and money".[37] Pay for performance assumes that rewards should be based on contribution to the bottom line, or *equity*, rather than based on belonging to the group, or *equality*.[38] Notions of equity are embedded in the contractual view of employment – "you get what you deserve";[39] notions of equality correspond to the social view – "you deserve what you get".

While it would be unthinkable for most American managers to consider implementing a system at home where the amount that family members are given to eat is related to their contribution to the family income, at work the notion of pay for performance seems quite logical. In contrast, in many African societies a collective logic prevails; the principles applied to family members also apply to employees. One multinational, in an effort to improve the productivity of the workforce by providing nutritious lunches, met with resistance and the demand that the cost of the meal be paid directly to the workers so that they could feed their families. The attitude was one of "How can we eat while our families go hungry?".

The dominant influence in American managerial thinking is the principle of equity, that individuals are rewarded according to their individual contribution and if not, are prepared to move on. This reveals cultural assumptions of individualism, control over nature, and achievement. Like the American hero, Horatio Alger, anyone can succeed if he or she just keeps trying. And the sky is the limit! Therefore at Apple Computer, for instance, there is no upper limit on the salary which means that star performers could be earning up to 200 percent of their core wage.

The idea of special rewards for special efforts may not be so readily accepted elsewhere. In the Danish subsidiary of one American MNC, a proposal for incentives for salespeople was turned down because it favored one group over the others. In addition the Danish employees argued that everyone should get the same amount of bonus, not 5 percent of salary, and some even insisted that there should be no differences in pay between bosses and secretaries.[40] This reflects strong assumptions of egalitarianism.

Pay for performance is also largely assumed to mean **individual** performance. This assumption was not shared in Indonesia, obliging ARCO Oil and Gas Company to adapt its reward system. According to the Human Resources Manager:

> Indonesians manage their culture by a group process, and everybody is linked together as a team. Distributing money differently amongst the team did not go over all that well; so, we've come to the conclusion that pay for performance is not suitable for Indonesia.[41]

Attempts to introduce merit pay have also provoked outcries in Japan for fear that this could ruin the harmony (*wa*) of the group and encourage short-term thinking, something that Japanese executives have long criticized in American companies. Some Japanese companies which have experimented with merit pay have found that rather than reducing labor costs, it has actually increased them, finding themselves unable to cut salaries since this would be a blow to employee self-esteem (loss of face). Thus they simply had to pay more to good performers without penalizing the others.[42]

In the United States, merit-based pay is now being challenged as demotivating, particularly in view of the movement towards team management which requires cooperation rather than competition among individuals. As companies are trying to create "high involvement"[43] or strong commitment to the company, rewarding individual achievement is seen as a potential handicap.

Assumptions regarding uncertainty, risk-taking, and control influence the preference for *variable* rather than *fixed* compensation. In one study American managers claimed to be prepared to increase the proportion of variable compensation to nearly 100 percent compared with Europe, where the variable portion of a salary should rarely exceed 10 percent.[44] In cultures which tend to avoid uncertainty and perceive less control, efforts to introduce discretionary incentives may be met with suspicion and fail to produce the desired effect.

Preference for *financial* or *non-financial incentives* is also culturally related. The relative importance of money, status, or vacation time varies across countries and affects their motivating potential. For example, in Sweden, given a choice between a bonus and time off, the latter is likely to be chosen. Monetary rewards are less motivating, because the egalitarian ethos breeds a reluctance to stand out financially (as do the high tax rates). Swedes are also more concerned with quality of life, with Sweden ranking highest on Hofstede's femininity dimension.

In Japan, on the other hand, there would seem little point in offering more time off when employees only take half of their 16-day holiday entitlement as it is (as compared to 35 days in France and in Germany). *Karoshi* (or death through overwork) is regarded as an occupational hazard by many white-collar workers in Japan; surveys show that a third of Japan's managers are seriously worried about falling victim to it.[45] Workers who take full vacation or avoid working overtime are labelled *wagamama* (selfish), a harsh criticism aimed at those who let down their peers. Concern for the company is supposed to override concern for oneself and even one's family.

Companies which operate internationally clearly have to appreciate the different values and evaluate their potential impact. The remuneration package is a very strong indicator of the culture and the behavior expected and can be used to encourage cooperation or competition, information sharing or information hoarding, and risk-taking or conservatism. For aspiring recruits, the remuneration package is a very important signal. The company can choose to align itself with local norms if it wants to attract the local elite or it can offer an "alien" package if it seeks to attract the more adventurous or less mainstream. In addition, it may attract those who are frustrated with local practices, and are looking to be rewarded for their efforts and success.

Career development

National culture also has an impact on career development. The preferred paths for advancement, the traits and behavior required for promotion are different. Young managers quickly learn what they can aspire to and what they have to do to get promoted. What it takes to get ahead, however, varies according to assumptions regarding *being* versus *doing* (who you are versus what you do), and beliefs regarding the nature of the managerial task, or what managers are supposed to do or be.

An interesting cross-national study, conducted by André Laurent, provides insight into what managers in different countries perceive to be necessary for career success.[46] For example, "drive and ability" are considered by American managers to be the most important determinants. This reflects a pragmatic, individualistic, achievement-oriented, and instrumental world-view.

While "achieving results" was considered important by 88 percent of American respondents, only 52 percent of the French managers agreed. It therefore comes as something of a surprise to American managers when they find out that the same criteria do not apply in countries where people may be promoted because of the schools they went to and their personal connections. As one disillusioned HR director in the American subsidiary of a French group observed, "Becoming a *cadre* through hard work alone does not seem to be part of the system – or if it is, it is highly unusual".[47] For the most part, becoming a manager (achieving *cadre* status) is determined by having attended an elite *grande école*.

For this reason, 88 percent of the French managers perceived being labeled as having "high potential" as the most important determinant of career success as compared with 54 percent of the German managers. In Germany, technical competence and functional expertise, or *Leistung* (achievement), are considered necessary for advancement.

In the same study, 89 percent of the British respondents selected "skills in interpersonal relations and communication" as the most important determinant of career success. The British score reflects the traditional belief that management is essentially an interpersonal, rather than a technical (German) or a conceptual (French) challenge. British firms tended to favor those with a more classical education and a broader, generalist approach to management. "Generally, it remains true to say that the promotion to top level posts of 'gifted amateurs' remains a uniquely British phenomenon."[48]

Favored career paths – staying within the same function, company, or industry – also differ. The possibility of switching in and out of companies or industries and the potential career leverage in doing so varies between countries. This is bound up with cultural assumptions regarding the importance of the individual versus loyalty to the group, doing versus being, and tolerance for uncertainty.

In large Japanese companies moving between companies, much less business sectors, was virtually unknown up until recently. Graduates have traditionally been the raw material from which companies fashioned their senior managers; hence the importance for companies of attracting university recruits of the highest caliber. Job rotation reinforces company-specific knowledge. Mid-career moves were therefore difficult or tantamount to treason and cause for family shame. Many Japanese sent by their companies to obtain MBA degrees in the United States or Europe found themselves emotionally torn between returning to their employer and taking a job (often with a foreign multinational) where they may be offered not only more money but also more responsibility and better career opportunities.

Career mobility is not particularly valued by German companies either. But the reason is not so much to do with loyalty, as with the preference for specialized know-how. Titles are job-specific and skills or experience acquired in one job are not perceived as transferable to another function or company. Senior managers are expected to have not only the technical skills, but also an in-depth understanding of the business and the company which comes from a long-term career therein.

Managers in the United States and Britain, having a more generalist view, are less worried about being in charge of functions or businesses which they do not technically master. Therefore moving into jobs with which they are unfamiliar is not considered to pose a problem.[49] In France, top managers also move in and out of companies from different industries and even from public service positions. This type of career path was held responsible for the recent financial problems of the French bank, Crédit Lyonnais, which was blamed on the former CEO's lack of understanding of how to run a bank rather than a government agency.[50]

Thus different patterns of career development are found in different countries. These patterns differ in terms of whether managers are developed internally or recruited externally, the stage at which those with high potential are identified (entry or later on), the type of work experiences acquired within or outside the company or industry (specialist versus generalist), and the criteria for selection and promotion. Distinct cultural patterns of career development labeled as the Latin, Germanic, Anglo and Japanese approach, have been proposed by Paul Evans as shown in Figure 6.1. (pp. 148–9)[51]

These different career patterns can cause problems for multinational companies in implementing their plans for management development. For example, Japanese Nissan Motor Company was frustrated in Italy and Spain where local managers, after extensive (and costly) training and development, readily accepted the offers of rival companies. For the Japanese, this job mobility prevents the accumulation of company expertise and inhibits their planning for human resource management. On the other hand, non-Japanese managers have little reason for loyalty when they discover the glass ceiling, or limited career opportunities, for foreigners.

MNCs have to ensure that the perceptions of what it takes to reach the top, and the patterns of career development do not exclude people with different skills, abilities, and perspectives. This could be done by reflecting on the composition of the top two or three layers of their company, and considering whether the over-representation of particular groups may be due to implicit biases in the identification and development of high potentials. Otherwise, there is the danger of exclusively promoting managers with the same profile and characteristics. While this likemindedness may create cohesiveness, there is the risk of serious blind spots.

What it means to have high potential and to be successful is highly context- and culture-specific. Many executives with excellent track records at home have learned this the hard way. MNCs should therefore take advantage of these differences in promoting and developing managers to be effective in different time zones.

Making HRM meaningful across cultures

When developing international HRM policies, there needs to be discussion about how much similarity or variation is necessary. Which practices should be designed centrally by an international team, and which ones need to be adapted locally? Furthermore, companies can benefit from these discussions as opportunities to develop new ways of thinking about HRM.

The decisions regarding which HR policies can be globally exported and which need to be locally adapted can only be effective if the cultural assumptions embedded in these policies are brought to light and the differences evaluated in terms of their likely impact.

This first step is vital in avoiding the possible alienation or low morale which comes from imposing HR policies that are ill-suited to the local culture, or the risks of confusion and lack of coherence which can arise when each local unit determines its own policies.

The discussion, however, often hides a political subtext, as each party wants to reserve the power and autonomy to do things as they see fit. For this reason, cultural differences may be invoked as a pretext for retaining local control, or ignored as a pretext for preserving head office prerogative. Comments such as ". . . but that will never work in Italy" or ". . . but this is the way we do business" need to become subjects for debate rather than accepted as given.

On one hand, increasing the breadth of the discretionary zone regarding implementation of HR policies, increases the opportunities for creative interpretation locally. Too much explicitness or imposition may provide a focus for resistance, whereas a certain vagueness may enhance local buy-in and receptiveness. For example, Pepsi Cola International has accepted that one local unit might develop an individual incentive plan for the general manager, tied to the sales of the local operation, while another unit might develop a group incentive plan for the entire top management team tied to the sales of the local operation.[52]

On the other hand, it is also worth remembering that there are different ways to ignore local norms. One extreme is to impose HR policies direct from HQ, out of ignorance of cultural differences or insistence on "one best way". Another possibility is to exploit the differences to make use of local blind spots, for example by recruiting from undervalued labor pools, as previously discussed.

At Nissan, striking a balance between adapting and imposing HR policies has been resolved by adopting a position of "clear ends and loose means". This means that as long as the means are in line with the realization of Nissan's company objectives, no standardized way is enforced. So while the Mexican plant is run in a typical Japanese style, the American one in Tennessee is run in an American way with American top management. The British plant in Sunderland is half British and half Japanese in style. The factors which determine how to operate include the location, ownership (greenfield investment or joint venture), past history, level of technology, the nature of the product, and the human resources available.[53]

However, HR policies which ignore or aim to segregate cultural differences are missing out on the potential benefits of utilizing them. A more ambitious approach would be to try to seize the opportunity of mutual dialogue to experiment with creative variations. The pursuit of divergent initiatives around an agreed-upon theme may be the key to strategic flexibility and learning.[54] These deviations should not be killed off but allowed to run their course, then assessed for viability. Those retained can then be considered as candidates for global diffusion.

For example, different interpretations of what is meant by "high potential" encourages managers with different profiles to be selected and promoted in different locations. This can significantly enrich the company's understanding of the meaning of "effectiveness", particularly in an international context. Having highlighted the challenges and trade-offs that face companies in creating effective international HR practices, we now consider the extent to which the HR function is prepared to take on this effort.

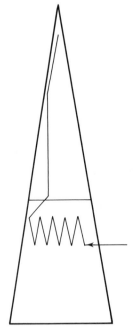

Potential development:
Functional ladders
• Functional careers, relationships and
  communications
• Expertise-based competition
• Multifunctional mobility limited to few
  elitist recruits, or non-existent
• Little multifunctional contact below level of
  division heads and *Vorstand* (executive
  committee)

Potential identification:
Apprenticeship
• Annual recruitment from universities
  and technical schools
• 2-year "apprenticeship" trial
  – Job rotation through most functions
  – Intensive training
  – Identification of person's
    functional potential and talents
• Some elitist recruitment, mostly
  of PhDs

Functional approach to management development: the "Germanic" model

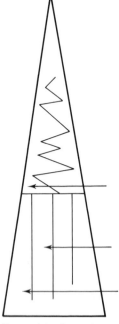

Potential development:
Managed potential development
• Careful monitoring of high potentials
  by management review committees
• Review to match up performance and
  potential with short- and long-term job
  and development requirements
• Importance of management
  development staff

Potential identification:
Unmanaged functional trial
• Little elite recruitment
• Decentralized recruitment for technical
  or functional jobs
• 5–7 years' trial
• No corporate monitoring
• Problem of internal "potential
  identification" via assessments,
  assessment centers, indicators
• Possible complementary recruitment
  of high potentials

Managed development approach to management development:
"Anglo–Dutch" model

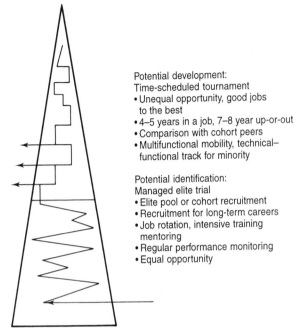

Potential development:
Time-scheduled tournament
• Unequal opportunity, good jobs
  to the best
• 4–5 years in a job, 7–8 year up-or-out
• Comparison with cohort peers
• Multifunctional mobility, technical–
  functional track for minority

Potential identification:
Managed elite trial
• Elite pool or cohort recruitment
• Recruitment for long-term careers
• Job rotation, intensive training
  mentoring
• Regular performance monitoring
• Equal opportunity

Elite cohort approach to management development: the "Japanese" model

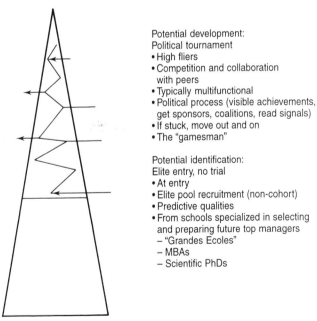

Potential development:
Political tournament
• High fliers
• Competition and collaboration
  with peers
• Typically multifunctional
• Political process (visible achievements,
  get sponsors, coalitions, read signals)
• If stuck, move out and on
• The "gamesman"

Potential identification:
Elite entry, no trial
• At entry
• Elite pool recruitment (non-cohort)
• Predictive qualities
• From schools specialized in selecting
  and preparing future top managers
  – "Grandes Ecoles"
  – MBAs
  – Scientific PhDs

Elite political approach to management development: the "Latin" model

Figure 6.1   Country patterns for career development. (*Source*: P. Evans, Y. Doz and A. Laurent (eds) (1989) *Human Resource Management in International Firms*, Macmillan, London.)

Internationalizing HRM

Internationalizing a company makes heavy demands of the HR function. First, it requires a sound understanding of the corporate strategy to make sure that the HRM policies are aligned. Second, it demands a thorough awareness of the cultural assumptions embedded in HR practices themselves, as well as those which prevail in local subsidiaries. And third, it requires the judgement to assess political concerns such that local resistance to HQ policies is really driven by cultural differences, or desire for local autonomy, or that HQ just wants to have its own way. Headquarters' HR personnel also have to be ready and willing to accept that they may have something to learn from their foreign subsidiaries and partners.

Unfortunately, the level of strategic, political, and cultural awareness required of the HR function to make it effective internationally is rarely achieved. A study of 1500 European HR executives reveals widely different levels of specialized HR training and of business experience.[55] Furthermore, it was found that HR managers rarely attain high levels in organizations (except in Scandinavia) and tend to be poorly integrated, if not isolated, from both operations and strategic planning. And while gaining competence in cross-cultural management was considered crucial by senior executives, very few HR directors considered this a priority. This creates an overwhelming challenge for HR managers, with the added headache of having to worry about internationalization.

One of the barriers preventing the HR function from fulfilling its role is its own lack of international experience. HR professionals, having very few transfer opportunities outside their home country, do not get the international exposure they need. HR jobs are thought of as fundamentally local, so HR positions are filled from outside only when a local solution is unavailable. The results of one survey indicate that only 30 percent of HR respondents considered international experience to be very important for promotion at corporate HR level; a mere 16 percent considered it to be very important for promotion to the regional HR group level.[56]

The lack of international perspective was revealed by a study conducted by Adler and Bartholomew[57] who found that a large number of American firms were *not* benchmarking excellence in global human resource management. Of the fifty HRM directors contacted, almost one-fifth could not name a single leading North American firm, more than one-third could not name a single excellent European firm, and one-half were ignorant of Asian examples. Paradoxically, then, the function in charge of implementing internationalization is itself rather parochial. This lack of international experience and understanding no doubt helps to explain why devising the appropriate international human resource strategies remains problematic for MNCs.

Companies also seem to make little effort to leverage the knowledge gained from operating in different cultural environments. Too often HR departments miss the opportunity to learn from the experiences of returning expatriates. In fact, it seems as if they pay little attention to these resources rich in cultural knowledge and do little to integrate this knowledge companywide. Apparently, only 20 percent of firms actively plan expatriates' return to specific, identified home positions.[58]

This means that returning executives often find that their new job does not encourage bringing home the international perspective developed abroad. With their experience so little valued, it comes as no surprise that among US firms 20 percent of repatriated managers leave their company within one year, and rates as high as 40–50 percent within three years have been reported.[59] Thus the company loses the very seeds needed for developing the international competence of the firm as a whole.

It is time to take stock of the lessons to be learned from the difficulties experienced by companies and indeed managers who have ventured abroad. It is also time to face the need for greater international experience overall, and the reality of the increasing international interactions in doing business anywhere. This means that individuals, teams, and organizations have to learn how to manage cultural differences which they will be confronting more and more on a daily basis, at home as well as abroad. Part III addresses these issues.

Questions to ask

Selection

How does local recruitment differ from home country policy?
How to interact with local networks?
Who is valued and why?

Socialization

How do local norms/expectations regarding socialization differ from home country policy?
Should managers at the local operation blend in with the local environment or do we want to differentiate ourselves?
Would a difference in values or attitudes inhibit internal dialogue?
To what extent should we articulate "the company way" in manuals?
To what extent should we organize exchanges of personnel?

Training

What sort of knowledge-aquisition is valued by the local organization?
Is this knowledge-acquisition complementary to that at HQ? To what extent will it inhibit communication and learning?
How important is it for the company to leverage knowledge across borders?
What does this mean for the nature and content of training sessions and who attends?

Performance appraisal

Is there a marked difference between the evaluation of performance from home country policy?
Is there a danger of alienating or demotivating the local team by imposing home rules?
Does the local operation have novel ways of delivering or depersonalizing negative feedback without demotivating?

Compensation and rewards

Do local preferences differ significantly from "home" ones?
Is the aim to instill competition or cooperation, information sharing or individual initiative?
Can these be encouraged by other than financial rewards?
Might an "alien" compensation package attract younger, more adaptable, or less typical managers disillusioned with local practices?

Career development

Do local mobility and poaching norms differ much from "home" ones?
What is the proportion of "foreigners" at HQ?
To what extent do company career paths favor some cultures over others?
Are there unintended biases in the identification of high potentials?

Notes

1. Evans, P. (1986) Apple Computer, Europe, INSEAD case.
2. Laurent, A. (1986) "The cross-cultural puzzle of international human resource management", *Human Resource Management*, 25(1), 91–102, 97.
3. Brewster, C. (1993) "Developing a 'European' model of human resource management", *The International Journal of Human Resource Management*, 4(4), 765–84.
4. Guest, D. (1990) "Human resource management and the American Dream", *Journal of Management Studies*, 27(4), 377–97.
5. Brewster, C. and Bournois, F. (1991) "Human resource management: A European perspective", *Personnel Review*, 20(6), 4–13.
6. Evans, P.A.L. (1984) "On the importance of a generalist conception of human resource management: A cross-national look", *Human Resource Management*, 23(4), 347–64.
7. "Selling is tough if you hate to smile", *Business Week*, August 1, 1994, 4.
8. Bartlett, C.A. and Nanda, A. (1990) Ingvar Kamprad and IKEA, Cambridge, MA, Harvard Business School case 9-390-132, 6.
9. Handy, C., Gordon, C., Gow, I. and Randlesome, C. (1988) *Making Managers*, London: Pitman, p. 2.
10. James, B. (1992) "New skills are knocking on French firms' doors", *International Herald Tribune*, February 6.
11. "Enarchy", *The Economist*, April 15, 1995, 27.
12. "Get 'em young, boss!", *Far Eastern Economic Review*, September 22, 1988.
13. Lasserre, P. and Probert, J. (1994) "Human Resource Management in the Asia Pacific Region", INSEAD Euro–Asia Centre Research Series, 18.
14. Adler, N.J. (1987) "Pacific basin managers: A Gaijin not a woman", *Human Resource Management*, 26(2), 169–92.
15. Rohlen, T. (1978) "The education of the Japanese banker", *Human Nature*, January, 22–30.
16. Van Maanen, J. and Laurent, A. (1993) "The flow of culture: Some notes on globalization and the multinational corporation" in S. Ghoshal and D.E. Westney (eds) *Organization Theory and the Multinational Corporation* New York: St. Martin's Press, 275–312.
17. Lewis, M. (1989) *Liar's Poker*, New York: W.W. Norton.
18. Lee, P. (1993) "Which is the real Goldman Sachs?", *Euromoney*, October, 50–7.

19. Adent Hoecklin, L. (1993) *Managing Cultural Differences for Competitive Advantage*, London: The Economist Intelligence Unit.
20. Schneider, S. and Inoue, R. (1988) Mitsuhoshi France, INSEAD case.
21. Stewart, R., Barsoux, J.-L., Kieser, A., Ganter, D. and Walgenbach, P. (1994) *Managing in Britain and Germany*, London: Macmillan.
22. Nonaka, I. (1991) "The knowledge-creating company", *Harvard Business Review*, November–December, 96–104.
23. Evans, P. (1986) Apple Computer, INSEAD case, 24.
24. Laurent, *Op. cit.*
25. Saner, R. and Yiu, L. (1994) "European and Asian resistance to the use of the American case method in management training", *The International Journal of Human Resource Management*, 5(4), 955–76.
26. *Ibid.*, p. 962.
27. Kolb, D.A. (1974) "Four styles of managerial learning" in D.A. Kolb, I.M. Rubin and J.M. McIntyre (eds) *Organizational Psychology: A Book of Readings*, 2nd edn, Englewood Cliffs, NJ: Prentice Hall, 27–34.
28. Evans, P.A.L. (1992) "Developing leaders and managing development", *European Management Journal*, 10(1), 1–9, 4.
29. Schneider, S.C. (1988) "National vs corporate culture: Implications for Human Resource Management", *Human Resource Management*, 27(2), 231–46.
30. Hofstede, G. (1980) *Cultures Consequences*, Beverly Hills: Sage.
31. Orleman, P. (1992) "The global corporation: Managing across cultures", Masters Thesis, University of Pennsylvania.
32. Trepo, G. (1973) "Management style à la Française", *European Business*, Autumn, 71–9.
33. Dowling, P.J. and Schuler, R.S. (1990) *International Dimensions of Human Resource Management*, Boston: PWS-Kent.
34. Orleman, *Op. cit.*
35. Kanter, R.M. and Corn, R.I. (1994) "Do cultural differences make a business difference?", *Journal of Management Development*, 13(2), 5–23.
36. Laurent, *Op. cit.*, p. 99.
37. Orleman, *Op. cit.*
38. Eretz, M. and Early, P.C. (1993) *Culture, Self-identity, and Work*, New York: Oxford University Press.
39. Pennings, J.M. (1993) "Executive reward systems: A cross-national comparison", *Journal of Management Studies*, 30(2), 261–80, 264.
40. Schneider, S.C., Wittenberg-Cox, A. and Hansen, L. (1991) Honeywell, Europe, INSEAD case.
41. Vance, C.M., McClaine, S.R., Boje, D.M. and Stage, H.D. (1992) "An examination of the transferability of traditional performance appraisal principles across cultural boundaries", *Management International Review*, 32(4), 313–26, 323.
42. Sanger, D.E. (1993) "Performance related pay in Japan", *International Herald Tribune*, October 5, p. 20.
43. Lawler, E.E. and Mohrman, S. (1989) "High-involvement management", *Organization Dynamics*, April, 27–31.
44. Pennings, *Op. cit.*
45. "Wages of death delight Japanese", *Sunday Times*, December 11, 1993, 1, 21.
46. Derr, C.B. and Laurent, A. (1989) "Internal and external careers: A theoretical and cross cultural perspective" in M.B. Arthur, D.T. Hall and B.S. Lawrence (eds) *Handbook of Career Theory*, Cambridge: Cambridge University Press, pp. 454–471; see also Derr, C. (1987) "Managing high potentials in Europe", *European Management Journal*, 5(2), 72–80.
47. Coale, D.J. (1994) "International barriers to progress", *Journal of Management Development*, 13(2), 55–8, p. 57.

48. Lane, C. (1989) *Management and Labour in Europe*, Aldershot: Edward Elgar, 92.
49. Stewart *et al.*, *Op. cit.*
50. "The old pals act" (1994) *The Banker*, May, 18.
51. Evans, *Op. cit.*
52. Fulkerson, J.R. and Schuler, R.S. (1992) "Managing worldwide diversity at Pepsi-Cola International" in S.E. Jackson (ed.) *Diversity in the Workplace*, New York: Guilford Press.
53. Schneider, S.C. and Asakura, A. (1993) Nissan Motor Co., Europe, INSEAD case study.
54. Burgelman, R.A. (1991) "Intraorganizational ecology of strategy making and organizational adaptation: Theory and field research", *Organization Science*, 2(3), August, 239–62.
55. Hiltrop, J.-M., Despres, C. and Sparrow, P. (1995) "The changing role of HR managers in Europe", *European Management Journal*, March, 91–98.
56. Gates, S. (1994) "The changing global role of the human resources function", New York: The Conference Board, Report No. 1062-94-RR, 22.
57. Adler, N. and Bartholomew, S. (1992) "Managing globally competent people", *Academy of Management Executive*, 6(3), 52–65.
58. Gates, *Op. cit.*
59. Black, J.S., Gregersen, H. and Mendenhall, M. (1992) *Global Assignments: Successfully Expatriating and Repatriating International Managers*, San Francisco: Jossey-Bass.

PART THREE

Managing cultural differences

On ne connait jamais un être, mais on cesse parfois de sentir qu'on l'ignore.

Malraux

(You can never really know someone, but sometimes you stop feeling like complete strangers.)

In Part II we described how culture affects management practice and how it may constrain the effectiveness or transfer of particular organizational structures, strategies, and HR systEms. In Part III we discuss how individuals, teams, and organizations manage these cultural differences. Here again we focus primarily on national culture. Nevertheless, much of what is said can be applied to other spheres of cultural influence: industry, corporate, functional, and professional. Cultural differences diagnosed at the different levels of culture as described in Chapter 2 – behavior and artifacts, values and beliefs, and underlying assumptions – are considered to be *generic*, visible in all spheres of cultural influence. For example, the importance of hierarchy can be seen in different company cultures, or the avoidance of uncertainty found in different functional cultures, such as R&D compared with marketing.

Seeing cultural diversity as an opportunity rather than as a threat obviously has intellectual, emotional, and moral appeal. Practically speaking, being able to manage this diversity is required for getting the job done, whether in daily contact with other colleagues, in cross-functional teams, or in cross-border alliances. Managing diversity, however, is easier said than done.

Throughout the book, we have placed a heavy emphasis on recognizing differences and confronting them, making these differences subject for discussion and negotiation. These prescriptions, more or less explicit, reflect our own cultural bias. We recognize that this may not be the norm in other cultures. Consider the Chinese perspective reflected in the following comment, "In the West, you are used to speaking out your problems. But this is not our tradition . . . In our country, we do not dissect ourselves and our relationships".[1]

The very processes of mutual adjustment are also culture-bound. This means learning how to confront differences in a culturally appropriate manner, such as being less direct (being more diplomatic), or going through a third party. Many managers, particularly Americans, are frustrated when these issues are not confronted head-on or when they do not get direct feedback. They complain, for example, that in Asia it is very difficult to know what the other is thinking or how the other is reacting to them. Nevertheless, managers from different cultures have to recognize the differences in what to say and how to say it in order to arrive at a strategy for working together.

Chapter 7 looks at how individuals manage cultural differences. What are the skills and competences necessary, given the increased and less predictable exposure to cultural diversity? The experience of expatriates is used as a starting point to consider the individual factors which contribute to managing effectively across cultures. This allows us to consider the personal histories, characteristics, or work experience which predispose managers to work well with different cultures. Today the notion of "international manager" has taken on new meaning, and with it new demands on managers to be effective. What challenges do international managers now face? How can they devise strategies for working with people from different cultures, both at home and abroad?

Chapter 8 examines the increasing use of multicultural teams. Pooling expertise across functional, company, and national boundaries promises to lead to better decision-making, greater creativity, more responsiveness to different customers, and easier local implementation of strategy. But in order to realize this promise, multicultural teams have to create the right tension between integration and differentiation, to build shared expectations while preserving the enriching differences.

This means identifying cultural similarities and differences and resolving two sets of issues, task issues and process issues. Team members must establish how they will structure their work – how decisions will be made, how to define roles and responsibilities, as well as how to assure participation, handle conflict, and promote learning. The aim is not to neutralize or contain cultural differences, but to build on them. Unless the multicultural team puts effort into creating cohesion and solidarity up front, diversity will become a liability, not an asset.

Chapter 9 examines the company strategies for managing cultural differences: ignore, minimize, or utilize. How can diversity create added value? We argue that treating diversity as a resource rather than a threat is essential for responding to the demands of a global market economy, for reaping the full benefit of cross-border alliances, and for enhancing organizational learning.

"Going global" means going beyond mere presence in the main trading blocks or having a globally recognized brand name. The real test of a global company is its ability to *utilize* cultural differences. In an era of global competition, drawing on the abilities of employees worldwide becomes a competitive necessity, not an ideological luxury.

CHAPTER SEVEN

The "international" manager

Let my house not be walled on four sides, let all the windows be open, let all the cultures blow in, but let no culture blow me off my feet.

Mahatma Gandhi

Traditionally, the **international manager** was synonymous with the expatriate manager. But as companies devise more sophisticated cross-border strategies, they increasingly search for executives who can leap borders in a single bound to do the implementing. This has prompted the call for a new type of cosmopolitan, multilingual, multifaceted executive who is operational across national borders (somewhat like James Bond). This search is especially frenetic in Europe where the global manager has spawned a sub-species, the Euromanager.[2]

The "international manager" has also come to mean an international elite of executives, drawn from the company's operations worldwide, portrayed as members of a global commando or SWAT team, living out of airplanes and recognizable by their constant jetlag. One story has it that a French IBM executive arriving at JFK airport in New York while searching for his entry visa pulled out his IBM identification card. The customs official, seeing it said, "Oh, it's OK, you're IBM, you can go ahead".

Companies having developed an international corps of executives, developed through frequent and multiple transfers, have often found that such an elite is difficult to integrate into the corporate mainstream; nor are those with "helicopter views" necessarily capable of doing the work of more down to earth experts.[3] Thus rumors of the existence of a "global" manager as someone who pursues a "borderless career", and whose corporate identity overrides that of country and even family,[4] may be somewhat exaggerated.

In any case, the mere fact of operating across national boundaries does not mean that the minds of international managers are also traveling across boundaries. It is sometimes questionable whether English-speaking, Hilton-based executives, with little local interaction, even warrant the international tag. This is internationalism on the "accidental tourist"[5] model (where the key character traveling to Europe is greatly relieved to find MacDonalds), making sure that nothing encountered abroad will differ too much from back home and bringing along all the supplies necessary for survival. International mobility does not necessarily enhance the ability to think internationally.[6]

Changes over the last decade or so have made business not just more international but also more interdependent. Global expansion is increasingly achieved through alliances and joint ventures, as well as cross-border mergers and acquisitions. Companies expect their employees to operate across borders, prehaps for short periods or as part of multi-disciplinary, multicultural teams. Furthermore, thanks to advances in communication and information technology, contact by fax, e-mail, and teleconferencing has become commonplace. So even those who rarely leave their home base may find themselves interacting with foreigners.

One of the most striking findings of a survey undertaken by Fiat was that 40 percent of managerial positions dealt with international work matters.[7] This survey suggests the extent to which even MNCs are underestimating the amount of international management being done by their employees, and that the notion of international responsibility is being interpreted too narrowly.

What is more, cultural sensitivity is now demanded at all levels of the organization. Front-line employees (such as security guards, chauffeurs, and receptionists) are the first to greet foreign visitors and a company's global pretentions are easily shattered when foreign clients or employees cannot get past the front door or beyond the receptionist. The international content of jobs clearly varies depending on the nature of the business, the company, the function, and the level of experience but being able to handle cultural differences is becoming more and more a part of everybody's job.

While the image of the global manager may be more myth than reality, the conventional distinction between international and domestic managers is fading, given the much broader distribution of international responsibilities. Increasingly, people from all over the world must work with each other and consciously manage their cultural differences. So, as Barham and Antal observe, companies need to focus less on *who* is an international manager, and consider instead *what* international tasks and responsibilities employees really do fulfill and use this as a basis for reviewing the actual competencies required for each job.[8]

Before looking specifically at the competencies needed by international managers, it may be worth considering what has been learned from expatriates who have been roaming the world for the past several decades. We will then consider the evolving portrait of the international manager, which now includes those who deal with cultural differences at home, not just abroad. This leads to a far wider definition of international manager and to reconsidering which skills and competencies are necessary. What personal histories, characteristics, or work experience predispose managers to work well with diversity? And finally, what can be done to manage cultural differences so that managers can navigate more effectively (whether abroad or at home) in international business.

Lessons from abroad

Much of what we know about managing cultural differences at an individual level comes from the experience of expatriates (missionaries sent out by companies as well as the

Peace Corps). Unfortunately, companies have not been particularly attentive when listening to feedback from expatriates and to learning from their experiences. So what can we learn from the expatriate experience about the trials and satisfactions of working abroad?

For many expatriates, international assignments turn out to be the most memorable career experience, but not always for the right reasons. Of course, there is the opportunity for greater challenge and responsibility, and for personal as well as professional development. Yet failure rates of up to 30 percent within US multinationals reveal the difficulties of adapting to a new culture. In fact, expatriate failure is estimated to cost US business $2 billion a year.[9] What are some of the potential reasons for these difficulties in adjusting?

Consider the experience of these two expatriates. First, the reaction of a German manager with IBM on arriving in England:

> Dieter Shultz took up his post as a product manager in 1986 and found that most lunchtimes and particularly on Fridays the vast majority of his management team decamped to the pub. "I stopped that right away", he says. "Now they are not allowed off the premises. It didn't make me very popular at the time but it is not good for efficiency. There is no way we would do that in Germany. No way."[10]

And the poignant testimony of an American manager sent out to head up a newly acquired operation in France:

> After months of trying my best to break down the barriers, I pretty much abandoned all hope of establishing trust with my staff. I had used up all my tricks within a year or so – setting clear goals, working longer hours than anyone, joining in the actual nuts-and-bolts work of each project, maintaining an open-door policy, roaming through the editorial offices (management by walking about like mad), and that ultimate seducer I had been advised would always work in France: taking them out to a good lunch one by one. They could never overcome the deep-seated belief that management was out to exploit them.[11]

Had Herr Schultz been assigned to a more distant country he might have better anticipated the cultural differences. That he reacted so strongly indicates that these differences were unexpected. His reaction, nevertheless, tells us as much about his home culture (and perhaps that of the company, IBM) as the host culture: concerns for efficiency and for absolute policies and procedures. IBM had a very explicit rule regarding alcohol consumption during the work day: none. As he saw it, the difference, or problem, lay in "the others". A critical step for managers working internationally is when they realize that the cultural difference also resides in them, and the company.

The exasperated American manager, having tried everything possible from his own repertoire of behaviors (or bag of tricks) to break down the barriers, finally tries the prescribed "French" way. His own approach is highly *instrumental* and task-oriented, setting clear goals, joining in the nuts and bolts. Even the lunch option is used as a last resort. This approach only serves to reinforce the feeling of exploitation and manipulation, that getting the job done is more important than the personal relationships. "Management by walking about" signals surveillance, not supportiveness. He has thus unwittingly fulfilled the prophecy of "the deep-seated belief that management was out to exploit them".

For expatriate managers, then, living in a foreign country produces constant and unexpected challenges to their ways of perceiving, acting, and valuing things, making it difficult to correctly process and act on information. Inevitably, this leads to committing cultural gaffes or *faux pas* that leave the expatriate feeling confused and uncomfortable. They may find it difficult to make sense of other people's behavior. Worse still, their own behavior does not have the expected impact. The techniques which worked back home simply fail to get results.

Indeed, the most often cited reason for failed assignments is the inability of expatriates and their families to adapt to the local culture. The strain is perhaps even greater on families, as the manager is often buffered by work from the more mundane cultural encounters. Thus, it is often the family that takes the shock full force. Therefore, it is important to understand the processes of adjustment and to recognize the warning signs of culture malaise.

The process of cultural adjustment

The process of adjusting to a foreign culture is said to follow a U-curve[12] comprising three main phases: an initial stage of elation and optimism (the honeymoon), soon followed by a period of irritability, frustration, and confusion (the morning after), and then a gradual adjustment to the new environment (happily ever after). Although the inevitability of these stages has been challenged, these emotional experiences are not uncommon. The intensity of these reactions often depends upon the motivation and prior expectations of the expatriates and their family to go abroad, the amount of cultural distance between the home and host countries, and the degree of uncertainty in job and/ or daily living activities.[13]

The same emotions may be experienced for the return journey. Indeed the shock of returning home can be more severe because it is less expected. Where expatriates may have a sense of *déjà vu* when going abroad, coming home can feel as if never having been there before; a sort of *jamais vu*. The returning manager is more often treated like the prodigal son than the conquering hero.

Attention has been drawn particularly to the phase following the "honeymoon", when cultural differences are no longer experienced as charming but rather annoying. This phase is when most assignments are at risk of failure. The increased involvement with the new culture brings the realization that there are unsettling differences in interpersonal behavior as well as work behavior. These can come as quite a surprise, especially in culturally or economically neighboring countries.

The term "culture shock", often used to describe this sense of frustration, is actually rather misleading. It tends to suggest a sudden impact with a single cause. More likely, it will result from a simmering reaction to a succession of minor events which are difficult to identify. It is more like tennis elbow than a dislocated shoulder. The symptoms of cultural malaise go from simple embarrassment, through homesickness and identity confusion, and can culminate in a fully fledged depression.

Given that culture shock or malaise is a kind of "rite of passage" in international assignments, there are reasons for welcoming its arrival. First, it signals that the expatriate manager is becoming involved in the new culture, not hiding out in an expatriate ghetto. Second, it provides the motivation, which may not have been there at earlier stages, to try to understand and come to grips with the cultural differences. However, if the anxiety of culture shock is too high, it may prevent people from learning.[14] The experience of culture shock and the various responses to it are summed up in Figure 7.1.[15]

Over time, it is thought that adjustment evolves through acquiring greater knowledge of the local culture and language and working together with others to achieve shared goals. When all goes well, greater cross-cultural interaction can foster greater perceived cultural similarity, reducing "we–they" stereotypes. More interaction also increases the likelihood of shared understandings, providing a greater sense of predictability and control.[16] This in turn facilitates adjustment. However, when cross-cultural interaction is marked by friction and frustration, stereotypes may indeed be reinforced, and conflicts can become entrenched, thus impeding adjustment.

Research has found that European managers based in other European countries than their own reported less cultural interaction than those based in the United States or Asia. This was attributed to less perceived cultural distance, and that Europeans were less likely "to mix" socially, having more support from "back home".[17] Paradoxically, it seems that being closer to home, both in terms of culture and geography, may limit the needed cultural interaction and potentially impair adjustment. Assumptions of similarity as well as assumptions of differences therefore need to be challenged.

In addition to resolving the challenges posed when confronting a new culture, the expatriate manager must come to terms with a number of inevitable dilemmas.[18] These tensions derive from the manager's position as mediator between the two cultures and the two parts of the same organization. For instance, a basic dilemma for expatriates is how much of their own way of doing things they are prepared to relinquish, and how much of the new ways they are willing to embrace. Remaining behind the closed doors of the expatriate community or "going native" may not be the most effective solutions.

Expatriate managers are also caught in the dilemma of reconciling responsibility and power, invested with a great deal of responsibility but having to depend on local management and employees to achieve their objectives. Furthermore, they have to manage their allegiances between parent firm and local operation.[19] Where head-office directives conflict with local values, expatriate managers gradually learn to pick those battles they can win and avoid those they cannot.

Being faced with conflicting demands or contradictory truths requires the ability to see situations from both angles and to assess the strengths and weaknesses from each perspective (a bicultural perspective). This means that dogmatic thinking, assuming there is one best way (my way), is doomed. What is needed is well-captured by American author, F. Scott Fitzgerald's remark, "Intelligence is the ability to hold two conflicting ideas in mind and retain the ability to function."

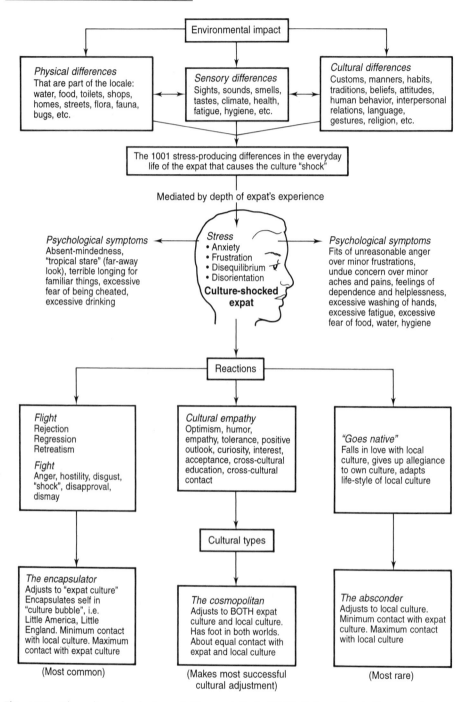

Figure 7.1　The culture-shocked expat. (*Source*: J. Craig (1979) *Culture Shock*, Times Books International, Singapore.)

Competencies for managing internationally

Having highlighted some of the challenges of working abroad, we can now consider what skills and abilities are needed in order to be effective, as shown in Table 7.1. Individuals clearly have different aptitudes for managing in new cultural surroundings.

Table 7.1   What it takes

Competencies for managing differences abroad
Interpersonal (relationship) skills
Linguistic ability
Motivation to live abroad (cultural curiosity)
Tolerance for uncertainty and ambiguity
Flexibility
Patience and respect
Cultural empathy
Strong sense of self (or ego strength)
Sense of humor

Managing differences abroad

Interpersonal skills

"Interpersonal skills" are often identified as crucial, if not *the* most important. The ability to form relationships helps the manager integrate into the social fabric of the host culture. Not only does this satisfy the needs for friendship and intimacy, but also facilitates the transfer of knowledge, and improves coordination and control. Establishing relationships and building trust allows the expatriate manager to tap into critical information, thus reducing the stressful uncertainties surrounding both work and personal life.

While many companies acknowledge the importance of interpersonal skills, it is rarely seen as a critical criterion for selection. In practice, expatriate managers are primarily selected on their strong track record at home, that is, their reputation for getting the job done. Companies also send abroad those who have been identified as high fliers, for the purpose of career development. Either way, expatriates are most often chosen based on technical or conceptual abilities rather than interpersonal skills.

Those having been placed on the fast track often arrive on assignment ready to prove themselves, to make their mark. Thus they tend to be quite focused on the task, and on achieving the objectives set by corporate headquarters. As assignments may only last 18 months, they have to move quickly to make things happen. This can create tension with the local staff, who refer to them as "birds of passage",[20] laying low waiting for this latest arrival to fly off again, until the next one arrives, with yet another personal agenda.

Time pressures and strong task orientation interfere with the need to build relationships and to establish trust. Often local staff feel exploited, as instruments to achieve goals that are not their own. This exacerbates feelings of mistrust and resentment towards head office. In fact, some experts argue that successful expatriates actually need to have *low task orientation*![21]

The need for more *people-oriented* managers is confirmed by the personnel director for the European division of ICI (a British chemical and pharmaceutical company) who looks for people who are "good at getting along with colleagues at home". This is deemed essential for the simple reason that any problems a manager has in dealing with colleagues, will be magnified in a foreign setting, where much more effort is needed to build understanding and trust. The former cochairman of Unilever, Floris Maljers, agrees by stating, "We tend to look for people who can work in teams and understand the value of cooperation and consensus".[22] Thus the ability to get along with others is considered to be an important passport to international business.

Linguistic ability

Linguistic ability is also important as it helps to establish contact. However, having total command of the other language may not be feasible and may be less important than trying to develop a feel for what matters to others, picking up bits of "conversational currency"[23]: local expressions, information, and interests. On short overseas assignments in particular, efforts to speak the local language may have more symbolic than practical value, but the impact is highly significant. It indicates an eagerness to communicate and to connect with host nationals. A resolute unwillingness to speak the other's language can be very damaging in that it may be taken as a sign of disdain.

Motivation to work and live abroad

Motivation to work and live abroad has been shown to be a key ingredient to the successful adaptation of the expatriates and their families. This is manifested as "cultural curiosity". Expatriates and their families should be selected based on a genuine interest in other cultures and new experiences. For Swedish managers, *Wanderlust* was rated as their top motive for going abroad.[24]

Ability to tolerate and cope with uncertainty

Ability to tolerate and cope with uncertainty and ambiguity is also needed. Action often has to be taken on the basis of insufficient, unreliable and/or conflicting information.[25] Circumstances change unexpectedly, the behavior and reactions of local employees may be unpredictable, so that the international manager has to be able to adapt almost instinctively. This requires, first of all, acknowledging that uncertainty and ambiguity exist, that everything is not as straightforward as it seems, and that multiple perspectives are possible. The inability to do so encourages dogmatic thinking and rigid behavior, which interfere with the flexibility and resourcefulness necessary for responding effectively.[26]

When AT&T went through a major corporate culture change in the mid-1980s, executives were evaluated on their ability to acknowledge uncertainty as well as their ability to cope with it. Training was then conducted specifically on how to cope with uncertainty.[27] Top executives at Colgate asked to identify the kind of executive who worked best in an international setting cited the main attribute to be flexibility. The consensus was, "You don't always go by the book".[28]

Faced with the threat of greater uncertainty and ambiguity of international assignments, managers often feel a strong need to reassert control. This response, in effect, interferes with remaining flexible. Research has shown that under conditions of threat, managers tend to engage in efforts to impose greater controls, restrict information flows, and revert to well-known behavior.[29] This can result in stereotypical responses, not necessarily well-adapted to the situation at hand. In these circumstances, expatriates may more often need to let go of control, to "go with the flow".

This is quite difficult especially when managers are used to being rewarded for being in charge and staying on top of things. This is particularly evident in cultures where control over the environment is an underlying assumption. Indeed, the success of Japanese company strategies (as in the case of Honda) is often attributed to their flexibility which enables them to capitalize on unexpected opportunities. This flexibility comes from their readiness to adapt rather than to impose controls over changing circumstances.

Patience and respect

Perhaps even more crucial for the international executive are patience and respect. Patience is necessary, not only because different cultures have different rhythms, but also because it takes time to "learn the ropes".[30] Expatriates have to avoid the temptation constantly to benchmark the new culture against the home culture, but must instead try to understand the local reasons for the way things happen. While having patience and respect may be the golden rule of international business, it seems to be the one most often broken.

Cultural empathy

Respecting the behavior and ideas of others requires empathy. Some individuals find it easier to appreciate the thoughts, feelings, and experiences of others. Focused listening and a non-judgemental approach help managers to understand the other person's viewpoint. But one's capacity for empathy is deeply rooted in one's character and may not be a skill easily acquired.

Narcissism, which evolves from one's psychological development, interferes with the capacity for empathy.[31] Narcissistic managers often treat others as mere extensions of themselves making it difficult to recognize, let alone appreciate, the attitudes and behavior of others, especially those who are different. These managers see others as objects or instruments to satisfy their own needs, or as mirrors to reflect their own glory. In their efforts to prove their worth, they fail to take into consideration the needs and the *value* of others.

Strong sense of self

On the other hand, expatriates do need a strong sense of self, or ego (healthy narcissism). This allows interaction with another person, or culture without fear of losing one's own identity. This also enables the expatriate to be self-critical and open to feedback. It permits expatriates to respond appropriately to failure, treating it as a learning experience rather than as a narcissistic injury, a blow to their self-image which can undermine their self-confidence.

A strong ego also reinforces the ability to handle stress. This is particularly critical in an environment where the manager is deprived of familiar surroundings and social support. The anxiety created by the uncertainties and frustrations of international experiences needs to be appropriately handled, rather than triggering dysfunctional coping devices, such as alcohol abuse.

Creating "stability zones"[32] – hobbies, diaries, favorite pastimes, meditation, or religious worship – can provide refuge into which the expatriate can temporarily withdraw and get refueled. Taking time-out is vital because it reintroduces the element of choice and control over the rhythm of involvement with the new culture and enables the manager to regain a sense of perspective, "observing ego".

Sense of humor

Finally, a sense of humor is one quality which is often cited but only in passing. Humor is actually important on two levels: as a coping mechanism and for relationship building. Retaining a sense of humor is seen as a way for managers to buffer the frustration, uncertainty, and confusion they are bound to encounter in an unfamiliar environment. Humor provides a way of distancing oneself from the situation, to regain a sense of perspective. Also, "the ability to laugh at one's mistakes may be the ultimate defense against despair".[33] Or in the words of one oil industry veteran, "The first few months in an international posting can seem like one long round of social gaffes and management blunders. If you didn't laugh, you'd cry".

Humor can also be used proactively to break the ice, to establish a link with others, and to deal with sensitive issues. A well-timed bit of humor can put people at ease, break the tension in an interaction, allowing a more open and constructive discussion to follow, and to say what might not be said otherwise. As the expression goes, "Many a true word is spoken in jest". Humor can serve to create the space for an "emotional time-out", to let off steam and alleviate tension.[34]

One person noted for his humor in international relations was Henry Kissinger.

> He made humor a tool of diplomacy. His banter inspired banter in others and usually led to a more relaxed atmosphere in the private, formal discussions or negotiations with world leaders. The humor opened the door to more frankness and less ritualized

recitations as well. In that regard, Kissinger lightened the whole heavy international diplomatic scene.[35]

But it must be remembered that what is considered funny in one culture does not necessarily translate to another. British humor often involves poking fun at oneself and others, dosed with a bit of sarcasm and wit (sometimes biting). In France, *se moquer* (or "to mock" self or others) has a different, more pejorative, connotation. Thus teasing or making fun of someone may be experienced as humiliation. For Asians this type of humor does not adequately "save face", protect self-esteem.

Humor can, in effect, be used to reinforce the power distance, in the form of "put downs", or one-upmanship. French comedy, for example, often depicts situations where different social classes are forced to interact. In the United Kingdom as well as in France, humor is often based on intellectual or linguistic prowess – witticisms or *jeux de mots*, that is, plays on words or double meanings. This demands a high level of language sensitivity which excludes most foreigners, even the most fluent. Humor, such as "inside jokes", can also reinforce notions of who's in and who's out. Thus the use of humor has great potential for facilitating or destroying cross-cultural interactions.

Most of the above skills and competencies, traditionally considered crucial for expatriate effectiveness are equally valid for those who deal with foreigners at home. The experiences of expatriates provide important lessons for handling this diversity. However, international management is no longer the exclusive domain of expatriates.

Managing differences at home

With more and more managers having international responsibilities, what are the new challenges, and how do the skills needed differ from those expected of expatriate managers? While there is much overlap between the demands made of expatriate managers and of those managing internationally, contrasting the two roles is instructive.

Understand interdependencies

To start with, managing internationally demands a more complete understanding of the interdependencies between different parts of the organization worldwide, and a wider appreciation of the impact that a course of action in one area will have on another. International managers do not just deal with straight up and down relationships between a subsidiary and head office, but engage in much more complex interactions across country and functional boundaries. They play multiple roles participating in multiple teams, as leaders in some, and as members in others.

Respond to different cultures simultaneously

The cultural awareness of the international manager therefore has to extend beyond expertise in a single culture. Dealing with people from many different cultures makes learning all their diverse customs, attitudes, tastes, and approaches to business a difficult, if not impossible, task. What is more, contact with other cultures is not sequential, as in the case of the expatriate manager, but *simultaneous*. In other words, "international" managers have to be able to deal with a mixed group of individuals all at the same time.[36] The conventional wisdom that expatriate managers are people who can get results from people who are very different from themselves is given an added twist: the international manager is actually someone who can get results from people who are very different from each other as well.

Recognize cultural differences at home

This task is rendered even more difficult by the tendency to overlook cultural differences "at home". Cultural differences are expected abroad, but at home it is often assumed that the foreigner will make the effort to adapt to "our ways" or to fit in with the dominant culture. Taking this view can alienate others, but more importantly fails to capitalize on the potential benefits of recognizing diversity and the unsuspected value added which outsiders can contribute from their different experience, skills, and perspective. Beyond that, it also ignores the shift in the balance of power between managers from various parts of the globe.

Be willing to share power

Relations between home country and foreign nations are no longer those of boss and subordinate. Companies with global aspirations can no longer assume, as in the past, that the most sophisticated customers, the most important market, and the leading suppliers are home-based.[37] The dispersal of key resources and markets means that head office is no longer all-powerful. And more and more shareholders are no longer necessarily compatriots.

Increases in economic power, wider access to business education, and the decentralization of organizations have put these relationships on a much more equal footing. This means that head-office representatives can no longer "tell" sophisticated foreign counterparts what to do, but have to "sell", just as they would with colleagues at head office. Furthermore, they may just find that the foreigner is their boss. Currently it is estimated that there are more than two million Americans working for foreign employers in the United States.[38]

Thus, the role of the international manager has evolved in two important ways. First, the pattern of cultural contact has changed; it is more varied and fragmented than it was, it is simultaneous rather than sequential, and it is not always recognized as such, since much of it happens on home turf. Second, the nature of the relationships has changed. The relations of power and dominance between HQ and subsidiaries are no longer what they were; and with competitive advantages harder to come by, MNCs can no longer afford to ignore learning opportunities from their foreign counterparts. Head-office managers therefore have to engage in a dialogue with subsidiary managers, and listen. So what additional skills are required to manage across cultures at home?

The changing demands on international managers described above mean that additional skills and competencies are required and may even differ from those required of the expatriate. Managers need cross-cultural skills on a daily basis, throughout their careers, not just during foreign assignments, but also on regular multicountry business trips and in daily interaction with clients or colleagues worldwide.[39]

Demonstrate cognitive complexity

For managers to be effective across cultures requires the ability to simultaneously recognize the need for differentiation while understanding the need for integration, at multiple levels and at multiple sites within and outside the organization. The ability to respond to the concurrent needs for local responsiveness and the demands for global integration means creating a "matrix of the mind".[40] The ability to think multidimensionally while seeing the interrelatedness of the dimensions has been labeled "cognitive complexity".[41] According to Jacques,[42] this ability is the determining factor of a manager's position in the hierarchy, and the degree of discretion in decision-making.

However, in international settings, this ability cannot be considered to be the preserve of an elite. This, in effect, is a key challenge for training and development. Job rotation, brief assignments, and joint seminars can facilitate the development of a better appreciation of the different pieces of the organization puzzle, and foster a better understanding of the potential synergies in their interrelationships.

Adopt a "cultural-general" approach

Furthermore, in dealing simultaneously with multiple cultures, managers need to develop a "cultural-general" approach. Rather than a thorough knowledge of one particular culture, international managers need to be aware of the cues signaling culture differences be they national, corporate, or functional. According to this approach (which is indeed the one favored by the authors), it is important to identify which dimensions of culture may be relevant, rather than knowing the central tendencies of each particular country represented in meetings, or encounters in the course of a day's work. This approach contrasts with the "cultural-specific" approach typically offered in training expatriates in the past.

While programs preparing expatriates for international assignments sometimes included language training, international managers cannot hope to master all the languages they need. But it is important, as one Dutch banker observed, "to learn a language – any language – simply to give yourself another perspective on the world". International managers must also learn to communiate more effectively, avoiding slang, pausing frequently, and speaking slowly and clearly (not loudly – it is not a problem of deafness). Although English may be the *lingua franca* of international business, strong regional accents (such as those in the deep South in the United States or Scotland in the United Kingdom) can leave even native English speakers at a loss. Training anglophone managers with international responsibilities to speak "middle English" may not be such a bad idea.[43]

Rapidly learn and unlearn

Finally, faced with the need to simultaneously manage multiple cultures, there is the need to *rapidly learn* and *unlearn*. This means constantly challenging basic assumptions and not falling into the comfortable trap of assuming that "since we have a common corporate or professional culture we see things the same way". It means being constantly ready to take on new perspectives and try new approaches. This can prove to be a highly demanding, if not exhausting, exercise. However, the energy derived from discovering exciting new possibilities and pursuing new horizons beyond those given, serves to replenish and reinvigorate. Thus faced with the challenges of managing cultural differences at home, additional skills are required, as shown in Table 7.2.

Table 7.2 . . . And more

Additional competencies for managing differences at home
Understand business interdependencies
Respond to multiple cultures simultaneously
Recognize the influence of culture "at home"
Be willing to share power
Demonstrate cognitive complexity
Adopt a "cultural-general" approach
Rapidly learn and unlearn

So what kinds of individuals are more likely to have these qualities, or to be able to develop them? We will consider, in turn, individual background and work experience.

Developing cultural competencies

Individual background

The invention of the bicycle is said to have led to a dramatic increase in the average distance separating the home towns of people getting married. Today, international travel means that more and more children have parents of different nationalities. This may mean that the children change countries several times when young, as well as growing up with two, if not more, languages in the home, neither of which may be the local language. Again this helps individuals acquire a certain receptiveness to cultural differences from an early age. According to Catherine Bateson, this early experience of other cultures develops better "peripheral vision", or other ways of seeing things.[44]

Such exposure to cultural differences is obviously more likely in some regions of the world than others. Europe, when compared with Japan, packs big cultural differences into small spaces, and would thus seem a useful training ground for would-be international managers. And within Europe, it could be argued that certain countries such as Belgium and Switzerland provide their inhabitants with a special head start, due to the cultural and language differences that exist within these countries. Unfortunately, this familiarity can breed contempt. Cultural differences in Belgium and Switzerland may be acknowledged but they are not necessarily valued.

Nevertheless, in these countries, television programs and cinema are available in several languages and subtitled in others, such as German and French. Living in international cities such as Brussels or Geneva, school children are quite likely to find classmates from the rest of the European or international community. Growing up in places such as New York, London, or Paris one is likely to take cultural differences for granted, as part of everyday life.

In terms of further education, there are increasing numbers of exchange programs on business courses at university level. European universities are becoming more involved in these initiatives because of the geographical proximity of distinctive cultures and EU-sponsored efforts to encourage exchanges for both students and staff. American universities have also planted stakes in Europe through alliances such as that of Northwestern University's Kellogg School of Business and IESE in Barcelona.

European business schools emphasize the international background of both their students and faculty as a competitive advantage over their US or UK counterparts.[45] For example, the distinctive competence of INSEAD is considered to be its genuine multiculturalism among both students and faculty. This multiculturalism is enforced by a policy which limits the proportion of students of any one nationality to less than 25 percent. This means that students confront cultural differences on a routine basis. Much of the work involves group assignments designed to maximize diversity by putting together individuals of different nationality, work experience, age, and gender. Indeed the *content* of the coursework may be secondary to the *process* of learning how to work across cultures.

Graduates from these international business schools are particularly attractive to multinational companies and large consulting firms. As employers see it, students from international business schools are well prepared to work globally due to their linguistic ability, their willingness to study abroad, and their experience in working in multicultural teams. As one human resource specialist with a large multinational saw it, "The most valuable service performed by [these schools] is not just training, but selection and socialization".

Work experience

While the background and education of individuals may help them to operate in an international context, those skills can be enhanced within companies. Early challenges and diversified experience are considered important in developing international managers. The idea behind sending people abroad is that they will learn to understand and appreciate cultural differences in management style and perspective. Consider the testimony of one Shell manager.

> I was trained as a geologist and spent the first seven years of my career trying to discover oil. One day when I was heading an exploration assignment, they called me to London and told me that they wanted me to take over the responsibility for a troubled

department of 80 maintenance engineers on the other side of the world. Geology is the noble elite, and maintenance engineering is somewhere between here-and-hell in the value system. I didn't want the job, and I told them that I knew nothing about maintenance engineering. "We're not sending you there to learn about engineering" they said, "We are sending you there to learn about management."[46]

The implicit assumption is that if managers are moved around enough, they will develop cultural sensitivity. Mobility is indeed considered the key to the internationalization of both managers and companies.[47]

While essential, it becomes clear that exposure to other cultures is not a sufficient condition to develop the skills needed to manage across cultures. It may happen that executives sent abroad can become more rigid in their thinking rather than less so. A colonial mentality can result when these executives are charged with implementing standardized policies and procedures dictated by the home office.

Furthermore, pressures created by performance expectations and time constraints inhibit experimenting with new approaches that may be more locally (and perhaps even more globally) effective. Companies provide too few chances for their executives to reflect on their experiences, to draw out the learning and assimilate it in new behavior in discussions with peers, coaches, or mentors. Also lost is the opportunity for the company to learn and develop through these experiences and discussions.[48]

A further problem with international development through mobility is that companies can spend a great deal of time and money identifying people who can work internationally, only to find that those individuals are actually unwilling to relocate. Perhaps more pertinent than whether they *can* be international managers is the question of whether they *want* to be. This is confirmed by one IBM executive who claims that, "Personal and family reasons, often genuine though sometimes as an excuse, are certainly the greatest inhibitor to moving people. And it is increasingly so with the dual career situation."[49]

The problem of mobility itself differs across cultures. For example, the proportion of managers with working partners is particularly high in Sweden. For this reason, Swedish companies often make it their business to assist spouses in finding jobs in the local community. Continental Europeans are also less inclined to live abroad, preferring to remain in close contact with their extended family. These family ties have greater importance than for British managers, who may be more accustomed to leaving their children in distant boarding schools.

Companies have found two ways of getting round this increased resistance to mobility. The first is to push managers out of the nest as early as possible, before family responsibilities enter into the picture. This approach is favored by Schlumberger, the French engineering company, which sends young (male) recently graduated engineers off to exotic places. One British company, ICI, does not wait for them to graduate, offering twenty university students two-month internships at an ICI site outside their home country. Trainees therefore can combine their operational apprenticeship with a cross-cultural experience, rather than making the two phases sequential.[50]

Procter and Gamble is another company which believes that exposing new graduates to cultural differences from the start is the best way to learn about them.[51] The head of recruitment for P&G in Brussels claims that the idea of a first job outside their country of origin appeals to more and more graduates. It is also believed that early experiences help these aspiring international managers to better manage cultural differences.

Besides foreign postings, managers can acquire a global perspective through working in mixed-nationality teams. Improvements in communications and transportation mean that it is increasingly feasible (and strategically important) to assemble geographically dispersed teams in project groups and *ad hoc* task forces. This exposes local managers to more global concerns without requiring extensive relocation of personnel.

For example, when 3M radically restructured its European operations, involving 21,000 people, it managed to limit relocation to only 40 managers. On the other hand, about 1,000 of their managers have been given permanent and/or project responsibilities across national borders; this involves them spending about one-third of their time outside their home country.[52]

Figure 7.2 provides a summary of the background and career factors which influence cross-cultural competence.

Personal strategies for managing across cultures

The traditional approach to preparing expatriates for international assignments focused on cultural briefings, language training, and "suggested" readings (How to do business in . . .). The implicit advice was "when in Rome do as the Romans do". That strategy is far less applicable today, since much of the cross-cultural contacts take place in yet another country or else on virtual territory (via satellites and video screens). Under these circumstances, the principle of "when in Rome . . ." becomes less meaningful.

Furthermore, with increasing exposure to other cultures, through media, travel, training and education, and through experience with international business ventures, familiarity with other cultures is growing. Thus it is not unlikely that each side has been prepared to adapt to the other.

Yet the degree of cultural familiarity may be asymmetrical. For example, a Malaysian may be more familiar with American culture than the American with Malaysian culture. Based on differences in the degree of familiarity with the other's culture, Weiss suggests different strategies in cross-cultural negotiations.[53] For example, using a go-between or third party is suggested when each party is unfamiliar with the other culture.

On the other hand, it may be possible to induce others to follow your "negotiating script" when they are more familiar with your culture than you are with theirs. Nevertheless when undertaking this strategy care should be taken to demonstrate that this approach is not taken out of ignorance of cultural differences (assuming that your way is universal) or from lack of respect for the other culture.

Another strategy is to embrace the other culture's way of doing things. This, however, requires high levels of familiarity, marked by language fluency and extensive experience with the other culture: being bilingual and bicultural. Finally, when both cultures are quite familiar with each other, there is more opportunity to create something better, beyond adapting to one or the other.[54]

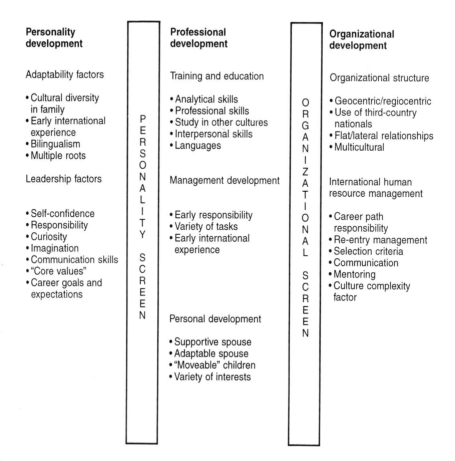

Figure 7.2 Creating cultural competence. (*Source*: K. de Vries and C. Mead (1991) "Identifying management talent for a pan-European environment", in S.G. Makridakis and associates, *Single Market Europe: Opportunities and challenges for business*, Jossey-Bass, New York. Copyright © 1991 Jossey-Bass Inc., Publishers.)

This allows something akin to jazz improvisation[55] wherein one musician picks up from where the other leaves off, leaving room for each party to display their virtuosity and even to go off in unexpected directions, based on personal interpretation. This requires that both parties know the score, the underlying structure of the music and key themes, and listen intently to be able to pick up from and build upon the contribution of the other.

Weiss also proposes criteria for selecting a culturally responsive strategy including its *feasibility* and *acceptability* in light of the manager's repertoire of behaviors and values, its *appropriateness* given the prevailing relationship and circumstances, and the need to insure *coherent interaction*.[56] For example, it may simply not be possible to behave as the other (kissing *à la russe* – on the lips of your counterpart) or to expect them to behave as you would (confronting conflict). Even if it were possible, behavior such as use of facilitating payments (bribes) may conflict with one's own value systems.

What is *appropriate* is determined by the nature of the relationship, notably the history of previous interactions and the balance of power. Appropriateness is also determined by the nature of the circumstances, such as timing constraints and the audience present. Highly public events and media attention may constrain the flexibility of those involved. In any event, the goal is to provide coherent interaction and to develop a viable relationship.

Familiarity can be increased by preparing cultural profiles, not only of the other culture, but also of one's own culture. In this way similarities can be identified which can serve as bridges to establish a common ground. Potential clashes due to differences can also be better anticipated and negotiated. While this can be done in advance, based on country-specific information and training, it needs to be modified in real time when faced with the actual people involved.

With the increasing international experience of individuals worldwide, managers can no longer assume that the person facing them will act in accordance with national norms. Many managers from around the world have been educated, or have spent a large amount of time, outside their home countries. Furthermore, they may be second or third generation immigrants, as in the case of the Chinese or Indian migration. Therefore, it is quite misleading to assume nationality based on name, physical appearance, or accent.

In addition, it is also risky to assume, for example, that American-born Chinese or UK-born Indians are the best suited to take on missions "back home". Although familiar with the culture and perhaps fluent in the language, the cultural identification of those managers born or educated abroad is not necessarily with the "homeland". Furthermore, the experiences and memories of their parents, or grandparents, may be far removed from the current realities. Nor are they immediately accepted by the local staff as there may be feelings of resentment for having had opportunities not available to the others (not to mention salaries that are often beyond their imagination).

It is also important to recognize that people belong to several cultures – professional or functional, corporate, or industry – as discussed in Chapter 3. Thus, creating a cultural profile of the other means focusing on the relevant dimensions of culture, not the specific national norms. This involves recognizing the visible cues of the relevant cultural dimensions, asking questions to discover core values and beliefs, and developing hypotheses regarding underlying assumptions as described in Chapter 2. Focusing on the cultural dimension relevant to the situation or issue at hand, rather than specific country norms, avoids the trap of stereotypes, encourages recognition of the individual apart from his or her national culture, and enhances the possibility of creating a shared culture for working together.

While creating cultural (not necessarily national) profiles provides an initial starting point, it must be recognized that the individuals involved, including oneself, may fall outside cultural norms (whether national or corporate). To further complicate matters, individuals may strongly adhere to certain cultural norms while being less wedded to others, as discussed by Mary-Yoko Brannen.[57] Which norms are relevant is a function of the situation or issue at hand. Thus according to the issue, different constellations of norms, and degrees of "normality" and "marginality" can be found.

Nevertheless, although you may consider yourself culturally marginal, for example less outgoing than your compatriots, the other may still see you as quite outgoing in comparison with their own behavior. The Johari window technique discussed in Chapter 1 can be useful as a tool for bringing to the surface and discussing these perceptions of cultural differences, and degrees of normality. It provides the opportunity for each party involved to come to grips with differences in perception of how we see us and how they see us, and to reduce the blind spots that can lead to cultural misunderstandings.

This technique can be revisited when confronted with key issues and situations. For example, in creating a new organization structure, it may be apparent that greater decentralization will require more delegation. While you may perceive your style to be highly participative, others may experience it to be fairly autocratic, particularly under pressure. Thus this technique can be used in an ongoing manner to provide feedback regarding your personal behavior, espoused values and beliefs, and underlying assumptions. In fact it was for this purpose that the Johari window was originally designed.

Furthermore, cultural interactions must not be regarded as static, but as evolving in a dynamic process. Borrowing Brannen's analogy,[58] rather than imagining this interaction as two billiard balls bouncing off of each other, one with the power to push aside the other, cultures interact and rub off on one another. Mutual adjustment evolves over time as the relationship develops.

As mentioned earlier, cultural interactions are no longer sequential, but simultaneous. This makes the above suggestions even more complicated to implement. It may be useful to consider how different people involved are likely to respond to the situation at hand, such as a corporate change effort or developing a new market strategy. For example, faced with a multicultural team, as will be elaborated upon in the next chapter, cultural differences regarding the task and process issues can be mapped.

Take a simple cultural artifact such as forms of address. If some members of the team prefer to be called "Herr Doktor" while others prefer "Joe", then it should be possible to use these forms of address, without assuming that one is trying to pull rank or that the other is behaving in an unprofessional manner. It is not that the behavior has to conform. Differentiated responses may even be more desirable as it encourages flexibility and learning.

What is necessary is that the other's behavior is no longer evaluated as good or bad as viewed through our own cultural filters. What is good or bad needs to be defined through discussion of the behavior, values and beliefs, and underlying assumptions considered necessary given the task at hand. It requires discussion and negotiation to arrive at an agreed upon way of working together, even if that means doing things differently (agreeing to disagree).

So where the conventional approach focuses on national culture, and the corresponding "do's and don't", the approach recommended here recognizes people as cultural composites. Here the focus becomes more personal, with different approaches to different people, and perhaps different approaches with the same person depending on the circumstances. As relationships evolve over time, international managers should be guided less by role and stereotype, and should become more attentive to the individual and the circumstance.

Triandis *et al.*[59] propose a model of managing workplace diversity that is useful, particularly given that cultural differences exist at home as well as abroad. They argue that perceived similarity creates greater interaction which, in turn, encourages greater perceived similarity. Several methods can be used to increase perceived similarity. For one, past history of conflict should be minimized (in Europe, for example, between the French and the English, and between the Germans and the Dutch). Secondly, perceived cultural distance can be reduced through learning about the other's culture and language. Perceived similarity is also greater when working with people from other cultures with whom one has common friends or colleagues (network overlap) and with whom one shares equal status. Furthermore, opportunities must be created for cross-cultural interactions that provide rewarding experiences such as achieving a shared goal. Of course, the relationship between perceived cultural similarity and interaction is further enhanced by non-ethnocentric attitudes, high task structure, and a society which encourages pluralism rather than homogeneity.

Easier said than done

Many of the recommendations regarding the handling of cultural diversity often sound like common sense: more recognition, more trust, more respect, more communication, more patience, more confrontation of differences. But the fact that the prescriptions are simple does not imply that they are easy. Recognizing and valuing cultural differences is fine in theory, but in practice remains elusive. For one, it means questioning our own ways of doing which can be perceived as a threat to our identity and autonomy. Many managers are concerned that managing cultural differences means adapting to the other culture and finding themselves lost at sea, without a point of reference.

That anxiety stems in part from a misconception about what it means to be an effective international manager. While recognition of cultural differences is vital, the cross-cultural message is not that managers need to accept everything about other cultures in order to be effective across borders. The idea is not to become some sort of cultural chameleon, receptive to every new view that comes along, and changing accordingly. As Evans puts it, "It is not a question of making some composite person. That would be the quickest way of making an individual into a schizophrenic".[60] At best, this would lead to "feeling at ease anywhere but belonging nowhere".[61]

Receptiveness to other cultures does not mean losing one's own values, as these provide the solid ground from which managers move forward. As Kets de Vries points out, "Truly global leaders need a set of core values that will guide them and provide support in whatever environment they may find themselves".[62] To be effective in a cross-cultural setting demands an ability to tap into one's roots when one is unsure. This provides a sense of who we are, a vital landmark when cultural differences seem overwhelming.

International managers have to consciously manage concerns regarding personal boundaries and control. They have to be sure of their own identity, to let others know where they stand. Having a strong sense of self is required to be able to acknowledge the identity of others. Having secure personal boundaries enables us to interact comfortably with others. Therefore, international managers need to have a strong sense of autonomy and control over their lives, to feel that they have freedom of choice in their actions and do not feel coerced. When this is the case, there is less sense of threat in allowing others autonomy and self-control, in other words, empowerment. With less fear of letting go, there is more opportunity for exposure to new experiences and new ideas, and a greater potential for learning.

The value of cross-cultural interactions, then, lies in learning new possibilities, new ways of thinking, new ways of behaving. While this experience is unlikely to change people's deep-seated assumptions, it can make them aware of what these might be and how they influence behavior. Far from leading to a loss of identity or individuality, contact with other cultures tends to make people more aware of themselves and their cultural heritage. To quote Kipling, "What know they of England, who only England know?".[63] Experience with other cultures leads to a better understanding of one's own culture. This in turn leads back to a better understanding of the other.

The challenge is to have the willingness to confront our own assumptions, to question them, and to hold on to the essential ones out of a sense of conviction rather than fear of something different. With that as an anchor, it becomes possible to share differences by creating openness and encouraging empathy, as well as to test them and disagree without destroying one's sense of self.[64] Cross-cultural recommendations may sound like little more than common sense but it takes considerable robustness, openness, and effort to see to it that common sense prevails.

Suggestions for managing differences

- Use a cultural-general approach – diagnose cultural dimensions not countries
- Avoid assuming differences or similarities where there are none. Seek similarities as well as differences
- Analyze different levels of culture: use multiple approaches of observation, questioning, and interpretation
- Recognize your own cultural profile. Anticipate clashes with others
- Recognize individual variance within your own culture as well as the other in terms of specific dimensions. You/they may be more or less "normal" on different dimensions
- Recognize that cultural interaction is not a static, but a dynamic process; look for rub-off effects and enjoy
- Depending on the degree of familiarity of each culture, use different strategies for interaction
- Confront concerns regarding identity and autonomy, both yours and theirs. People need to feel valued and not coerced.

Notes

1. Thubron, C. (1987) *Behind the Wall*, London: Penguin, p. 158 (as cited by Weiss, 1994).
2. "The elusive Euro-manager", *The Economist*, 1992 (November 7), 81.
3. Bartlett, C.A. and Ghoshal, S. (1992) "What is a global manager?", *Harvard Business Review*, September–October, 124–32.
4. Ouchi, W.G. and Jaeger, A.M. (1978) "Type Z organization: Stability in the midst of mobility", *Academy of Management Review*, 3(2), 305–41.
5. Tyler, A. (1985) *The Accidental Tourist*, New York: Knopf.

6. Barham, K. and Oates, D. (1991) *The International Manager,* London: The Economist Books.
7. Auteri, E. and Tesio, V. (1990) "The internationalization of management at FIAT", *Journal of Management Development,* 9(6), 6–16.
8. Barham, K. and Antal, A. (1994) "Competences for the pan-European manager' in P.S. Kirkbride (ed.) *Human Resource Management in Europe,* Ch. 14, London: Routledge, 222–41.
9. Black, J.S., Gregersen, H. and Mendenhall, M. (1992) *Global Assignments: Successfully Expatriating and Repatriating International Managers,* San Francisco: Jossey-Bass; Tung, R. (1988) *The New Expatriates: Managing Human Resources Abroad,* Cambridge, MA: Ballinger.
10. Cope, N. (1992) "In search of Euroman", *Management Today,* June, 50–3.
11. Johnson, M. (1993) "Doing le business", *Management Today,* February, 62–5.
12. Lysgaard, S. (1955) "Adjustment in a foreign society: Norwegian Fulbright grantees visiting the United States", *International Social Sciences Bulletin,* 7, 45–51.
13. Brett, J.M., Stroh, L.K. and Reilly, A.H. (1992) "Job transfer" in C. L. Cooper and I.T. Robinson (eds) *International Review of Industrial and Organizational Psychology,* Chichester: Wiley, pp. 93–138; Black *et al., Op. cit.*
14. Brislin, R.W. (1981) *Cross-cultural Encounters: Face-to-face Interaction,* New York: Pergamon Press.
15. Craig, J. (1979) *Culture Shock!,* Singapore: Times Books International.
16. Triandis, H.C., Kurowski, L.L. and Gelfand, M.J. (1994) "Workplace diversity" in H.C. Triandis, M.D. Dunnette and L.M. Hough (eds) *Handbook of Industrial and Organizational Psychology,* Vol. 4, Palo Alto: Consulting Psychologists Press, Ch. 16, 769–827.
17. Janssens, M. (1995) "Intercultural interaction: a burden on international managers?", *Journal of Organizational Behavior,* 16, 155–67.
18. Osland, J.S. (1995) *The Adventure of Working Abroad: Hero Tales from the Global Frontier,* San Francisco: Jossey Bass.
19. Black, J.S. and Gregersen, H. (1992) "Serving two masters: Managing dual allegiances", *Sloan Management Review,* Summer, 66–71.
20. La Palombara, J. and Blank, S. (1977) *Multinational Corporations in Comparative Perspective,* New York: The Conference Board, Report 725.
21. Kohls, L.R. (1979) *Survival Kit for Overseas Living,* Yarmouth, ME: Intercultural Press.
22. Hagerty, B. (1991) "Companies in Europe seeking executives who can cross borders in a single bound", *The Wall Street Journal,* January 25, p. B1.
23. Brein, M. and David, K.H. (1973) *Improving Cross-cultural Training and Measurement of Cross-cultural Learning,* Vol. 1, Denver: Center for Research and Education.
24. Borg, M. (1988) *International Transfers of Managers in Multinational Corporations,* Uppsala: Studia Oeconomiae Negotorum.
25. Lobel, S. (1990) "Global leadership competencies: Managing to a different drumbeat", *Human Resource Management,* 29(1), 39–47.
26. Frenkel-Brunswik, E. (1949) "Intolerance of ambiguity as an emotional and perceptual personality variable", *Journal of Personality,* 18, 108–43.
27. Schneider, S. and Powley, E. (1984) "Changing images: The case of AT&T", INSEAD case series.
28. Hagerty, *Op. cit.*
29. Staw, B.M., Sandelands, L. and Dutton, J.E. (1981) "Threat rigidity cycles in organizational behavior", *Administrative Science Quarterly,* 26, 501–24.
30. Ferraro, G.P. (1990) *The Cultural Dimension of International Business,* Englewood Cliffs, NJ: Prentice Hall.
31. Kets de Vries, M. and Mead, C. (1992) "Development of the global leader" in V. Pucik, N. Tichy and C. Barnett (eds) *Globalizing Management,* New York: John Wiley, 194–205.

32. Ratui, I. (1983) "Thinking internationally: A comparison of how international executives learn", *International Studies of Management and Organization*, XIII (1–2), 139–50, 144.
33. Ferrano, *Op. cit.*, p. 151.
34. Van Maanen, J. and Kunda, G. (1989), "Real feelings: Emotional expression and organizational culture", *Research in Organizational Behavior*, Vol. II, Greenwich, CT: JAI Press, 43–103.
35. Valeriani, R. (1979) *Travels With Henry*, Boston: Houghton Mifflin, 9.
36. Adler, N. and Bartholomew, S. (1992) "Managing globally competent people", *Academy of Management Executive*, 6(3), 52–65.
37. Reich, R. (1990) "Who is us?", *Harvard Business Review*, January–February, 53–64.
38. Rosenzweig, P.M. (1994) "The new 'American Challenge': Foreign multinationals in the United States", *California Management Review*, 36(3), 107–23.
39. Adler and Bartholomew, *Op. cit.*
40. Ghoshal, S. and Bartlett, C.A. (1990) "Matrix management: Not a structure, a frame of mind", *Harvard Business Review*, July–August, 138–45.
41. Barham and Antal, *Op. cit.*
42. Jacques, E. (1990) "In praise of hierarchy", *Harvard Business Review*, January–February, 127–33.
43. Kiyoi, M. (1995) "Dear English speakers: Please drop the dialects", *International Herald Tribune*, November 3, 9.
44. Bateson, M.C. (1994) *Peripheral Vision*, New York: Harper Collins.
45. "Les MBA font un retour en force", *Le Nouvel Economiste*, March 30, 1995, 66–7.
46. Evans, P.A.L. (1992) "Developing leaders and management development", *European Management Journal*, 10(1), 1–9.
47. Evans, P., Doz, Y. and Laurent, A. (eds) (1989) *Human Resource Management in International Firms*, London: Macmillan.
48. Barham and Antal, *Op. cit.*
49. Evans *et al.*, *Op. cit.*
50. Hagerty, *Op. cit.*
51. Beslu, E.-X. and de Vendeuil, R. (1991) "Cadres: Manager les différences", *L'Express*, December 19, 160–64.
52. Lorenz, C. (1993) "Here, there and everywhere", *Financial Times*, November 10, 11.
53. Weiss, S.E. (1994) "Negotiating with 'Romans' – Part 1", *Sloan Management Review*, Winter, 51–61.
54. *Ibid.*
55. Weick, K.E. (1995) "Improvisation as a mindset for organizing", Academy of Management Meetings, Vancouver, BC.
56. Weiss, S.E. (1994) "Negotiating with 'Romans' – Part 2', *Sloan Management Review*, Spring, 85–99.
57. Brannen, M.-Y. *Negotiating Cultural Change: Dynamics of Work Culture Formation in a Japanese Takeover*, Oxford: Oxford University Press, forthcoming.
58. *Ibid.*
59. Triandis *et al.*, *Op. cit.*
60. Wood, L. (1990) "The Euromanager: Is it a myth or a real Superman?", *Financial Times*, February 14, 16.
61. Osland, *Op. cit.*, p. 5.
62. Kets de Vries and Mead, *Op. cit.*, p. 193.
63. Kipling, R. (1987) "The English flag", quoted in *The Everyman Dictionary of Quotations and Proverbs*, London: Cathay Books.
64. Irene Rodgers, Personal communication.

CHAPTER EIGHT

The "multicultural" team

> When we sit together as Germans, Swiss, Americans, and Swedes, with many of us living, working, traveling in different places, the insights can be remarkable. But you have to force people into these situations. Mixing nationalities doesn't just happen.
>
> Percy Barnevik, CEO and President of Asea Brown Boveri[1]

Today, more and more companies are turning towards teams as a way of managing increasingly complex and dynamic environments. Teams are now seen as solutions to problems of external adaptation, responding to complexity by bringing together a variety of perspectives while responding to dynamic changes by encouraging teams to make decisions at the front line, where the action is.

Yet in order for teams to be effective, to provide successful solutions to problems of external adaptation, they need to find solutions to problems of internal integration. This means developing strategies for managing the team's primary task as well as its process. This is all the more difficult when team members hold different cultural assumptions about how teams should function.

Finding solutions to problems of internal integration requires a balance of individual and collective effort. The very idea of teams as a solution is now being promoted in highly individualist cultures, such as the United States. In fact, the use of team approaches, such as quality circles, contributed to the initial popularity of Japanese management techniques among Western managers. In other cultures, such as in eastern Europe where Communist ideology has promoted collectivism, the current emphasis is on increasing individualism, with the aim of encouraging entrepreneurship and personal initiative. Teamwork is disparaged due to its association with the old regime. Some consider it unfortunate that in the former Yugoslavia, well-known for its self-managing teams in the early 1970s, managers are not building upon or benefiting from this tradition.[2]

Nevertheless, teams are cropping up all over the map (as well as in cyberspace). And given the likely evolution of information and communication technologies, teams of the future may be found anywhere and anytime. For teams to become effective solutions in an international context, there has to be an appreciation of the impact of culture on receptiveness to teams, and its impact on all the ingredients that go into making them viable. For multicultural teams to deliver on the promise of better performance through diversity, there is a need to develop culturally appropriate strategies to manage the task as well as the process.

In solving these problems of external adaptation and internal integration, teams in effect, create their own culture. Over time group members come to share behavior, values and beliefs, and assumptions which may be more or less aligned with the dominant national or corporate culture. In fact, sometimes teams are created with the express purpose of violating corporate norms, and developing a counter-culture, such as skunk works, in order to develop new business ideas.

Why multicultural teams?

Increasingly, companies are promoting the practice of employees participating in multiple teams for multiple purposes. They are setting up greater numbers of temporary and permanent work groups – project teams, task forces, steering committees, commissions, and boards – designed to formulate or implement strategies. People drawn from different functions, units, and levels within the organization and from the outside are having to learn to work together.

For example, new product development teams may not only include representatives from different functions within the organization, but also may bring in customers and suppliers from the outside. Corporations are also pooling their expertise across national boundaries in the hope that this will lead to more successful marketing to different types of customers, as well as enhancing local commitment to strategic directions and facilitating implementation. These changes are bringing together people not only with different expertise and perspectives, but also different behavior, values, and beliefs, that is, cultures: national, functional, and corporate.

As boundaries within and between companies, industries, and countries are breaking down due to the competitive pressures and globalization of business activities, teams are becoming more and more multicultural. Managers may, in fact, find themselves, simultaneously, in many teams, in many places, at many times, among many different cultures, as shown in Table 8.1.

These transnational teams can contribute to what Paul Evans refers to as the organization's "glue technology"[3]: encouraging cohesiveness among otherwise independent, autonomous national subsidiaries and other business and functional units. Transnational teams also create *lateral networks* which can improve communication and information flow between subsidiaries and HQ and among subsidiaries.[4]

Transnational teams provide development opportunities for the team members to understand international issues better, and to appreciate better the interdependencies between units. These teams also provide the opportunity for managers and the organization to learn how to function effectively within different cultures, be it with suppliers,

Table 8.1   Types of transnational teams

Major types of transnational teams

---

1. Business development/product launch
   Team members of multiple nationalities responsible for developing or launching a product
   which has multinational sales potential

2. Regional headquarters
   Several nationalities, primarily from throughout a single region (e.g. Scandinavia, Asia Pacific),
   responsible for strategic coordination

3. Functional
   Team members of multiple nationalities working in a particular functional area (e.g. R&D,
   quality assurance)

4. International joint venture
   Two or more nationalities are represented in nearly equal proportions

5. Corporate headquarters
   A corporate-level team composed of multiple nationalities

Source: Adapted from C.C. Snow *et al.* (1993) "Types of transnational teams", from *Transnational Teams Resources Guide,* Transnational Teams Project, sponsored by ICEDR.

customers, or employees. They send an important message to the rest of the organization, and to outsiders, regarding career opportunities, thereby facilitating recruitment of local managers with high potential. Thus there may be wider strategic reasons for creating such teams: organizational integration, organizational learning, and managerial development.

Sometimes these transnational teams are multicultural as an inevitable consequence of drawing team members from different parts of the company, and from different countries. At other times, multicultural teams are designed as a deliberate attempt to promote better decision-making, and to encourage greater creativity and innovation. The payoff of multicultural teams is presumed to be in creating richer quality of decisions.

The benefit of using multicultural teams and utilizing their inherent diversity has intuitive appeal. Given the greater complexity and speed of change in the international business environment, it seems obvious that bringing together people with different cultural backgrounds will enhance the quality of decisions taken.[5] Given the greater uncertainty and ambiguity in decision-making, these cultural differences provide a greater range of perspectives and options. Cultural differences can also contribute to new ways of looking at old problems, creating the opportunity for greater creativity and innovation.

Multicultural groups can also help to minimize the risk of uniformity and pressures for conformity that can occur in groups where there are too many like-minded individuals.[6] Bringing together people with different cultural backgrounds is thought to be a good antidote. However, as Percy Barnevik, President and CEO of ABB, puts it,

> Multinational teams do not happen naturally – on the contrary, the human inclination
> is to stick to its own kind. If in selecting a manager the choice is between a compatriot

with a familiar background, and a foreigner whose credentials appear strange and whose language is difficult to understand, objective criteria tend to lose out.[7]

The very richness of this diversity makes the group dynamics much more complex. These differences can create interpersonal conflict and communication problems.[8] There is a greater potential for frustration and dissatisfaction, which can lead to higher turnover of team members. Thus despite the appeal and logic of teams, multicultural or otherwise, effective teamwork does not happen spontaneously. Teams have to actively manage their task and process to avoid lost investment of time and resources, missed opportunities, and disappointing outcomes, as indicated by the old saying which goes, "A camel is a horse designed by a committee".

Teams have been shown in the past to either enhance or impede productivity, and this is even more true for multicultural teams. Research seems to indicate that multicultural teams tend to perform either much better or much worse than monocultural teams.[9] Other evidence suggests that heterogeneous teams can outperform homogeneous ones.

Research conducted on group performance in the United Kingdom by Meredith Belbin indicates that teams composed of members with different profiles were more effective than teams made up of "star" performers (the best and the brightest), or with members having similar profiles. Teams which had included a mix of profiles such that there was a balance of roles performed better.[10] Preliminary evidence suggests that certain cultures have preference for different roles: the French for coming up with bright ideas, the Germans for structuring the task, and the Swedes for obtaining the necessary resources.[11] Thus the case for bringing together people with different profiles, personal or cultural, grows stronger.

Recent research has further demonstrated that, once settled, multicultural teams performed better than monocultural ones in "identifying problem perspectives" and "generating alternatives".[12] The problem is "how to get settled" or how to arrive at a common ground. Diverse groups have to confront differences in attitudes, values, behavior, experience, background, expectations, and even language. When team members have similar profiles, there appears to be less trouble in finding "a style of operation which suits all the members".[13]

Consider the following case. Three well-known, internationally sophisticated companies – IBM, Siemens, and Toshiba – decided to form a joint venture, Triad, in order to develop a computer chip.

> Siemens scientists were shocked to find Toshiba colleagues closing their eyes and seeming to sleep during meetings (a common practice for overworked Japanese managers when talk doesn't concern them). The Japanese, who normally work in big groups, found it painful to sit in small, individual offices and speak English . . . IBMers complained that the Germans plan too much and that the Japanese – who like to review ideas constantly – won't make clear decisions. Suspicions circulate that some researchers are withholding information from the group.[14]

The failure to address these cultural differences and to agree on task and process strategies can sabotage any group effort.[15] Sue Canney Davison labels this problem, the "rush to structure".[16] In an extensive study of multinational teams, she found that most newly

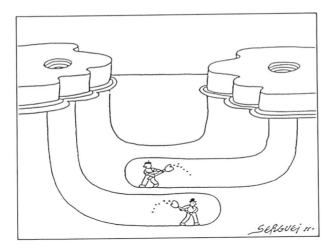

Figure 8.1   Making ends meet. (*Source*: *Le Monde*, 1985. Reproduced by permission of *Le Monde*; artist: Serguei.)

formed teams jumped straight into a discussion of the nuts and bolts of the task. They did not devote enough time to considering the interactive process through which the task is achieved: what patterns and style of communication are needed; how meetings are to be conducted, how relationships are built, and how decisions will be made. In neglecting to deal with these differences upfront, the teams in question were storing up problems for later on. "You have to start slowly and end faster; by starting too fast, you run the risk of not ending at all", as shown in Figure 8.1.[17]

Prescriptions for effective teams are easy to come by. Generally they recommend creating a common purpose, setting specific performance goals, having the right mix of skills (technical, problem-solving, and interpersonal), having the necessary external support and resources, establishing task and process strategies, and evaluating and providing feedback on team performance.[18]

But cultural differences are expressed in different expectations about the purpose of the team and how the team is supposed to operate. Some of these expectations are related to *task* strategies: how the task is structured, roles or who does what, and when, and how decisions will be made. Other expectations relate to *process* – team building, language, participation, ways of managing conflict, and team evaluation. These expectations have to be negotiated for both task and process. Table 8.2 below summarizes the task and process strategies, the underlying cultural assumptions, and the questions to ask in order to draw out the differences.

The purpose of Table 8.2 is not to provide a checklist or recipe but rather to stimulate discussion among team members. This framework should not be taken as comprehensive, as unsuspected cultural dimensions may well emerge en route. It does, nevertheless, provide a starting point.

The purpose of the ensuing discussion is to develop a shared strategy of how the team will work together. It provides the opportunity to surface cultural differences and to

Table 8.2   Strategies for managing multicultural teams

Task strategies	Cultural determinants
Creating a sense of purpose	
● What is the team's mission?	Task versus relationship
How explicit should this be?	Being versus doing
● What are the team's goals and objectives?	Hierarchy
To what extent can they be measured?	Individual versus collective
● Who should be a member?	High versus low context
● What are the team's priorities?	Monochronic versus polychronic
(Schedule? Budget? Quality?)	
Structuring the task	
● To what extent should agenda be structured?	Uncertainty avoidance
● To what extent should the "rules of the game" be clearly spelled	Monochronic versus polychronic
out?	High versus low context
● What needs to be accomplished? By whom?	
● How should time be managed?	
How important are deadlines?	
What happens if deadlines are not met?	
● How will work be divided? Then integrated?	
● What can be done together? Apart?	
Assigning roles and responsibilities	
● Who does what? Who is responsible for what?	Individual versus collective
● Should a leader be assigned?	Power and status
Based on what criteria?	Uncertainty and control
Competence? Interpersonal skills? Hierarchical position?	Task versus relationship
● What is the role of leader? To take decisions? Facilitate	
discussions? Obtain resources?	
● Who needs to attend meetings and when?	
Reaching decisions	
● How should decisions be made?	Individual versus collective
By vote? By consensus? By compromise?	High versus low context
● Who is expected to make the decision? The leader versus team?	Hierarchy

Process strategies	
Team building	
● How is trust developed?	Task versus relationship
● How much time for social activities?	Monochronic versus polychronic
	High versus low context
Choosing how to communicate	
● What is the working language? Who decides?	Power
● How to address imbalance in levels of fluency?	Individual versus collective
● What type of communication technology can be used?	High versus low context
● What is an effective presentation?	Monochronic versus polychronic
Eliciting participation	
● How can we ensure participation of all members?	Power
● To what extent are some members given more credibility than	Individual versus collective
others?	
● Does it appear that the input of some members is being ignored?	
● Who listens to whom?	
● Who interrupts who?	
Resolving conflict	
● How is conflict managed?	Task versus relationship
Avoided? Confronted?	Power
● Who accommodates whom? Is collaboration sought?	Individual versus collective
● To what extent do we compromise? Is negotiation seen as win/	
lose, lose/win or win/win?	
Evaluating performance	
● How and when to evaluate performance?	High versus low context
● Is evaluation a two-way process?	Power
● How direct can feedback be?	Individual versus collective

allow them to be discussed, rather than ignored, in the hope that they will go away. By putting cultural differences on the table rather than pushing them *under* the table, the potential problems can be anticipated and addressed and the potential opportunities can be brought to light.

Some of the cultural differences can be spotted in artifacts such as the use of titles and first or last names, the presence and form of meeting agendas, and the amount of social versus task activity engaged in. Beliefs and values elicited in these discussions indicate expectations regarding, for example, the roles of leaders and members and the structure of meetings (preferred degrees of hierarchy and formalization). Underlying assumptions regarding power, individualism, and time, among others, can then be interpreted. The rest of this chapter will explore in greater detail the different approaches to these strategies and the underlying cultural assumptions.

Task strategies

Creating a sense of purpose

One of the most important elements of successful teams is having a "shared sense of purpose". This purpose has to be developed within the team whether or not its mandate comes from on high. Often teams are formed with no clear idea of their rationale, other than it seemed like a good idea at the time. These groups quickly lose their motivation, unless able to turn the situation into one of defining their own reason for being. Yet creating a sense of shared purpose is not an easy task, particularly when first allegiances may be to functional, business, or country units. In addition, different cultures have different assumptions about the reason for teams: to share information and discuss problems, to make decisions and take actions, or to renew contact and build social relationships. This will determine issues such as the frequency of meetings and contacts, who should attend, whether the meetings can take place through conference calls or need to be face to face, and the time needed to be set aside expressly for socializing.

Take the example of an alliance among three companies, French, German, and Danish. A high-level working group met monthly to operationalize the intended goals of the alliance. The German and Danish managers came to the meetings expecting to negotiate decisions that would then be implemented. Thus they prepared seriously, arriving with a well-planned agenda, and making sure that decisions were duly noted in the minutes. They were annoyed at what they perceived as the lack of preparation, and the lack of focused discussion from their French counterparts. The French managers were in turn surprised, and amused, at the earnestness of the others. For the French, the working party was consultative; its purpose was to share information and make suggestions. Only the boss would eventually make decisions. This was never openly discussed, culminating in nine months of frustration.[19]

German managers are typically well-prepared for meetings, as they value technical competence and specialized expertise. British managers, given their more generalist perspective, may well have skimmed through the papers on the plane and may still be leafing through them during the meeting. Yet this will not prevent them from offering their point of view. These differences led to problems in one joint venture between a German and a British firm, where the German managers were systematically irritated by the uninformed questions of their British counterparts during meetings. The German managers tended to refrain from making comments when they did not have the relevant knowledge and had no desire to demonstrate their lack of knowledge by asking stupid questions. The British managers did not see the need to demonstrate technical competence or expertise and took the opportunity to ask naive questions which they saw as critical to providing the broader perspective.

For those cultures with strong informal networks, what goes on at the bar, over coffee, or during lunch may be as important as what is said in meetings. The real decisions are taken outside the meeting room. Thus the purpose of the meeting may be more to encourage and to assess members' willingness to implement the decision. This is particularly frustrating to those who expect that the purpose of the meeting is to arrive at decisions, not to confirm them. This may be the case of negotiating teams where the responsibility for decision-making is diffuse, and probably lies outside the team.

The perceived purpose of the team will determine "who needs to be involved". In task-oriented cultures, only those who are directly concerned, and with the appropriate knowledge and skills will be invited. The objective is to get the job done. In cultures where hierarchy is important, members may be assigned to teams because of their power and influence in the organization, rather than their knowledge *per se*. The presence of powerful members may signal the importance attached to the team, as well as the likelihood of a decision being made. The idea of team members being drawn from more or less the same hierarchical level, so as not to have any one member pull rank, would seem like a bizarre idea.

In relationship-oriented or collectivist cultures, more members are likely to be included, regardless of whether their knowledge is relevant to the task at hand. The purpose of the team is to create a sense of belonging, to reaffirm relationships, and to reinforce identification with the group. Being left out would create malaise, as it could be experienced as social ostracism.

Creating a sense of purpose not only means agreeing on what the group is expected to accomplish overall, but also "setting specific performance goals and objectives". Given the different expectations of the purpose of teams, these goals and objectives may differ. In fact, common prescriptions for making shared purpose explicit and setting precise goals and objectives can be taken as somewhat naive, if not impossible. In high-context cultures, the sense of purpose may be more implicit. Spelling it out, clearly articulating a vision, is seen as robbing it of some of its subtlety or sophistication. Purpose or vision is experienced more as a feeling, something more intuitive, rather than concrete and tangible.

Some members expect the purpose of the team to evolve over time, and as such cannot be agreed upon upfront, nor within a particular time frame. The latter approach would be viewed as limiting flexibility and stifling creativity. This reflects different notions of time. Where a monochronic view of time prevails, task strategies can be expected to be dealt with in a sequential way, within a limited time frame. But where time is seen as polychronic, the process is likely to be far more iterative, and the purpose of the team, or its objectives, can be revisited at any point in time. This is the problem with putting forth prescriptions, such as five steps to better team performance.

Insisting on precise performance goals and objectives may also be seen as too instrumental, too task-oriented, and insensitive to the individual member's needs, or the social needs of the group. Not enough time is devoted to relationship-building and developing a sense of rapport, including time for socializing. Furthermore, in cultures where there is low sense of control over the environment, setting performance objectives may be experienced with discomfort, as members feel that they are being held responsible for something over which they have no perceived control.

Furthermore, it is not obvious that team members share the same sense of priorities. For example, some members may feel that it is more important to achieve time deadlines, while others are more concerned with achieving higher quality despite possible delays. Constant reminders regarding cost targets may annoy those who feel that cost overruns may be necessary in order to achieve time or quality targets. These differences may be due to assumptions regarding time, as limited or expandable. It may also reflect different values regarding pragmatism, coming up with a solution that works rather than one that is "ideal".[20]

Structuring the task

Teams also have to decide on how they will structure the task: setting agendas, when and where to have meetings, what needs to be done by when, and who needs to do what.

Setting agendas

Setting agendas is one area where cultural differences can be a source of potential confusion and friction. Indeed cultures differ in expectation as to whether an agenda is set at all, or whether the flow of the meeting should take its own course.

In Germany, the *tagesordnung*, or agenda, plays a critical role. Statements and reports have been prepared which correspond to specific items on the agenda. Thus there is great reluctance to deviate from that agenda. This created problems in an American–German joint venture, frustrating one American manager, ". . . because there are all these associated issues that are getting behind and you are not quite sure whether they will ever come back to these issues or not".[21] This frustration was attributed to differences in the desire to reduce uncertainty, which is greater for Germans than for Americans.[22]

French managers, on the other hand, do not appreciate the systematic, one agenda item at a time, approach. They tend to advance discussion on several fronts at once, and prefer to consider all the issues together, as they may well be interrelated. This is liable to frustrate American managers who see time passing and no decisions being made on any particular agenda item. They may become restless sitting through what they perceive as "endless talk", and "going round in circles".

Consider the reactions of these two expatriates in a Franco–American merger.[23]

An American manager, who was visiting Paris for the first time was invited to a full-day meeting which began with a two hour presentation during which the 12 participants in the meeting spontaneously split into various sub-groups, which had separate, private clashing conversations about the topic at hand. Occasionally, someone was loud or interesting enough to get everyone quiet and have the full group listen – but not for long. There was tremendous debate, and people loudly challenged the ideas of other people. The American was shocked by the rudeness of the group and lack of courtesy towards the consultant. Several times, the American had tried to make a point, but no one would listen. The American left the meeting feeling quite frustrated.

A French expatriate, at his first American meeting, could not believe what was taking place. The clock seemed to control everything. The meeting began exactly at the time stated; there were no side conversations, and the leader of the meeting made sure that each agenda item was discussed at the time and for the duration the agenda had specified. Decisions were made, and people accepted "action items", the responsibility to take action based on the decisions made. For the most part, one person spoke at a time, and few ideas were challenged. One person even said, "Excuse me, please let me finish" when someone interrupted her! When it was all over, people left the room talking about what a productive meeting it had been. The French expatriate left the room feeling very confused and uncomfortable.

These reactions reveal different notions of time – monochronic or polychronic. In monochronic cultures, agenda items are expected to be dealt with systematically, decisions taken, deadlines respected, and one person speaks at a time. In polychronic cultures, rigid agendas are likely to be perceived as inhibiting creativity in meetings, deadlines serve more as guidelines than unalterable facts, and it is, on the whole, more acceptable for several people to talk at the same time without it being experienced as chaos.

These different views of time also lead to different notions of what is considered to be acceptable behavior in meetings. The polychronic manager may not instruct the secretary to hold calls or ask unscheduled visitors to wait outside. That would be inexcusably rude to friends or colleagues who are accustomed to dropping in unannounced. Similarly, polychronic managers may leave to make calls or attend to paperwork if the discussion is not immediately relevant to them. Monochronic participants get particularly irritated when meetings start late or overrun. Announcements for meetings in France often have a start-time specified but no end-time.

Another important cultural difference in setting agendas is *high* and *low context* – the degree to which things are spelled out versus inferred. German managers are often admired for their ability to structure meetings, and frequently use techniques such as Metaplan. However, they often frustrate others in their need to spell out all the details. This is also true of Americans. At an international management conference in Paris, American organizers both amused and annoyed the European audience by going over the conference sessions in detail, spelling out what was clearly already outlined in the conference program. They also went as far as to put in writing how the American participants were supposed to behave with an international audience.

Assigning roles and responsibilities

Teams also need to decide who is to do what. This means *assigning roles* and *responsibilities* within the team. In more individualistic cultures, team members often prefer a "go it alone" approach and are eager to split up the tasks so that everyone can go off and work on their own. Later on, the different pieces are expected to be integrated through group discussion, or indeed by one person taking responsibility for pulling it all together.

In more collectivist cultures, assigning individual responsibility seems somewhat strange. They expect the work of the group to be done together, interdependently. The idea that each goes off and does their own work independently makes no sense. Thus team members from collectivist cultures, having been assigned their part may go off and do nothing, much to the frustration of their counterparts from more individualist cultures. One frustrated Swedish expatriate manager in Hungary complained that team members did not seem to realize that reaching a decision in the meeting was not enough: something had to be done between meetings.

The very fact of working in a team is more appealing to some than to others. Rugged individualists tend to feel constrained by teams and have little patience when it comes to trying to understand the other's point of view, and having to reach consensus. Furthermore, they want to be rewarded for their individual effort and resent "free riders", those members of the group that do not pull their weight.

People from collectivist societies are more used to and comfortable working in a team, do not keep accounts of who did what, and are reluctant to assert their own ideas above the others. Rewarding individuals rather than the team is seen to destroy the harmony needed to sustain working relationships. Research on Chinese, American, and Israeli managers demonstrated that managers from more individualist cultures performed better working alone, whereas those from the collectivist cultures worked better when part of a group.[24]

The importance of taking individual initiative and personal responsibility, and being held accountable is stressed in cultures that are not only individualist, but also where there is perceived control over the environment. This is expressed in the belief that "The buck stops here", as championed by President Truman. If something goes wrong, Americans believe, they have only themselves to blame. Thus, they are often frustrated when trying to get managers from more collectivist cultures, notably in Asia or in eastern Europe, to take individual responsibility and to be held personally accountable. Why take responsibility for something over which they have no control?

When Americans readily take responsibility for an item on the agenda, for the Japanese this means that there are no mitigating circumstances. That person has to deliver, regardless. The Americans taking responsibility assume that this means giving it their best effort, but that if the situation is untenable, they expect to be absolved of that responsibility.[25]

The roles and responsibilities of team leaders and members also differ significantly between cultures. The preferred choice of team leader is clearly influenced by different cultural assumptions. For instance, in Germany the team leader must demonstrate technical competence to have credibility. In France or Italy, the team leader is chosen based on the power and political influence he or she holds with the organization.[26] Many prescriptions from American gurus stress the importance of choosing a team leader with good interpersonal skills and who can serve as a facilitator, particularly warning against choosing team leaders on the basis of narrow, task-specific knowledge or hierarchical position.[27]

In cultures where the hierarchy is important, the team leader is expected to chair the sessions and have the final word on any decisions. Latin Europeans expect strong control from the chair regarding the agenda and the discussion. French managers have difficulty believing that a group can make a decision; that is the boss's job. In more egalitarian cultures, team members may rotate chairing the meetings and decisions are expected to be arrived at through consensus. Roles and responsibilities among the members are expected to be shared. Nordic managers, for example, expect the chair to play more of a facilitation role.

In keeping with the need for structure, team leaders in Germany are expected to take a strong hand in running the meeting. Team members who signal their desire to contribute are duly noted, their names written down, and then taken in turn. In one German–American joint venture, the German participants were left feeling disoriented when the leader did not control and direct the flow. As Professor Heinz-Dieter Meyer puts it, "I have observed otherwise very articulate German managers reduced to silence in American-style meetings where the senior person did not play the orchestrating role".[28]

In keeping with the different notions of the role of a team leader, there are also different expectations of the role of team members. These differences are particularly noticeable during brainstorming sessions which rely on speaking out, challenging authority, and participating on equal terms in decision-making. These types of behavior are difficult in cultures where respect for age, titles, or authority is the norm. The assumption that members are on equal footing just does not hold.

Reaching decisions

Culture also influences how teams decide and on what basis decisions are taken: majority rule, consensus, or compromise. Reaching decisions by voting, or majority rule, may be seen as fundamental to the democratic process wherein individual opinions are represented. Voting rests on assumptions of egalitarianism, and individualism; everyone's vote counts equally. It neglects the role of voice and silence, and of power and influence.

When asking "All those in favor? All those opposed?", Americans often assume that silence means agreement. This approach also often neglects the formation of coalitions and the subtle pressures for conformity or willingness to go along with the group. Voting also creates winners and losers which may create problems in cultures where consensus is valued and saving face is more important.

There are also different ways of looking at consensus. Consensus can be seen as a way of synthesizing divergent views or gaining compliance for adoption of the best idea. On the other hand, consensus may be seen as a way of preserving social harmony rather than necessarily ensuring task integrity. One Danish manager complained, "Danish managers would rather have a consensus than a good decision. We can all agree and we can all be wrong".

In Japan, it would be unthinkable to put forward a proposal which did not already have universal approval. The "official" meeting is not a place for discussion, but rather the place for confirming consensus. All the spadework, *Nemawashi*, takes place in advance of the meeting, to avoid conflicts which would result in loss of face for the defeated party.[29]

However, reaching consensus may be time-consuming and does not necessarily guarantee the best solution. Research has demonstrated that better decisions are achieved through active debate among members representing conflicting alternatives.[30] In conflict avoiding cultures, this prescription would be difficult to follow.

Managers from the United States and Britain are likely to adopt an attitude of "let's split the difference" to satisfy individual interests. In this way they are more concerned with arriving at "what's fair" in order to promote team spirit and commitment to the solution. This may result in a compromise rather than in arriving at the best solution.

For the French, why go for a compromise if the perfect solution can be found? Decisions should be based on the best intellectual argument. Thus, compromise in Anglo cultures may be seen as a fair solution to divergent positions, but for the French it can also be interpreted as a suboptimal solution, even damaging to one's position. *Compromis* for the French signifies jeopardizing opportunities or plans.

The degree of explicitness, or high context versus low context also plays a role. In French meetings, a decision may well be made and understood, yet not be written down. Americans, who are used to a higher level of explicitness and formalization (more low context) may not recognize that any decision has been reached unless it is formally brought to the table (not "tabled" as the British would say, which for an American means postponed), voted on, and clearly noted in the minutes.

Thus multicultural groups have to actively negotiate the task strategies in order to arrive at a common approach to working together. They also have to explicitly negotiate process issues, which have more to do with the way members interact than with how the task is structured.

Process strategies

Building a team

When it comes to building teams, North American managers tend to have a more task-oriented, mechanistic view. As they see it, teams can be put together by assembling a group of individuals, setting the objective, oiling the wheels (a little socializing, some extra resources), and then expecting them to function effectively, or fixing them (exchanging parts) if they fail to do so. Team-building efforts, such as *Outward Bound*, are designed to demonstrate (to groups of rugged individualists) the need to cooperate in order to survive.

Following the merger of a British and French company, the members of the top management team flew to the middle of the Arabian desert. Upon arrival they found a jeep, a map, and a note from the president giving them one week to find their way to Riyadh. Having to survive together in the desert for one week was thought to be good preparation for planning company survival. The second week was spent in a luxury hotel, formulating strategy.[31]

Teams that perceive themselves as actively doing something together rather than coordinating information or expertise, work harder to integrate themselves and their activities.[32] However team building may create the sense of forced comradery. These efforts may be seen as manipulative, an instrumental use of relationships and may therefore backfire. These exercises may also be rejected, as they violate the line between professional and personal relationships. Thus making explicit attempts to create team identity (through artifacts such as T-shirts, slogans, and so forth) may run into resistance.

Consider the example of a French medical equipment maker, taken over by General Electric in 1988. GE decided to boost the morale of its new French employees by calling a training seminar for French and other European managers. In their hotel rooms, the company left colorful T-shirts emblazoned with the GE slogan "Go for One". A note urged the managers to wear the T-shirts "to show that you are members of the team". The French managers wore them, grudgingly, to the seminar, but as one of them recalled, ". . . forcing us to wear uniforms . . . was humiliating".[33]

Team-building exercises are also designed to establish trust. Trust is thought to develop faster where teams are exposed to moderate risk and team members have to learn to rely on one another for support.[34] For this reason, companies will sometimes deliberately understaff transnational teams. This forces team members to cooperate in order to make up for the missing person(s).

Yet while trust is considered universally important, it is built up and sustained in different ways. Americans tend to trust first until proven wrong. For Germans the reverse is generally the case. "Americans operate by a 'extend good will unless you have reason to distrust' rule, while Germans operate by the opposite *caveat emptor* [buyer beware] rule: 'distrust until you have reason to trust'."[35]

Americans build trust by being friendly and informal. The Germans build trust by proving competence and demonstrating technical knowledge. This may result in Germans creating various "tests". As an American project leader of an American–German joint venture described,

> Now the interesting phenomenon is that of our seven or eight issues, all of which [they considered as] blocks to proceed forward, in the next meeting were never mentioned again . . . [It was a] process of checking us out. [At later meetings] a good half dozen [of] what I would call "tester red herrings" just came out of left field. Once again, about half of them I already knew the answers and knew . . . that they were not issues.[36]

In Germany, trust is based on a person's integrity and predictability: delivering on promises, honesty, dependability, and punctuality. If a task is not going to be completed by a promised date, the deadline must be renegotiated in advance to let people make arrangements. This reflects the high task orientation. In more relationship-oriented cultures, what counts is the person's integrity and predictabilty in relation to other people: care, concern, and support. Furthermore, not meeting a deadline is not considered to be critical and will not necessarily lead to a loss of trust where time is more elastic (polychronic), and words and statements are taken less literally (high context).

Building trust is further complicated by problems communicating across cultures. Misunderstandings can often occur in situations where trust is low. Disagreement and suspicion may therefore be magnified out of all proportion. The misunderstanding serves as additional proof of lack of trustworthiness. There is no benefit of the doubt.

People get hung up on a word and it flies up into a huge event, and becomes a focus for all sorts of displaced anger and frustration – a bit like domestic quarrels caused by leaving the lid off the toothpaste.[37]

Choosing how to communicate

How teams talk reveals and influences team dynamics. In her study of cross-functional teams in one US company (3M), Professor Anne Donnelon used sociolinguistics to recognize and interpret patterns in team dynamics.[38] She argued that teams do their work through language and that the work they do is conversation. The ways in which teams "talk" creates thoughts and feelings, enhancing or inhibiting relationships, problem-solving, and learning. "Team talk" also reveals how issues of identity, interdependence, power, social distance, conflict, and negotiation are managed. Thus being able to decipher language and communication patterns is extremely important to negotiating strategies for working together.

One of the first items to agree on is the working language. The choice of language may cause friction, especially if the team is a bicultural one, perhaps the product of a joint venture or cross-border merger. One Franco–Swedish team decided to adopt English as the working language. While this seemed like a reasonable compromise, the French managers' mastery of English was considerably weaker than that of the Swedes. Thus the French felt at a disadvantage.

Choice of language can create "winners or losers" as language dominance is often synonymous with power and influence.[39]

A story is told of an American, whose company had been acquired, present for the first time at a meeting of the strategic committee. One board member suggests they speak in English as a courtesy to the guest. CEO changes his mind saying "Gentlemen, this meeting is going to be in Italian". It was a brutal impact. That man must have understood next to nothing . . . "Wrong, [said another manager hearing the story]. He understood that he'd been bought."[40]

Teams have to guard against vesting all the power in managers from the host country, from the parent company, or in members with the same mother tongue. Assumptions of power, however, are particularly difficult to address directly and language may be used, consciously or not, as a way of keeping power. Even power-sharing discourse in dominant cultures is often undermined by subtle colonial or imperialist world-views. It is easy to talk about empowerment or bringing issues into the open as long as it is in English. The very fact that English has become the *lingua franca* of business reinforces this power issue. Thus anglophones, those most likely to preach empowerment or to favor brainstorming, tend to dominate group discussion ignoring that the differences in ability to speak English create an unequal playing field, as shown in Figure 8.2.

Efforts can be made to render the issue less emotional by insisting that the language chosen does not belong to a particular clique, but represents the best solution, given the composition of the team and the levels of fluency. At the very least, care must be taken to establish a process which addresses any imbalance created by language fluency.[41]

"Look, everyone here loves vanilla, right? So let's start there."

Figure 8.2 We all speak English? (Reproduced by permission of the Cartoonists and Writers Syndicate; artist: P. Steiner.)

Paul Orleman, manager of the global training and development team at Rhône-Poulenc Rorer, a French–American joint venture in pharmaceuticals, offers the following advice,[42]

> We make several rules for participants: speak slowly; ask for clarification at any point; and if anyone gets too frustrated in trying to make a point in English, the participant can revert to his or her native language and someone will translate. Though rarely used, this "native language safety valve" has proved helpful on several occasions.
>
> Even if there is no one to translate, the switch to native language releases pressure and frustration; and other participants often learn something about the individual's "true personality". There is often an amazing transformation in body language, tone of voice, facial expression and confidence when someone switches to his/her native language.

It is also useful to summarize, paraphrase, and keep a visual record. Leaders of multicultural groups have to learn to rephrase questions in a number of ways to continuously monitor that everyone understands the same thing by what is being said and agreed. A more low-context approach may be necessary, as it cannot be assumed that people can read between the lines, or will understand the allusions and *sous-entendus* (implied meaning) of another culture.

It may even require a symbolic gesture of giving up something precious by the team leader, such as the mother tongue. This, however, is quite difficult to do, particularly as it means giving up a major source of power and a significant sense of competence. This clearly becomes more difficult in some cultures than others, for example in the United Kingdom and in France, where the sophisticated use of language is highly regarded, and taken as a sign of competence.

Aside from language fluency, patterns of language also differ. Use of silence for example is under-appreciated by Americans despite the motto, "Silence is golden". These differences were strikingly confirmed on one international management course where executives from five nations were thrown together for five weeks (Michigan Leadership Program).[43] In the initial meetings, the Americans tended to jump in and grab control, while the Japanese preferred to wait and listen.

The Americans later found out that the Japanese have a saying which goes, "He who speaks first at a meeting is a dumb ass". Sobered by this implication, the Americans decided to give the Japanese more chance to talk by introducing a two-second rule: when someone else stops talking, wait two seconds before speaking to give others a chance. Furthermore, the Japanese adopted the sporting time-out signal in order to request a break for explanations when the language became too confusing.

Language facility and how free people feel to speak up or interrupt greatly affect people's participation. Japanese managers value silence and measure their words carefully before uttering them. As one Japanese MBA student put it, "The Western communication style is like a tennis match whereas the Japanese communication style is like bowling. The participants in bowling do not face one another, and can choose their own pace".[44]

In southeast Asia and some Scandinavian cultures the norm is not to interrupt, but even to leave an appreciative silence between utterances. Interrupting is considered to be rude. Research comparing negotiations in Japan, United States, and Brazil found that Brazilian negotiators interrupt each other twice as often as either the Americans or the Japanese.[45]

Language, or syntax, to some extent determines the possibility of interruption. For example, since English has the subject, verb, and object at the beginning of the sentence it is easier for Anglo–Saxons to interrupt one another as they can guess the ending. This is not the case for German which has the verb, tense, and necessary degree of respect all at the end of the sentence. You have to wait until the end to get the full meaning.[46]

Increasingly, the issue of ongoing communication among team members involves use of technologies such as groupware, electronic and voice mail, teleconferencing, and fax machines. These technologies have significantly facilitated communication among team members in different geographic locations. Groupware enables team members to brainstorm ideas without having to meet face to face, to participate more actively, and to overcome problems related to group pressures and language difficulties. Electronic mail and faxes make time zones irrelevant, and teleconferences come close to providing the richness of face-to-face meetings. However, these technologies can never hope to capture the full range of sensory information, feelings, and context. According to one senior product development manager, "All things considered, the most effective communication, especially in the beginning of a project, is a handshake across a table to build mutual trust and confidence. Then and only then can the electronics be really effective".[47]

Furthermore, these tools cannot be considered as culturally neutral and can be expected to be met with varying degrees of receptiveness. For example, communication by e-mail tends to be more direct (low context) and impersonal, without the subtlety or diplomacy, or indications of status, necessary in some cultures. As one senior British manager with ICI complained,

I hate e-mail. I think it is intrusive. I feel emotionally aggravated by it. I am a bit status conscious and e-mail is so bloody egalitarian. I suspect it is also because my surname begins with a T and I always find myself near the bottom of the list. It irritates me and it is so impersonal. It does not say, "Dear Peter, . . . Regards, so and so". It comes spitting out with some code at the front, and some code at the bottom.

Or again, consider the case of teleconferencing. According to advice given to teams by O'Hara-Devereaux and Johansen in their recent book *Global Work*, "The agenda should be time-blocked with decision points clearly identified so that people will be prepared for both the allotted time per activity as well as when and how they will be asked to make a decision".[48] One can imagine that team members more from polychronic cultures might not feel comfortable with such a tightly scheduled agenda and be less disciplined about sticking to such protocols.

Embedded in the use of teleconferencing are cultural assumptions regarding trust and the nature of truth. As one German engineer with considerable experience in the use of this technology explained,

I am never sure that my colleagues at the other end will not tape me, to use my own words against me. I know it is silly, because I am not scared of being taped on the phone, but videoconferencing meetings still create many more formal commitments than a simple phone call.[49]

To be useful, these technologies must be accepted by team members. Therefore, multi-cultural teams must discuss and negotiate which technologies will be used, as well as when and how they are to be used, while providing flexibility to take into account the cultural differences in communication.

Eliciting participation

Given differences in how language is used and in language fluency, efforts to elicit participation need specific attention. Unless a conscious effort is made to integrate the diverse contributions, the very reason for its presence is undermined and the experience only serves to reinforce the idea that diversity does not add value. Thus, some restraint of dominant members and encouragement of quieter members may well be needed. More insidious is the experience of "token" foreigners, where the individual is listened to but rarely heard, as shown in Figure 8.3.

Making sure that all members are heard, that their views are properly aired and considered requires sensitivity and courage. This is needed to identify and confront underlying differences and prejudices that exclude certain team members. This means not just listening to, but also acknowledging their contribution. Too often, the foreigner, whether the only American in a group of French managers or the only French manager in a group of Britons, feels ignored.

Sometimes cultural differences are interpreted as "personality problems". A team member may be considered difficult or sabotaging group efforts (perhaps by remaining silent or by forcefully arguing their point of view) when that person is merely responding to a different set of cultural norms. The person is then treated as a deviant and ignored, or

"That's an excellent suggestion, Miss Triggs. Perhaps one of
the men here would like to suggest it."

Figure 8.3 Speaking out. (*Source*: *Punch*, 8 January 1988; artist: Duncan.)

is pressured to conform, thus losing his/her potential contribution. Furthermore, in blaming the individual, one fails to critique the situation, where the dominance of one culture over the others, or the nature of the interaction, may be discouraging participation.

Meaningful participation does not mean that everyone has to speak the same amount. A person may speak only occasionally and yet regularly come up with crucial input. Meaningful participation means that everyone has helped move the team forward, in their own way. In fact, the team can define upfront the very meaning of "meaningful participation", and how to ensure it. Multicultural teams should not fall into the trap of trying to force contributions. Team members may be more comfortable discussing issues on a one-to-one basis, than bringing them forward in a team meeting.[50]

In Finland, for example, many things get said in the sauna that are not said in more formal meetings. This may mean structuring meetings so that there are more opportunities for people to speak among themselves or to contribute on a more personal basis as public statements may cause discomfort. The assumption that what goes on in the meeting is all that counts, paying little attention to social occasions or corridor talk, restricts valuable input.

Using techniques such as brainstorming or teleconferencing to encourage participation may, in fact, prove counter-productive. Brainstorming works against people who do not master the language or who have different participation norms. And however difficult it is to understand other team members face to face, teleconferences will only make it worse.

One HR executive from Digital Equipment suggests distributing colored cards and asking everyone to write their ideas regarding a certain issue, such as their objectives for the team. Cards are then placed on a board, grouped by themes, and then periodically reviewed.

Resolving conflict

For teams to function effectively they need to establish mechanisms or ways of resolving conflict. This presents a problem for multicultural teams, given different norms for managing conflict. Modes of conflict resolution have been classified according to degrees of assertiveness and cooperativeness: competing, collaborating, compromising, accommodating, and avoiding.[51] While this model acknowledges differences in personal styles, cultural patterns tend to be ignored.

Gladwin and Walter[52] recommend different modes given the situation such that the importance of the stakes involved and power should determine degree of assertiveness, while the nature of the relationship and interests will determine cooperativeness, as shown in Figure 8.4. Here, cultural dimensions are relevant in attitudes towards power, individual versus mutual gain, and in what is considered to be important (stakes).

For example, in individualist countries where power is unequally distributed, such as France, conflict is likely to be managed through *avoidance* (referred up the hierarchy) and then *confrontation*, or force. This often provokes a violent reaction or counterforce, like strikes. One French HR director insisted that the word "conflict" not be used in a seminar on managing cross-functional teams because, "Once you get to conflict there's no return. It's finished". In countries like Sweden, where power is supposed to be shared equally and where there is more concern for relationships and mutual gain, conflict is more likely to be resolved through *collaboration*.

Accommodation is likely in cultures which are relationship-oriented and where interests are perceived or defined as mutual. Also when perceived power is low, the subordinate expects (and is expected) to submit to the boss. Accommodation also rests on the notion of interdependence and mutual obligation – the need for parties to take care of

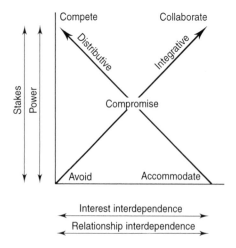

Figure 8.4   Resolving conflicts. (*Source:* T.N. Gladwin and I. Walter (1979) *Multinationals under Fire*, John Wiley, New York. Copyright © 1979. Reprinted by permission of John Wiley & Sons Inc.)

each other as in the case of the buyer–seller relationship in Japan where the buyer is obliged to take care of the seller (*amae*).

Avoidance of conflict, as mentioned earlier in the case of France, may also be used when power is low, where little hope for mutual gain is perceived, or where there is little interest in pursuing a relationship. Avoidance can also be a powerful tactic. In negotiations, Japanese managers know that if they keep silent long enough, the Americans will finally agree. However, avoidance is also common in countries where it is of utmost importance to maintain relationships by saving face. Japanese avoid conflict in public in order to preserve relationships as well as to maintain maximum flexibility in satisfying mutual obligations.[53]

Thus individualist cultures are more likely to push for or assert their own ideas. The assumption is that conflict of interests is inherent in negotiations. In such cultures, negotiations are seen as a zero-sum game, with a winner and a loser (distributive versus integrative). As the "pie" (or amount of resources available) is perceived as fixed, the prime concern is to gain as much of that pie as possible. This goal takes priority over building up the relationships. Thus they put more stake in winning and therefore come to the negotiation table armed with unassailable arguments to support their case.

One research study found that in negotiations Americans were satisfied with less pie equally split, while Japanese found ways of increasing the size of the pie, but were less concerned with the idea that it should be equally shared.[54] Team members from collective cultures are more likely to look for mutual gain (integrative), to focus on building and maintaining the relationship, and to come to the table in a "humble", not assertive, posture. This should not be confused with weakness.

Avoiding rather than confronting conflict may thus preserve team harmony and the leader's authority. One team leader from India explained that due to his culture he could live with more ambiguity and did not feel the need to resolve everything at meetings. This did not go down well with American and British team members, who wanted more clarity and sense of direction. He, however, did not want to bring conflict to a head by clarifying different viewpoints and actively resolving differences. In his culture it was not polite to do so. He complained that the Americans (both women) were quite aggressive in their positions, not tolerant of other views, tended to polarize the issues, and then wanted to "fight them out". He was also fed up with the Anglo need to vote on everything. For him, ambiguity served to buffer conflict, and was his way of keeping the power in making decisions later on. This had worked for him in previous assignments in India and Mexico, where differences in power are expected and accepted.

Clearly, unresolved cultural differences can create conflict and can have a significant negative impact on the team by closing off communication channels, wasting group energy, and creating excessive amounts of turnover. But too little conflict is not necessarily a good sign either. It may mean that the cultural differences are being ignored or suppressed rather than exploited, and that minority views have succumbed to the dominant majority. This can result in complacency and the inappropriate use of routine approaches to address new problems. A certain amount of "constructive tension" is therefore desirable.

Evaluating performance

To ensure effectiveness, teams have to evaluate their progress continuously, both in terms of task and process. Furthermore, it is necessary to provide opportunities to reflect and learn as a team.[55] This requires setting aside time to evaluate how the team and its members are doing, to discuss the dynamics and resolve the differences. While not easy to do in any culture, some cultures are more prepared to give and receive feedback than others. This makes the process of evaluating performance a potential cultural minefield.

When a group or team member seems to be having problems, American managers believe in direct intervention. As they see it, problems can be put right by designing processes and providing a forum in which individuals can articulate their needs, clarify their expectations, and resolve their differences. Americans, given the heterogeneous nature of their culture, find it necessary to deal with differences by confronting them and working them out. This, incidentally, tends to be our own bias, which is more or less implicit throughout this book! In Japan, given its homogeneous nature, differences tend to be smoothed over, thus preserving harmony. Being different is a threat in Japan; in the United States it is a given, something to be managed, or overcome.

Even the boss may expect and even request constructive feedback from subordinates as well as peers, as in the practice of 360 degree feedback favored by many multinational companies, such as Pepsi International.[56] In Latin European countries which are more attached to hierarchy, such as France, the thought of the team giving feedback to the leader, and the leader accepting it, is difficult to imagine.

In Britain, where communication is less direct (more low context) than in America, critical feedback is likely to be veiled or couched in humor.[57] Thus, in a multicultural context, the message is likely to be lost. In many Asian countries, feedback is less direct still, and may occur outside the workplace altogether, certainly not in a team meeting. Differences will be dealt with in private, often through the informal network. In Japan, team members may be able to address issues while drinking together after hours.

It is necessary therefore to agree upon ways of giving feedback and discussing the group's interaction. For example, one team used three simple learning styles: red (action-oriented), green (people-oriented), and blue (ideas-oriented). This made it possible to suggest to one team member that he might like to be less red and become more green. He, being Chinese, was able to take the suggestions without losing face.[58]

Multicultural teams have to find ways of describing and bringing differences to the surface in ways that are not personally threatening. Learning about cultural dimensions which are relevant to their working together provides team members with a vocabulary to talk about their differences, and a tool for understanding critical incidents within the group.

For instance, one multicultural team of MBA students, having just learned the notion of polychronic versus monochronic time (discussed above) teased an Italian student who turned up late to their next session for "being polychronic". This served to mark his "violation" of team norms without attacking him personally. Rather than getting annoyed with the particular individual, his colleagues gave him the "benefit of the doubt" by ascribing his lateness to cultural programming. However, care must be taken that differences do not get used as excuses for justifying one's own or others' behavior, and become non-negotiable.

Reweaving differences: Joseph's coat

Multicultural teams are now a fact of organizational life. Rather than worrying about whether a multicultural team is better than a monocultural one, the focus should be on how these teams can best work together, acknowledging differences, negotiating interaction process, and reweaving the differences to create, like Joseph, "a coat of many colors".

Discussing cultural differences, however, is a high-risk activity for the team since all sorts of value-laden preferences and prejudices are exposed. This requires high levels of sensitivity, trust, and a real commitment to integration. The differences have to be identified, discussed and channeled, rather than accommodated, absorbed or ignored. Sometimes, according to one HR manager in a French–American company, this means that if these differences are truly integrated, everyone ends up feeling somewhat uncomfortable, as they have had to give up some of their taken-for-granted assumptions. High-performing transnational teams are those, however, that risk identifying their differences to create more intricate and colorful patterns of interaction.

The problem is that the differences are not always apparent or accepted. For example, while it may be readily acknowledged and accepted that marketing has a different perspective from manufacturing, differences between organizational members due to nationality, ethnicity, or gender may be less obvious or well-accepted – "After all, we all work for the same company".[59] On the other hand, cultural differences may be observed, but misinterpreted. For example, polychronic behavior (talking or doing several things simultaneously), if not understood, can be taken as "rude".

Multicultural teams must be willing to identify, and negotiate differences in expectations regarding the task strategies and the processes of interaction. The aim is not to neutralize differences, but to build on them. Embracing diversity is not the same as containing it. If differences are not recognized or discussed, they cannot be valued or utilized, and can become a handicap when we pretend that they do not exist. The promise of multicultural teams lies in *using* differences, not just living with them.

When individuals in a group share a common culture, be it national, corporate, or professional, the solutions to the problems which emerge, may be more spontaneous, requiring less conscious effort, than when members come from different cultures. Some argue that cross-functional teams are more difficult to manage than cross-national teams or that the problems in joint-venture teams are more due to corporate than national culture. Regardless of which cultural differences are in play, the solutions that evolve from the different cultural assumptions of the individual members become part of the cultural legacy of that group.

The team culture which emerges needs to preserve rather than homogenize the differences in order to reap their benefits. It makes no sense to bring together people from different backgrounds, for the very purpose of capturing differences in expertise and perspective, and then trying to make everyone look alike, think alike, talk alike, and act alike. This is the real risk of relying on corporate culture or professional cultures to override culture differences. The issue, therefore, is not whether differences in national culture are more important than funtional culture, but rather to understand what these differences *are* and to develop a team culture which builds upon them.

From her study of cross-functional teams, Donnelon concludes that,

> The tension of team work occurs *within teams* as they grapple with the dilemma of how to integrate their differences, *within individuals* as they try to adjust to being team members, and *within organizations* as they shift about to make sense of, and room for, teams as a new form of professional work.[60]

Managing this tension requires creating conditions of both security and challenge.[61] Conditions of security refer to the need for members to feel safe in order to disclose their own ideas and opinions, and to challenge those of others. This can be helped by acknowledging differences, respecting uniqueness, recognizing competence, affirming mutual goals, and ensuring shared status.

Conditions of challenge, on the other hand, require a different set of efforts, aimed at provoking diversity. These include actively seeking out alternative views, building in a procedure for critique, and ensuring that all members participate in meaningful ways. Teams with divergent views require more time to establish working relationships and to gain confidence with the decision-making process. A supportive climate is necessary for constructive controversy.

A vital tool for achieving this is humor. Humor both fosters a sense of belonging as well as providing a channel through which individuals can challenge group norms without seriously threatening group cohesiveness. Humor serves as a means of putting the cultural differences "on the table" and making them discussable. The level of shared humor within a group therefore serves as a kind of barometer of team integration. Shared laughter is a concrete sign that a group is creating an identity for itself, and that the individuals are becoming a team. The team's independent existence is marked by the creation of its own jokes, jesters, and external "fools".

Teams reinforce their norms and values by what they laugh at. Mocking the red tape within the company or the lack of resources at their disposal, is a way for teams to forge a sense of joint purpose. Jokes based on shared experiences and setbacks are invented and become the exclusive property of the team. This kind of humor may not be very amusing to outsiders, but it is very powerful to those inside. It derives its humor from the specific relationship between the people who were there at the time. It is, in fact, meaningful only to them. This creates a sense of community. "If team members have reached a high level of emotional security and can laugh, joke, question and play devil's advocate with each other while completing the task, then they have done well."[62]

Successful multicultural teams are those which have found ways of integrating the contribution of their members, and have learned to find solutions that add value *due* to their diversity not in spite of it. They have also learned to have fun, to experience the discovery of cultural differences as opportunities for surprise, learning, and shared laughter.

Questions to ask

Task strategies

What is the purpose, process, and timing of meetings?
To what extent does the mission need to be made clear and explicit?
Is it more important to achieve cost targets or are cost overruns OK given time/quality targets?
What does "on time" mean?
What is the priority of time?
What are the importance and priority of deadlines?
Is it more important to achieve time deadlines, or to delay for higher quality?
What do we do about missed commitments?
To what extent does the agenda need to be clearly structured and followed?
To what extent do the rules of the game need to be spelled out?
To what extent do roles and responsibilities need to be formalized and written?
Who needs to attend, when?
What is the role of the leader? Of team members?
How will the tasks be divided up and then integrated?
What work can be done together or apart?
What technologies can be used (videoconferencing, e-mail)?
What is an effective presentation?
What is needed to be convincing: facts and figures, philosophy, feelings?
How will information be passed? To whom? When? Formally or informally? Within the team or outside?
How, where and when do we make decisions? Consensus, majority rule, compromise?

Process strategies

How will we manage relationships – dive right into business versus take time to socialize?
To what extent will we socialize together, and when?
What is trust and how is it earned?
How will we address people? First/last name? Titles?
How formal or informal will we be?
What language(s) will we use?
How will differences in language fluency be managed?
To what extent does participation reflect potential contributions?
Who dominates?
Who listens to whom?
Who talks to whom?
How are interruptions managed?
How is conflict managed? Forcing, accommodating, avoiding, collaborating, compromising?
How is negotiation viewed? Win/lose, or win/win?
How is feedback provided? Face to face, third party, direct?

Suggestions for managers

- Ask each team member: For you, what are the characteristics of an effective team? An ineffective team?
- Build a "code of conduct" or "team charter" which defines task and process guidelines.
- Periodically assess "reality" against the charter.
- Use a facilitator who can debrief re: levels of participation, domination, approach to conflict.
- To ensure participation, use diverse approaches: Metaplan, paired discussions, round robin/round-table discussions (asking for input from each participant).
- Prepare/provide a written cultural brief, summarizing aspects of each culture represented on the team.
- Use scientific method (e.g. TQM tools) for pro–con analysis, problem definition.
- Ask each team member to identify a surprise they have experienced working with another culture, a challenge and how they resolved it.
- Provide training for the team in cultural dimensions which gives a framework and language for discussing differences.
- After a meeting, ask participants from each culture how the meeting would have been different if all participants were from their own culture.
- Ask each person to describe their "vision of success" for the team. What will the output be? What will the process for producing it look like?

Source: Paul Orleman, HR manager, Rhône-Poulenc Rorer

Notes

1. Taylor, W. (1991) "The logic of global business: An interview with ABB's Percy Barnevik", *Harvard Business Review*, March–April, 91–105, 95.
2. Professor Slavica Singer, University of Osijek, Croatia, personal communication.
3. Evans, P. (1992) "Management development as glue technology", *Human Resource Planning*, 15(1), 85–106.
4. Ghoshal, S., Korine, H. and Szulanski, G. (1994) "Interunit communications in multinational corporations", *Management Science*, 40(1), 96–110.
5. McLeod, P.L. and Lobel, S.A. (1992) "The effects of ethnic diversity on idea generation in small groups", *Proceedings of the Annual Academy of Management Meetings*, 227–31; Maznevski, M.L. (1994) "Understanding our differences: Performance in decision making groups with diverse members", *Human Relations*, 47(5), 531–52; Kirchmeyer, C. and McLellan, J. (1991) "Capitalizing on ethnic diversity: An approach to managing the diverse workgroups of the 1990's", *Canadian Journal of Administrative Sciences*, 8(2), 72–8.
6. Janis, I.L. (1971) *Victims of Groupthink*, Boston, MA: Houghton Mifflin.
7. Barnevik, P. (1994) "Making local heroes international", *Financial Times*, January 17, 8.
8. Cox, T. (1991) 'The multicultural organization", *Academy of Management Executive*, 5(2), 34–47.
9. Adler, N. (1991) *International Dimensions of Organizational Behavior*, Boston: Kent Publishing Company, 135.

10. Belbin, R.M. (1981) *Management Teams*, London: Heinemann.
11. Haberstrom, N., INSEAD presentation.
12. Watson, W.E., Kumar, K. and Michaelsen, L.K. (1993) "Cultural diversity's impact on interaction process and performance: Comparing homogeneous and diverse task groups", *The Academy of Management Journal*, 36(3), 590–602.
13. Belbin, *Op. cit.*
14. Browning, E.S. (1994) "Side by side . . .", *Wall Street Journal*, May 3.
15. Gersick, C.G. (1988) "Time and transition in work groups: Towards a new map of group development", *Academy of Management Journal*, 31(1), 9–41.
16. Snow, C.C., Canney Davison, S., Hambrick, D.C. and Snell, S.A. (1993) *Transnational Teams – A Learning Resource Guide*, ICEDR Report, 30.
17. Canney Davison, S., Snow, C., Snell, S. and Hambrick, D. (1993) *Creating High Performing Transnational Teams: Processes, Phases and Pitfalls*, ICEDR Report, 122.
18. Hackman, J.R. (1987) "The design of work teams" in J.W. Lorsch (ed.) *Handbook of Organizational Behavior*, New York: Prentice Hall, 315–41; Gladstein, D.L. (1984) "Groups in context: a model of task group effectiveness', *Administrative Science Quarterly*, 29, 499–517.
19. Evans, P.A.L. (1993) "Dosing the glue: Applying human resource technology to build the global organization" in *Research in Personnel and Human Resources Management*, Supplement 3, Greenwich, CT: JAI Press, 21–54.
20. Orleman, P., Personal communication.
21. Meyer, H.-D. (1993) "The cultural gap in long-term international work groups: A German–American case study", *European Management Journal*, 11(1), 93–101.
22. *Ibid.*
23. Orleman, P.A. (1992) "The global corporation: Managing across cultures", Masters Thesis, University of Pennsylvania.
24. Earley, P.C. (1993) "East meets West meets Mideast: Further explorations of collectivistic and individualistic Work Groups", *Academy of Management Journal*, (36)2, 319–48.
25. "Doing business in Japan", Video produced by the Japan Society: New York.
26. Canney Davison *et al.*, *Op. cit.*, p. 125.
27. Altier, W.J. (1986) "Task forces: an effective management tool", *Sloan Management Review*, Spring, 69–76.
28. Meyer, *Op. cit.*, p. 100.
29. Black, J.S. and Mendenhall, M. (1993) "Resolving conflicts with the Japanese: Mission impossible?", *Sloan Management Review*, Spring, 49–59.
30. Schweiger, D.M., Sandberg, W.R. and Rechner, P.L. (1989) "Experiential effects of dialectical inquiry, devil's advocacy, and consensus approaches to strategic decision making", *Academy of Management Journal*, 32, 745–72.
31. Evans, *Op. cit.*
32. Canney Davison *et al.*, *Op. cit.*
33. Nelson, M. and Browning, E.S. (1990) "GE's culture turns sour at French unit", *Wall Street Journal*, July 31, 4.
34. Snow *et al.*, *Op. cit.*, p. 22.
35. Meyer, *Op. cit.*, p. 98.
36. *Ibid.*, p. 96.
37. Irene Rodgers, Personal communication.
38. Donnelon, A. (1996) *Team Talk*, Boston: Harvard Business School Press.
39. Canney Davison, S. (1994) "Creating a high performance international team", *Journal of Management Development*, 13(2), 81–90.
40. Botti, H. (1992) "The internationalization paradox in Parodi: A research tale", *Scandinavian Journal of Management*, 8(2), 85–112, 106.
41. Canney Davison (1994), *Op. cit.*
42. Orleman, *Op. cit.*, p. 30.

43. Main, J. (1989) "How 21 men got global in 35 days", *Fortune*, June 11, 57–60.
44. Yasuyuki Inoue, "Searching for synergy effects from cultural diversity", INSEAD MBA thesis, 9.
45. Graham, J.L. (1985) "The influence of culture on business negotiations", *Journal of International Business Studies*, XVI(1), 81–96.
46. Canney Davison (1994), *Op. cit.*
47. De Meyer, A. (1991) "Tech talk: How managers are stimulating global R&D communication", *Sloan Management Review*, Spring, 49–58.
48. O'Hara-Devereaux, M. and Johansen, R. (1994) *Global Work: Bridging Distance, Culture, and Time*, San Francisco: Jossey-Bass, 127.
49. De Meyer, *Op. cit.*, p. 56.
50. Canney Davison, S., Personal communication.
51. Thomas, K. (1976) "Conflict and conflict management" in M. Dunnette (ed.) *Handbook of Industrial and Organizational Psychology* Chicago: Rand McNally, 889–935.
52. Gladwin, T.N. and Walter, I. (1980) *Multinationals Under Fire*, New York: John Wiley.
53. Black and Mendenhall, *Op. cit.*
54. Graham, J.L. and Sano, Y. (1989) *Smart Bargaining: Doing Business With the Japanese*, New York: Harper & Row.
55. Canney Davison *et al.* (1993), *Op. cit.*
56. Fulkerson, J.R. and Schuler, R.S. (1992) "Managing worldwide diversity at Pepsi-Cola International" in S.E. Jackson (ed.) *Diversity in the Workplace*, New York: Guilford Press.
57. Barsoux, J.-L. (1993) *Funny Business: Humour, Management, and Business Culture*, London: Cassell.
58. Canney Davison (1994), *Op. cit.*, p. 133.
59. Maznevski, *Op. cit.*
60. Donnelon, *Op. cit.*
61. Kirchmeyer and McLellan, *Op. cit.*
62. Canney Davison *et al.* (1993), *Op. cit.* p.135.

CHAPTER NINE

The "global" organization

A company is made of [people] with different backgrounds, different cultures, different inclinations, different aspirations . . . different jobs . . . All of these [people] . . . of different ages and cultures, with different jobs, have to produce the miracle of their own striving together so that the company's balance sheet can be good. Today and tomorrow.

Giovanni Agnelli, retired CEO, Fiat

So far in Part III of this book we have looked at how individuals and teams manage cultural differences. In Chapter 7 we asked: How do individual managers react to cultural differences? What does it take to be an effective international manager, whether at home or abroad? Where can those competencies be found and how can they be developed?

In Chapter 8 we considered the *raison d'être* of multicultural teams. We explored cultural differences in how teams function, both in terms of task and process strategies. We also provided a set of questions to guide teams in thinking through how to manage these cultural differences, so that different perspectives can be captured to fulfill the promise of enhanced effectiveness and greater innovation and creativity.

We now address the question of how organizations manage cultural differences. What are the best strategies? What does it take to become an international, or truly global, company and how can organizations actually go about doing it?

We start by considering three basic organizational strategies for managing cultural differences: ignore, minimize, or utilize. These strategies, discussed more or less explicitly by international management scholars, are embedded in the nature of relationships between headquarters and subsidiaries, which often correspond to different stages of internationalization. These strategies also drive the way in which multinational companies manage the often conflicting demands for global integration and local responsiveness.

For example, relationships between headquarters and subsidiaries have been classified by Heenan and Perlmutter[1] according to the degree to which they are ethnocentric, polycentric, regiocentric, or geocentric. Where the relationship between HQ and subsidiaries is **ethnocentric**, all policies and procedures come from the top (HQ decides what and how). Where the relationship is **polycentric**, how policies and procedures are implemented is determined locally (HQ decides what, locals decide how). In the case of **regiocentric** relationships, regional HQ serves as a buffer, negotiating between home country HQ and host country subsidiaries in a particular region, for example northeast Asia, Latin America, or central and eastern Europe. Where a **geocentric** relationship prevails, policies and procedures, the *whats* and the *hows*, are developed with input from both HQ and subsidiaries, as well as across subsidiaries.

These different approaches tend to evolve over time as multinationals develop their activities abroad. Many companies start with an ethnocentric approach, and move to a polycentric one when they realize that the local product standards, markets, or rules of the game are very different. The regiocentric approach evolves in response to needs to rationalize or to better coordinate business activities among countries in a particular region. Many companies today are moving to a geocentric approach, such as worldwide product divisions or business units, in efforts to become more global. Paradoxically, creating global business or product divisions may appear to be a return to an ethnocentric approach, as was the case when one American multinational moved its European regional headquarters from London to New Jersey (USA).

According to management scholars Prahalad and Doz[2] and Bartlett and Ghoshal,[3] multinationals have to manage between the often conflicting demands for local responsiveness, global integration, as well as searching for ways to stimulate innovation and learning. Innovations, for example, can be developed by HQ and then diffused to local subsidiaries (global for local), developed by subsidiaries for the local market (local for local), or diffused to the wider organization (local for global). Given these options, relationships between headquarters and subsidiaries can be better differentiated in order to satisfy these demands.

Strategies for managing cultural differences

Underlying these different approaches to managing multinational companies are different strategies for managing cultural differences. Embedded in them are assumptions of culture as irrelevant, as a problem or threat, or as an opportunity for learning and innovation, and as a source of competitive advantage as shown in Table 9.1.

Professor Nancy Adler[4] of McGill University asked a group of organization development (OD) consultants in Montreal to what extent cultural differences between francophone and anglophone Canadians were important to their work. Two-thirds reported that culture was not an issue. Of those that acknowledged its impact, only 1 out of 60 described it as having a positive impact. Based on further research and experience, she argues that the most common approach is to ignore differences. It remains difficult to find companies that use cultural differences as a source of competitive advantage.

These strategies – ignore, minimize, utilize – have implications for relationships between headquarters and subsidiaries, as well as for managing the conflicting demands for global integration, local responsiveness, and organizational innovation and learning as discussed above. We recognize that many companies use several strategies simultaneously, and that the examples are not entirely pure. Nevertheless, we do think it

Table 9.1   Strategies for managing cultural differences

	Ignore	Minimize	Utilize
Assumptions: culture as			
	Irrelevant	A problem/threat	An opportunity A source of competitive advantage
Headquarter/subsidiary relationships:			
	Ethnocentric	Polycentric/regiocentric	Geocentric
Expected benefit:			
	Standardization Global integration	Localization Responsiveness	Innovation and learning
Performance criteria:			
	Efficiency	Adaptability	Synergy
Communication:			
	Top down	Top down Bottom up reporting	All channels
Major challenge:			
	Gaining acceptance	Achieving coherence	Leveraging differences
Major concern:			
	Inflexibility Missed opportunities	Fragmentation Duplication of effort and loss of potential synergy	Confusion Friction

is important for companies to question the extent to which they are achieving their aspirations to become more international or truly global. We encourage companies with global aspirations to recognize their implicit strategies for managing cultural differences and to challenge themselves as to whether they are not missing opportunities for creating competitive advantage.

Ignoring cultural differences: business is business

When companies choose to *ignore* cultural differences, they are operating on the assumption that business is business, and that managers, engineers, or bankers are the same throughout the world. They assume convergence in management practice due to economic and technological development, a universal desire for modernization, and the diffusion of professionalism through management education and management consultancy.

For these companies, policies and practices developed in the home country are considered to be readily transferable. And host country subsidiaries are expected to apply them to the letter. This, they argue, is necessary in order to maintain product quality, to uphold customer service and technological standards, and ensure that the corporate culture is shared by all employees. Such companies may even create their own training centers or universities to inculcate the necessary management practices and behavior, core beliefs and values. While compliance may be achieved at the surface level of behavior and espoused values and beliefs,[5] it is not evident that underlying assumptions are truly shared.

Perhaps due to their strong belief in universalism, American companies, such as MacDonalds, Disney, and IBM, provide the best examples of this approach. At the level of artifacts and behavior, this can be seen in insistence on uniform dress codes and standardized procedures. For example, some say that you used to be able to spot an IBM manager anywhere in the world by the way they are dressed (as penguins: dark suits, white shirts, and narrow ties) and the way they make presentations. Conformity with the rules of behavior, spoken or not, was expected. Breaking the rules could result in being derailed from one's career track, or being sent to a distant location for "time out".[6]

One of the commandments at IBM is "Thou shalt not drink alcohol during the working day". IBM insists that no alcohol be served in the company dining room, even in France and Germany where wine and beer are considered to be an integral part of the meal. After much deliberation, IBM France was finally allowed to serve alcohol, but IBM's European HQ, right next door, was not.

Another example is the insistence of Disney executives, when they landed in Europe, on the same dress codes for employees as in the United States and Japan: minimal make-up, short nails with no colored polish, earrings no larger than the size of a franc (none for the men), no more than one ring per hand, no dark stockings for women, and neither long hair nor beards for men, all spelled out in a nine-page document. Disney even put a shower scene in a video shown to potential recruits to get across the message that Disney cast members must show up "fresh and clean every day" upholding the "squeaky clean" image of Disney.[7] This created quite an uproar among French employees who brought their displeasure to court.

While personal appearance and dress codes are understandable for cast members "on stage" (in the park), these policies also apply to office workers, managers included. One Irish MBA stated that she did not mind the dress code as it coincided with her own style (not surprisingly), but she did resent being told what she had to wear.

Even customers ("guests") are expected to behave properly. They are reminded that they cannot eat while waiting in line for attractions, that they cannot bring food into the park, and that they must keep their shirts on even when temperatures reach 40°C (105°F). The responsibility for crowd control lies not only with the unobtrusive security force but also with the sweepers. While Disney controls the entire "cast", the cast in turn, control the "guests".[8] The painstaking attention to and use of language ("cast", "on stage", "guests") is another indication of the extent to which shared artifacts and conformity in behavior are expected.

Standardized procedures may also be held sacrosanct. MacDonald's Hamburger University insists on split-second timing of hamburger flipping and service delivery and holds contests to encourage this spirit. Standards of cleanliness are scrupulously upheld. Potatoes for french fries have to meet certain taste and size requirements to ensure product standards. This meant shipping in potatoes from the United States to Russia where the local potatoes were too small – at least until they were able to source them from "nearby" Holland.[9]

While many customers appreciate the consistency in quality, service, and cleanliness of MacDonalds worldwide, local adaptation is not totally ruled out. While the golden arches remain clearly visible, MacDonald's now serves beer and wine in Europe as well as adapting the menu to local tastes. Even Disney has now allowed alcohol beverages to be served within the park, at sit-down restaurants.

Although these companies may make concessions to satisfy customers, they are often less willing to adapt to satisfy employees. Local adaptation is only made under duress. The prevailing attitude of headquarters to subsidiaries is one of "universalism", the idea being that there is one best way; and "ethnocentrism", that what has been tried and tested at home will work best in the local country. Paradoxically, according to Nancy Adler, this universalist view of business is actually quite "parochial".[10]

There are, of course, examples of successful MNCs which have not paid much attention to cultural differences. Here managers do not see much evidence that culture makes a difference, or at least not one worth worrying about. In fact competitive advantage may be perceived as derived from standardized ways of operating worldwide. This may be particularly true in industries which are engineering-driven, such as oil or construction, or rely on high technology, such as telecommunications. Indeed, many multinational companies may seek to hire accounting firms which promise to use the same standards and procedures worldwide. Even Disney found out that their Japanese partner wanted Disneyland Tokyo to be "just like America".[11]

The assumption of "one best way" means that management practices just require fine-tuning for optimal effectiveness. A study of eight foreign acquisitions of US firms found that while cultural differences were easy to identify, they did not seem to have important operational consequences. Problems were more readily attributed to contextual, structural, and political factors. Sensitivity to cultural differences and willingness to deal with related problems were considered important only insofar as they improved mutual respect and communication. This finding led to recommendations to follow the golden (universal) rules: finding the right strategy and structure, the right amount of interpersonal sensitivity and communications, limiting politics, and preserving managerial autonomy.[12]

Cultural differences may indeed represent convenient excuses for failure to make an effort on other fronts. For instance, cultural problems are easily invoked to explain failed mergers, when the business merits of the merger may have been doubtful in the first place. Invoking culture as the reason for failed mergers is like invoking communication problems for failed marriages. There is a need to dig more deeply to understand what are the underlying problems and how culture may play an important part.

Nevertheless, failure to consider the potential consequences of cultural differences when implementing policies and procedures abroad can prove costly. Although the debate continues as to whether the problems of Disneyland in Europe are cultural, strategic, or financial, one Disney executive reckoned that the company could have saved millions of dollars had they taken cultural differences into consideration *before* rather than *after* the set-up. This is a familiar lament among managers that have been sent to set up operations abroad.

Minimizing cultural differences

Another strategy for managing cultural differences is to try to *minimize* its impact. This approach recognizes cultural differences as important, but mainly as a source of problems or threats to efficient and effective operations. Trying to minimize cultural differences means finding ways of homogenizing them, creating sameness, or of isolating them, creating segregation, in order to reduce potential conflict. This can be done by developing a "global" corporate culture or allowing autonomy while relying on rigorous sytems of reporting and financial control.

These companies assume that a strong corporate culture can be created to serve as a melting pot to reduce the impact of the different national cultures. Or they assume that they can allow subsidiaries to "do their own thing" (polycentric approach) as long as they deliver results. However, it is difficult to implement standardized systems and procedures or to create a global corporate culture that does not reflect the head-office national practices and culture, and thus may resemble an ethnocentric approach. For this reason, these global corporate practices, systems, and values are often resisted.

Creating a global corporate culture – the melting pot

Percy Barnevik, the Swedish CEO of ABB, argues that when trying to integrate international operations, adopting the corporate culture of any single nationality will create problems. He has therefore worked round the clock (and around the world) to develop a global corporate culture for all members of ABB. English was chosen as the common language, although it is the mother tongue of only a minority of its 218,000 employees. A sophisticated management information system, called Abacus, is used to keep its 1,300 separate companies and 5,000 profit centers in line. Corporate conversion relies on "the bible" (policy manual), and on the charisma of Percy Barnevik, who spends a large part of his time on the road, giving speeches to the masses, and handpicking his devoted followers. In the case of ABB, the culture bearer is clearly the CEO, which creates some concern for what will happen after he is gone.[13]

Integration is achieved by global business leaders in charge of teams of local managers who are, in turn, held responsible for day-to-day operations, also known as the "business strategist and global optimizer". He or she decides which factories make what, which export markets to serve, and how to pool expertise and research, as well as tracking the 60–70 most talented managers.[14] Furthermore, an "elite cadre of 500 global managers, a Praetorian Guard" is responsible for carrying the corporate practices and culture around the globe. Headquarters in Zürich is limited to under 200 people (from 19 different countries). Nevertheless, Barnevik has also recognized the importance of local cultures. According to his philosophy, the way to manage a complex global company is by making it simple and local, "[In Norway] We must be a Norwegian company to work effectively in many businesses . . . This means that ABB Norway is a Norwegian company with a Norwegian CEO". In these ways, ABB tries to manage the demands for global integration and local responsiveness.

Other companies chose to assign senior management from the parent company culture to head up the local subsidiary, someone that has been sufficiently "socialized" to serve as a *cultural transfer agent*, the official bearer and custodian of the head-office culture.[15] This is often the European approach, which relies more on behavioral control that is normative (based on shared norms and values) rather than on reporting control, which is considered more calculative and coercive.[16]

Parent company executives may frequently visit subsidiaries and meet with local managers to discuss how things are going, using personal contact to resolve problems and to help get things on line. Local managers may also be invited to spend some time at "home", headquarters, to become familiar with the parent's policies and procedures as well as to immerse themselves in the preferred behavior and values.

For example, when Electrolux acquired Zanussi, Swedish board members visited Zanussi's headquarters in Pordenone for two days once every two months, to review activities and progress, to tour the facilities, and to engage in preplanned meetings with Zanussi's top management.[17] This type of headquarter–subsidiary relationship, often found in Swedish multinationals, is referred to as "mother–daughter" as it is built on trust and information sharing, visits and involvement, and ultimately partnership.[18]

Many Japanese companies try to minimize the influence of local cultural differences by combining frequent personal interaction between head office and expatriate Japanese with strong socialization practices for locals. Subsidiary heads, mostly Japanese nationals, remain in close contact with headquarters, making frequent trips back (sometimes monthly), as it is vital to keep informed and to maintain the network of contacts in order to get things done. Local nationals are carefully screened to match desired company values and behavior. Local workers receive intensive training not only in work techniques but also in philosophy, and are then often sent to Japan to observe and experience the Japanese way of doing things.

However, many non-Japanese managers, even those who speak fluent Japanese, are not able to develop the necessary personal network and, according to their Japanese counterparts, would never really be able to understand the Japanese way of doing things. This was the justification given by Matsushita for sending over 700 Japanese expatriates on 4–8 year assignments. According to one Matsushita expatriate, "This communication role . . . almost always requires a manager from the parent company. Even if a local manager speaks Japanese, he would not have the long experience that is needed to build relationships and understand our management processes".[19] In 1982, when Matsushita president Yamashita launched "Operation Localization", three Americans were named among the six US company presidents reporting to the Japanese CEO of MECA (Matsushita Corp. of America in New York City). But it was not until 1994 that Matsushita finally appointed an American to head up its American subsidiary.

While these approaches take into account national cultural differences, they aim to assimilate these differences into an overriding corporate culture. This, according to Giovanni Agnelli, former CEO of Fiat, requires ". . . the ability to deal with and manage cultural differences relating to other national contexts, without invalidating the values expressed by the company's own individual culture".[20] Thus the corporate culture is assumed to remain paramount.

Efforts to create a strong corporate culture in order to reduce cultural differences often meet with resistance because the parent company culture (which is often embedded in the national culture) remains dominant. This results in local managers feeling like minorities in their own countries. Even when the company culture is concocted in a melting pot, national cultural differences tend to be absorbed, not utilized. Thus differences may add some spice, but risk losing their distinctive flavor.

Separate but equal – cultural segregation

Another way of minimizing the impact of culture is to isolate the different cultures, thus avoiding clashes. This approach reflects a polycentric approach to headquarter–subsidiary relations; each local company has the autonomy to make operating decisions, to do as it sees fit, provided targets are met. In other words, the parent company determines what has to be done, and the local subsidiary is free to figure out how. This is often the case when foreign business is important due to historical or strategic reasons. Strategy formulation is centralized, while strategy implementation is a local decision.

The case of Royal Dutch Shell provides a good example:

> The principle of decentralization and autonomy to local operating companies has been Shell's basic organizational philosophy for the last 40 years. Thus Shell Oil is an independent U.S. company, while Deutsche Shell in Germany is expected to function as a German firm. Nevertheless, Shell functions as an integrated group . . . .
>
> As Lo Van Wachem, the former chairman of the group, is reputed to have said: "There are three things that hold this group of autonomous companies together. The first is the common logo, the Shell pecten and the values of quality that this represents. The second is common financial system – the rationale behind the performance evaluations is the same for all operating companies. And the third and most important source of cohesion is management development – close attention to common training principles and particularly to career management".[21]

While the above approach utilizes corporate culture – the logo and management development – to homogenize operations, it also relies heavily on frequent and extensive reporting of targets, figures, and sales forecasts. Compliance with systems and procedures is stressed. And any missed target quickly sets off warning bells.

The same is true at Matsushita. In addition to heavy doses of socialization to fortify the corporate culture and clear targets set by headquarters Japanese expatriates are then sent out to achieve their mission.

> Although parent company units set detailed sales and profits targets for their overseas subsidiaries, local managers were told they had complete autonomy on how to achieve the targets. [However] failure to meet targets [means] forfeited freedom: "Losses show bad health and invite many doctors from Japan who provide advice and support".[22]

The use of standardized and sophisticated reporting procedures and systems is also common among American multinational companies. European managers in US companies often complain that they spend most of their time gathering information for head office and that they are judged solely on results without concern for local conditions.

They also complain that this leads to an obsession with numbers and to short-term thinking.

Indeed European MNCs often provide the best examples of a "multidomestic" (or polycentric) business approach for historical reasons (notably two world wars and several economic recessions) and because of different national technical standards and market requirements. Michael Porter[23] argues that most European business, German pharmaceuticals being an exception, is still very local and is therefore more sensitive to local needs and better at delegating decisions to local management. As a result, European companies tend to do well in businesses that are not very global but depend on local responsiveness. This has resulted in national organizations having a high degree of autonomy, including the possibility of saying "no" to their parents.

The Dutch electronics company, Philips, is a case in point.[24] Founded in 1892, the strategic decision to focus on light bulbs led Philips to expand abroad as early as 1899. External historical events further strengthened the power of national subsidiaries at Philips. All this was compounded by country-specific conditions relating to different technical standards, such as television standards, and to differences in market demand, which required greater local responsiveness.

Unfortunately, this led to too many local princes protecting their fiefdoms. It had serious consequences for implementing company-wide strategy, such as getting innovative technology to markets. For example, in the 1980s, the North American subsidiary refused to adopt the Philips video recorder (V2000), although it was considered technically superior. They opted instead for the rival Japanese (JVC) model, the VHS, stating that they had to take into account the interests of their shareholders. It took nearly two decades of trying to "tilt the matrix" – for example, by creating international production centers (IPCs) – before Philips was finally able to move, in 1987, to four worldwide product divisions (geocentric).

While the polycentric approach acknowledges cultural differences and allows local firms to do it their way, encouraging pluralism, many firms are finding this approach costly and are discovering a greater need for regional integration and rationalization. This is particularly evident now in Europe in light of the Single European Market, which allows for a greater flow of goods, capital, and people across borders of the now fifteen member states. This has stimulated a search for a pan-European approach.

For example, with the aim of improving pan-European logistics, companies such as Philips, and Jacobs Suchard, the Swiss chocolate company, are rationalizing factories. Indeed, more and more independent local (national) units are being drawn into the web of integration. Nevertheless, some consumer companies continue to segment product lines and marketing approaches within Europe to accommodate cultural differences between the north and south.[25]

Creating a buffer

In order to balance the need for global integration while remaining sensitive to local conditions, many MNCs have created regional headquarters (regiocentric approach). Regional headquarters help to improve coordination between national organizations and to seek out potential synergies between them. Regional headquarters also help to reconcile local responsiveness and global integration by mediating between local conditions and global strategic directives from headquarters. The idea is to provide a "buffer" between national units and head-office cultures. Functions such as marketing and HRM, where local sensitivity is often considered more important, may be delegated to the regional level, while finance and R&D may remain centralized at headquarters.

Honeywell, as early as the 1970s, created a regional headquarters for Europe as previous efforts to coordinate national organizations had failed. In addition, they created vice-president positions for different regions within Europe, Centers of Excellence responsible for pan-European business, and the European Policy Committee. Another committee, the HR Advisory Board, took up the challenge of developing a corporate culture campaign to find the *ONE* in *HONEYWELL*. Starting with the one-page list of "Honeywell Principles", they turned into a colorful booklet which was translated into several languages.

Despite these efforts, many European senior managers complained that the regional headquarters was "too American". In particular the marketing and HRM functions which were being run by Americans were not considered sufficiently sensitive to the different local market and labor conditions. It was not until 1986 that European headquarters had its first non-American President.[26]

While models with a regional headquarters may provide a balance of local responsiveness and global integration, this proves a difficult juggling act, often creating tensions and dilemmas. Often regional headquarters are set up as a step towards a geocentric, or global organization, for example, on the way to establishing global products or business groups.

Whether using regional headquarters as buffers or creating complex matrices to resolve balancing demands for global integration and local responsiveness, the logic remains one of reducing the impact of national cultural differences. This tends to ignore the potential value-added of the local units in terms of innovation, not just in products and technology, but also in management practices. Strategic thrust, transfer of technology, and learning are still seen as a top–down affair.

And even global products can have different consumer perceptions. While consumer tastes may be converging, many companies deny that convergence means homogenization. While the Germans and British may be drinking more wine, and the French and Italians more beer, the Germans consume six times as much beer per capita as the Italians, and the French six times as much wine per capita as the British. "Going global does not make things simpler by reducing everything . . . to one standardized reality. . . . If anything it makes them more complex."[27] This means having to create a complex menu of options and possibilities, and deciding which elements to standardize and leaving local managers an important strategic role, as well as space for autonomy and creativity.

Utilizing differences – going global?

Many MNCs are trying to improve integration between national companies by developing global business areas or product lines. ABB, Philips, and Honeywell are just some examples. National organizations are matrixed with these global business or product lines creating a dual reporting structure, to a country manager and a business/product manager. While country heads are seen to be very important to preserve local responsiveness, business or product heads are responsible for optimizing global integration. Local resistance is high as formerly powerful country heads see their power and autonomy being diminished.

Efforts to achieve greater integration may be sabotaged unless local managers are committed to a regional or global perspective. It is therefore necessary to involve country heads in developing global plans and enlarging their sphere of influence. This may include giving them responsibility for coordination, as well as career opportunities outside their local operations, not waiting until they reach 45 years old to do this, but exposing them much earlier in their careers to international management experience. In this way, cultural differences are brought into the mainstream.

However, local managers cannot be expected to work successfully with other nationalities if they are not provided with appropriate language and cultural training. Nor can they be expected to cooperate with people in other units if there is no mechanism nor incentive to do so. For example, IBM is introducing performance measures to reward managers for cooperating with colleagues around the world.[28] And Unilever has 25,000 employees using Lotus Notes to share their globally acquired expertise with others.[29]

Cross-border cooperation can also be encouraged by structural mechanisms. Companies can build interdependencies into their structures. For example, Nestlé has a network of some twenty research and technology centers dotted around the world.[30] In 1983, it established a new research center in Singapore. To accelerate the center's integration into its network of research units, it was given responsibility for quality assurance for the whole of the Far East region.

This structural interdependence forced intensive communication between the existing units and the new operations. Had the Singaporean operation been given strictly an R&D role, it would have taken far longer for the informal connections to build up in that area and for the center to contribute actively to the organization. Furthermore, Nestlé benefited from Singapore's culture. The emphasis on the accrual of factual knowledge, and the pursuit of detail fitted well with the mandate for quality assurance.

To ensure that such cultural advantages can be utilized, managers from different countries need the skills to operate across country boundaries, such as cultural and language skills, and an infrastructure (such as information and accounting systems, structures, and incentives) to make that happen. They also need to understand and even **create** interdependencies among units, as well as having an important role in the broader organization.[31]

Capitalizing on cultural differences requires finding the proper balance between responsiveness to local needs and central control. This is an ongoing dilemma for most multinational companies today. For historical as well as cultural reasons, the balance is different between Europe, the United States, and Japan. Typically, European MNCs have been more aware of and responsive to local needs and are now trying to get more global.

Meanwhile, Japanese firms have run into difficulties in internationalizing, particularly at senior management level, and are now striving to become more local.[32] American MNCs are now more concerned with global integration, as overseas markets become more and more important in contributing to the bottom line.

These differences may be in part culturally driven. American expansion overseas, particularly in Europe, has tended to be regiocentric, in part due to the lack of understanding of the different cultures within Europe. Many American companies have in some ways treated Europe as one country, a mistake which some say may now serve as a competitive advantage. In addition, the American penchant for standardization may come from a history of accepting foreigners (that is, cultural differences) but expecting them to conform to local practice, to become Americans. This means that the rules and procedures apply to everyone, such is the American desire for universalism.[33] This may explain their somewhat "ethnocentric" approach.

The same can be said for Japan, where everyone is expected to fit into the group, to succumb to social pressures for conformity. Being different is considered a stigma, and outsiders can never hope to be fully integrated. This does not help Japanese to recruit and retain highly talented locals. While creating greenfield sites provides the control that Japanese firms are accustomed to, acquiring local firms creates more problems, as Nissan learned painfully in Spain.[34] Thus Japanese companies are trying to become more international and to be more receptive to local cultures.

Many Europeans consider themselves in the best position for going global and incorporating cultural differences, as they are more accustomed to living closely with neighbors of different cultures.

> More than many Americans or Japanese, Europeans are often very comfortable in international situations. The better run companies – like Nestlé – have corporate boards that closely resemble the UN Security Council . . . Our diversity is a huge asset . . . Europeans are better equipped for globalization.[35]

The consequences of these different approaches can be seen in a study of Hungarian firms involved in joint ventures with American, German, and Japanese companies. Hungarian managers resented the imposition of American systems and procedures, as well as the heavy-handed socialization tactics of Japanese partners. They preferred the German partners transfer of technology and techniques without the accompanying pressures to comply, either in terms of systems or behavior.[36]

While trying to manage the tensions created by balancing demands from headquarters and subsidiaries, there is the need to step back and to consider how to be most effective on a worldwide basis (geocentric approach). This means searching for new constellations of business activities, redefining the role and meaning of headquarters and subsidiaries, and discovering opportunities for organizational innovation and learning.

> The "multicultural multinational", as some are calling this new animal, is based on [the idea] that innovation is the key to success. An organization that relies on one culture for its ideas and treats foreign subsidiaries as dumb production-colonies might as well hire subcontractors.[37]

Creating added value

Although international competitive advantage may depend on national conditions which stimulate innovation, it is increasingly evident that competitive advantage is also a matter of creating assets across borders, such as human capital or R&D.[38] Companies are having to search outside national boundaries to develop their capacity fully.

One such example is Otis Elevator, a subsidiary of United Technologies.

> Being deployed globally helped Otis Elevator Inc . . . to develop the customized Elecvonic 411 at the lowest possible cost. The elevator . . . was developed by six research centers in five countries. Otis' group in Connecticut [USA] handled the systems integration, Japan designed the special motor drives that make the elevators ride smoothly. France perfected the door systems, Germany handled the electronics, and Spain took care of the small-geared components. Otis says the international shuttling saved more than $10 million in design costs and cut the development cycle from four years to two.[39]

Other examples include placing functional, product, and business unit headquarters in countries where the best resources are available. Thus, software development might be located in Bangalore (India) which has one of the highest number of well-trained software engineers per capita.[40] Swatch has placed its design units in Italy and production engineering in Switzerland (ETA).[41] R&D laboratories could be situated wherever conditions such as university facilities or government grants were likely to encourage technological innovation (such as Denmark or France).

Several MNCs have in fact taken steps in this direction. ICI, for instance, has four of its nine business units located outside Britain. Nestlé put its confectionary business headquarters in the United Kingdom (following the takeover of Rowntree) and its pasta business (Buitoni) in Italy.[42] Philips has transferred its digital audiotape business to Japan and its medical equipment business to the United States because of the high levels of market and technological development.[43]

Some of the more innovative Japanese companies are also taking this route. For example, one pharmaceutical company, Eisai, realized that to maximize its chances of finding a "blockbuster" drug it needed to locate in Europe, which is at the forefront of pharmaceutical research. As a result it has set up research labs (headed by locals in order to tap into the local research networks) notably in Britain, which enjoys world leadership in molecular and cellular biochemical research.[44]

Similarly, Shiseido, the cosmetics company, realized that the only way to become a leader in the perfume business was to relocate its R&D in France, which represents both the most competitive market and the center of expertise in the field. France boasts the best glass bottle manufacturers, the leading perfume specialists, and the top source of skilled labor in the cosmetics industry. By short-cutting the traditional sequence of international expansion and decentralizing R&D early on (rather than later, following sales and production) Shiseido has stolen market share from its bigger and more established rival, Kao.

The rationale behind such moves is that product or business groups should have a home base wherever world strategy is set, core R&D takes place, and a critical mass of sophisticated production occurs.[45] The idea is to benefit from the competitiveness of the most advantageous country, rather than being tied unnecessarily to the country of origin. This characterizes a new model of the multinational firm – or transnational – where specialized units are coordinated into integrated networks.[46] Rather than being an assemblage of semi-independent units which contribute individually to HQ coffers, the MNC becomes a heterarchy with many centers playing a strategic role in formulating as well as implementing strategy. This fosters a broader range of strategic thinking, and encourages a global mentality among all employees. The company comes to resemble a hologram, as information regarding the whole is contained in each part.[47]

These approaches provide opportunities for organizational innovation and learning from any direction. They encourage reflecting on which local innovations may have applications in other national units or might even warrant global diffusion. They force companies to consider what is the opportunity or incentive for "local for global" organizational learning, or transfer of "best practice" from the subsidiaries to headquarters.[48]

The ability to benefit from local thinking and to tap into the roots of pluralism and diversity for innovation, was seen in the case of P&G in India. By positioning products to take advantage of the preference (and legislation) for using natural herbal products (based on the ancient Ayurvedic system of medicine) P&G was able to gain an important share of the market. According to Gucharan Das, a global manager for P&G, strongly tied to his local (Indian) roots,

> Globalization does not mean imposing homogeneous solutions in a pluralistic world. It means having a global vision and strategy, but it also means cultivating roots and individual identities. It means nourishing local insights, but it also means reemploying communicable ideas in new geographies around the world.[49]

While he believes that the key to success is local passion, pride, and ownership of brands, Das reminds local managers to "think global". Taking ideas from elsewhere and adapting them to new circumstances requires humility, flexibility, and open mindedness. But local managers also must seek to develop local insights which have potentially universal appeal. After all, the benefit of being a multinational company is to have talented people in different parts of the world seeking opportunities and solving problems for common products and brands.

Thus the challenge for multinational companies is one of how to capture the benefits of cultural differences rather than trying to minimize their effects. But in order to capitalize on it, companies have to honestly assess their level of internationalism, because few companies are as international as their managers would like to believe.

Less global than we thought

Given all the talk about going global, it may be worth considering to what extent business is truly international.

> We are living in a world which is about as integrated as the world of the 19th century. Trade in goods and services is only slightly larger now as a fraction of gross world product than it was before 1914. Measured against GDP, US imports are only slightly

bigger now (11 percent) than they were in 1880 (8 percent). The world of 1913 had many of today's earmarks of globalism, including multinational companies whose linkages spanned the world [e.g. German pharmaceuticals which brought Bayer aspirin to America]. Fewer than 10 percent of the businesses that inquire about going global actually try it.[50]

Answering the question, "Just how international are we?" may therefore require some pretty painful self-examination. In this respect, the process undertaken by Fiat, the Italian automaker, is instructive.

Fiat, with a $34 billion turnover, operates in 52 countries, and has 290,000 employees, one-fifth of whom are abroad. Given the extent of operations and people outside Italy, Fiat management wanted to define what internationalization really meant, to know how they measured up, and how to become more international.[51] Working groups were set up to address issues such as the nature of international positions, the profile of the international manager, and the appropriate HRM systems. Despite its presence in many countries, and its long history of international operations, Fiat discovered that it had a lot to do to become more international.

In analyzing the international nature of jobs, they found four types of managers: transnationals (300) who lived abroad mostly on airplanes, multinationals (1700) who traveled extensively but lived in Turin, "open locals" who received foreigners, and locals, who had little international contact. They also realized that more than 40 percent of managerial positions dealt with international work matters and that three-quarters of these jobs were in Europe. On the basis of these findings, Fiat management began developing ways to recruit, train, and develop international managers, both within Italy as well as abroad. They also planned to create a "company culture that is increasingly sensitive to the international context . . . [which required] greater participation and integration of managers in various national contexts within the culture and values of the Fiat group".

A closer look at so-called global companies raises similar concerns. "Going global" means more than operating in markets in many countries or having products that sell around the world. Having global products, like Levi jeans and MacDonald's hamburgers, or having sales offices and bank branches in the far reaches of the world, or having done business internationally for over 200 years is no indication of an international mind-set. Head offices and most of the functional and product/business unit heads often remain firmly planted in the home country. Even the international division is often housed in the same building, or just next door.

This was confirmed by a gobal leadership study of 1500 executives from 12 large companies around the world which described themselves as global. Out of 34 dimensions considered vital to competitiveness, they rated last the ability to cultivate a global mind-set in their organization. A **global mind-set** was defined as "the capacity to appreciate the beliefs, values, behaviors, and business practices of individuals and organizations from a variety of regions and cultures".[52]

It is therefore important to take a good look in the mirror.

Don't believe in your own press releases. It's too easy to think that you're a global company because you keep saying you're a global company. Search for measurable indicators that your organization is behaving more globally than it was last year and the year before. Believe in behaviors not rhetoric. Celebrate your progress, but never allow yourself to become fully satisfied that you have made it. Holding on to that nagging anxiety is what being globally minded is all about.[53]

The real test of a global company is the extent to which strategic thinking actually benefits from cultural diversity. How many members of the managing board are not from the same country? How many of the top 200 managers? Can a company really be considered global if the top 200 are all French, Dutch, or Belgian? The composition of the management board is thus revealing,

> The boards of directors in both U.S. and foreign-owned global corporations remain almost exclusively a native affair . . . in major U.S. corporations the same percentage of board seats were held by foreign nationals in 1991 (2.1%) as were held ten years earlier. In Asian corporations, . . . "foreign board members are as rare as British sumo wrestlers". Similarly, stock ownership is almost always concentrated in the home country.[54]

Even within MNCs which do include a vice-president or board member who is French, Brazilian, Chinese, or female, the undertow of the dominant culture is often strong enough to silence them. Despite representation of foreign managers in top management, at the board level, or across the board in any function (structural integration), what is often more revealing is the extent to which foreign managers are involved in informal networks and social activities, or informal integration.[55]

And even then, non-Japanese managers may go out drinking with the boys after work but will never be considered one of the boys. In Switzerland, as in Israel, top management is connected through continuing military service, although less so than in the past. And in France, half of the CEOs of the top 200 companies come from the top six *grandes écoles*, making it very difficult for outsiders to break in to senior management. Furthermore, out of the 144 CEOs of the top French MNCs, only 16 had foreign managerial experience. Even now, "The typical top management team remains remarkably like those of the past: very French, very male, and very elite".[56]

So, there remains quite a gap between the global representation within many MNCs and their global pretensions. Even companies such as Philips, with its long history of developing international businesses, still had a long way to go. According to an interview with CEO, Wisse Dekker in 1989,

> Not long ago the membership of both of these boards [management and supervisory] was completely Dutch. Now the supervisory board has Americans, a German, a French-man, a Belgian, and an Englishman as well as some Dutchmen, while the management board includes a German and a Belgian.[57]

While this may be a step in the right direction, the presence of western Europeans on the board, is hardly revolutionary. The mark of a truly global company is not the tradition of operating abroad, nor a product that appeals around the world, but the multiple nationalities of the top and senior management ranks involved in formulating strategy, not just in implementing it. The central question is to what extent national strengths and cultural differences are drawn upon to create global synergies. It may just be true that, "The fittest – those who survive – are those who cooperate best with other living things".[58]

Creating culturally strategic alliances

Perhaps the best model for managing diversity can be found in strategic alliances and joint ventures. Given the competing interests of nationalism and globalism, companies may operate more like political federations, in which each company retains local owner-ship and governance but seeks an alliance to accomplish difficult or expensive missions. Thus companies retain independence, avoiding antitrust regulations, and retain local identity, keeping political ties and the facility to raise capital.

For example, in March 1992 a consortium of insurance companies agreed to form a pan-European insurance group. This consortium included insurance companies from The Netherlands, the United Kingdom, Sweden, and Denmark. Each national company was responsible for and had full autonomy in its home market. In a joint effort to take on Europe, they took significant cross-holdings, creating a headquarters "shell" of ten people with a rotating chairman. In their vision to create a pan-European financial services company, they extended their reach to include a Portuguese bank. In creating this alliance, one of the most important tasks to be accomplished is to make clear to each partner the benefits of cooperating, and to encourage the sharing of best practice. One of the key concerns that has to be addressed is preserving the autonomy of each partner.

Take also the example of Airbus, a European consortium supported by the French, German, British, and Spanish governments. Many thought that the idea of bringing together experts from four separate, and sometimes hostile, cultures to build and market a complex piece of machinery was sheer folly. Adam Brown, now director of strategic planning, recalls, "To be frank, none of us really thought this project had much chance of taking off".[59]

Though heavily subsidized, the Airbus venture has proved successful and is regarded by its French CEO as the model of high-tech multinational cooperation. "Aeronautical engineers tend to think beyond national boundaries . . . We are an international frater-nity. We have invented our own system." This included establishing a corporate culture which transcended nationalities, insisting that all business meetings and official com-munications should be in English, and designing planes in inches and feet to be user-friendly to mechanics around the world used to working with American aircraft.

Clearly, boundaries between sectors and nations are becoming less and less distinct. Companies can engage in joint ventures or strategic alliances with companies worldwide, sometimes even with rival companies. Firms might have very different relationships in different markets or businesses; they could be partners in one, competitors in another, and suppliers and customers of one another in a third. Marriage, divorce, and remarriage are not unlikely.

For example, Rover, the British car group, linked up with Honda in order to acquire technology and management skills, while Honda gained market access in Europe. Ten years later BMW came along with a better offer, facilitating Rover's entry into the long-abandoned US market while enabling BMW to move into the small car market.[60]

With collaboration being in constant flux, the need for a reputation for being trustworthy is absolute. "Managers thus need to acquire skills important to the diplomat and politician such as cultural sensitivity and a talent for discerning shared interests."[61]

Whether seeking to leverage local innovations globally, or to collaborate with foreign competitors, the lessons are the same. Companies need to be able to spot the value-added that is embedded in each culture while focusing on shared interests both within and outside the organizational boundaries. Or, in the words of the Director of Human Resources of Sony France,

> The cultural split between the intellectual flexibility of the French and the team spirit of the Japanese is an obvious enrichment for each party.[62]

In 1990, a joint venture was created between the French company Rhône-Poulenc and American company Rorer with the vision of becoming a global corporation, RPR.[63] Although both were in pharmaceuticals, Rhône-Poulenc was a large, nationalized, bureaucratic French conglomerate with no outside shareholders, while Rorer was a mid-sized, entrepreneurial, publically traded American company. In 1991, Rhône-Poulenc Rorer (RPR) sales totaled $3.8 billion and products were marketed in more than 140 countries, the North America market represented 25 percent of total sales, the European market 61 percent.

According to RPR Chairman and CEO, Rob Cawthorn (British),

> We've abolished the idea of a domestic and international business. We're not French – we're not American – we're global. The fact that neither of the two cultures is fully dominant can be an advantage. The different backgrounds and different ways of looking at things can cause innovation. Not just in France and the U.S., but everywhere around the world. From two "OK" companies in the pharmaceutical business, we've been given the opportunity to create something great.

Initially, however, each company felt taken over by the other. This reaction was countered by publically stating that RPR would be a global company, respecting all cultures. An executive council was created consisting of French, American, British, Austrian, and Australian members. Dual HQs were established, one in Philadelphia and one in Paris. Key functions were globalized, such as R&D, finance, and HR, while sales and marketing were regionalized. Heavy investments were made in technology – global e-mail, video-conferences – and travel to encourage face-to-face relationships. Short-term exchanges (one week to three months) were organized, even among secretaries.

Top management openly talked about cultural issues and each team was encouraged to define its own culture. The 150 expatriates were chosen based not solely on job competence but on being adaptable, having a sense of adventure, being a detective or investigator in order to be able to "get at what's really going on". Good support was provided before and after expatriation by outside consulting firms (e.g. relocation). Training was provided, depending on the needs of the expatriates and others throughout the organizations. And training itself was globalized, using methods, materials, and trainers from different cultures. Nevertheless, three years later the rank and file closely watch who gets the next available senior management position, French or American?

While many of the above examples demonstrate the benefits of capturing strategic or structural differences in creating global companies, the question remains as to how to utilize cultural differences in order to provide competitive advantage.

Gaining competitive advantage from cultural differences

A truly multicultural organization can be defined as one wherein diversity is *valued* and *utilized* rather than just contained.[64] The strategy of *utilizing* cultural differences can create competitive advantage. Thus, rather than one culture overriding another, or compromising to find "safe" solutions that will antagonize neither, the challenge is to discover solutions that capture the differences in creative ways so that the sum of the parts is greater than the whole.[65] "Diversity is taking people from different backgrounds, with different expectations and at different stages of life and melding them into a force that will drive the company's profitability and competitiveness."[66] Unfortunately most companies do not think about cultural differences as a source of competitive advantage.

While much of the literature on managing diversity comes from American companies' efforts to integrate women and minorities in the workforce, some lessons can be taken for managing national diversity. In many cases, being a minority means being the only French manager in a team of Germans, or the only American senior manager in a Japanese firm.

Cox and Blake[67] argue that competitive advantage derives from cultural diversity, in the ways shown in Table 9.2. The most obvious reason given for utilizing cultural differences is greater sensitivity to different markets. Product development teams composed of people from differing cultures are more likely to develop products that appeal to

Table 9.2 Advantages of cultural diversity

1. Marketing argument: increases the ability to respond to cultural preferences of local markets

2. Resource acquisition: increases ability to recruit employees of different national backgrounds, and host country elites

3. Cost argument: reduces cost incurred by turnover of non-home country managers

4. Problem-solving argument: improves decision-making through wider range of perspectives and more thorough critical analysis

5. Creativity argument: enhances creativity through diversity of perspectives and less emphasis on conformity

6. Systems flexibility argument: enhances organizational flexibility and responsiveness to multiple demands and changing environments

Source: Adapted from T.H. Cox and S. Blake (1991) "Managing cultural diversity: Implications for organizational competitiveness", *Academy of Management Executive*, 5(3), 45–56.

the different tastes of customers. Diversity also can enhance problem-solving capability, innovation, and creativity, as discussed in the previous chapter. Top management teams designing strategy require different perspectives to reflect the complexity of operating in an international arena, emphasizing national differences, while providing the forum for integrating those perspectives.

Ernie Drew, CEO of Hoechst Celanese, quickly embraced the idea of diversity as a source of strength in problem-solving when, at a management meeting composed of 150 top (mostly white male) managers and 50 women and minorities drawn from the ranks, he saw that diverse teams came up with broader solutions. In addition, he discovered that productivity had surged at plants where the workforce was more diverse. Thus he made diversity a top priority in the following ways.

First he made diversity a business objective: creating a target of 34 percent at *all levels* of the organization by the year 2001. Then he required 26 top executives to join in two groups where they were a minority. The company favored sources supplying recruits of diverse backgrounds (universities), and took care in the event of downsizing to ensure that minorities were not the primary casualties.[68]

This points to another reason for creating diversity, which is the cost of not being able to attract or retain top local talent. In fact the most common complaint heard among managers working for foreign MNCs is a sense of always being an outsider, not eligible to join the inner circle. Meanwhile, these companies complain that they cannot tap into the local elite, or lose valuable local managers after much investment, for example, in training and development. In many multinational companies, the top management remains reserved for home-country nationals, whether in Europe, Japan, or the United States. Thus limited career opportunities is one reason that many qualified managers jump ship.

The best and brightest locals tend to prefer to join and stay within national firms, albeit for different reasons. For some, such as the Japanese, it may be a sense of national duty or pride. For others, such as the French, it may represent a source of social prestige or sensitivity to foreign control. And for others still, particularly for Americans, it is attributed to strong cultural needs for autonomy and independence. It is difficult for people from dominant cultures to realize that the other culture is calling the shots. "Americans are used to seeing the dog, not the tail of the dog"[69]; in other words, the Americans are used to being in charge.

Another interesting argument for the benefit of using cultural diversity is that it creates systems flexibility. Given the complexity of the current business environment, there is a need for organizations to match that variety internally, to have what is known as "requisite variety".[70] In addition to the complexity, the pace of environmental change requires the ability to live with, even thrive on, ambiguity and chaos in order to achieve maximum organizational flexibility and adaptability. Multicultural organizations foster both the variety of perspectives and the practice of managing ambiguity. Less is taken for granted, and there is not the assumption of one best way of doing things.

Furthermore, there is evidence that non-Western, non-white, and non-males (Asians, Africans, women) have different cognitive styles: issues tend to be seen as "both–and" rather than as "either–or", the links between things are viewed more in relational than hierarchical patterns (collaborate versus control), and there is greater sensitivity towards the more affective or "non-rational" components of arguments.[71] Furthermore, bilinguals have been found to have higher levels of divergent thinking and cognitive flexibility.[72] Thus other ways of seeing and thinking may be particularly useful, as business paradigms need to be constantly questioned. As André Laurent puts it, "It is the very richness in the diversity of cultures that makes them an asset to international companies. Each culture has some specific and unique insights and some specific and unique blind spots".[73]

The argument in favor of embracing cultural diversity clearly has moral undertones. It is an argument which upholds equal opportunities and which condemns cultural imperialism. It can therefore seem somewhat utopian. But this should not overshadow its firm practical foundations. In any case, the reality of demographics indicates that most of the workforce by the year 2000 will not be white males, from the northern and western parts of the world map, who presently compose the top management teams of many multinational companies. Thus the ability to utilize cultural differences can provide companies with competitive advantage.

Digital Equipment is one company which firmly believes in this philosophy.[74]

> In the early 1980s Digital developed a management approach called "Valuing Differences". This approach encourages employees to pay attention to their differences as unique individuals and as members of groups, to raise their level of comfort with differences, and to capitalize on differences as a major asset to the company's productivity.
>
> The philosophy is anchored in the conviction that the broader the spectrum of differences in the workplace, the richer the synergy among employees and the more excellent the organization's performance. It is a belief in the constructive potential of all people. It assumes that each person's differences bring unique and special gifts to the organization.[75]

At Digital, "core groups" were established, which met on an ongoing basis to encourage dialogue, becoming an important vehicle for establishing and developing relationships. This effort was conducted with the firm belief that it would contribute to Digital's reputation as the best place to work and would stimulate greater innovation, higher productivity, and more effective global competition.

Returning to the case of Fiat, better integration between Italian and non-Italian management was achieved. There are now more country meetings, more exchanges among the different companies, and greater visibility of corporate top management in different countries. Furthermore, the management development system has been extended to include non-Italians, new training programs on cross-cultural and global issues have been initiated, and recruitment is now pan-European. "In two years, more than 69 young Europeans have started work in different environments, preparing themselves to become citizens of the world of Fiat."[76]

Other European companies are also making efforts to actively recruit and train nonnationals, and to track their careers more closely. For example, France's Rhône-Poulenc and Germany's Henkel are "Europeanizing" their personnel strategies, and Finnish

Nokia has opened training to managers from other European countries. The European round table, an association of forty of Europe's biggest companies, has arranged for members to swap managers for short periods.[77]

Prescriptions regarding managing cultural differences are inevitably culturally biased. Even our tendency to stress the need to raise differences, confront them, and utilize them points to our own cultural programming – explicit (low context), egalitarian (low power distance), and instrumental (doing, not being). Nevertheless, we need to begin to take actions such that competitive advantage can indeed be derived from cultural differences.

Start at the top

What is the nationality of the corporate leader? The head of McKinsey is Indian, that of JP Morgan is British, the CEO of Coca-Cola is Cuban-born, and the PDG of L'Oréal is British. The representation among the rop ranks of non-national managers sends the signal that capability not passport is what counts. Involvement of top management in selection and promotion, even mentoring, of other nationalities is crucial. Even Disney is getting the message. According to a recent interview with CEO Michael Eisner, ". . . 'non-American born' executives will play a much more important role in the management of the company. I think you will see names in our top management that are hard to pronounce as time goes on".[78]

Create opportunities for learning

Learning across cultures means learning to be open to self-awareness and to be willing to analyze one's own cultural baggage. It means being able to assess views of own and others' culture, to evaluate the effectiveness of interaction, and to develop strategies for dealing with differences. Above all, learning across cultures means continuously learning how to learn about cultures.

Training seminars provide the opportunity for face-to-face interaction among different nationalities, and for developing problem-solving skills in multicultural teams. Unilever brings hundreds of managers from around the world to its training center in the United Kingdom.

The program goals for cross-cultural training, more specifically, include developing observation and interview skills, being able to recognize the role of emotions and values in cross-cultural interactions and the avoidance of sensitive issues, and being able to define problems and gather information in real time.[79]

Check the pulse

Employee surveys need to be conducted to check on attitudes and perceptions regarding how the company is dealing with diversity, the representation of foreign nationals at various levels, as well as their career experiences. Auditing HR systems is needed to ensure that recruitment, performance appraisal, compensation, and career tracks do not undermine attempts to attract and retain talented foreigners.

And the corporate culture has to be checked for biases. The degree to which an organization is truly multicultural can be evaluated by the degree of prejudice and discrimination that exists, using survey feedback (as do Xerox and P&G) and the degree of intergroup conflict which is based on national or cultural differences.[80] A greater mix of nationalities enhances identification with the company by erasing the distinction between insiders and outsiders, and reduces the "them and us" mentality based on nationality.

Le défi: the global challenge

The challenge, then, is to find ways to capitalize on differences, to utilize cultural differences in order to gain competitive advantage. But to do this, differences have to be acknowledged and accepted as legitimate. This means they have to be discussed. They must also be seen as an opportunity and not as a threat to efficiency, to existing power bases, nor to harmony. It is easier to try to dominate, to assert that our way of doing things is better, more efficient, more effective, and so on. After all, it has always worked in the past.

It is difficult to acknowledge that there may be a better way, one which involves many people of different nationalities, races, religions and gender trying to figure it out together. Acknowledging differences may threaten individual identity (how are we different?) or threaten the cohesiveness of the group (one big happy family). Acknowledging differences raises the possibility of conflict, which may upset the harmony. Ignoring or denying differences, however, means losing the richness of diversity.

MNCs have understood the changes that need to take place in order to become global companies. Many are in the process of adapting their strategies, structures, and systems accordingly. But globalization has to happen in people's minds too. Ethnocentric thinking, "our way is best" has to change. Multiparadigm thinking is necessary. To derive the potential benefits from cross-cultural interactions, we need to open our minds to alternative perspectives, and be willing to go towards others, rather than hide behind sameness. Cultural mosaics, where each culture preserves its uniqueness, not melting pots where cultures are merged losing their distinctiveness, can create multiple patterns that better reflect and respond to the complexity of operating in a global arena.

This is the challenge for managers, organizations and nation states. There is no other way to move forward than to take on this challenge, quickly. Otherwise, we will stay mired in the mess we see around us today, where one culture tries to impose its ways on the other, where turf battles continually multiply, and where the hope for economic and political integration, not least for a global civilization, is shattered.

Suggestions for managing cultural diversity

Build face-to-face relationships.
Create international project groups.
Develop international management training and development.

Build shared values, while encouraging local interpretation.
Promote divergent values to provide seeds for flexibility.

Questions to ask

To what extent are cultural differences open to discussion and negotiation?
To what extent do different interpretations of company culture, values, and behavior exist in the organization?
To what extent are ideas from outside HQ listened to and implemented?
To what extent do HR initiatives, selection and recruitment, training programs, performance appraisal and compensation, and career systems, reflect cultural bias?
What opportunities exist for learning from other cultures?
To what extent does top management "walk the talk" of valuing and utilizing cultural differences?
To what extent are different nationalities present in top management? Top 200?

Notes

1. Heenan, D.A. and Perlmutter, H.V. (1979) *Multinational Organizational Development*, Reading, MA: Addison-Wesley.
2. Prahalad, C.K. and Doz, Y. (1987) *The Multinational Mission: Balancing Local Demands and Global Vision*, New York: Free Press.
3. Bartlett, C.A. and Ghoshal, S. (1989) *Managing Across Borders: The Transnational Solution*, Boston, MA: Harvard Business School Press.
4. Adler, N. (1991) *International Dimensions of Organizational Behavior*, Boston, MA: PWS Kent.
5. Sathe, V. (1983) "Implications of corporate culture: A manager's guide to action", *Organizational Dynamics*, Autumn, 5–23.
6. Pascale, R. (1984) "The paradox of 'corporate culture': reconciling ourselves to socialization", *California Management Review*, 27(2), 26–41.
7. Nehrer, J. (1991) "France amazed, amused by Disney dress code", *International Herald Tribune*, December 26.
8. See Van Maanen, J. (1991) "The smile factory: Work at Disneyland" in P.J. Frost, L.F. Moore, M.R. Louis, C.C. Lundberg and J. Martin (eds) *Reframing Organizational Culture*, Newbury Park, CA: Sage, pp. 58–76; also Van Maanen, J. and Laurent, A. (1993) "The flow of culture: Some notes on globalization and the multinational corporation" in S. Ghoshal and D.E. Westney (eds) *Organization Theory and the Multinational Corporation*, New York: St. Martin's Press, 275–312.
9. Presentation at INSEAD by George Cohn, CEO MacDonalds Canada, with Video of MacDonalds in Russia.
10. Adler, N.J. (1983) "Organizational development in a multicultural environment", *Journal of Applied Behavioral Science*, 19(3), 349–65.
11. Brannen, M.Y. (1992) "'Bwana Mickey': Constructing cultural consumption at Tokyo Disneyland" in J.J. Tobin (ed.) *Remade in Japan: Everyday Life and Consumer Taste in a Changing Society*, New Haven: Yale University Press, 216–234.
12. Kanter, R.M. and Corn, R.I. (1994) "Do cultural differences make a business difference?", *Journal of Management Development*, 13(2), 5–23.

13. Barnevik, P. (1994) "Making local heroes international", *Financial Times*, January 17, 8; "The ABB of management", *The Economist*, January 6, 1996, 62.
14. Simmons, R. and Bartlett, C. (1992) Asea Brown Boveri, Harvard Business School Case.
15. Edstrom, A. and Galbraith, J. (1977) "Transfer of managers as a coordination and control strategy in multinational organizations", *Administrative Science Quarterly*, 22, 248–63.
16. Doz, Y. and Prahalad, C.K. (1984) "Patterns of strategic control within multinational corporations", *Journal of International Business Studies*, 15(2), 55–72; Baliga, B.R. and Jaeger, A.M. (1984) "Multinational corporations: Control systems and delegation issues", *Journal of International Business Studies*, 15(2), 25–40; Etzioni, A. (1988) *The Moral Dimension*, New York: Free Press.
17. Haspeslagh, P. and Ghoshal, S. (1992) Electrolux Zanussi, INSEAD case.
18. Hedlund, G. (1980) "The role of foreign subsidiaries in strategic decision-making in Swedish multinational corporations", *Strategic Management Journal*, 9, 23–6.
19. Lightfoot, R.W. (1992) "Philips and Matsushita: A portrait of two evolving companies", Harvard Business School.
20. Auteri, E. and Tesio, V. (1990) "The internationalization of management at FIAT", *Journal of Management Development*, 9(6), 6–16.
21. Evans, P.A.L. (1993) "Dosing the glue: Applying human resource technology to build the global organization" in *Research in Personnel and Human Resources Management*, Supplement 3, Greenwich, CT: JAI Press, 21–54, p. 35.
22. Lightfoot, *Op. cit.*, p. 13.
23. "A conversation with Michael Porter", *European Management Journal*, 1991, 9(4), 355–59.
24. Lightfoot, *Op. cit.*
25. Blackwell, N., Bizet, J.P., Child, P. and Hensley, D. (1991) "Shaping a pan-European organization", *The McKinsey Quarterly*, No. 2, 94–111.
26. Schneider, S.C., Wittenberg, A. and Hansen, L. (1990) Honeywell, Europe, INSEAD case.
27. Riesenbeck, H. and Freeling, A. (1993) "How global are global brands?", *European Business Report*, 2Q, Summer, 12–17.
28. "The discreet charm of the multicultural multinational", *The Economist*, July 30, 1994, 59–60.
29. "Don't be an ugly American manager", *Fortune*, October 16, 1995, 99.
30. DeMeyer, A. (1993) Nestlé, S.A., INSEAD case.
31. Blackwell, N., Bizet, J.P., Child, P. and Hensely, D. (1992) "Creating European organizations that work", *The McKinsey Quarterly*, No. 2, 31–43.
32. Kriger, M. and Solomon, E.E. (1992) "Strategic mindsets and decision-making autonomy in U.S. and Japanese MNCs", *Management International Review*, 32(4), 327–43.
33. Hampden-Turner, C. and Trompenaars, F. (1994) *The Seven Cultures of Capitalism*, London: Piatkus.
34. Asakura, A.E. (1989) Schneider, S.C., Nissan, Europe, INSEAD case.
35. Hofheinz, P. (1993) "Europe's tough new managers", *Fortune*, September 6, 20–3.
36. Child, J., Markoczy, L. and Cheung, T. (1992) "Managerial adaptation in Chinese and Hungarian strategic alliances with culturally foreign partners", Paper presented at the British Academy of Management Annual Conference, Bradford, September.
37. *The Economist*, July 30, 1994, *Op. cit.*, pp. 59–60.
38. Dunning, J.H. (1993) "Internationalizing Porter's diamond", *Management International Review*, 33(2), 7–15.
39. "The stateless corporation", *Business Week*, May 14, 1990, 52–59, 55.
40. Gargan, E.A. (1993) "India's Silicon Valley moves to state of the art", *International Herald Tribune*, December 31.
41. Taylor, W. (1993) "Message and muscle: An interview with Swatch titan Nicolas Hayek", *Harvard Business Review*, March–April, 99–110.

42. *European Management Journal* (1991), *Op. cit.*
43. Lightfoot, *Op. cit.*
44. K. Asakawa, Professor Keio Business School, Japan.
45. *European Management Journal* (1991), *Op. cit.*
46. Ghoshal, S. and Bartlett, C.A. (1990) "The multinational corporation as an inter-organizational network", *Academy of Management Review*, 15(4), 603–25.
47. Hedlund, G. (1986) "The hypermodern MNC: A heterarchy?", *Human Resource Management*, 25, 9–35.
48. Bartlett and Ghoshal (1989), *Op. cit.*
49. Das, G. (1993) "Local memoirs of a global manager", *Harvard Business Review*, March–April, pp. 38–47, p. 38.
50. Farnham, A. (1994) "Global – or just Globaloney", *Fortune*, June 27, 49–51.
51. Auteri and Tesio, *Op. cit.*
52. *Fortune*, October 16, 1995, *Op. cit.*
53. *Ibid.*
54. Farnham, *Op. cit.*
55. Cox, T. (1991) "The multinational organization", *Academy of Management Executive*, 5(2), 34–47.
56. Schmidt, V.A. (1993) "An end to French economic exceptionalism: The transformation of business under Mitterand", *California Management Review*, Fall, 75–98, 94.
57. Stone, N. (1989) "The globalization of Europe: An interview with Wisse Dekker", *Harvard Business Review*, May–June, 90–5, 91.
58. Perlmutter, H.V. and Heenan, D.A. (1986) "Cooperate to compete globally", *Harvard Business Review*, March–April, 3–8.
59. Labich, K. (1992) "Airbus takes off", *Fortune*, June 1, 26–30.
60. Done, K. (1994) "Don't cry over Rover", *Financial Times*, February 1, p. 19.
61. Farnham, *Op. cit.*
62. *L'Express*, December 19, 1991, p. 8.
63. Orleman, P.A. (1992) The global corporation: Managing across cultures, Masters thesis, University of Pennsylvania.
64. Cox, *Op. cit.*
65. Adler, N.J. (1980) "Cultural synergy: The management of cross-cultural organizations" in W.W. Burke and L.D. Goodstein (eds) *Trends and Issues in OD: Current Theory and Practice*, San Diego: University Associates, 163–84.
66. Noble, B.P. (1994) "'Diversity' fails to catch on", *International Herald Tribune*, November 10, 9.
67. Cox, T.H. and Blake, S. (1991) "Managing cultural diversity: Implications for organizational competitiveness", *Academy of Management Executive*, 5(3), 45–56.
68. Rice, F. (1994) "How to make diversity pay", *Fortune*, August 8, 44–9.
69. Rosenzweig, P.M. (1994) "The new 'American Challenge': Foreign multinationals in the United States", *California Management Review*, Spring, 107–23, 115.
70. Ashby, W.R. (1956) *Introduction to Cybernetics*, London: Chapman & Hall.
71. Noble, B.P. (1993) "On women's 'difference': Companies are listening", *International Herald Tribune*, August 18, 9, 11; see also Tannen, D. (1994) *Talking From 9 to 5*, New York: William Morrow.
72. Cox and Blake, *Op. cit.*
73. Laurent, A. (1987) "Vive la différence!", *Strategic Direction*, March, 18.
74. Walker, B.A. and Hanson, W.C. (1992) "Valuing differences at Digital Equipment Corporation" in S. Jackson and associates (eds) *Diversity in the Workplace*, New York: Guilford Press, Ch. 6, 119–37.
75. *Ibid*, pp. 119–120.
76. Auteri and Tesio, *Op. cit.*, pp. 15–16.
77. "The elusive Euro-manager", *The Economist*, November 7, 1992, 81.

78. Sims, C. (1994) "Disney wants to learn languages", *International Herald Tribune*, April 28, 9, 11.
79. Lobel, S.A. (1990) "Global leadership competencies: Managing to a different drumbeat", *Human Resource Management*, 29(1), 39–47.
80. Cox, *Op. cit.*

CHAPTER TEN

Citizens of the world: business ethics and social responsibility

L'éthique, c'est le désir d'une vie accomplie, avec et pour les autres, dans le cadre d'institutions justes.

Paul Ricoeur[1]

(Ethics is the desire for a life accomplished, with and for others, within the framework of fair institutions.)

We now come to the end of our journey. In navigating the seas of international business, we have come to recognize culture as a powerful force which can either undermine our best intentions and efforts or push forward our business activities. We have used as our guide a map which indicates the cultural terrain, or key dimensions, and suggests methods for discovery through observation, questioning, and interpretation. This map can also serve to reveal different spheres of cultural influence – regional, industry, and corporate – and to consider the consequences of their interaction. We then examined the evidence of how and why culture influences management practice: in designing organization structure and processes, strategies, and human resource management practices. And finally, we brought to light the issues and concerns of how to manage these cultural differences as international managers, as multicultural teams, and as global organizations.

Throughout this journey we have demonstrated the impact of culture on management practices around the world. In this concluding chapter, we question to what extent notions of business ethics and social responsibility are also culture-bound, and whether we can ever hope to arrive at a culturally shared understanding of and response to ethical dilemmas and social responsibility. What, indeed, is the role of managers and companies as **global citizens** and what is the best path to follow in conducting international business?

We start by recognizing a long tradition of different cultural assumptions regarding business and profit, which are also revealed in theories of economic growth and of the firm ("why firms exist"). These different assumptions provide the fuel for the debate over "ethics versus profit"; do they go hand in hand or are there inherent, irreconcilable trade-offs? Despite this debate, ethical and socially responsible behavior can be considered to be an imperative for conducting business on a global scale. Indeed, attempts to establish a "level playing field" have already created cultural shock waves around the world.

Nevertheless attitudes and behavior towards ethics among managers and companies differ across cultures. Here we consider the *evidence* and explore *reasons* for similarities as well as differences. We question whether it is best to adopt a policy of "When in Rome do as the Romans do", or to impose home country or company ethical standards and risk being accused of "cultural imperialism". In addressing these questions, managers and companies can better define their role as citizens of the world, and develop guidelines to keep them on track in their continuing journey towards a global civilization.

Taking care of business

According to David Vogel, Professor of Business at the University of California at Berkeley, the current interest in business ethics represents "an ongoing moral dialogue with deep secular and religious roots" regarding the nature of market economy and human nature.[2]

> [As] medieval Catholic thought held that money-making was morally suspect . . . a moral businessman was thus a contradiction in terms . . .
>
> It was by morally sanctifying the pursuit of profit that Protestantism made business ethics possible . . . Not only could one serve God by working, but the correct use of wealth was precisely to improve it for the glory of God. Consequently, the pursuit of profit and the pursuit of heaven become not only compatible, but mutually reinforcing . . . In short, the Reformation made it possible for the first time to be both a good person and a successful businessman.[3]

In the Catholic church, profit was sanctioned for the benefit of the community, not for individual enhancement. The role of the hierarchy was to intervene on behalf of the people to ensure collective well-being and to mediate in upholding the word of God. For Protestants, access to God was more direct (no intermediary was necessary). Work, rather than a necessary evil, was considered to be the means to redemption. "The profile of the PWE [Protestant work ethic] believer then is of an independently minded, competitive, hard-working individual who is prepared to persevere at a task to achieve desirable ends."[4] This Protestant work ethic encouraged a strong need for individual achievement, perceived control over the environment, an instrumental approach, and the belief of a just world (equity).[5] It was this work ethic which, according to Max Weber, promoted capitalism.[6] Vogel argues that the doctrine of corporate social responsibility can be understood in part as the ongoing effort to reconcile the intentions and results of capitalism.

In France, for example, making money has long been viewed with some suspicion. Status and prestige came from family lineage and relationships – better to be an indebted aristocrat (*ancien pauvre*) than *nouveau riche*. Your personal value is derived from what you *are* rather than what you *do* or earn (ascription versus achievement).

In Russia, the power of the ruling elites and the concern for the collective in both traditional Russian culture, as well as under Communist ideology, also led to suspicion and mistrust of business. Engaging in business and making profit are still held as evidence of selfishness and unethical motives. Parents are ashamed of children who go into private business to make money.[7]

Economic development is also thought to be rooted in culture. Hofstede found that country GNP strongly correlated (0.82) with rankings on individualism.[8] He then went on to explain the more recent impressive economic growth of southeast Asian "tigers" as related to "Confucian dynamism" which includes values of persistence, thrift, well-defined social roles, and a long-term, future orientation.[9]

Why firms exist

The very reason for "why firms exist", or the theory of the firm, is also strongly influenced by culture. Many Western business schools preach profit maximization as the ultimate goal to be *achieved*. They promote the idea that firms exist in order to provide benefits to shareholders, or to reduce transaction costs. These notions reflect underlying assumptions of organizations as instrumental, and of managers as "rational economic" actors, driven by self-interest (individualism).

In contrast, the idea that firms exist in order to promote the well-being of society (social responsibility) reflects assumptions of organizations as "systems of relationships", and of managers as "paternalistic", driven by concern for the "collective" (multiple stakeholders). These notions can be found in a growing number of company mission statements. Consider the following excerpts from Matsushita's creed and philosophy.

> Through our industrial activities, we strive to foster progress, to promote the general welfare of society, and to devote ourselves to furthering the development of world culture.

> The purpose of an enterprise is to contribute to society by supplying goods of high quality and low prices in ample quantity.

> Profit comes in compensation for contribution to society . . . [it] is a result rather than a goal.[10]

This vision clashes with assumptions underlying free market ideology; the *raison d'être* is not necessarily to provide shareholder benefits, nor to improve efficiency in market-driven economies. Responding to the question, "Is the only real goal of a company to make a profit or should the well-being of the various stakeholders be taken into account?", 47 percent of US managers chose the profit motive; this was true for a mere 4 percent of the Japanese.[11] The very meaning of profit may also be subject to cultural differences in interpretation. A study conducted with US and Japanese business students found such differences.

> For the Japanese, only one factor emerged. Profit is the reward to businessmen for taking risks to produce innovations society needs to develop the future. The American students had multiple concepts of profit, some emphasizing personal gain, some social value. To the Japanese, however, only one concept of profit exists and in it social and self interest are the same.[12]

In Portugal, one may find a more or less explicit theory of the firm including the belief that it exists to take care of workers. This theory reflects values of paternalism (hierarchy) and collectivism which makes the idea of layoffs in economic downturn particularly difficult to accept or implement. Moreover, this is reinforced by law.[13] For many Europeans (both west and east) and Asians, Americans are seen as behaving unethically when closing factories, laying off workers, and neglecting their social obligations. This lack of social conscience is what is perceived as "harsh capitalism". It comes as a shock to many to see the huge gap between the rich and poor in the United States, or the ratio of CEO to employee salary (Japan 17:1, Europe 21:1, US 155:1),[14] taken as evidence of unethical exploitation.

When Reader's Digest decided to withdraw from the Japanese market after 24 years, having been profitable for only 11 of those years, they were accused of a "crime akin to child abandonment". The affected labor union placed advertisements in the *New York Times* saying that the company's behavior was "unfair, unscrupulous, and irresponsible".[15]

Also, although it is common for Americans to change jobs often, and to trade up (change company for an increase in pay), company-hopping is seen as immoral in Japan; even if changing companies is now becoming more acceptable, frequent moves remain suspect. Faced with economic recession and increased competition, many European and even Japanese companies are restructuring (downsizing), creating moral *angst* over the breakdown of the psychological contract: employee loyalty in return for lifetime employment and company commitment to employee welfare.

Nevertheless, many American companies also make it their business to be socially responsible. These companies take seriously their role in improving society and providing benefit to multiple *stakeholders*, not just shareholders. Johnson & Johnson's credo makes it clear that providing benefits to shareholders is not first on the list of priorities, as shown in Figure 10.1. The strength of this credo, or corporate philosophy was credited with the socially responsible behavior of recalling Tylenol from market shelves. Thus different theories of the firm can be found in different cultures, both national and corporate.

These different underlying assumptions regarding the purpose of the firm – economic or social – drive the debate regarding the relationship between profit and social responsibility. Does profit represent an end in itself or does it provide the means for creating a better society? Does social responsibility make economic sense or is it a moral imperative? While some managers may remain cynical faced with such discussions, the social role and responsibility, particularly of global organizations, can no longer be side-stepped.

Making economic versus moral sense

The motivation for ethical behavior and for social responsibility has recently become a hot topic in the business press and within academic circles. What *really* drives such behavior: corporate philanthropy or corporate profit? For example, the furniture company, Herman Miller, banned the use of certain species of wood in order to prevent the destruction of rainforests (no more rosewood). While the corporate concern for ethics

Our Credo

We believe our first responsibility is to the doctors, nurses and patients,
to mothers and all others who use our products and services.
In meeting their needs everything we do must be of high quality.
We must constantly strive to reduce our costs
in order to maintain reasonable prices.
Customers' orders must be serviced promptly and accurately.
Our suppliers and distributors must have an opportunity
to make a fair profit.

We are responsible to our employees,
the men and women who work with us throughout the world.
Everyone must be considered as an individual.
We must respect their dignity and recognize their merit.
They must have a sense of security in their jobs.
Compensation must be fair and adequate,
and working conditions clean, orderly and safe.
Employees must feel free to make suggestions and complaints.
There must be equal opportunity for employment, development
and advancement for those qualified.
We must provide competent management,
and their actions must be just and ethical.

We are responsible to the communities in which we live and work
and to the world community as well.
We must be good citizens — support good works and charities
and bear our fair share of taxes.
We must encourage civic improvements and better health and education.
We must maintain in good order
the property we are privileged to use,
protecting the environment and natural resources.

Our final responsibility is to our stockholders.
Business must make a sound profit.
We must experiment with new ideas.
Research must be carried on, innovative programs developed
and mistakes paid for.
New equipment must be purchased, new facilities provided
and new products launched.
Reserves must be created to provide for adverse times.
When we operate according to these principles,
the stockholders should realize a fair return.

Johnson & Johnson

Figure 10.1 Johnson & Johnson credo. (Reproduced by permission of Johnson & Johnson, New York.)

dates back to 1923, thanks to the founder, D.J. DePree, a devout Baptist, top management also argues that these initiatives, such as recycling, make economic sense.[16]

In the United Kingdom, Anita Roddick's Body Shop, a soaps and cosmetics company, has made a fortune selling "natural" products. Company practices appeal to the consumer's conscience by recycling bottles, sourcing natural materials from the rainforest and other exotic locations, and setting up operations in developing countries under the slogan "Trade not Aid".[17] Their policy of "no animal testing" in developing products (and the highly visible campaign to stop such industry practices) came under attack, when they were accused of not upholding their own policy and of playing on political correctness. Despite such criticism, since the stock went public in 1984, the stock price (by 1992) had increased by over 10,000 percent.[18]

Interest in investing in "ethical" companies or "ethical" funds has grown. These funds (the first ethical fund, Pax World, was set up in the United States in the early 1970s) are restricted from investing in companies, for example, that produce alcohol and tobacco, or defense contractors. Supporters of these funds argue that paying attention to stakeholders as well as shareholders will, in the long term, boost profits by motivating the workforce, developing community goodwill, and avoiding fines. US and UK charities constrained to invest in ethical funds did, in fact, marginally outperform others not so constrained.[19]

Economists, however, protest that "ethical fund investing is a clever marketing tool that dupes people into thinking they are doing something moral".[20] They argue that the stock market carries no moral value, merely a price. German investment firms argue that "we couldn't offer an ethical investment because if we offered a moral alternative that would mean that other investments were not moral".[21]

Many managers believe that there is an inherent trade-off between being profitable and socially responsible. For this reason, John Shad, former SEC chairman, gave Harvard Business School $30 million in order to convince students that "Ethics pays: It's smart to be ethical".[22] A survey of business school deans and congressmen found 63 percent agreement with that notion. However, David Vogel, professor at Berkeley, argues that the statement "ethics pays" undermines its very intention. He insists that "it is unethical to base the case for ethics on economic self interest". Sometimes ethics costs, making decisions to engage in ethical behavior far from trivial, nor devoid of moral choice.[23]

Acts of corporate social responsibility may in fact be the consequence of profitability rather than the cause. It is easy to be magnanimous when things are going well. The real test is when there is a choice between acting ethically and making a profit, as in the case of the decision of US jeans company, Levi-Strauss, to pull their $40 million business out of the lucrative Chinese market in protest against human rights violations. While being a family-held business means that there is less need to worry about shareholders, Levi-Strauss has a long tradition of upholding core values (called aspirations) that have been promoted by family members over several generations.[24]

The relationship between profit and ethics (or morality) may be doomed to an eternal debate between the "economists" and the "humanists", or on the front lines, between the finance and human resource departments. The question remains whether morality and personal (or corporate) self-interest are necessarily mutually exclusive. Does ethics make good business sense, or does it represent a personal (or organizational) "way of being", or integrity?[25] (What you are versus what you do.) Or should ethics be considered a fundamental necessity, an unassailable assumption, in conducting international business?

> No free society or free economy can long survive without an ethical base . . . a shared moral foundation, a set of binding rules for fair conduct . . . Far from being a luxury, a sound business ethic is essential to the preservation of free enterprise.[26]

Some may argue that this statement can be taken as evidence of cultural imperialism. According to a report in the *Financial Times*, many Asian leaders are rejecting such Western liberal democratic ideas, insisting on economic growth "the Asian way".

> . . . Neoconfucianists argue that authoritarian governments such as China's are acceptable, even essential, because discipline is necessary to bring prosperity to developing countries. Full democracy as understood in the west would lead to chaos. Freedom of expression is undesirable . . . because it encourages instability and could provoke conflict between ethnic groups. The rights of individuals must be respected only insofar as they do not impinge on the greater rights of the community as a whole . . .
>
> The west should stop arrogantly trying to impose inappropriate western standards of human rights, democracy and environmental protection on Asia, especially since Asia is on the rise and the west is declining as the "Pacific century" approaches.[27]

Others contend that ethical behavior provides the moral underpinnings of a free society and a free economy and can thereby be justified as an **imperative of globalization**. Yet notions of what is moral and ethical do not necessarily translate across national borders. For example, does the notion of "human rights" in China have a different meaning than in the West? Still, the push towards globalization is causing culture shocks in the way business is conducted around the world, as shown in Figure 10.2.

"It's either a shift away from Reaganomics, a shift in moral values, or an earthquake!"

Figure 10.2 Culture shocks. (*Source: Harvard Business Review*, May–June 1989. Adapted and reprinted by permission of *Harvard Business Review*. Copyright © 1989 by the President and Fellows of Harvard College, all rights reserved.)

The globalization imperative

The globalization of business activities calls for a "level playing field" where the rules of the game are clearly spelled out and apply to everyone. Clearly embedded in this imperative are assumptions of *universalism* and *fairness*. "Being fair" means providing equal opportunities and access to markets, not playing favorites, nor protecting home interests. It also implies distributive justice, such that everyone should get their "fair share". However these assumptions may not be shared in cultures that are relationship-driven and rely on personal networks, where belonging is more important than performing, and where *les droits du seigneur* (the rights of the lord) apply. After all, what does "equal access" or "fair share" mean in the context of a family and, more specifically, in the relationship between parent and child?

Nevertheless, as business continues to globalize, the role of multinationals and their missionaries in establishing and adhering to a shared set of business practices needs to be addressed. This is the case whether the primary motivation is to create a better world or simply to reduce the personal and company liabilities or perils of operating abroad, and now even at home.

Titans tumble

In many countries, chief executives and senior managers are waking up to some harsh realities of doing business across borders, as when the CEO of a French conglomerate found himself locked up in a Belgian jail. Indeed many senior executives are faced with some surprising consequences of becoming international players, finding themselves in jail in their own countries.[28] The "clean hands" (*mani pulite*) campaign launched in Italy in February 1992, for example, caused the resignation of top company and country officials, including ex-prime ministers, as well as the suicides of several prominent businessmen.[29] Many practices formerly considered "business as usual" are coming into public scrutiny, in Europe and in Asia, creating economic and political havoc.

The impact of the globalization imperative, that the rules of the game need to be the same for all players, is particularly evident in the financial industry. It started with scandals in the United States: E.F. Hutton gets nailed for check kiting schemes, Bank of Boston for laundering money, Citibank for parking funds off shore in the Caribbean, and Wall Street millionaire heroes (Mike Milliken, Dennis Levine, Ivan Boesky) are convicted of trading insider information. Questionable practices caused the sudden death of Drexel Burnham and the near death of Solomon Brothers (caught in treasury bond fiasco).

It may be that the nature of the industry plays an important role here. In investment banking, the "gray areas" are often where the money is to be made (no risk, no gain). Walking the thin line of legality provides the thrill as vividly portrayed by Michael Douglas as Gordon Gecko in the movie, *Wall Street*. Or, the corporate culture may be the culprit. The "profit above all" culture of GE was considered to be partly responsible for the Kidder Peabody scandal, as was the highly competitive "score at all costs" culture at Salomon Brothers.[30] But different countries also have different assumptions about what is considered "business as usual".

At first, many Europeans did not understand what all the noise was about in the United States. Insider trading, for example, was considered the normal state of affairs in the "City" (London). Then, in 1987 British courts convicted Ernest Saunders, then CEO of Guinness, of stock fraud. In Germany, insider trading was not considered illegal; "It's part of the culture here, and traders accept it as their due".[31] Nevertheless, Deutsche Bank has had to face up to its share of problems. The recent scandals of questionable financial trading practices at Metallgesellschaft and of Jurgen Schneider, who ended up owing the bank $3 billion, have challenged fundamental assumptions regarding the role of banks and business in Germany.[32]

In France, cultural aftershocks have been felt ever since the 1989 Pechiney insider trading fiasco and continue in more recent scandals involving shareholder- or taxpayer-financed home improvements, kickbacks, and political party contributions. These scandals have shaken up the "Gallic old boy network", and challenged the previously tight relationship between the judicial system and the government. This has resulted in a more open and accountable power structure where "the boss is no longer a sacred image".[33]

Continuing east, the banking scandals in Japan in 1991, and the bribery and corruption scandals in India and South Korea have seriously shaken economic and political stability in these countries. Thus the globalization imperative has challenged fundamental business, as well as cultural, assumptions in many countries: the long-cherished relationships between companies, or with customers in Japan, between banks and companies in Germany, or between companies and government in France.

Throughout the world, the resulting public outcry has challenged the long-entrenched social power structures, resulting in the growing demand for greater transparency and accountability to the public interest. In Japan this greater concern is attributed to the increasing vote (and louder voice) of women in society. Such cultural and political upheaval is due in part to globalization. Indeed, the very hope of arriving at "global civilization" depends upon being able to establish a shared meaning of what is considered to be ethical and socially responsible behavior. But to what extent is this really possible? The key question "what is ethical?" is itself a cultural minefield.

Are ethics culture-free?

St Thomas Aquinas, the thirteenth century philosopher, argued that there exists a "natural law" that transcends national boundaries and which "encompasses the preservation of human life, the promotion of family life, an orderly social life, and the quest for knowledge".[34] And throughout history, philosophers have been arguing over the proper criteria for determining ethical behavior: utilitarianism (Bentham and Mill), rights (Kant and Locke), justice (Aristotle), or filial piety (Confucius).

These criteria clearly reflect underlying cultural assumptions. For example, utilitarianism (the greatest good for the greatest number) implies an instrumental, functionalist approach. And rights, by what right: by hierarchy, or, as D'Iribarne argued,[35] by role as in France, by contract as in the United States, or by consensus as in The Netherlands? Does ethics take on different shades of truth on different sides of the Pyrenees (as stated by the sixteenth century French philosopher, Michel de Montaigne), or different sides of the Atlantic and Pacific oceans for that matter?

To address this issue we need to consider what is shared (*etic*) and what is culture-specific (*emic*), and perhaps more fundamentally, *why* we find similarities and differences. Only then can we consider the possibility of arriving at a shared understanding of the issues (such as corruption) and a shared way of responding to those issues, or an agreed upon code of conduct. Again, rather than imposing our own standards, the hope is to find ways of utilizing different cultural assumptions in order to become truly global citizens. With this aim in mind, we first consider the research evidence for cultural differences and similarities in attitudes and responses to issues of ethics and social responsibility. We then search for the underlying reasons. Let us consider the case of corruption.

What is corruption?

Corruption can be defined as

> . . . the misuse of authority as a result of considerations of personal gain which need not be monetary and includes bribery, nepotism, extortion, embezzlement, and utilization of resources and facilities which do not belong to the individual for his own private purposes.[36]

More recently sexual harassment has been added to the list.

In 1977, following scandals which implicated ITT in the effort to overthrow then President Allende in Chile and bribery at Lockheed, the United States passed the Foreign Corrupt Practices Act which made "unethical" behavior abroad subject to the same penalties as at home.

As certain practices, such as bribery, were sometimes considered the only way of doing business in certain environments, American companies had to find other ways or had to leave. IBM managers, for example, sign ethics pledges, swearing to uphold the Foreign Corrupt Practices Act and the company's ethics policies. ITT managers, having signed similar documents, are regularly audited (unannounced). Other companies hire local "watchdogs" to monitor their employee's lifestyles.[37]

Yet differences in local business practices continue to challenge international managers when confronted with what at home would be considered corrupt practices. And managers from different countries report different attitudes when faced with these situations.

For example, in a comparative study of US and European managers,[38] bribery was more often considered the price of doing business or necessary given the competitor's behavior by French (55 percent) and German (38 percent) managers than by US (17 percent). Forty-seven percent of American managers said that the action called for in the scenario presented was a bribe and therefore unethical, illegal, or against company policy (as compared with 15 percent French or 9 percent German). While bribery is illegal at home in France (French Penal Code, 1960) and in Germany, there is no such legislation that applies abroad.

In the same study it was found that all managers indicated similar concern in cases involving personal injury or protecting society. However, different reactions to such scenarios were evident. French and US managers were found more likely to blow the whistle (report on organizational activities to outside authorities) than were German managers. In addition, managers in France and Germany were more willing to let slide a minor infraction concerning pollution (despite having major environmental laws since early 1970s), than were American managers. The greater likelihood of enforcement in the United States was considered a key factor in explaining the differences found in this study.

Another study found both similarities and differences when comparing attitudes of managers in the United States and Hong Kong.[39] While differences were evident with regard to attitudes towards patent protection and price-fixing, almost all managers agreed on reporting defective or unsafe products to superiors even if their job was potentially jeopardized (94 percent HK versus 99 percent US). Although Hong Kong managers indicated that they were less inclined towards whistle blowing (50 percent HK versus 77 percent US), they reported often having to compromise personal principles to conform (92 percent HK versus 41 percent US).

Differences were also found in the way of resolving ethical dilemmas: US managers were more likely to consult with their boss (42 percent US versus 26 percent HK), while Hong Kong managers were more likely to discuss the issue with a friend (20 percent HK versus 6 percent US). These differences can be taken as evidence of greater collectivism when compared to the United States: sharing of information and consensual agreements, loyalty, and pressures for conformity.

The study also asked managers to rank the factors which they considered to contribute to unethical behavior. Neither group considered the society's moral climate or personal financial needs as important determinants. For both groups, the most important factor was the behavior of superiors. US managers placed more importance on the behavior of peers as a determining factor, while for managers in Hong Kong company policy and industry norms were given more importance.

According to the authors of this study, laws and regulations were considered unnecessary in Hong Kong due to the strong social controls created by intense interpersonal relationships. For example, insider trading is not considered a criminal offense; public exposure, loss of face, is considered to be sufficient punishment. Nonetheless, 82 percent of Hong Kong citizens indicated a need for regulation to improve ethical conduct in business. Apparently, more formal guidelines would be welcomed.

Codes of conduct

Codes of conduct provide such formal guidelines. One study conducted by the Conference Board found that by 1986, 92 percent of US companies had codes of conduct, 36 percent had ethics training, 16 percent indicated board level discussion of ethics, and 11 percent had assigned an ombudsman.[40] Another study compared codes of conduct in the top 200 firms in the United Kingdom, France, and (West) Germany and compared the results with that of a US survey of "Fortune 500" firms. Differences in the existence and content of codes of conduct were found not only between US and European firms, but among European firms as well.[41]

Codes of conduct were defined as "A statement setting down corporate principles, ethics, rules of conduct, codes of practice or company philosophy concerning responsibility to employees, shareholders, consumers, the environment or any other aspects of society external to the company". While 75 percent of the US "Fortune 500" firms surveyed has such codes, 59 percent of the 189 European companies responding did not. Most of the European companies had introduced codes in 1986 and only 56 percent intended to introduce them by 1990. These findings were taken as evidence of an "ethics gap" between the United States and Europe.

Differences within Europe were also found: only 30 percent of the French firms surveyed had codes of conduct, compared with 51 percent of the firms in Germany, and 41 percent in the United Kingdom. Controlling for local companies which were US affiliates, the "ethics gap" was found to be even greater: only 33 percent of European firms had codes – in France 18 percent, Germany 47 percent, and in the United Kingdom 31 percent. Of the US affiliates, only 2 percent did *not* have such codes.

The content of these codes of conduct was also found to be different. While all of the European company codes addressed the question of employee conduct (as compared with 55 percent of US firms), differences were found in what that meant. For US firms, it meant treating employees with "fairness and equity", for example, ensuring equal opportunity. The French and British codes stressed the importance of employees to the organization, reinforcing a sense of belonging and collective goals. In Germany, the rights of codetermination and shared responsibility were emphasized, as were specific expectations that the company had of its employees: reliability and loyalty. Thus the European codes focused on employee attitude and behavior towards the company (the collective), while in the United States the focus was placed on company policy towards employees (the individual).

Other differences in the content of codes were also reported: 60 percent of German companies stressed the importance of technology and innovation, and in France 93 percent addressed customer relations. This may indicate efforts to compensate for what is perceived as country-level competitive weaknesses discussed earlier: the reputation of German firms as not being terribly innovative and French firms not being particularly customer- or service-oriented. Given the French interest in high technology, it may not be surprising that one French construction company, Bouygues, included the use of advanced computerized information systems as its 11th commandment.

Other differences found to be culture-specific related to concern for political issues. For US managers this referred to the legal environment and was taken to mean being law-abiding. For the German publisher, Bertelsmann (Germany), this was expressed more generally as support for "a free, democratic and socially responsible society". Despite these differences, the study found that most ethical issues transcended national barriers: fairness and honesty; and concern for customers, suppliers, and community.

In the studies discussed above, it appears that there are concerns which cut across cultural boundaries, concern for society and for employee and customer safety, for example. However, differences were found in how they would respond to these issues. This difference was related to the legal context (regulation and enforcement) as well as the cultural context (hierarchy and collectivism).

Yet the questions remain: Why has this issue attracted so much attention in the United States? Is there indeed an "ethics gap"? Are US companies and managers more moral than their European and Asian counterparts? Or do they manage this issue in ways that are just more explicit, and public? Is insisting on ethical behavior, for example with regard to human rights, an excuse for meddling in internal national affairs, as China's Prime Minister has asserted? To what extent can a shared approach to business ethics be hoped for?

Reasons for differences

David Vogel, Professor at Berkeley, believes that there are persistent fundamental national differences in terms of how business ethics is defined, debated, and judged which are due to distinctive institutional, legal, social, and cultural contexts.[42]

Notions of ethics in the United States, for example, are more legalistic and universalist, based on rules and regulations that apply to everyone. These are often made explicit (low context), in written codes of conduct or lists of principles displayed proudly throughout the company, or distributed on wallet-sized cards. This approach annoyed one French manager of a firm acquired by Americans,

> I resent having notions of right and wrong boiled down to a checklist. I come from a nation whose ethical traditions date back hundreds of years. Its values have been transmitted to me by my church and through my family. I don't need to be told by some American lawyers how I should conduct myself in my business activities.[43]

In contrast with the United States where ethical decisions are considered personal, moral judgements, requiring individual responsibility and accountability, in Europe and Asia moral standards are considered to be more "consensual". "Legitimate moral expectations for a company are shaped by the norms of the community not the personal values or reflections of the individual."[44] Ethics is thus *particularist*, applied according to specific circumstances, and strongly affected by the nature of one's social ties and obligations.[45] As such, greater emphasis is placed on informal, social control.

The importance of this more collective, consensual approach is that outsiders, very often entrepreneurs, are the first to take the fall (Bernard Tapie in France, Resaat El-Sayed in Sweden. Even Saunders and Maxwell in the United Kingdom, and Milliken and Boesky in the United States are outsiders in these predominantly Anglo–Saxon Protestant cultures). The economic power of the entrepreneurial overseas Chinese makes them a target for local economic or political problems, as in Malaysia and Indonesia.

For the Japanese, the insider/outsider (*uchi/soto*) ethic is extremely powerful, making it difficult to do business without the proper connections. According to an old Japanese saying, "When you see a stranger, regard him as a thief".[46] Thus outsiders are viewed suspiciously, as they may not share the same values, nor be concerned for the welfare of the group.

In many Asian countries, the teachings of Confucius, which serve as moral guidelines, promote the importance of authority and the collective expressed as clearly structured role relationships. This means that morality is more likely to be defined in terms of others, in terms of interdependence rather than independence.[47] Japanese mothers, for example, coax their children to eat their vegetables by having them consider the feelings of the farmer who produced them.

Notions of reciprocity result in common practices of gift giving and exchanging favors, of saving face and giving face. Shame serves as the most powerful form of social control. Not living up to obligations results in being seen as unreliable, and may lead to ostracism. In Japan, taking individual responsibility has even more serious implications; mitigating circumstances are no excuse. This led to the suicide of the CEO of Japan Airlines following a plane crash.

In contrast, America's Protestant heritage encourages *individual* moral scrutiny and self-criticism (if not self-righteousness). "Ethics [is] considered as a question of personal scruples, a confidential matter between individuals and their consciences."[48] Feelings of guilt rather than shame rest upon living up to internalized ideals rather than external expectations. Morality is based on having to live with yourself rather than with others.

The insistence on individualism thus requires universalism, that the same set of morals or rules and regulations apply to everyone. This results in the US legalistic approach to ethics. The emphasis on individualism results in attributing ethical behavior to the CEO, as in the case of Tylenol, and downplaying the possibility that this behavior may not have happened without the supporting organizational culture. The legalistic approach may also result in an emphasis on compliance (*doing*) rather than on encouraging integrity (*being*).[49]

While the above discussion points to different cultural determinants of ethical behavior, institutional factors need to be considered as well. Some of the institutional reasons may have to do with the roles of government and legislation, of the media, and of the stakeholders, shareholders as well as consumers. For example, the more vocal concern for ethics in the United States may be due to stricter government disclosure laws and more active enforcement, more aggressive journalism (or less fear of libel suits, as in Britain) and "best company" rankings in the business press, and greater risk of shareholder activism and consumer boycotts.

Role of government

Vogel argues that the prevalence of private rather than state ownership in the United States makes corporate social responsibility and philanthropy "primarily an American phenomenon".[50] In Europe, until very recently, business has been largely state rather than privately owned, and populated by small rather than large organizations. Thus the responsibility of business was more narrowly defined. The government was considered primarily responsible for economic development and social welfare.

In the United States private ownership and "big" business put more of the onus and spotlight on company behavior. According to Vogel, "Because the public's expectations of business conduct are so high, the invariable result is a consistently high level of public dissatisfaction with the actual ethical performance of business".[51] It seems more likely, however, that the experience with big business has been such that there is a greater perceived need to be vigilant. Given a history of questionable business practices, some of the richest Americans, the Rockefellers, Carnegies, and Kennedys, were held morally (and legally) suspect in how they made their fortunes.

In fact, in the last ten years, two-thirds of American business has been found to be involved in illegal behavior.[52] And public perceptions of business ethics are indeed quite negative: 59 percent of Americans surveyed believed corporate executives to be dishonest, 58 percent thought ethical standards of business fair or poor, and 49 percent thought business crime was *very* common (41 percent *somewhat* common).[53]

Rather than the "values of 'business civilization' [being] so deeply engrained", as Vogel argues, it is more likely that the perceived excesses of capitalism have to be carefully checked. For example, the oil shortages in the 1970s were viewed by the public as having been manipulated by the oil companies for profit at their expense. This created an outcry that turned some of them into corporate philanthropists, demonstrating concern for social responsibility by creating foundations and by providing highly visible endowments to the arts.

Regulation: the legal context

Differences in legal context, the nature of regulation and the likelihood of enforcement, also play an important role. In Germany, strict environmental laws make these issues more salient. Still, there are few laws against bribery, kickbacks and pay-offs in the corporate sector.[54] In France, the "commission des operations de la bourse" has become a more powerful watchdog. However, in Britain, enforcement remains infrequent, despite the conviction of Ernest Saunders in the Guinness affair. Many were surprised at the lenient ruling on the Maxwell brothers, accused of misappropriating pension funds.

In the United States, between 1988 and 1990, financial penalties have increased by a factor of eight. This cost Exxon $100 million in fines for the Valdez disaster (oil spill), Salomon $200 million, and Drexel Burnham $650 million (which put it into bankruptcy). US managers have learned that crime does not pay.[55] In response to federal guidelines that went into effect on November 1, 1991, many US companies have adopted codes of conduct and training programs to reduce liabilities and potential fines: $1–2 million fines could be knocked down to $50,000 if they had comprehensive programs such as codes of conduct, ombudsmen, employee hotlines, and mandatory training programs.[56]

At Citibank, for example, ethics training tools were designed such as "Work Ethic" which poses ethical dilemmas for managers to solve, such as that shown in Figure 10.3.[57] Implementing such programs may be viewed cynically as a way to avoid fines rather than as the right way of doing business. Indeed, no amount of ethical programs can make a company immune. The existence of a business conduct committee since 1976, did not stop Dow Corning from continuing to manufacture potentially dangerous breast implants.[58] Compliance with these guidelines does not address the fundamental ways of doing business which may put company integrity at risk.

The role of the media

Public scrutiny of ethical behavior in companies has been made possible by the increased attention to these issues by the media. Ethical breaches have become front page news:

Ethics: part of the game at Citicorp

■ Citicorp managers, ever circumspect, do not like to call their newly designed training tool, the Work Ethic, a game. But it is.

Players move markers around a game board by correctly answering multiple-choice questions presented on cards. Each card poses an ethical dilemma a bank employee might encounter in the office or with customers. As the game progresses, players are "promoted" from entry-level employee to supervisor, and eventually to senior manager. As the rank in the company rises, the score for a correct answer drops.

Should you talk to a credit applicant about his loan in public at a cocktail party? If you know not to and you're a supervisor, you gain 30 points; if you're an executive, add only 10. What if the manager of a competing bank calls to suggest colluding on interest rates? If you pick "ask to meet him and discuss it further", you're "fired for cause", and out of the game.

Citicorp thinks the game, which is still under development, could become part of its comprehensive corporate-ethics training program. Says Citicorp assistant secretary Christopher York: "We wanted to increase people's involvement by adding a little bit of competition to the training exercise."

After successfully completing a complex deal for a Japanese client, he presents you with a vase to express his appreciation. It's an expensive item and accepting a gift of such value is clearly against Citicorp policy. Yet, returning it would insult your client.

You:
a) return the vase to the client and explain diplomatically that it's against Citicorp policy to accept gifts from clients.
b) accept the gift because you can't risk insulting an importamt client.
c) accept the gift on behalf of Citicorp, log it with premises management as a furnishing, and display it in a public area of the office.
d) accept the gift and use it as an award for an employee who displays service excellence.

Citicorp likes answer c.

Figure 10.3 Citibank's ethics game. (*Source*: *FORTUNE*, 26 October 1987. Reprinted by permission.)

Exxon's Valdez oil spill, Union Carbide's Bhopal disaster, the BCCI débâcle, and the Barings fiasco. Journalists are increasingly becoming the "moral watchdogs" of corporate behavior. This has led to the dictum for managers: "Don't do anything that you wouldn't want to read in the newspaper".

The CNN coverage of the Anita Hill/Clarence Day affair made sexual harassment a global concern, highlighting the role of the media in the debate and definition of ethics. While Europeans tend to view the American public as excessively moralistic, puritanical, and hypocritical, some were nevertheless impressed with the openness and the transparency with which such ethical concerns were addressed, or publicly aired.

Media attention can also promote "good behavior". Companies have come to realize that well-publicized ethical actions can provide a competitive edge in the "caring nineties" (public backlash to the 1980s as the decade of corporate greed). Company image is enhanced not only with consumers but also with the internal workforce. Company pride can serve as a powerful motivator. Best company rankings provided by business journals such as *Fortune* or *Business Week* (which take into account ethical behavior) not only attract investment and customers but also top talent. Anita Roddick of the Body Shop recognizes the value of media attention in promoting public relations; the company does not advertise.

The role of stakeholders

Company stakeholders – the local community, customers, employees as well as shareholders – play an increasingly important role in monitoring ethical behavior. Striking employees protest over the closing of factories. Employees may also "blow the whistle" on unethical activities, such as employee safety practices in the famous case of Karen Silkwood. A Japanese engineer at Honda recently testified against the company's safety practices, sending shock waves in Japan where whistle-blowing is unheard of, akin to high treason.[59]

Customers boycott companies engaged in questionable practices, for example refusing to buy grapes picked by migrant workers in California. Local communities have become much more active in insisting on environmental protection, as in the case of Swiss pharmaceutical company Sandoz, which was burned in effigy, accused of polluting the Rhine. US government agencies are prohibited from doing business with suppliers or distributors that do not uphold affirmative action guidelines.

There is also growing pressure to hold company boards of directors more accountable. In the United States, members of the board are subject to increased personal liability for company actions and risk landing in jail or receiving heavy fines. Shareholders have become more vigilant and vocal in questioning the behavior of top management. In France this has led to the resignation of CEOs accused of using company resources for private purposes.

Despite the reasons, both cultural and institutional, for similarities and differences in ethical behavior, as discussed above, the question remains: to what extent should personal values, parent company, or home-country values and rules apply? Head-office efforts to insist on ethical practices or to install ethics programs in foreign subsidiaries may be taken as another sign of cultural imperialism. These efforts may even be disparaged as moral hypocrisy. Americans are often accused of excessive self-righteousness, and worse yet, of missionary zeal. Should we play by the local rules? Or is it possible to find a better way?

Strategies for managing ethical dilemmas

While the globalization imperative has challenged fundamental cultural and business assumptions throughout the world, many practices which may seem objectionable, remain firmly embedded in the host-country environment. The decision has to be made whether to impose parent company or home-country rules in host countries or to play by the local rules of the game. Journalist Roger Williams argues that,

> Corporations are not formed to effect change but to sell goods. It can be pressured into treating employees more equitably. But it cannot be expected to challenge the laws of a society. Those who insist otherwise are trying to get a businessman to do the job of a diplomat or a soldier.

However, during investigations of Italy's bribery scandals, the activities of foreign multinationals operating in Italy (such as ABB, Siemens, and Ericsson) came under scrutiny. Although kickbacks had been considered necessary to win public contracts, as openly acknowledged by top Italian industrialist, Carlo Di Benedetti, many major multinationals and their executives, both foreign and domestic, found themselves under arrest.

In fact, succession planning at some of the major Italian multinationals has been held up pending outcomes of such investigations. This experience provided a literal warning that the advice "when in Rome . . ." had serious limitations.[60]

Apparently, few American companies were implicated. This was attributed to taking seriously US anticorruption legislation and corporate ethics policies. At Honeywell Europe, the Italian Vice-President responsible for southern Europe acknowledged that while upholding company principles regarding ethical behavior sometimes meant walking away from certain markets, most managers felt pride in being able to do this.[61] But to what extent does imposing home country or company rules reflect cultural imperialism? In the words of Citibank,

> We must never lose sight of the fact that we are guests in foreign countries. We must conduct ourselves accordingly. Local governments can pass any kind of legislation, and whether we like it or not, we must conform to it. Under these circumstances, Citibank can survive only if we are successful in demonstrating to the local authorities that our presence is useful to them.[62]

Consider the case of South Africa, under apartheid, where different decisions were taken for different reasons. Some companies such as Polaroid or General Motors chose the path of "civil disobedience", operating in ways to bring about social change by breaking the rules of apartheid. Insisting on the corporate ethic of racial equality and opportunity, for example, these companies integrated factory washrooms and community neighborhoods.[63] Over one hundred (125) of the US "Fortune 500" companies (accounting for $2.5 billion in US FDI in Africa) signed up promising to adhere to the Sullivan Principles, a code of conduct for operating in South Africa.[64] These principles are shown in Figure 10.4.

The Sullivan Principles

• Non-segregation of the races in all eating, comfort, locker room, and work facilities
• Equal and fair employment practices for all employees
• Equal pay for all employees doing equal or comparable work for the same period of time
▶ Initiation and development of training programs that will prepare blacks, coloreds, and Asians in substantial numbers for supervisory, administrative, clerical, and technical jobs
▶ Increasing the number of blacks, coloreds, and Asians in management and supervisory positions
▶ Improving the quality of employees' lives outside the work environment in such areas as housing, transportation, schooling, recreation, and health facilities

Figure 10.4 The Sullivan principles. (*Source*: "The case for doing business in South Africa", *Fortune*, 19 June 1978. Reprinted by permission.)

Other companies chose to play by the host-country (apartheid) rules for reasons such as those expressed by Citibank. Eventually, economic sanctions imposed by the US Comprehensive Anti-Apartheid Act in November 1986 forced forty-nine US firms (including IBM, GM, and P&G) to withdraw from South Africa, and another forty the year after.

Several European companies, however, were reluctant to pull out, given the substantial amounts of investment, notably by British and West German firms less subject to the same kind of sanctions and shareholder pressures as in the United States. "The big difference between American and European business is the lesser moral tone".[65] However, British bank Barclays did pull out in 1986 after pressure from local special interest groups.[66] Dutch interests also succumbed to external pressures. Other foreign investors, particularly Asian companies, went in, buying up companies at fire-sale prices. The same has since happened in Burma.

Thus, as the case of South Africa demonstrates, different countries and different companies adopt different decisions when faced with these ethical dilemmas. Powerful multinational companies, such as Shell or IBM, may be able to convince local governments to play by the company rules or not to play at all. Thus the relationship of the home company or country to the host country, being considered an insider, powerful, and important, is critical.[67] Nevertheless, despite instances of countries agreeing to impose economic sanctions or boycotts for political reasons (Bosnia, Iran, Israel), arriving at a common approach to operating in other countries for economic reasons remains elusive. French President Chirac's recent promotion of business activities in China, to the chagrin of US President Clinton, may be a case in point.

In choosing to play by the local rules or to impose home-court rules, the following questions need to be open for discussion: Is following the dictum "when in Rome . . ." an easy way out, the path of least resistance? Does this mean that there is no difference between cultural relativism and ethical relativism, that there is no absolute good versus bad, right versus wrong? By accepting that different cultures have different notions of what is considered moral behavior, are we respecting cultural differences or are we contributing to social problems?

As Alan Christie, Director of Community Affairs, Levi-Strauss Europe, puts it, "The private sector may not be able to answer the social problems of the world – but it can stop being part of those problems". But does this mean that it is better to pull out or to stay and insist on doing it your way? Is it better to refuse to play (withdraw) or to fight the system from within? Which was more effective in the case of South Africa: economic sanctions or civil disobedience?

While it may not always be clear what is right and wrong (acute dilemmas), it may also be the case that one knows what is right or wrong but fails to do it (acute rationalization).[68] What are the appropriate criteria for judging ethical behavior: "How would it look in the press" (the "best disinfectant is sunlight"); or "How it would look in the mirror"? Is it enough to consult your personal sense of right and wrong?[69] Or is this an individual or collective (company, community, or national) process? These issues need to be addressed by both managers and their companies, in order to define their role as global citizens.

Global citizens: the role of managers and companies

Individual managers need to take stock not only of their own cultural and moral baggage, but also that of their company, industry, or host country. It is important to assess how these different spheres of cultural influence contribute to ethical behavior. While one's own moral position needs to be well defined ("To thine own self be true"), one must recognize how these external pressures, however subtle, may influence our judgement. In this way, morality is both an individual and collective affair.

In a study of recent Harvard MBA graduates, most reported using the "sleep test" to resolve ethical dilemmas and that the family was the primary source of ethical wisdom. They also reported company pressure to act unethically in the following messages: performance is what counts – meet your numbers, be loyal, be a team player, do not break the law, and do not overinvest in ethical behavior.[70]

In today's competitive environment, performance pressures are ever-increasing, making it more and more necessary to establish realistic performance goals. Pressure to achieve objectives above all else has led to a "means justify the ends attitude". Indeed, one study reports 20–30 percent of middle managers wrote deceptive internal reports, and 12–24 percent of job applicants deceptive resumés.[71]

Four rationalizations are found to be common in explaining unethical behavior: it is not really illegal or immoral; it serves the best interest of the individual or corporation; it is safe because it will never be found out or publicized; the activity helps the company and therefore will be condoned and protected.[72] These arguments reflect psychologically primitive systems of defense (denial). According to psychoanalyst, Abraham Zaleznik, this type of thinking derives from a narcissistic sense of entitlement that weakens conscience. Also, more than greed, there is the thrill of flirting with danger and a similar high to that of being on a winning streak, which may represent meglomania or a cover for depression.[73]

These rationalizations also reflect stages of moral development. An individual's sense of morality is developed quite early on. Kohlberg identified a sequence of six stages of moral development in children (ranging from obedience and fear of punishment if caught through adhering to universal principles of justice and welfare) which he considered to be invariant and universal.[74]

A study of Hong Kong managers found that although what managers said they would do corresponded to specific stages of development as described by Kohlberg, what they actually did when faced with different scenarios demonstrated reasoning at several stages simultaneously.[75] While some cultural differences were found when compared with American managers, the key issue was being able to capture what managers of whatever nationality would actually do or have done, rather than what they say they would do.

Using Kohlberg's model, different stages of moral development can also be found among companies, as shown in Figure 10.5.[76] **Amoral** organizations are driven by "winning at all costs", by greed, and short-term orientation. Their approach to ethics is "we won't get caught". **Legalistic** organizations are driven by concerns for economic performance. Their approach is reactive: "Don't do any harm", and obey the law to the letter. They avoid writing codes of ethics, as this can create legal problems later on. In

A summary of the moral development of corporations

Stage in moral development	Management attitude and approach	Ethical aspects of corporate culture	Corporate ethics artifacts	Defining corporate behavior
Stage I – the amoral organization	Get away with all you can; it's ethical as long as we're not caught; ethical violations, when caught, are a cost of doing business	Outlaw culture; live hard and fast; damn the risks; get what you can and get out	No meaningful code of ethics or other documentation; no set of values other than greed	Film Recovery System Numerous penny stock companies
Stage II – the legalistic organization	Play within the legal rules; fight changes that affect your economic outcome; use damage control through public relations when social problems occur; a reactive concern for damage to organizations from social problems	If it's legal, it's OK; work the gray areas; protect loopholes and don't give ground without a fight; economic performance dominates evaluations and rewards	The code of ethics, if it exists, is an internal document; "Don't do anything to harm the organization"; "Be a good corporate citizen"	Ford Pinto Firestone 500 Nestlé Infant Formula R. J. Reynolds Philip Morris
Stage III – the responsive organization	Management understands the value of not acting solely on a legal basis, even though they believe they could win; management still has a reactive mentality; a growing balance between profits and ethics, although a basic premise still may be a cynical "ethics pays"; management begins to test and learn from more responsive actions	There is a growing concern for other corporate stakeholders other than owners; culture begins to embrace a more "responsible citizen" attitude	Codes are more externally oriented and reflect a concern for other publics; other ethics vehicles are undeveloped	Procter & Gamble (Rely Tampons) Abbott Labs Borden
Stage IV – the emerging ethical organization	First stage to exhibit an active concern for ethical outcomes; "We want to do the 'right' thing"; top management values become organizational values; ethical perception has focus but lacks organization and long-term planning; ethics management is characterized by successes and failures	Ethical values become part of culture; these core values provide guidance in some situations but questions exist in others; a culture that is less reactive and more proactive to social problems when they occur	Codes of ethics become action documents; code items reflect the core values of the organization; handbooks, policy statements, committees, ombudsmen are sometimes used	Boeing General Mills Johnson & Johnson (Tylenol) General Dynamics Caterpillar Levi Strauss
Stage V – the ethical organization	A balanced concern for ethical and economic outcomes; ethical analysis is a fully integrated partner in developing both the mission and strategic plan; SWOT (Strengths, Weaknesses, Opportunities, Threats) analysis is used to *anticipate* problems and analyze alternative outcomes	A total ethical profile, with carefully selected core values which reflect that profile, directs the culture; corporate culture is planned and managed to be ethical; hiring, training, firing, and rewarding all reflect the ethical profile	Documents focus on the ethical profile and core values; all phases of organizational documents reflect them	????????

Figure 10.5 Stages of moral development. (*Source*: R.E. Reidenbach and D.P. Robin (1991) "A conceptual model of corporate model development", *Journal of Business Ethics*, 10, p. 282. Reprinted with kind permission from Kluwer Academic Publishers.)

responsive companies there is a growing concern for balance between profits and ethics, and for stakeholders. Nevertheless, their approach remains somewhat cynical: ethics pays. The fourth stage, the **emerging ethical** organization demonstrates an active approach to ethics, providing support and measures of ethical behavior, to encourage people to do the "right" thing, developing shared values of ethical behavior. Finally, the **ethical** organization thoroughly integrates questions of ethical behavior with developing strategy and mission, thereby addressing the fundamental issue of organizational integrity – what a company *is* rather than what it *does*.

Harvard Professor Lynne Paine provides the guidelines for developing strategies for integrity, as shown in Figure 10.6. Thus for managers and companies, the ethical decisions taken and the corresponding rationale, for legal (fear of getting caught) versus moral reasons, reflect different stages of moral development. In fact, by making something legal, it may no longer be considered as an ethical issue. This may be one way of creating a level "ethical" playing field, albeit to the lowest moral common denominator.

While it may help to clarify what is ethical and what is legal, this does not necessarily resolve the moral dilemma. Consider, for example, making corruption illegal (as did the United States). Although it may be legally permissible to give payments to officials to facilitate routine government action (so you can pay $25 to get your belongings through customs) or to use other legal kinds of currency, such as information, prestige, and contacts, does this not avoid the ethical issue? Is there a difference between a bribe and providing infrastructure or building a hospital? Or by having the country's president visit another country in order to get a government bid accepted? Or are we (as George Bernard Shaw argued in his indecent proposal) quibbling about the price, not the act? Why should best price be more valued than best relationship?

Thus there are many gray areas that need to be resolved. Creating a legal/ethical matrix can help to provide guidelines for conduct: what is neither ethical nor legal should be avoided; what is both legal and ethical can be embraced. But managers will still have to decide whether being legal or illegal makes it ethical or not: legal/unethical or illegal/

1. Guiding values and commitments make sense and are clearly communicated

2. Company leaders are personally committed, credible, and willing to take action on the values they espouse

3. Espoused values are integrated into the normal channels of management decision-making and are reflected in the organization's critical activities

4. Company systems and structures support and reinforce its values

5. Managers throughout the company have the decision-making skills, knowledge, and competencies needed to make ethically sound decisions on a day to day basis

Figure 10.6   Developing corporate integrity. (*Source*: L.S. Paine (1994) "Managing for organizational integrity", *Harvard Business Review*, March–April, p. 112.)

ethical (such as prostitution, child labor, birth control, abortion, designated mothers and fathers, assisted suicide, genetic engineering). Many such ethical dilemmas are outside the law, which cannot keep up with advances, say in technology and medicine.[77] Consider the ethical issues provoked by the Internet and subsequent calls for censorship.

Towards a global civilization

In order to address these issues of what is ethical and what guidelines need to be followed, companies need to provide opportunity for open discussion, without fear of punishment. It may be that ". . . levels of moral reasoning and judgment are likely to be higher when managers get together and discuss ethical issues than when these choices have to be made in solitude".[78]

Most ethics courses designed for managers or MBA students have been criticized as too theoretical (deontology/Kant), too general (questioning economic and political systems), or too impractical.[79] De Bettignies recommends that such courses need to be experiential, conceptual, practical, prospective, and imaginative, where ethical dilemmas can be brought into the open and debated publicly by multidisciplinary and multicultural teams.[80]

> The purpose of these discussions and debates is not to impose values or give solutions but to enhance awareness, to provide frames of reference, to give analytical tools to explore in-depth tradeoffs among short and long term alternative decisions, to involve individual managers in assessing their own values and paradigms in order to be more lucid and responsible in their own choices.[81]

Puffer and McCarthy recommend creating a framework of what is considered ethical/unethical in each country to clarify the issues and to provide the starting point in working together to develop mutually acceptable ethical standards. This helps managers to recognize where there are differences and to understand the reasons for these differences. For example, the ambiguity and ambivalence about business ethics in Russia are strongly related to the current political and economic uncertainties, as well as the previous methods found necessary for survival. Nevertheless, both US and Russian managers were found to share universal values of honesty, integrity, trust, and fairness.[82]

Thus certain ethical standards may be universal: honesty, integrity, and protection of society, customer, and employees. Others may remain culturally specific: reciprocity (gift-giving), whistle-blowing, profit maximization, social welfare, patent protection, and price-fixing. These reflect cultural differences in importance placed on what is good for the group, rather than what is good for the individual, on achievement rather than belonging, and on social harmony rather than adherence to abstract principles.

What is important is to recognize where there are similarities and where there are differences, what are the cultural or institutional reasons for these differences, and how to arrive at some shared way of resolving them. One recommendation made by Dunfee is "to identify and make explicit diverse ethical norms and evaluate them against certain universal, but minimalist, moral principles".[83]

Efforts have been made to create a common set of business ethics, at the supranational level such as the United Nations code of conduct for multinationals and at the industry level. According to a report in the *Financial Times*,[84] in 1994, business leaders from Europe, Japan, and the United States met in Switzerland to develop an international code of ethics; to set a world standard against which business behavior could be measured and a benchmark to help companies devise their own codes. The Caux Round Table sought to identify shared values and reconcile differing values in an attempt to reduce trade tensions with Japan. A seven-point set of principles for doing business was drawn from two ethical traditions: Japanese *kyosei* ("living and working together for the common good of mankind") and human dignity.

Ultimately, the way that these decisions are taken by companies and managers will most likely remain culturally determined. Those from **individualist** cultures, such as Americans, will look within themselves, asking if they can personally live with the decisions taken. Those from **collectivist** cultures will look to those around them and ask how the others will live with them. In **low-context** cultures, ethical standards are likely to be made explicit, to be found in writing, and in law. In **high-context** cultures, ethical standards are likely to be more implicit, assumed to be shared by members of the community. This may result in some countries adhering to the letter of the law, in other cultures to the spirit of the law. In cultures that are **universalist**, the laws will be expected to apply to everyone; in **particularist** cultures, more attention will be paid to the situation and people involved.

Perhaps globalization of the economy will necessitate the convergence of rules and regulations for doing business, and perhaps even ethics. Nevertheless, the assumptions underlying economic and political integration, however deeply rooted (or near to one's heart), need to be acknowledged and challenged. The very ideologies of free market, of democracy, and of equal opportunity carry with them ethical baggage. We too often accept them as given. The lack of questioning of their own world-view is what leads to the perception of Americans as "playing moral police" in their mission to "make the world safe for democracy".

Yet, there are perhaps some fundamentals which need not be questioned. It may be possible to arrive at a shared view of morality and ethical behavior, in line with such efforts as the Helsinki agreements (against torture and murder). To arrive at such criteria for global citizenship requires acknowledging and utilizing cultural differences, enabling us to choose from a broader menu of desirable values: life, liberty, and the pursuit of happiness; liberty, equality, fraternity; filial piety, frugality, and hard work; Do unto others . . . . For Aristotle, "moral" simply meant "practical". He thus advocated "virtue", which meant toughness, "willingness to do what is necessary" as humanely as possible. Virtue also includes courage, fairness, sensitivity, persistence, honesty, and gracefulness.[85]

Now, coming to the end of our journey, rather than finding a global village, we discover yet another road. This road (whether paved with yellow bricks or gold) will hopefully lead towards a "global civilization". This destination promises greater riches through a fruitful coexistence of differences, and sharing of fundamental values. In the words of Harold Perlmutter, Professor of International Business at Wharton,

By the first global civilization we mean a world order, with shared values, processes, and structures: 1) whereby nations and cultures become more open to influence by each other, 2) whereby there is recognition of identities and diversities of peoples in various groups, and ethnic and religious pluralism, 3) where peoples of different ideologies and values both cooperate and compete but no ideology prevails over all the others, 4) where the global civilization becomes unique in a holistic sense while still being plural-ist, and heterogeneous in its character, and 5) where increasingly these values are perceived as shared despite varying interpretations, such as we currently see for the values of openness, human rights, freedom, and democracy.[86]

Thus rather than corporate soldiers sent out to the battlefield to wage economic warfare, managers become global citizens engaged in making the world a better place through economic development.

Notes

1. Ricoeur, P. (1990) *Soi-même comme un Autre*, Paris: Seuil.
2. Vogel, D. (1991) "Business ethics: New perspectives on old problems", *California Management Review*, Summer, pp. 101–17.
3. *Ibid.*, p. 103.
4. Furnham, A. and Koritsas, E. (1990) "The protestant work ethic and vocational prefer-ence", *Journal of Organizational Behavior*, 11, 43–55, p. 44.
5. Furnham, A. (1990) *The Protestant Work Ethic: The Psychology of Work-related Beliefs and Behaviors*, London: Routledge.
6. Weber, M. (1905) *The Protestant Ethic and the Spirit of Capitalism*, New York: Scribners.
7. Puffer, S.M. and McCarthy, D.J. (1995) "Finding the common ground in Russian and American business ethics", *California Management Review*, 37(2), pp. 29–47.
8. Hofstede, G. (1991) *Culture and Organization: Software of the Mind*, London: McGraw-Hill.
9. Hofstede, G. and Bond, M.H. (1988) "The Confucius connection: From cultural roots to economic growth", *Organizational Dynamics*, Spring, pp. 4–21.
10. Ghoshal, S. and Bartlett, C.A. (1987) "Matsushita Electric Industrial (MEI) in 1987", Harvard Business School case.
11. Trompenaars, F. (1993) *Riding the Waves of Culture*, London: The Economist Books.
12. Japan study, source unknown.
13. Santos, J.P., International executive and professor of management, Universidade Catolica Portuguesa, personal communication.
14. Cole, R.E. (1992) "Work and leisure in Japan", *California Management Review*, 34(3), pp. 52–63.
15. Grundling, E. (1991) "Ethics and working with the Japanese", *California Management Review*, Spring, 25–39, p. 33.
16. "Herman Miller: How green is my factory", *Business Week*, September 23, 1991, pp. 57–8.
17. Bartlett, C. (1993) "The Body Shop International", Harvard Business School case No. 9-392-032.
18. "Body Shop International: What selling will be like in the '90s", *Fortune*, January 13, 1992, pp. 47–8.
19. Bruce, R. (1992) "Can 'ethics' square money and nature?", *International Herald Tribune*, March 14–15, p. 14.

20. Baker, M. (1992) "Get rich, feel good: Is this moral?", *International Herald Tribune*, March 14–15, p. 15.
21. *Ibid.*
22. "Can ethics be taught? Harvard gives it the old college try", *Business Week*, April 6, 1992, p. 36.
23. Vogel, D. (1988) "Ethics and profits don't always go hand in hand", *Los Angeles Times*, December 28, p. 7.
24. "Managing by values: Is Levi Strauss' approach visionary – or flaky", *Business Week*, September 12, 1994, pp. 38–43.
25. Paine, L.S. (1994) "Managing for organizational integrity", *Harvard Business Review*, March–April, pp. 106–17.
26. Simon,W.E. (1976) "A challenge to free enterprise" in I. Hill (ed.) *The Ethical Basis of Economic Freedom*, Chapel Hill, NC: American Viewpoint, pp. 405–6.
27. Mallet, V. (1994) "Confucius or convenience? Asian leaders say their ideology must be taken seriously by the west, but critics say the philosophy is cynically self serving", *Financial Times*, March 5, p. 26.
28. "Something's rotten in France, Spain . . .", *Business Week*, June 20, 1994, pp. 16–18.
29. Glover, J. (1994) "A death in Tangentopoli", *Institutional Investor*, May, pp. 55–63.
30. Hager, B. (1991) "What's behind business' sudden fervor for ethics", *Business Week*, September 23, p. 39.
31. "Now it's Germany's turn for a scandal", *Business Week*, September 23, 1991, p. 17.
32. "Something's rotten in France, Spain . . .", *Business Week*, June 20, 1994, pp. 16–18.
33. Toy, S. (1994) "The real scandal in France is over", *Business Week*, July 25, p. 18.
34. Becker, H. and Fritzsche, D.J. (1987) "A comparison of the ethical behavior of American, French and German managers", *Columbia Journal of World Business*, Winter, 87–95, p. 87.
35. D'Iribarne, P. (1989) *La Logique de l'Honneur*, Paris: Seuil.
36. Muzaffar, C. (1980) "The scourge of corruption", Presented at the seminar of *Corruption and Society*.
37. Worthy, F.S. (1989) "When somebody wants a payoff", *Fortune*, Pacific Rim, pp. 91–3.
38. Becker and Fritzsche, *Op. cit.*
39. Dolecheck, M.M. and Dolecheck, C.C. (1987) "Business ethics: A comparison of attitudes of managers in Hong Kong and the United States", *The Hong Kong Manager*, April–May, pp. 28–43.
40. Berenbeim, R.E. (1986) *Corporate Ethics*, New York: The Conference Board.
41. Langlosis, C.C. and Schlegelmilch, B.B. (1990) "Do corporate codes of ethics reflect national character? Evidence from Europe and the United States", *Journal of International Business Studies*, Fourth quarter, pp. 519–39.
42. Vogel, D. (1992) "The globalization of business ethics: Why America remains distinctive", *California Management Review*, Fall, pp. 30–49.
43. *Ibid.*, p. 45.
44. *Ibid.*, pp. 44–5.
45. de Bettignies, H.-C. (1991) "Ethics and international business: A European perspective", presented at the Tokyo Conference on the Ethics of Business in a Global Economy, Kashiwa-shi, Japan.
46. Grundling, *Op. cit.*, p. 27.
47. Markus, H.R. and Kitayama, S. (1991) "Culture and the self: Implications for cognition, emotion, and motivation", *Psychological Review*, 98(2), pp. 224–53.
48. Vogel, *Op. cit.*
49. Paine, *Op. cit.*
50. Vogel, *Op. cit.*
51. *Ibid.*, p. 43.

52. Gellerman, S.W. (1986) "Why 'good' managers make bad ethical choices", *Harvard Business Review*, July–August, pp. 85–9.
53. De Bettignies, H.-C., Professor INSEAD, lecture notes.
54. Nash, N.C. (1995) "Germans look to their corporate ethics", *International Herald Tribune*, July 21, pp. 1, 10.
55. Vogel, *Op. cit.*
56. *Ibid.*
57. "Ethics: Part of the game at Citicorp", *Fortune*, October 26, 1987.
58. "The best laid ethics program", *Business Week*, March 9, 1992, pp. 59–60.
59. Weiser, B. (1996) "An ex-employee as hostile witness: Honda faces unusual critic", *International Herald Tribune*, March 6, pp. 13, 17.
60. "When in Rome . . .", *Business Week*, June 7, 1993, p. 20.
61. Schneider, S.C. and Wittenberg-Cox, A. and Hanson, L. (1990) Honeywell, Europe, INSEAD case.
62. Schmidt, E. (1980) *Decoding Corporate Camouflage: U.S. Business Support for Apartheid*, Institute for Policy Studies, Washington, DC, p. 78.
63. "Companies try a new tack: Civil disobedience", *Business Week*, October 13, 1985, p. 27.
64. Sherman, S.P. (1984) "Scoring corporate conduct in South Africa", *Fortune*, July 9, pp. 168–72.
65. "As Americans pull out of South Africa, Europeans and Asians move in", *Business Week*, March 17, 1986, pp. 22–3.
66. Rolfe, R. (1988) "South Africa: The next wave of pullouts", *International Management*, April, pp. 51–5.
67. Gladwin, T.N. and Walter, I. (1980) *Multinationals Under Fire*, New York: John Wiley.
68. Stark, A. (1993) "What's the matter with business ethics?", *Harvard Business Review*, May–June, pp. 38–48.
69. Worthy, *Op. cit.*.
70. Badaracco, J.L. and Webb, A.P. (1995) "Business ethics: A view from the trenches", *California Management Review*, 37(2), pp. 8–28.
71. Labisch, K. (1992) "The new crisis in business ethics", April 20, *Fortune*, pp. 99–102.
72. *Ibid.*
73. Magnet, M. (1986) "The decline and fall of business ethics", *Fortune*, December 8, pp. 65–72.
74. Kohlberg, L. (1981) *Essays on Moral Development*, San Francisco: Harper & Row.
75. Snell, R.S. (1996) "Complementing Kohlberg: Mapping the ethical reasoning used by managers for their own dilemma cases", *Human Relations*, 49(1), pp. 23–49.
76. Drummond, J. (1994) "Management: Saints and sinners – How to achieve an ethical balance in business operations", *Financial Times*, March 23, p. 12.
77. De Bettignies, lecture.
78. Posner, B.Z. and Schmidt, W.H. (1984) "Values and the American manager: An update", *California Management Review*, 26(3), pp. 210–12.
79. Stark, *Op. cit.*
80. de Bettignies, *Op. cit.*
81. *Ibid.*, p. 15.
82. Puffer and McCarthy, *Op. cit.*
83. Stark, *Op. cit.*
84. Dickson, T. (1994) "The search for universal ethics: The launch of a new set of business principles", *Financial Times*, July 22, p. 11.
85. Stark, *Op. cit.*
86. Perlmutter, H.V. (1991) "On the rocky road to the first global civilization", *Human Relations*, 44(9), 897–920, p. 898.

Index